THE RADICAL EYE

THE ADICAL EYE

MODERNIST PHOTOGRAPHY FROM THE SIR ELTON JOHN COLLECTION

TH RAD

THER

LEYE

DICA

HERA

EYET

ADICA
DICA

THERA
HERA

EYET
EYE T

DICAL
OICAL

MODERNIST
PHOTOGRAPHY FROM
THE SIR ELTON JOHN
COLLECTION

EDITED BY
SIMON BAKER AND
SHOAIR MAVLIAN
WITH NEWELL HARBIN

WITH CONTRIBUTIONS FROM
SIR ELTON JOHN, DAWN ADES,
SAMUEL GLANVILLE,
JANE JACKSON, EMMA LEWIS
AND ZMIRA ZILKHA

aperture

"When I make a picture, I make love."
Alfred Stieglitz

"Wherever Elton goes, there is love."
Bob & Tamar Manoukian

CONTENTS

The Sir Elton John Photography Collection is recognised as one of the greatest privately owned photographic collections in the world, reaching in scope from the beginning of the twentieth century to the present day and containing masterpieces by the world's most influential photographers. With over 8,000 works, it represents an incredible achievement for a British collector and shows the ongoing commitment of both Sir Elton John and David Furnish to the photographic medium over the long term and for the future. Such collections are rarely made available to public view and so it was with great excitement that Tate began a collaboration with Sir Elton and his team to assemble the exhibition *The Radical Eye: Modernist Photography from The Sir Elton John Collection.*

The exhibition takes as its subject the birth and development of what is known as 'modernist photography', from around 1920 to 1950, the period when photography really came into its own as a medium, and which is, in many ways, the most exciting and dynamic time in its history. Tate, which only began collecting photography seriously and strategically in 2009, has very little material from this seminal moment in its collection, and today many vintage prints from the period are beyond the reach of a national collection. This project has given our curatorial team the opportunity to make an exhibition showing the greatest photographers of the twentieth century, including key figures such as Imogen Cunningham, André Kertész, Tina Modotti, Man Ray and Aleksandr Rodchenko, drawn entirely from one incredible collection. The resulting exhibition, which this book accompanies, draws out the major themes and approaches that characterise the radical innovation and originality of modernist photography, from the Bauhaus in Germany to the surrealists in Paris and the great pioneers of photography in the United States and Latin America. Although the exhibition covers a range of material from abstract experiments and still life, to architecture and social documentary practice, perhaps the most significant and unique aspect is the exemplary collection of portraits. Assembled by a collector who is no stranger to presenting a dynamic public image, the portraits in *The Radical Eye* show the full range of technical and psychological styles. From Man Ray's portraits of the key surrealist artists and thinkers, to Edward Steichen's marvellous veiled Gloria Swanson, to Alfred Stieglitz's depictions of Georgia O'Keeffe, Berenice Abbott's portrait of Jean Cocteau and Tina Modotti's studies of Edward Weston, these are the finest photographic portraits of the twentieth century, brought together in the United Kingdom for the very first time.

Inevitably, an exhibition of this scale and complexity is the result of many individual contributions. First and foremost, however, we would like to recognise the generosity and great enthusiasm of both Sir Elton John and David Furnish for allowing Tate access to their collection, and their homes, in order to work on this project, and for their willingness to part with so many great works for the period of the exhibition. We would also like to thank especially Newell Harbin, Director of The Sir Elton John Photography Collection, for her unstinting work and good humour in all aspects of the exhibition's research and conceptual development, as well as for co-editing this book: the show simply could not have happened without her. Likewise Jane Jackson, who played a seminal role in building the collection with Sir Elton and who has been supportive throughout the project. Thank you also to Luke Lloyd Davies, Chief Operating Officer, Rocket Entertainment, for his tireless work, and to his team Elanzo Burgess, Rebecca Davies, Alex Hall, Beth Harrold and Kevin O'Duffy for all the time and energy dedicated to the exhibition. Thank you additionally to John T.D. Murphy, Myott, Charlie McCullers, Audrey Jackson, Lucy Hernadez, Erika Simpson and Joseph Guay, along with Sarah Morthland and Vicki Harris, who have been a huge support throughout.

For Tate, Shoair Mavlian, Assistant Curator, International Art, has made an important and insightful exhibition, working with Simon Baker, Senior Curator, International Art (Photography). The logistical oversight of the exhibition was the responsibility of Helen Sainsbury and her team, Carol Burnier Magno and Rachel Kent, while the exhibition design and installation were overseen by Phil Monk, Justina Budd and Glen Williams. We would also like to thank everyone else in the curatorial team at Tate Modern for their contributions behind the scenes, but especially Helen O'Malley, as well as all our colleagues in the conservation department, press office and marketing team. Thanks for their exemplary work on this book are due to Bill Jones, John Stachiewicz and Roz Young at Tate Publishing, project manager Kate Bell and copy-editor Denny Hemming, as well as Melanie Mues at Mues Design. We are especially grateful to Dawn Ades, Emma Lewis, Zmira Zilkha and Samuel Glanville for their collaboration and insightful contributions. Further thanks are due to Sir Elton for the interview he granted, and to Jane Jackson and Newell Harbin for their editorial contributions. We would, of course, also like to thank the artist and the artists' estates.

The exhibition has been made possible by the provision of insurance through the Government Indemnity Scheme. Tate Modern would like to thank HM Government for providing Government Indemnity and the Department for Culture, Media and Sport and Arts Council England for arranging the indemnity.

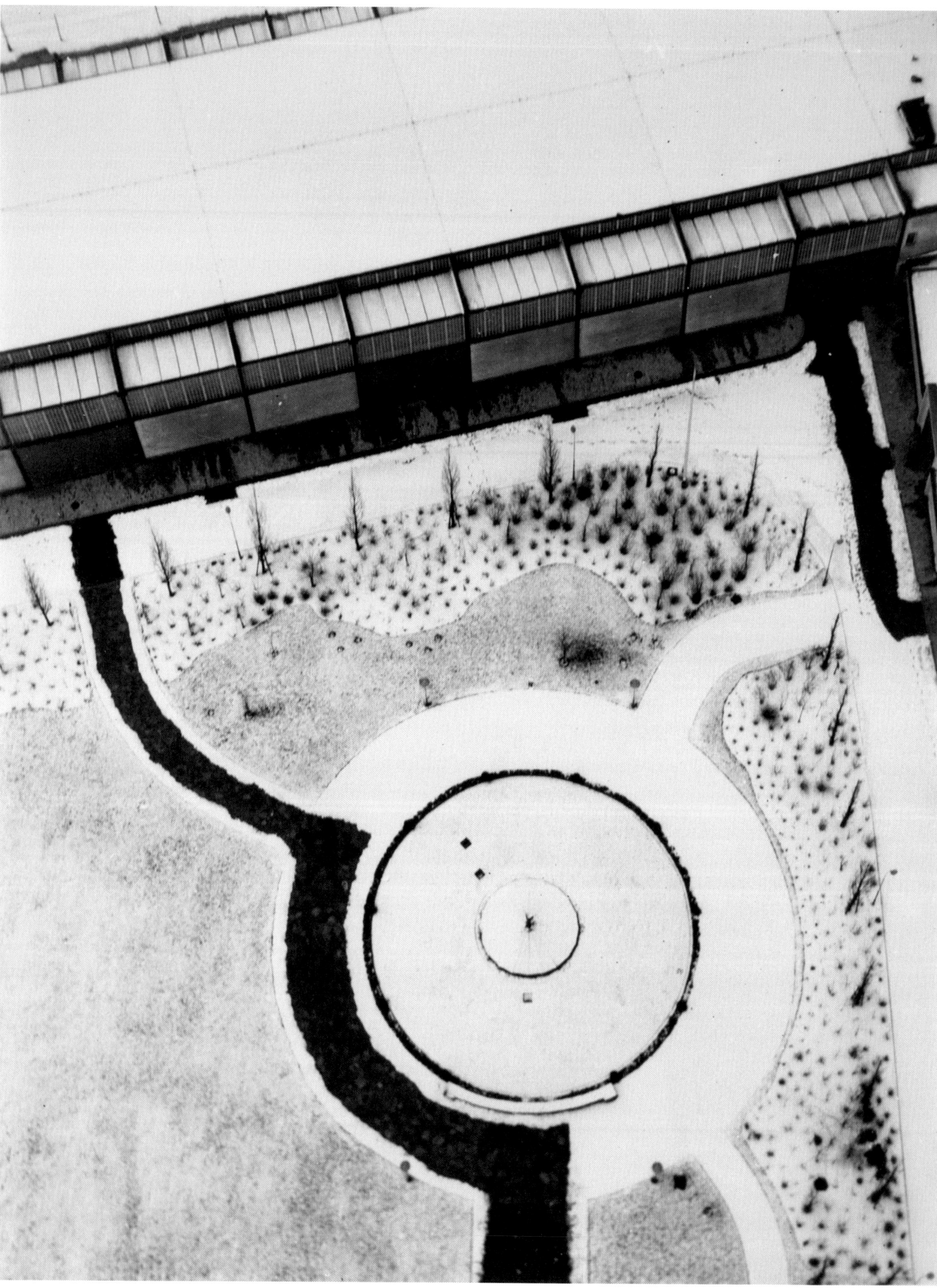

In 1927, one hundred years after the production of the first light-sensitised image, László Moholy-Nagy was able to write that the invention of photography had contributed to a radical revolution in vision. 'We may say,' he wrote, 'that we see the world with entirely different eyes'. But so much of what had happened since 1827 was nothing compared to the complete re-writing of the visual lexicon that happened in the years after the First World War and into the 1920s. What is now commonly referred to as 'modernist photography', and what Moholy-Nagy called 'the new vision', was not only a new way of seeing the world, expanding on the limitations of human sight, but also a new way of producing art, bringing technology into play creatively to an extent never before imagined.

Both in the classrooms of the Bauhaus school in Germany and in the workshops and publications of their Soviet counterparts, debates raged about the potential of a medium being re-imagined for the modern world. As one critic wrote: 'The task of photography is to comprehend its own specific forms and methods.' Photography, in other words, should stop trying to be artistic by resembling painting, and instead find its own visual language. The photographer and theorist Aleksandr Rodchenko was very clear how this might be achieved: 'Do you understand now,' he wrote, 'that the most interesting viewpoints for modern photography are from above down and from below up, and any others rather than belly-button level?' Both Moholy-Nagy and Rodchenko would champion what they called 'bird's eye' and 'worm's eye' views, raking perspectives on the everyday world

that transformed photographs from descriptive images of things to complex compositions with energy and dynamism. But in addition to looking in new ways, photographers concerned with the modernity of their medium sought to make images that could only be produced by photographic means; through the magic combination of lens, shutter and darkroom. Beginning with the powerful effects of light and shadow transformed into black-and-white images, the radical new approach quickly took in arrested movement, distortions, double exposures, negatives, and a whole host of darkroom tactics that exploded from the 1920s onwards until photography had reinvented not only its own rules but also avant-garde art in general. 'The mere fact of transposing something seen to a photograph,' wrote the surrealist painter Salvador Dalí, is 'the recording of an UNPRECEDENTED REALITY.'

The Radical Eye offers a complete account of the breadth and scope of the new approaches to photography that were pioneered in the 1920s and established by the 1950s. Organised according to the priorities of the new photographic avant-garde, it ranges from the objective clarity of the modernist portrait to the experimental magic of darkroom manipulations that tend even towards abstraction. From the technical purism of the Bauhaus, and social commitment of early documentary practice, to the wild imagination of surrealism, photography was employed to push the boundaries of the possible, changing the world through the ways in which it was seen and understood.

LÁSZLÓ MOHOLY-NAGY
View from the Berlin Radio Tower
1928, printed c.1941
24.1 × 18.4 cm

All photographs are gelatin silver prints on
paper unless otherwise specified

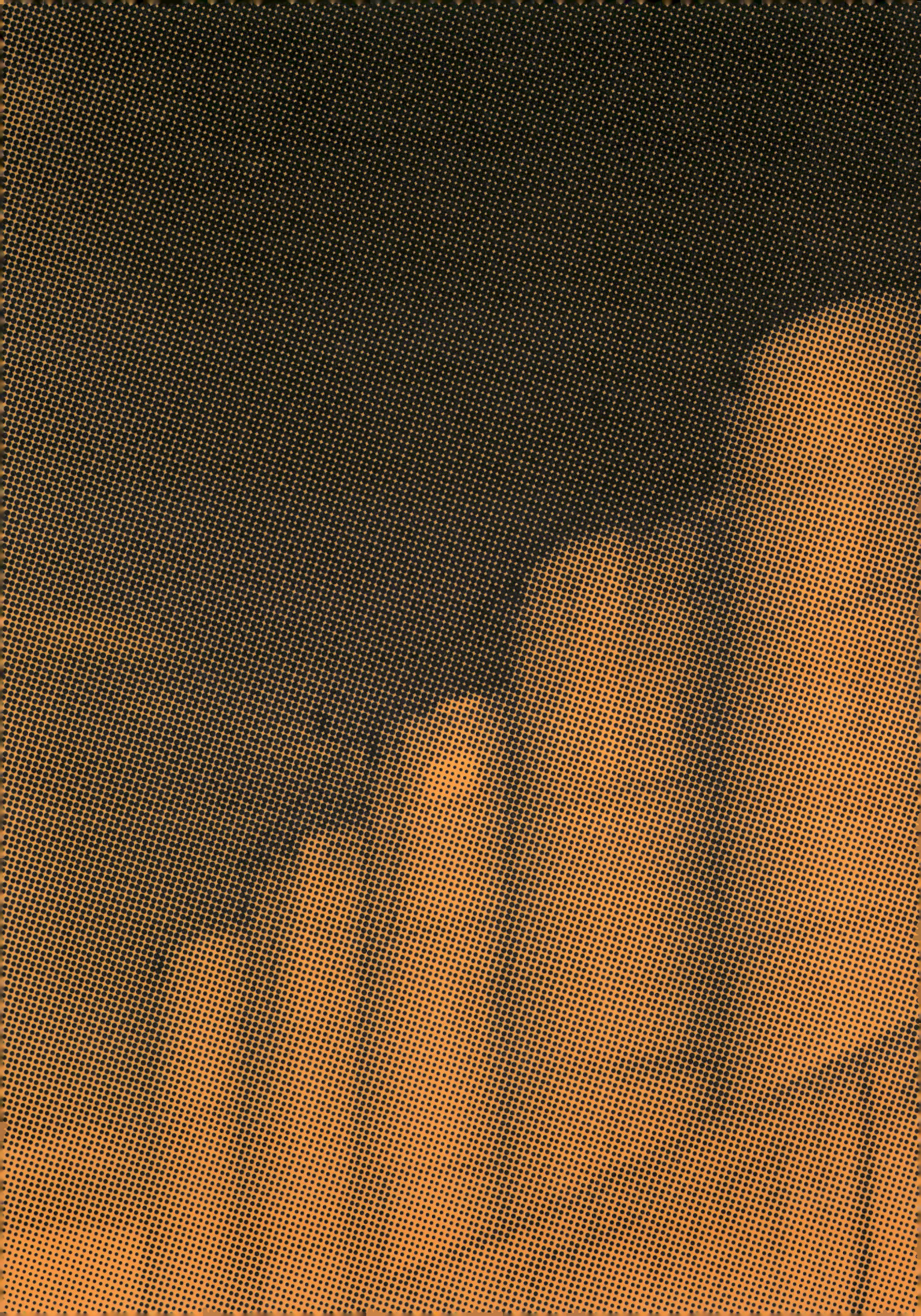

In January 2016 curator Jane Jackson visited Sir Elton John at his Los Angles home to discuss his passion for collecting photographs in general and the specific works to be included in Tate Modern's *The Radical Eye* exhibition in particular. Ms Jackson first met Sir Elton John in 1990 and was one of a select group of international gallery owners who, through the years, have helped him to build his impressive collection. In 2003 Jackson sold her gallery in Atlanta and became the first Director of The Sir Elton John Photography Collection (2003-12). Here, she discusses with Sir Elton John the important role photography has played in his life, the ethos of collecting and connoisseurship, his personal response to and appreciation of the medium, its history and its artists, and his desire to share his collection with others.

JANE JACKSON: Let's start by going back to the days after you came out of rehab. The therapists had said the best thing for you to do was to go someplace where you could be with supportive friends and ease yourself back into the world again. Perhaps we could begin by talking about that time because that's when you first discovered photography as fine art.

SIR ELTON JOHN: After rehab in 1990 I went to France to spend time with friends who owned a chateau in Cahors. They had helped to organise a photography festival there and photography exhibitions were everywhere, even on the outside of buildings. I'd never really noticed photography as an art form before. I had had my picture taken by lots of wonderful photographers through the years, including Norman Parkinson, Terry O'Neill and David Bailey, but seeing this artistic side of the medium was very different. Also staying there was the LA gallery owner David Fahey and the photographer Herb Ritts. David had brought with him photographs by Ritts, Horst P. Horst and Irving Penn. They were all in black and white, and mostly of fashion subjects. I looked at them and thought, oh my God, these are so beautiful – I bought about twelve on the spot. I suddenly became intensely interested in photography.

JANE: And at the time when you were in Cahors, photography as a collectable art form was still really young. It wasn't like it is now, when it's seen in every gallery and museum, and even in every interiors magazine. In 1990, even though there were photography dealers and galleries all over the world, the collecting base was still rather small. All of the dealers and collectors knew each other personally. It was a small sub-sect of the art world.

ELTON: Yes, the timing for me couldn't have been better. Photographs were very undervalued then. If I had started collecting twenty years later, most of the vintage works would no longer have been available and the prices would have been drastically different. I wouldn't have been able to amass the collection I've got now.

JANE: Would you say that becoming sober opened your eyes to photography and to starting a new collection?

ELTON: It's funny but after rehab I wasn't interested in anything that I'd collected before. I love objects. I've always loved objects. As a child, my parents argued a lot, so I found comfort in objects and my collections were always pristine – my records, my toys, they were all beautifully kept. Then as I started making money, I got interested in art deco and art nouveau. Before I went into rehab, I sold it all in a big one-week auction at Sotheby's.

JANE: Do you think your alcohol addiction changed into another type of addiction, an obsession with acquiring photographs?

ELTON: Absolutely. It's a much healthier addiction to buy photographs, so I just switched. I felt as if my eyes were opened by photography. It was the most beautiful thing because I was getting sober, and feeling great about myself, and entering a new phase of my life. Photography became this incredible companion. It went hand in hand with my sobriety, which was also fresh and a release. I was like a kid in a candy store. I started with these ten or twelve photographs and then I happened to come to your gallery in Atlanta. I think the first things I bought were an Elliott Erwitt, a Harry Callahan and a Ray Metzker.

JANE: Yes, I think those were some of your first purchases and I gave you a stack of books. At the time I didn't know you were such a voracious reader, so I was surprised when you came back to the gallery that you had read all the books and were full of curiosity.

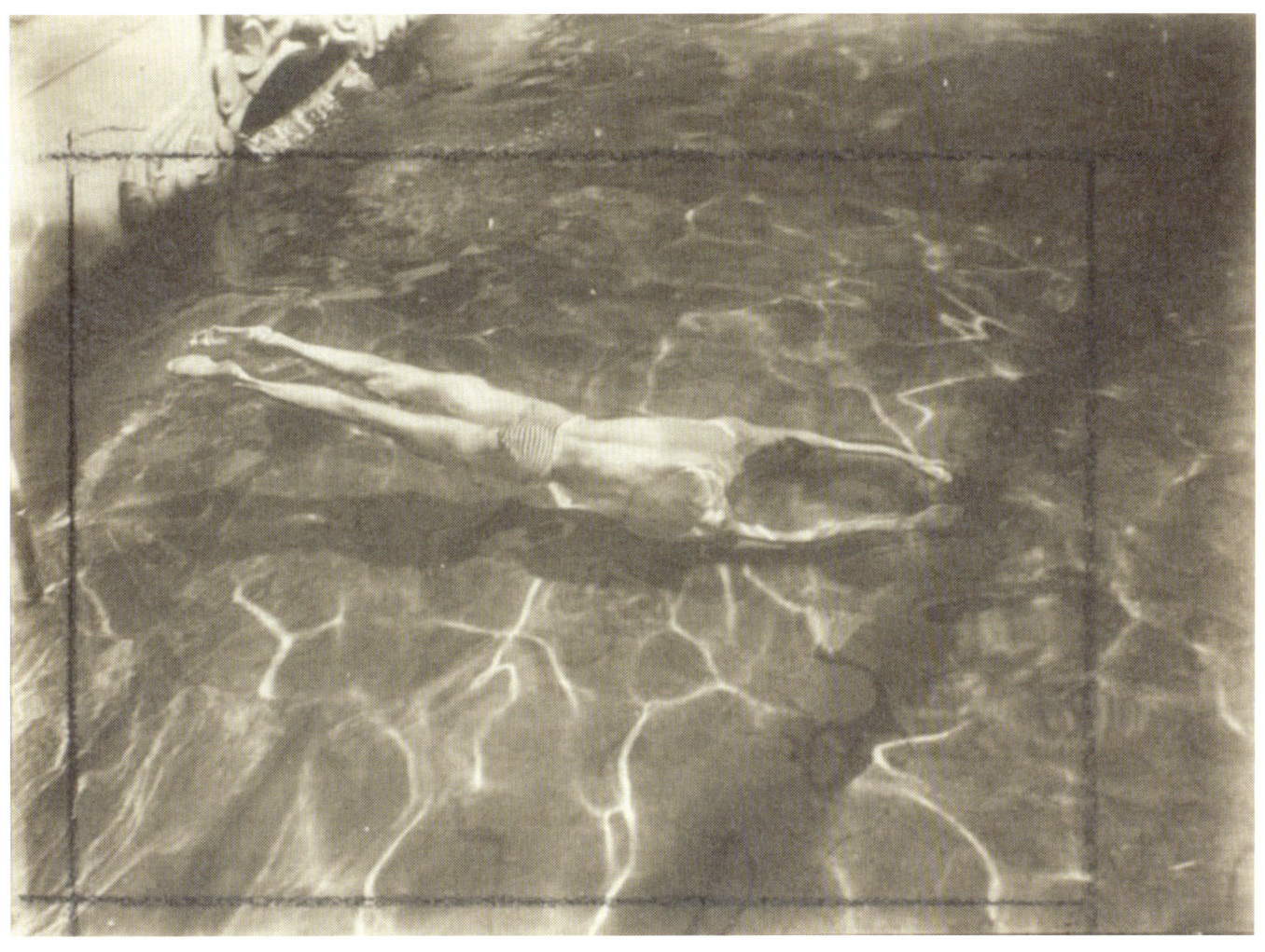

André Kertész
Underwater Swimmer,
Esztergom, Hungary,
30 June 1917
4.1 × 5.7 cm

ELTON: I just couldn't believe that I had been so ignorant about something. When I collected art nouveau and art deco, I'd read up about it. I was knowledgeable about it. And I couldn't believe that there I was, forty-three or forty-four years of age, and I'd never noticed photography, yet I'd grown up in a business that the greatest photographers worked in. I'd been completely unaware of it.

JANE: When you first started collecting photographs, you bought fashion, flowers and portraits. These were by photographers who all worked in a very controlled manner. Later, as you saw and learned more about photography and its history, you became interested in the experimental work of the 1920s, 1930s and 1940s. This is the work that Tate Modern will be featuring in its 2016 exhibition.

ELTON: Yes, as I learned more about photography, I saw that these artists were able to do things that I thought only a painter could do. When I first saw Kertész's distortions (p.90) or Man Ray's rayographs (p.218) or Edward Quigley's light abstractions (p.213), I couldn't believe people were able to do that with photography. I thought that was the realm of painters. I was just astonished. The Kertész *Underwater Swimmer* (p.13), done in 1917, blew me away. And then to understand that this incredible image later influenced other artists made me realise even more the importance of photography.

JANE: You have always loved Kertész's work and have some fabulous vintage photographs by him. Initially you had been given a modern print of the *Underwater Swimmer* as a gift but you wanted a vintage print. Tell me why you think your vintage print is so special because you had to wait a long time before you were able to acquire it.

ELTON: I had a modern print of the *Underwater Swimmer*, printed in the late 1970s, but I really wanted a vintage print. Over time I had been offered a couple that were said to be vintage but they weren't 'true' vintage prints. I wanted one printed in the same year it was first taken, 1917, in Hungary. I waited years. Then one day, Peter MacGill phoned me up and said that he had the original contact print of the swimmer and he'd like to sell it.

JANE: So this is the original contact print that Kertész made with the initial crop marks on it. Your print shows what the full negative looked like and then how all the future prints would be cropped.

ELTON: Yes, that's why it's so special because it shows his original vision. When people ask me, 'What was the most influential photograph of the twentieth century?', I say that

one without question because it has influenced so much and yet it looks as if it had been taken yesterday.

JANE: And what do you think of the importance of buying a vintage print over a modern print? You still have the modern print of the *Underwater Swimmer*, the print that was made in the late 1970s, and you have the original print from 1917. There is a huge difference when you look at the two of them together, but they are still similar. When you see a vintage print and a modern print, how do you react to them?

ELTON: I'm not a snob when it comes to that, but I would rather have the vintage print because of the story that's attached to it. There's something about the fact that this was actually printed at that time. The vintage print captures that initial, original thought of the artist. But if I like an image, and I can't get a vintage print, then I'll have a signed modern print.

When I was a kid I used to buy Man Ray posters. There was a shop in Oxford called Athena Reproductions and they'd have all these beautiful paintings, but they used to have reproductions, too, and I bought a poster of the Man Ray *Lips* because that was all I could afford. A lot of people can't afford to buy the original, so making art available in other forms is just wonderful. I'm lucky enough to be able to have the original. Even though the later or modern prints are typically printed from the original negative, you want to have the vintage one if you can.

JANE: It's about connoisseurship and buying the best you can afford from what's available. For example, take Paul Strand's photograph *Wall Street, New York* (p.202). You have the photogravure, not a vintage silver or platinum print. This photogravure was published in the last issue of Alfred Stieglitz's highly respected photographic journal *Camera Work*, but some collectors would say, well, it's a photogravure, that's not significant – but we have looked for a rare vintage print...

ELTON: And we can't find an early vintage print that is in good condition. It's always important to buy things that are in good condition if you are a collector. We're constantly monitoring the condition of our photographs and doing rotations within our homes. They are beautiful works of art and most are irreplaceable. So you have to be patient and then something will come along. It's funny how things find their way into my collection. How did we get the Edward Weston *Circus Tent, Mexico* (opposite)?

JANE: That was pure luck. I discovered it in a house that was up for sale in an old neighbourhood of Atlanta. I remember turning the corner into a hallway and seeing a print of the *Circus Tent*. I had only ever seen this image in books and was stunned to see it hanging in a metal frame that was falling

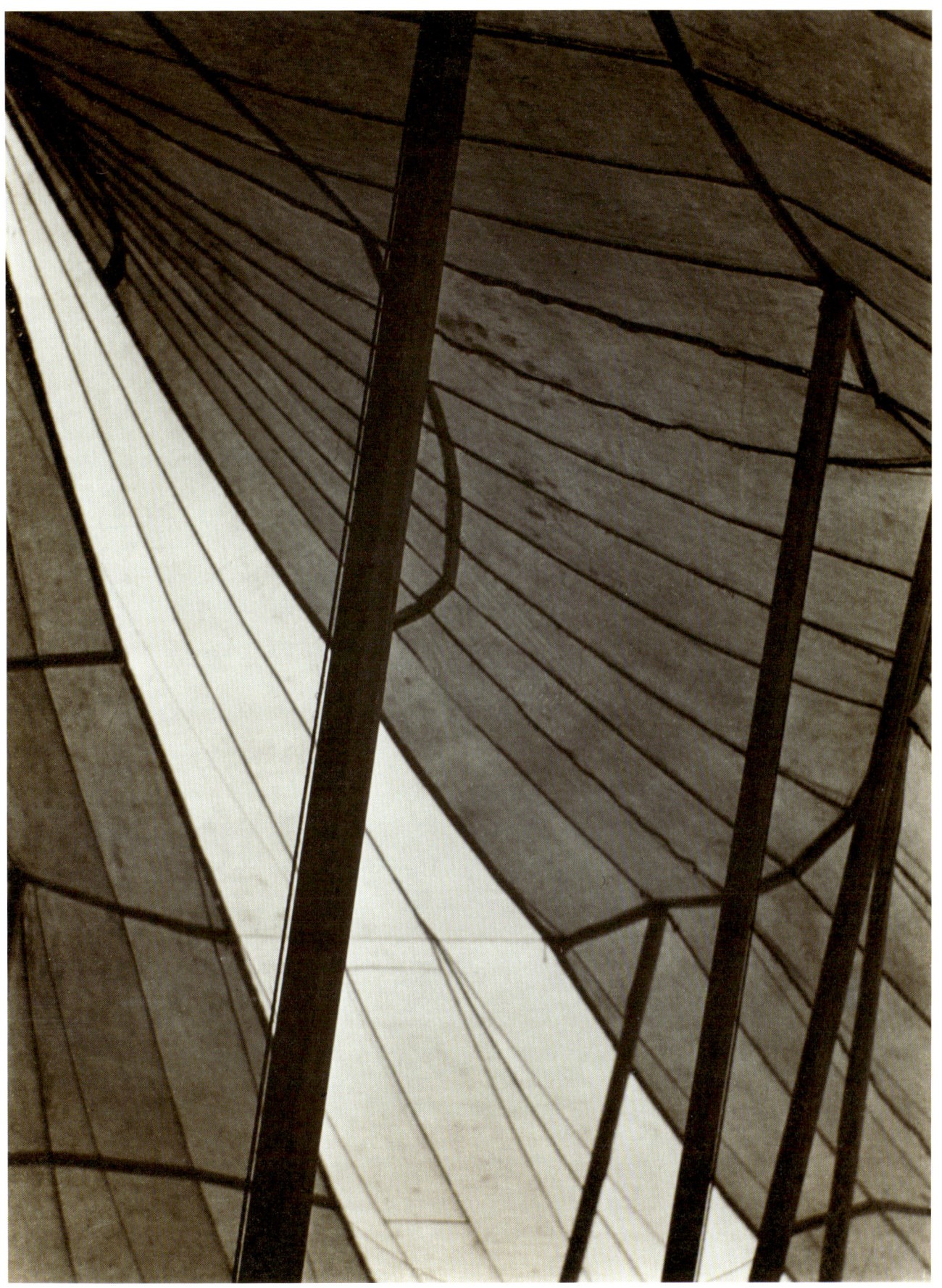

EDWARD WESTON
Circus Tent, Mexico 1923
24.8 × 18.4 cm

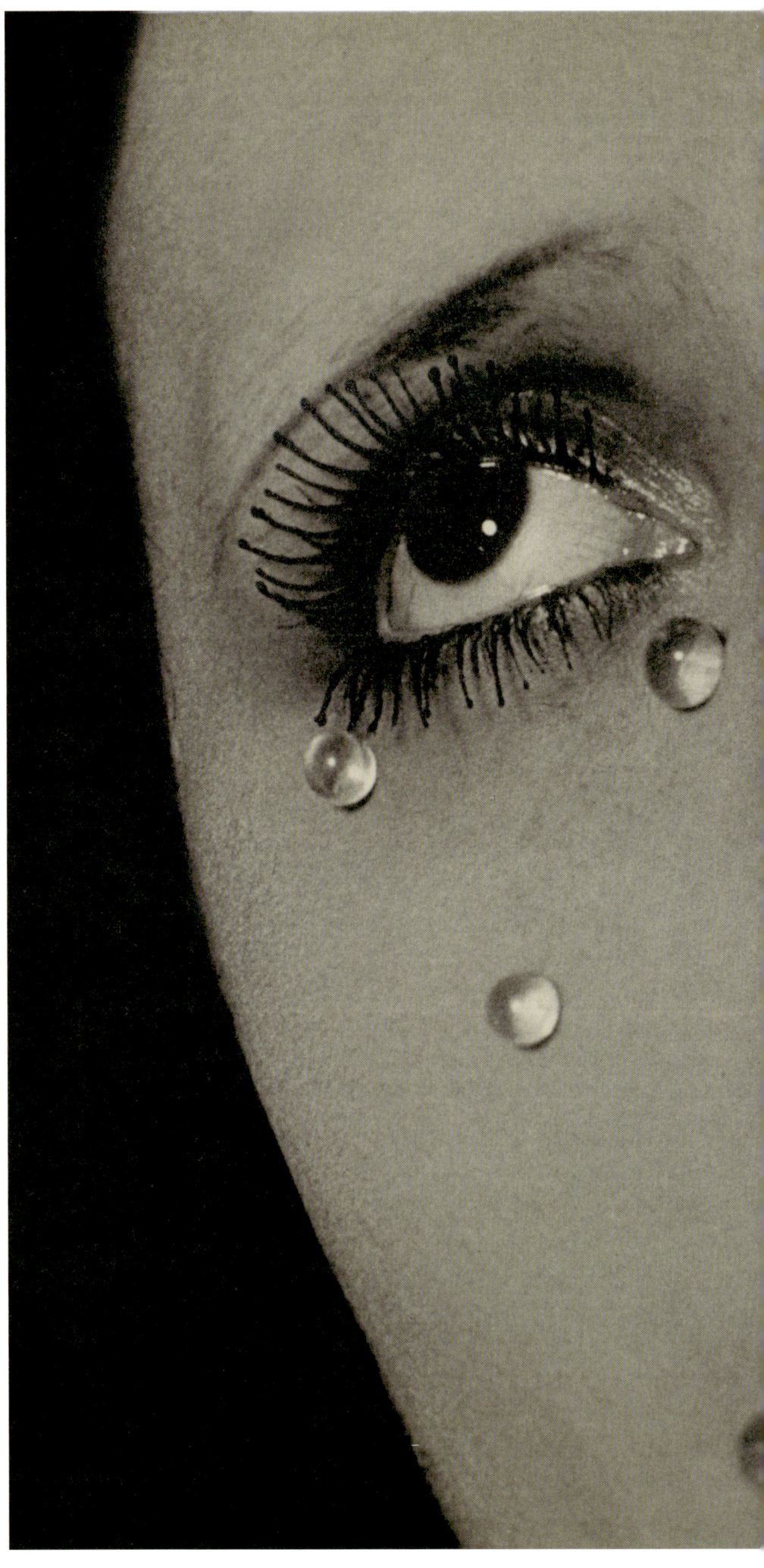

Man Ray
Glass Tears 1932
22.9 × 29.8 cm

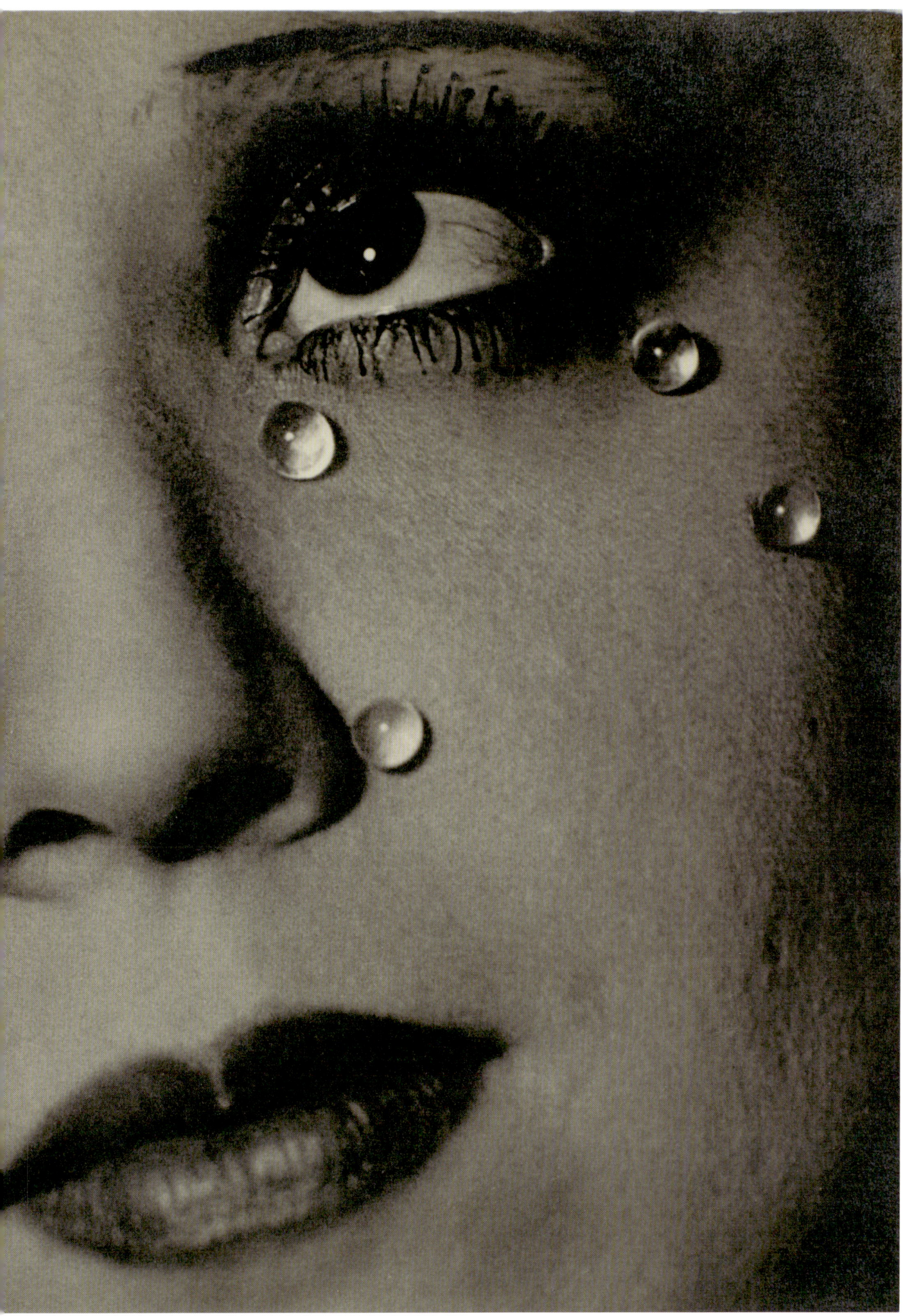

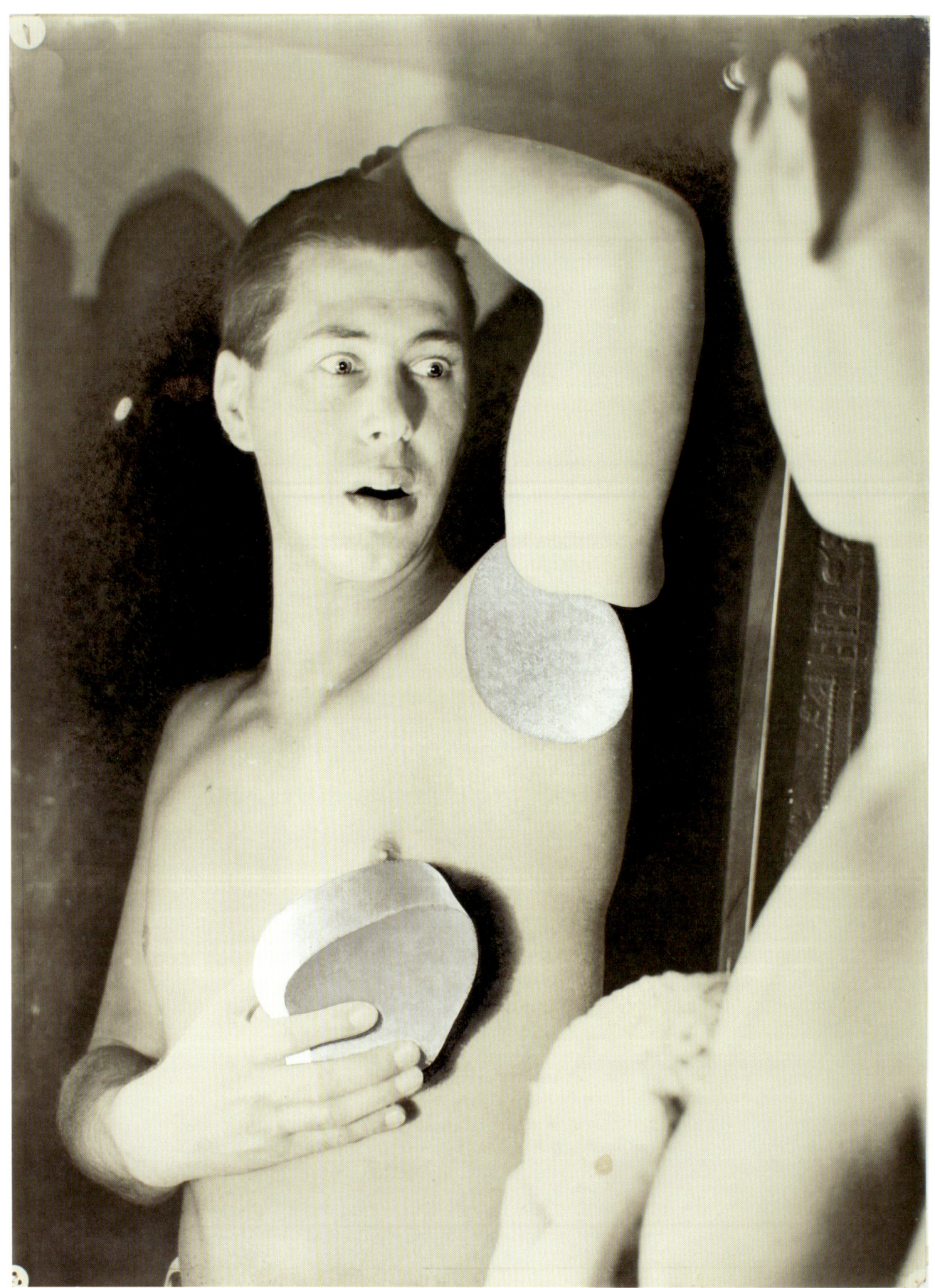

HERBERT BAYER
Humanly Impossible (Self-Portrait) 1932
photomontage, bromoil gelatin silver
print with gouache and airbrush
39.4 × 29.5 cm

apart at the corners. The owner had inherited the photograph from her mother. After some negotiating, a price was settled upon and it went into your collection.

ELTON: The *Circus Tent*. Now that is an abstraction. I didn't know what that was when I bought that.

JANE: When Weston was living in Mexico with his mistress, Tina Modotti, they both went to this circus to take pictures. She photographed the people and he photographed the abstractions, the bones of the tent.

ELTON: And then, in California, Weston photographed that fragment of the knees (p.153). Oh my God, how sexy is that. It's just the composition of it. And again, it was not a result of happenstance. It shows you how sex doesn't have anything to do with sexual organs, or anything. Something as simple as the knees can be sexy. The first Weston I ever bought was the one of the white church (p.170). It's beautiful, and it's peaceful, and you're wondering what's behind that door. And it's white, and it's pure, and it's got a certain spirituality about it. It's got a sense of sereneness, of calm - it's just a door but it says so much more.

JANE: What was the moment when you realised you were becoming a serious collector?

ELTON: One of the biggest moments I had was when I bought Man Ray's *Glass Tears* (pp.16-17). I thought I had gone stark raving mad but I had to have it. I think I bought it in 1993.

JANE: It was the cover lot of an auction in London.

ELTON: Yes, and it set a world record price for a single photograph sold at auction - I think the news made the front page of the *LA Times*, *New York Times* and the London *Times* - but when you think of it now it was a steal. That image stayed with me from the time I first saw it and I just could not resist it. I thought I'd lost my mind. Friends thought I'd lost my mind. I remember telling Gianni Versace and he said, 'You have the negative?' I said 'No, no, you don't get the negative' - he could never understand that if you bought a photograph you didn't get the negative. Gianni said, 'I would never do this, I just want the negative'. It's astonishing. I think that's when I knew I was serious about collecting, when I bought that print.

JANE: It's interesting because, when that happened, at first people didn't know it was you but then rumours started going around - Elton bought it, Elton bought it! I remember an older dealer Harry Lunn called me at that time and he was so excited that photographs were finally achieving these prices. You really were a catalyst for expanding the photography market in the 1990s.

ELTON: I never collected anything to make a profit. Never in my life have I done that. I've just bought things that I like. I've been fairly lucky. It's given me so much joy and I'm still finding things out, finding that there are still so many photographers whose work I don't have in my collection. Newell [Newell Harbin, current Director of The Sir Elton John Photography Collection] is always saying, 'What about this artist? We don't have any of his or hers?', and I go, 'Oh my God, we must get that work in the collection!'

JANE: I think part of what's great about your collection is you've spent little money on some things, you've spent a lot of money on other things, but you've always bought things that really spoke to you. It's not about impressing people and trying to say, 'Well, I've got a such and such on the wall over here…'.

ELTON: I hate trophy art. I buy what I like and if it's not fashionable I don't care. The more you collect, the more sophisticated your eye becomes. I can go straight to the piece that I know will work perfectly in the collection.

JANE: Why do you think today's art world seems to appreciate contemporary photography more than vintage works?

ELTON: Because people want the showy big stuff. And it's good stuff. But a lot of people who buy photography don't take the time to learn the history of the medium, and to realise the importance and the rarity of the earlier vintage works.

JANE: Do you think there is a lack of connoisseurship in collecting today?

ELTON: Many people are investing their money in photography and art rather than having it in the bank or in stocks and bonds. Which is great. I love it. They want something they can see in the morning and I'm all for that. It's great for artists too. But many collectors don't have the understanding that they should have. Some collectors hire advisors to choose work for them, instead of taking the time to learn and train their own eye. I'd rather walk into a house that is full of really mediocre stuff, but the owners love it and they've bought it themselves, than to see trophy art on the wall. 'Oh, hi. Look. I've just got this great Stieglitz' or 'I've got this great Picasso'. It's like, yes, but do you really like it or have you just been told about it. I think that people now don't have discernment. They're advised what to buy, they buy it as an investment, whereas for me photography is a journey of discovery.

JANE: 'Photography is a journey of discovery' - that is quite a significant declaration. Please elaborate why you feel that way.

ELTON: Photography has given me so much pleasure. I can't think of anything else, other than music, that's given me so much pleasure in an artistic way. For example, in Atlanta I wake up with Man Ray's *Noire et Blanche* (pp.82-3) above my head. It seeps into your skin. I love creativity. Everything visual around me has an impact on me and helps my wellbeing. The photographs make me feel happy, and sad, and wondrous. They make me realise there is so much more for me to do creatively.

JANE: There's a quote in *Essays on Art* by Julian Barnes that I would like you to respond to with regard to works in your collection. 'It is a rare picture that stuns, or argues, us into silence. And if one does, it is only a short time before we want to explain and understand the very silence into which we have been plunged.' Are there photographs in your collection that make you feel this way?

ELTON: Oh, yes. Like the Herbert Bayer self-portrait (p.18). The one with him looking in the mirror, holding a section of his arm. It's like, what is going on here? What was Bayer thinking? Is the image about him or is it about Germany in the 1930s? It really makes you wonder. And that one is the original photomontage from which other prints were made. It's incredible.

And then there is the Hank Willis Thomas photograph, *Priceless*, from 2004. It shows the funeral of his cousin who was killed for his gold chain. Hank superimposed the Mastercard logo and words like an advertisement over the photograph. It's sad, and makes you stop and think about violence, greed and poverty.

Also, Steichen's *Gloria Swanson* (opposite). I've never seen anything so beautiful. This photograph is so perfect and has such a tactile look that it seems like you could actually touch the lace. And then there is the hidden meaning of this famous silent actress behind the veil.

JANE: Yes, Steichen was an amazing portrait photographer. Your print is spectacular. It almost looks three-dimensional. The way the lace falls on her face. Steichen and Swanson had been working for hours to get the perfect shot and then Steichen came up with the idea of the veil over her face. She totally understood that it would make her look like a camouflaged tigress.

In your collection, you have a significant number of portraits. What attracts you to portraits?

ELTON: I still love painting but to me, and this is going to cause a stir, there's not a portrait in paint that could ever compare to a photographic portrait. Take the group of Man Ray portraits that I have. Those six Man Rays, including the one I call the 'Phil Collins' which is of the artist Yves Tanguy (p.23), were all of such important men of that time, yet Man Ray photographed them so simply that the images are timeless.

JANE: Let's talk a little bit about the modernist aesthetic. After the First World War, especially in Europe, people were left with all this destruction and emptiness. And a lot of artists didn't quite know how to relate, either mentally or artistically, to what had happened or to their current surroundings. They couldn't go back to the way things were. The world had changed and their art had to change as well. Many became anti-bourgeois, they experimented with new forms of art and they stayed away from realism. Why do you think you are attracted to this experimental style of photography?

ELTON: Just the timing of it. I mean first off, the fact it was done so long ago. And as you say, it was done after the First World War when people were completely and utterly devastated. Same with the Second World War. So where do you go from there? They just started afresh. And they started afresh in the most incredible way, I mean in the most daring way. It was like a revolution, not just in photography but a revolution in art. And the things they were doing were astounding. In photography it was boundary-breaking and quite astonishing because cameras weren't sophisticated in those days.

JANE: And the majority of these photographers had a background in painting and drawing. They understood the fundamentals of art. Photography was a new tool for them to use and experiment with.

ELTON: Yes. And you can see the excitement in these images, the energy. Can you imagine the reaction when Man Ray started doing solarisations and created that beautiful portrait of Dora Maar (p.97), or Josef Breitenbach's early experiments with colour pigment (p.88)? Like, wow, this is amazing. It was so different from anything that had ever appeared before. It's like music – new inventions like the electric guitar or the Hammond organ totally changed the future of music. It was revolutionary.

Artists like Funke and Drtikol understood the principles of composition, lighting and form. They produced sculptural photographs in a way. They planned these works using shapes, shadows and the texture of the paper. It was all choreographed. It's like when Richard Avedon photographed me. He took an hour just getting my body and my fingers in the right pose on the piano. He was a master. Once he was confident with the pose, he took only about ten shots and we were done.

JANE: You also have a fabulous group of vintage documentary work in your collection. During the 1930s and 1940s there weren't a lot of women working in photography. Dorothea Lange was one of them and she had a quote from the English philosopher Francis Bacon hanging on her darkroom wall. It read: 'The contemplation of things as they are, without error or confusion, without substitution or imposture, is in itself a nobler thing than a whole harvest of invention.'

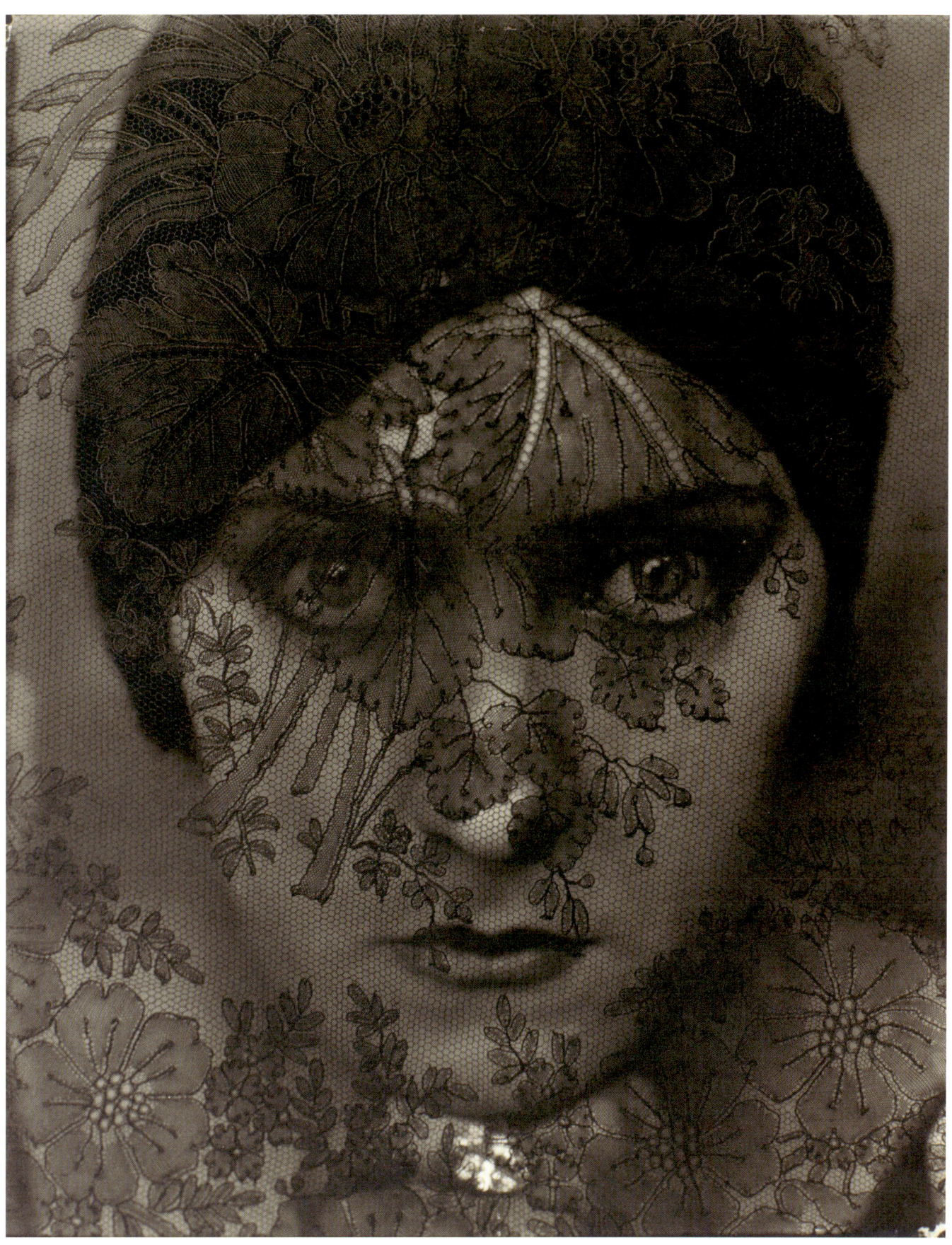

Edward Steichen
Gloria Swanson, New York 1924
24.1 × 18.1 cm

Elton: Wow.

Jane: Yes. She always said that she was trying to 'grab a hunk of lightning', meaning to capture photographically the precise moment that would make a big impact. One of the things Lange also said was 'Beauty appears when one feels deeply, and art is an act of total attention.' Whenever she was photographing, she needed to be thinking of nothing else other than making an image. Everything else was blocked out.

Elton: She also wanted to tell the world about the truth, to tell everyone about the Great Depression in America. And these photographs that she took, the pain in them - it just grabs you. The sadness, and the pain, and the suffering. She just gets it more than anybody else. The portraits and pictures of these people, she got inside their souls. Look at the *Migrant Mother* (p.24) - it's not so much a sad photograph as a resignation of this woman's suffering. It's an exhausting photograph. It's like, 'What else can I do? Where am I going? What does the future hold for me or for my family? Here are my children and what hope is there in this photograph?' It's such a despairing photograph.

Jane: The Lange photograph of the damaged child (p.112) that you own is, I think, especially important because of way she titled it in her own handwriting on the back of your specific print.

Elton: Yes, on the back she wrote 'The Damage is Already Done'. So much more poignant than the title *The Damaged Child* that you always see in books. The little girl with the black eye looks like she's experienced the emotions of a ninety-year-old woman. She's just so dark. It's incredibly touching when you think these are all little stories on their own. That's what I love about photographs. They're all stories. And look at the Walker Evans of the fantastic sign there on the tree, *Christ or Chaos?* (p.115). I love that. It really sums up what was happening at the time.

Jane: Yes. So Walker Evans and Dorothea Lange were both photographing for Roy Stryker of the Farm Security Administration and showing us the power of photography to make change. In the mid-1930s, Walker Evans and the writer James Agee would collaborate on what would eventually become the acclaimed book *Let Us Now Praise Famous Men*, in which Allie Mae Burroughs (p.117) and Floyd Burroughs (p.116) were featured.

Elton: Yes, and have you ever noticed that the damaged girl in Lange's photographs looks so much like a younger version of Evans's Allie Mae Burroughs? The hairline, the pursed lips. That is extraordinary. They should hang together.

Jane: When we talk about the power of photography for social change, I think of your own foundation. I remember being at an Elton John AIDS Foundation event where they showed some of the photographs which your husband David had taken of people that your charity was helping in Africa. What do you think of the role of photography as a means of increasing awareness and change?

Elton: After 9/11, Ingrid Sischy [writer, art critic and editor of *Interview Magazine* from 1989 to 2008] and I went to Ground Zero and we visited this store called Here is New York, which was selling prints taken by amateurs and professionals of the horrors of 9/11. I think the proceeds went to help the families of the victims. I purchased about 2,000 photographs and I keep them in portfolios to remind me of this tragedy. There were images of the shops that had been covered in mounds of dust and debris, and the reactions on peoples' faces looking up at the Twin Towers. The most horrible subject matter but the most moving photography. Jane, you've been there with me when I get those photographs out, or when I show them to people - I always cry. I always cry.

Jane: There are a number of photographers whose work you have collected extensively, such as Robert Mapplethorpe and Irving Penn. You also acquired a lot of Norman Parkinsons. through Tim Jefferies at Hamiltons. What attracted you to his work? Was it because he was British, or were you more attracted to his fashion work?

Elton: Yes, Tim was also there from the very beginning. I love Parkinson's fashion work and I love the fact he loved his wife so much. He was bit like an English Irving Penn. But he also took great photographs, like *After the Shower, Trafalgar Square, London* (p.203). I was photographed by him. He was just such a gentleman, so charming and wonderful. I like to think incredibly underrated, too. If he had been an American, it would've been a different situation. And I think he was a really fabulous photographer.

Jane: Conversely you also acquired the gritty New York City photographs by Weegee [Arthur Fellig]. He was an interesting photographer, don't you think?

Elton: Well, in his own way he was one of the first paparazzi. By his choice, he wasn't interested in stars. He was interested in the general public and crimes, murders. Reportage photography. He used to listen to a police radio in his car, so he could get to the crime scenes quickly. One of my favourite of Weegee's photographs is *The Critic*. And I also like the experimental work he did later with distortions (fig.8, p.39) and double exposures.

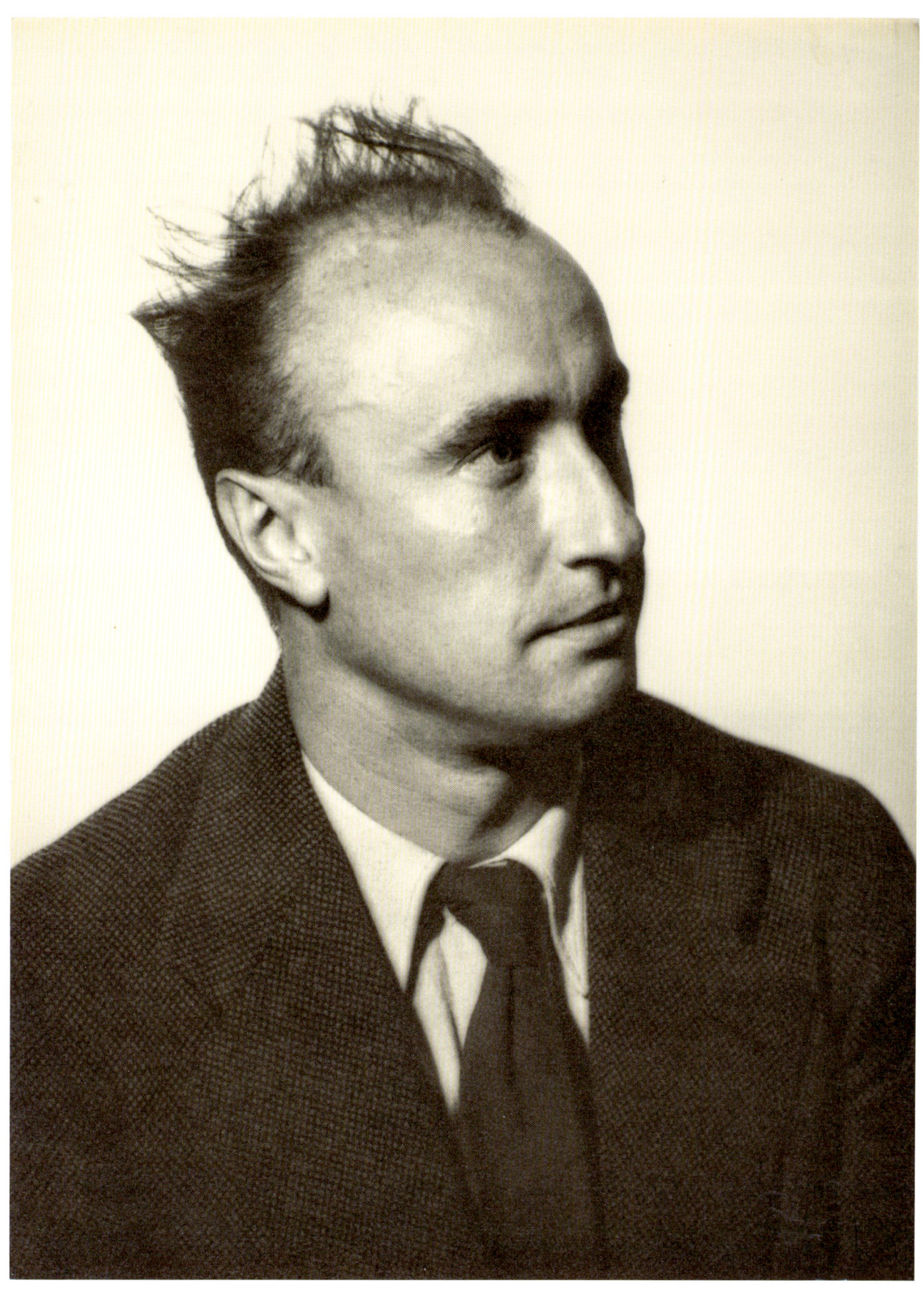

Man Ray
Yves Tanguy 1935
23.5 × 17.8 cm

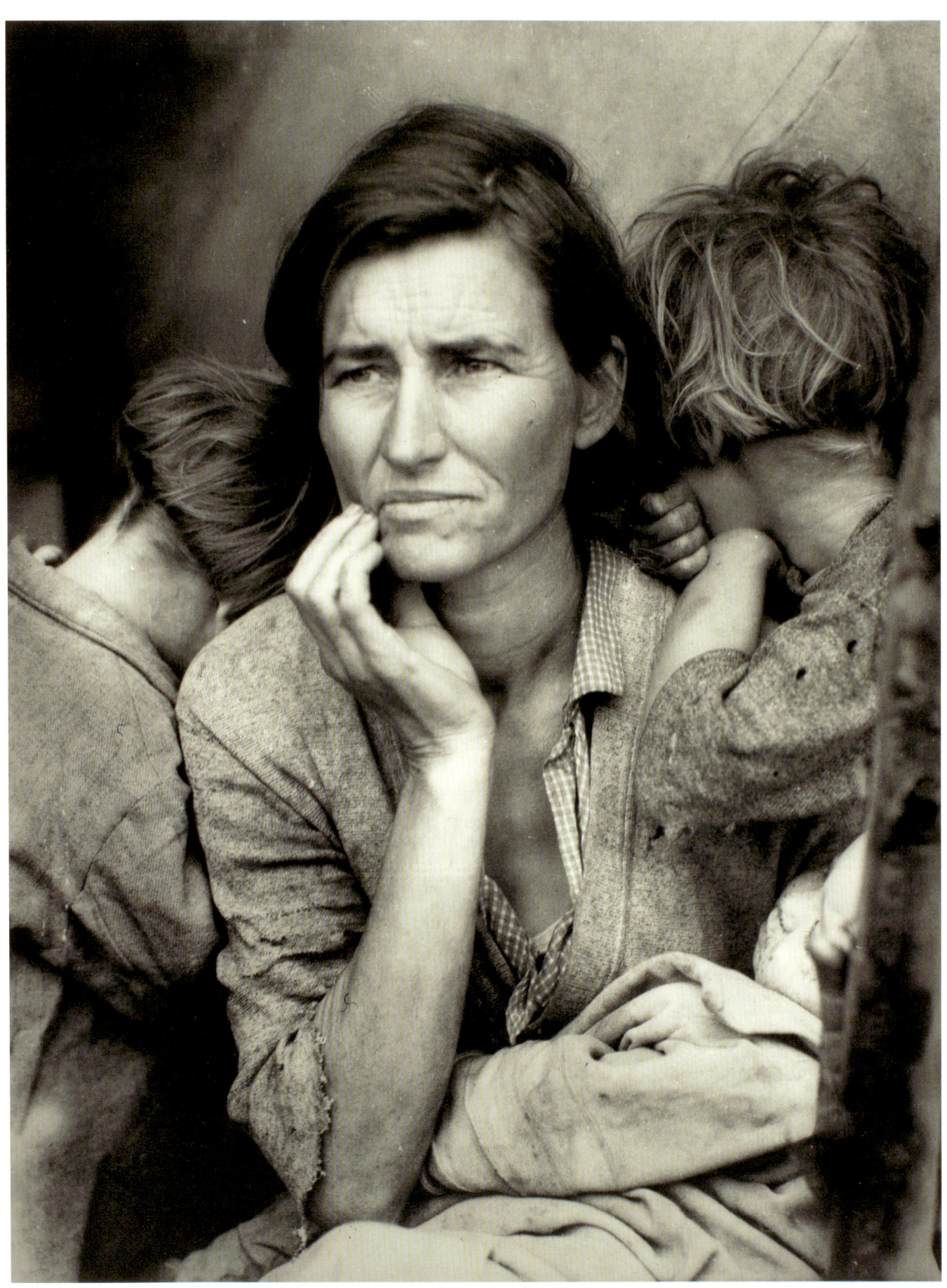

Dorothea Lange
Migrant Mother 1936
printed c.1950, 31.8 × 24.1 cm

JANE: Yes, Weegee did his double exposures in the darkroom by putting two negatives together. When he looked through the enlarger he knew exactly what the outcome would be. Others like Harry Callahan were more experimental and would do the double exposures in the camera, so they would be surprised by the outcome. And then you have solarisations. Again, some artists would solarise when making the print and others would solarise when processing the negative.

ELTON: I love this small photograph by Modotti of Weston in the window (p.64). It was taken in Mexico, right?

JANE: Yes, she captured him writing either a letter or entries in his Daybooks. We don't know for sure which. There is a story that he was writing a letter home to his youngest son, Cole, reminding him to brush his teeth. Although Weston was away in Mexico with Modotti, he never forgot about his four sons. Chandler lived with him in Mexico for a while and, later, so did Brett. Edward really respected Brett's work as a photographer.

ELTON: I adore my solarised male torso by Man Ray (p.139). I read that it was actually his assistant, Lee Miller, who accidently discovered the solarisation technique and then Man Ray saw it as a new creative process. It's a beautiful, sexy photograph. The shape of the body, the way it's leaning slightly, the hand held behind the back and the neck bending down - that didn't happen by accident.

He posed him. Man Ray obviously had an androgynous streak because he could make men look sexy as well as women. He was a very sexual man as well. I think anything went in those days. And then the Man Ray photograph of the neck (p.134). You don't know if it's a man's neck or a woman's. I remember when I first saw it - it was like, I have to have that.

JANE: What do you want people to get out of the Tate Modern exhibition?

ELTON: What I want them to get out of it is a sense of awe. I want them to think, 'I've never seen anything like that before, never knew this kind of thing existed' - just as I did when I first saw these photographs.

JANE: Do you think people will be surprised?

ELTON: I have no idea what to expect. People have no idea I've got this collection. But art should be seen. That's why I'm so happy that it is going to be shown in London. Then they can make of it what they like.

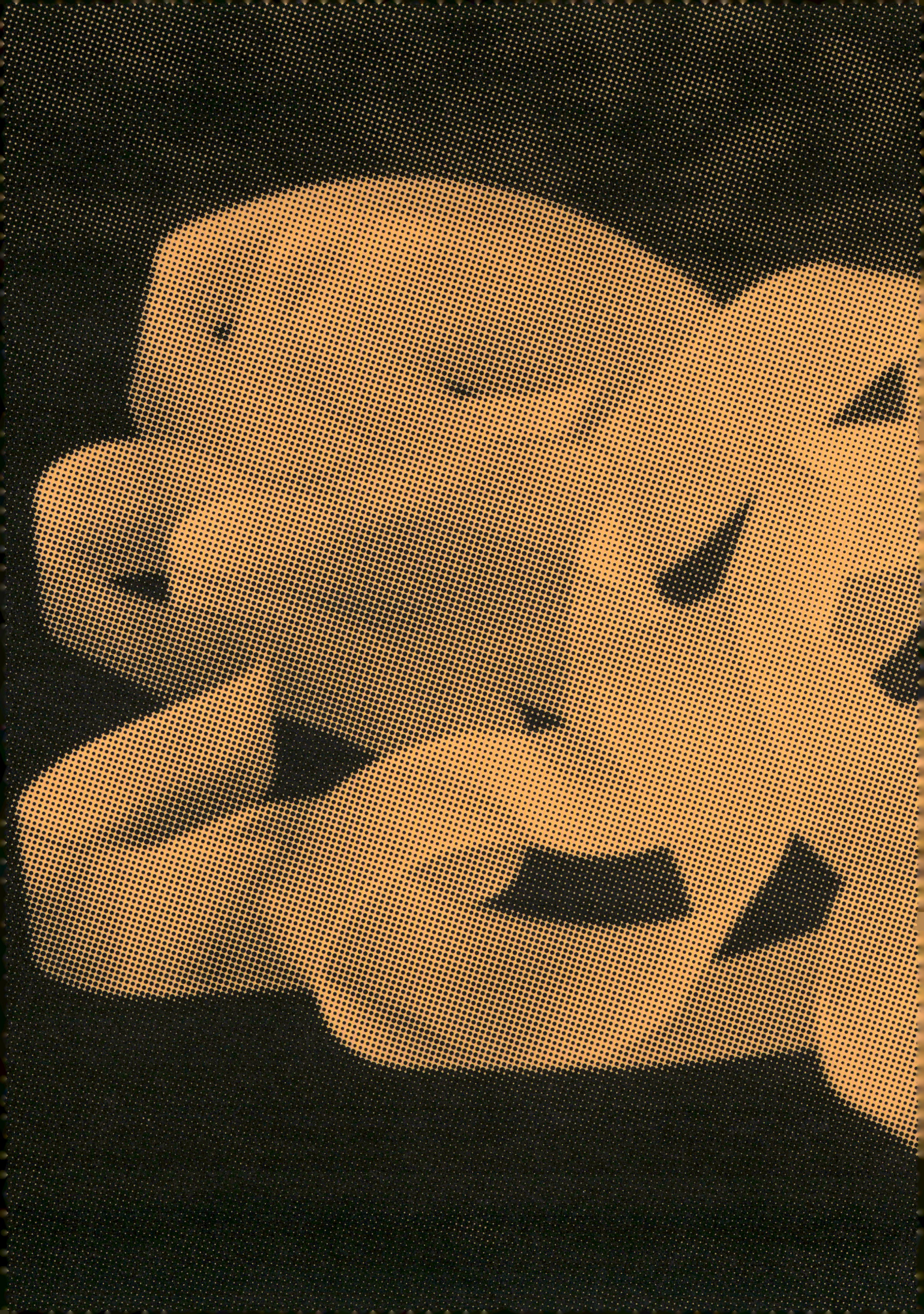

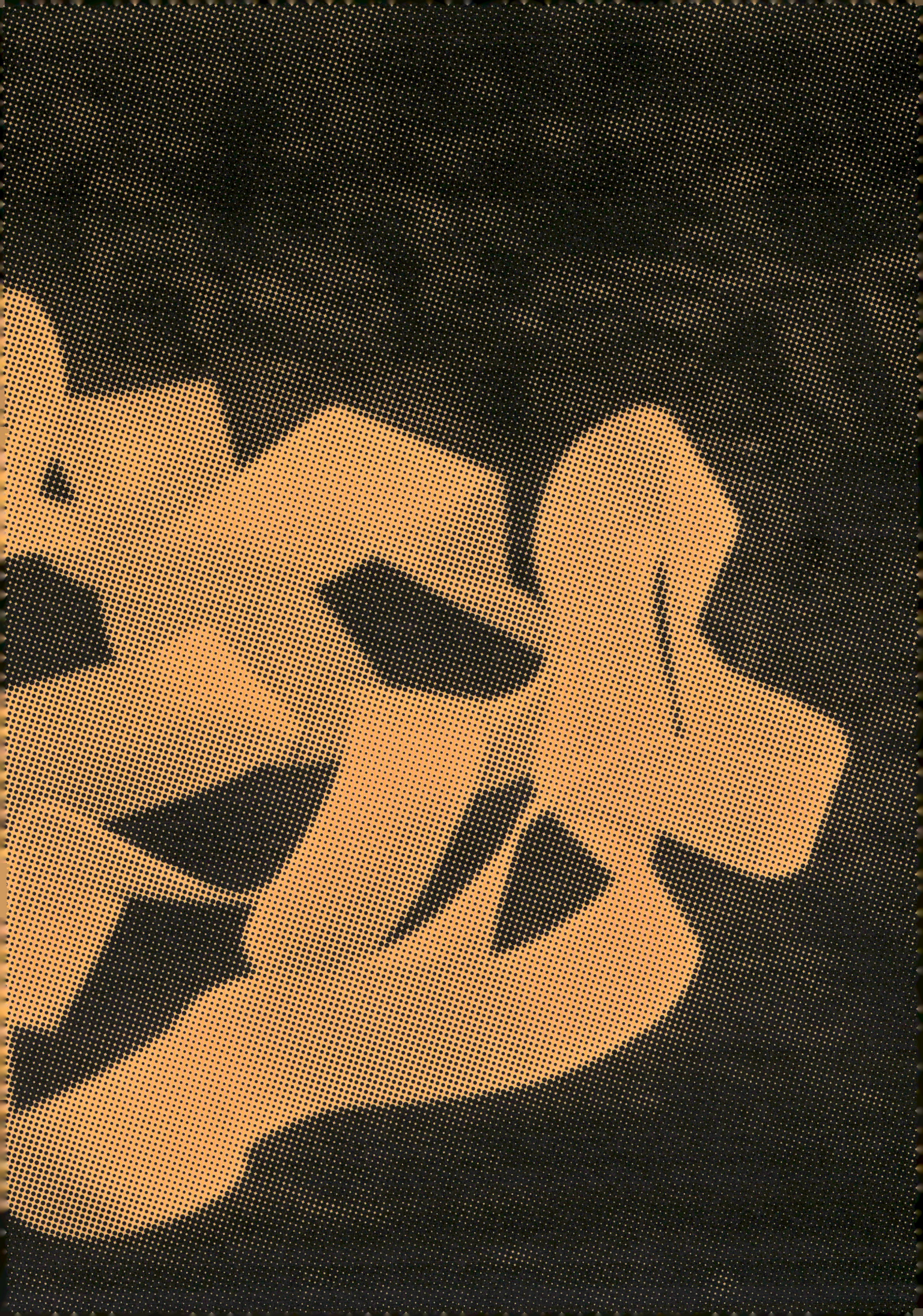

INSTRUMENT OF A NEW VISION:
PHOTOGRAPHY IN THE FIRST MACHINE AGE
DAWN ADES

It cannot be too plainly stated that it is quite unimportant whether photography produces 'art' or not. Its own basic laws, not the opinions of art critics, will provide the only valid measure of its future worth.[1]

László Moholy-Nagy, the most influential and far-sighted theorist and practitioner of photography in the inter-war years, was one of the first to summarise its 'basic laws'. In 'A New Instrument of Vision' (1932) he outlined the specific, and purely technical (not artistic), elements of photography that had enabled it to become 'one of the primary objective visual forms': Abstract seeing (the photogram); Exact seeing (reportage); Rapid seeing (snapshots); Slow seeing (prolonged time exposures); Intensified seeing (micro-photography and filter photography); Penetrative seeing (x-rays); Simultaneous seeing (superimposition); Distorted seeing (optical jokes, lenses fitted with prisms, reflecting mirrors or manipulation of the negative).

Moholy-Nagy was in no doubt that what he was arguing for, described and illustrated in spectacular plates in *Painting Photography Film*, his great Bauhaus manifesto of 1925, was a revolution in vision, affecting all mediums and pointing to the development of new ones, and he pursued the expansion of 'seeing' into every aspect of what he called optical creation. It was above all through film and photography that 'we see the world with entirely different eyes', but the capacities of the camera had hitherto only been explored 'in a secondary sense'. His was a call to action, with a strong tinge of constructivist ideology, to establish objective vision. 'Everyone will be compelled to see that which is optically true, is explicable in its own terms, is objective, before he can arrive at any subjective position. This will abolish that pictorial and imaginative associative pattern which has remained unsuperseded for centuries and which has been stamped upon our vision by great individual painters.'[2]

A key factor in the flowering of photography after the First World War and through the 1920s and 1930s, and its peculiarly intense relationship with that period which it seems visually to represent most fully, was the number of avant-garde artists, like Moholy-Nagy, who were drawn to it. In fact photography constituted an avant-garde in itself. 'The photographers who went over from figurative art to photography not on opportunistic grounds, not by chance, not out of sheer laziness, today constitute the avant-garde among their colleagues, because they are to some extent protected by their background against the greatest danger facing photography today, the touch of the commercial artist.'[3]

By no means a new medium – a good eighty years old by the end of the First World War – photography seemed suddenly to be the right mode of expression. The artists did not flock to photography because it had gained the status of art. Quite the contrary. It was more because it was free, as Moholy-Nagy put it, of the old 'pictorial and imaginative associative' patterns that they turned to it. This is what Man Ray meant when he said: 'I maintain that photography is not artistic! Grounds for complaint for some, plaudits for others.'[4] Some would complain that it was conceived of as art, others that it wasn't. Photography had been dogged throughout the nineteenth century by attacks motivated by the misdirected application of the essentially anti-technical concepts associated with art. The philosopher Walter Benjamin quoted a German newspaper that accused photography of blasphemy because it was using mechanical means to reproduce the features of Man, who is made in the image of God. 'Here we have the philistine notion of *art* in all its overweening obtuseness, a stranger to all technical considerations, which feels that its end is nigh with the alarming appearance of the new technology.'[5]

From the other end of the spectrum modern artist-photographers were still gnawing away at the problem in the twentieth century. In 1922 Alfred Stieglitz sent out a questionnaire asking, 'Can a photograph have the significance of art?' to which Marcel Duchamp brusquely and famously replied:

Dear Stieglitz
Even a few words I don't feel like writing.
You know exactly what I think about photography.
I would like to see it make people despise painting until something else will make photography unbearable.
There we are.[6]

Duchamp, who abandoned painting in 1918 and experimented with the camera (both film and photography), mostly in collaboration with Man Ray, congratulated his friend on having done likewise: 'Je suis enchanté de savoir que tu t'amuses bien et surtout que tu as lâché la peinture.'[7] Why on earth do in painting what a camera can do better? Man Ray's comment in 1930 that 'Painting is dead, finished' seemed conclusive. He preferred to connect photography not with the visual arts, but with poetry.

HOW PHOTOGRAPHY WAS SEEN, 1915–1939
The idea that photography had usurped the role of painting was widespread. Acceptance of it as an art was not. Stieglitz produced the magazine *Camera Work* from 1903 to 1917 with a missionary

1 Paul Strand
Abstraction, Twin Lakes,
Connecticut 1916

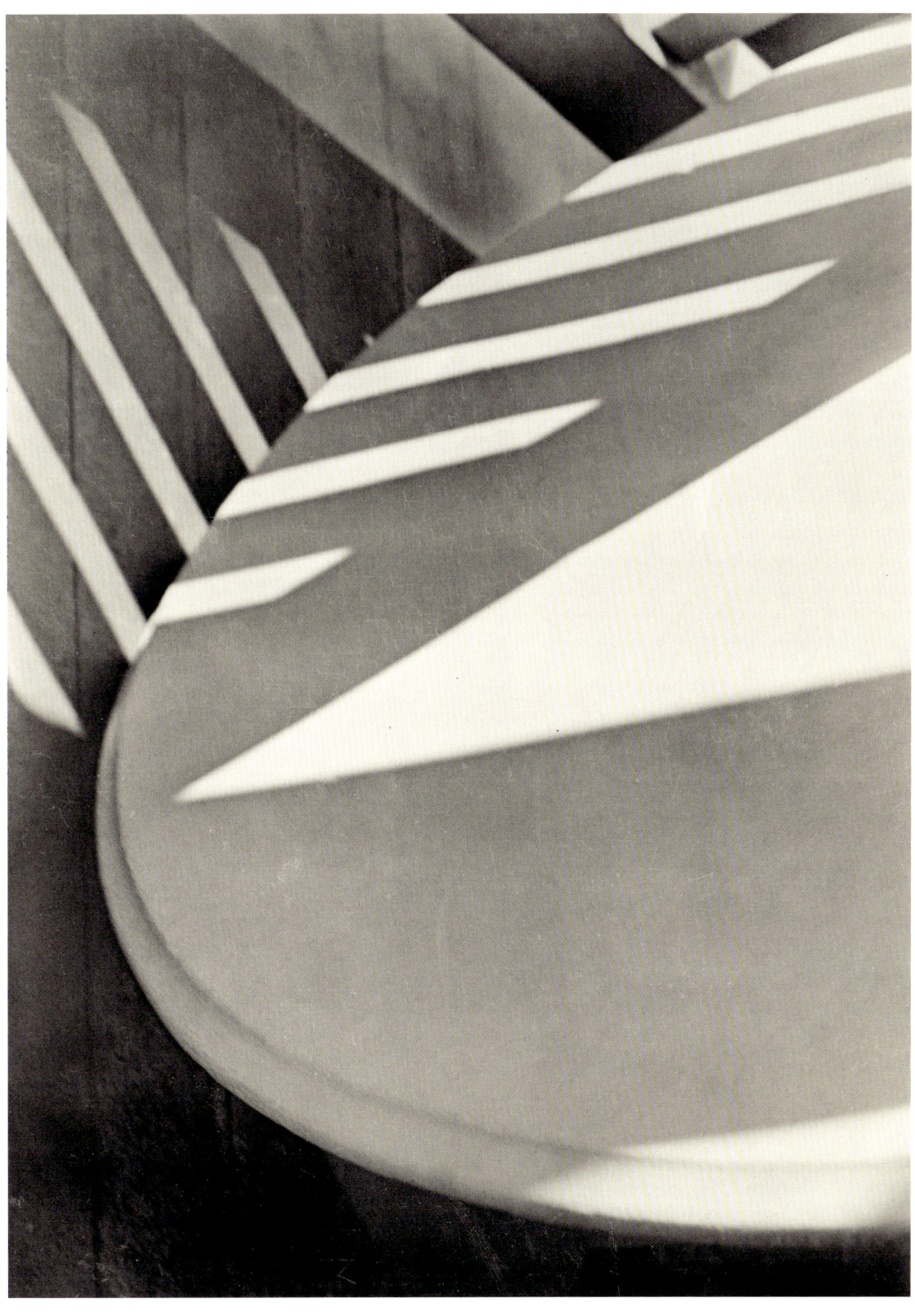

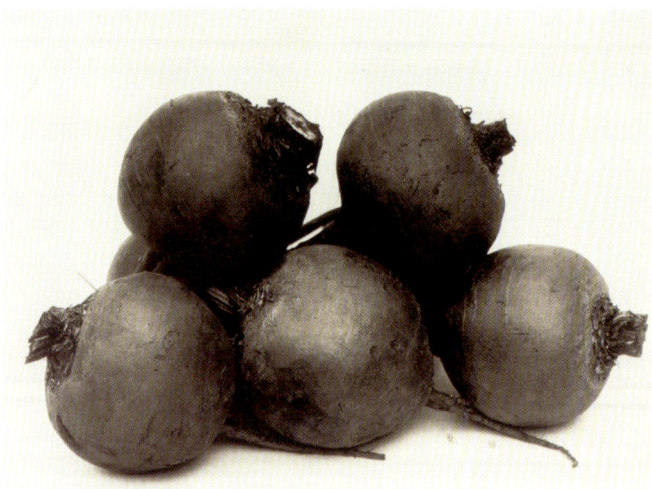

zeal. *Camera Work* had been a bastion of pictorial photography from its inception in 1903, but underwent a conversion when Stieglitz experienced a kind of epiphany before Paul Strand's New York street scenes. 'His work is pure. It is direct. It does not rely upon tricks of process.'[8] Strand's *Wall Street, New York* (p.202) is as iconic in its way as Stieglitz's *The Steerage* of the same year, 1915.[9] The vast, regular, dark rectangles in the walls dwarf the irregular knots of passing humans in a hard-edge city version of the sublime. Strand's photographs in the final issue of *Camera Work* in 1917 could hardly be further from the pictorial photography of its early years, which was often almost indistinguishable in the high quality textured reproductions from prints of impressionist landscape painting. These close urban studies of the patterns of light and shadow on constructions – one is straight-line geometrical, the other curvilinear – are almost abstract (fig.1).

Open as *Camera Work* was to a variety of opinions about photography and its relation to art, its editor Stieglitz had felt embattled as he struggled to maintain it as one of the few places where 'the tradition that photography is an art is still kept up'.[10] This, Stieglitz pointed out, was by no means the common view of photography: 'the word photographic in the minds of the general public is synonymous with pedantic exactitude, illogical selection, absence of imagination and feeling in general; in fact, an anti-art.'[11] Between this popular rejection of photography and the recognition that successive attempts to prove that photography could rival painting were proving self-defeating and futile, *Camera Work* felt isolated. The 'old fashioned toilers at composite photography' like O.G. Rejlander and H. Peach Robinson, who believed photography could be manipulated to rival historical, mythological and landscape painting, had

been eclipsed by naturalism such as George Davison's *Onion Field* (1890). *Camera Work* steadfastly kept the debate about photography as art open and the text 'Is photography a new art?' focused on this recurrent theme. But the terms of the argument were changing. Comparisons with the arts of painting and sculpture were increasingly regarded as not just unhelpful but irrelevant: photography as a medium with its own techniques and technology had its own distinct aesthetic possibilities. In the final issue of *Camera Work*, dated June 1917, Strand wrote that photography, the 'first and only important contribution thus far of science to the arts, finds its raison d'être, like all media, in a complete uniqueness of means'.[12]

Lucia Moholy understood that the relationship between photography and its 'technique' was unusual. 'Every art has its technique. So has photography.' Photography just has more technique, or technology, than most. The technique had an existence and use independent of photography as an art, was not exclusively linked to it and defined by it, as is the case of oil paint or watercolour, and this was one of the reasons for its ambiguous status. 'There is more equality of rights between the two than there is between the other arts and their techniques. Hence the widespread conclusion that photography is not an art at all.'[13]

The two most authoritative historical accounts of photography at the time, Benjamin's 'A Small History of Photography' (1931) and Moholy's *A Hundred Years of Photography 1839–1939* (1939), bring the story up to date but spend by far the most time on its early years. (Moholy, like Moholy-Nagy, her ex-husband, was a photographer, Benjamin a critic and theorist.) For both it was important to establish that this history was by no means a triumphant progress.

Moholy-Nagy's *Painting Photography Film*, unlike the two histories, demonstrates the avant-garde adoption of photography; it looks fully modernist, of its moment, in its typography, design and illustrations.

All three agree that the particular (and constantly evolving) technique/technology of photography distinguishes it from other forms of visual representation but do not all draw the same conclusions. Different values and interpretations are given to core issues: realism and reality, objective and subjective, document and invention. For Moholy-Nagy the mechanical nature of photography, which appeared to reduce the role of the hand and to limit its use as personal expression, was precisely one of its greatest strengths. He called for 'objective vision', and for him the question of whether photography was or was not an art was redundant. The camera had changed our relationship with the world and with what he called 'present-day optical creation': 'We cannot … express hostility towards representational art but must demand that in conformity with our interest in and feeling for the world at large, up-to-date consequences are drawn: that painterly methods of representation suggestive merely of past times and past ideologies shall disappear and their place be taken by *mechanical means of representation* and their as yet unpredictable *possibilities of extension*.'[14]

Benjamin by contrast is concerned with aesthetic and ideological issues in relation to photography. He looks back nostalgically on what he considers its golden age: the flowering of photography came in its first decade, before industrialisation. While Benjamin adulates what he calls the 'aura' of these early photographs, it is – somewhat puzzlingly – precisely the banishing of the aura that he welcomes in the work of the twentieth-century photographers that he admires: Eugène Atget, August Sander, Karl Blossfeldt. Atget 'initiates the emancipation of object from aura which is the most signal achievement of the latest school of photography'.[15] Setting aside for a moment the question of what exactly he meant by aura, the special quality he saw in the work of the earliest photographers – Louis Daguerre, Alexander Hill, Nadar, Julia Margaret Cameron, Victor Hugo – was the marriage of a technique at a particular moment in its rapid development with the subject of the photograph. In the early period 'subject and technique were as exactly congruent as they became incongruent in the period of decline that immediately followed'.[16] Everything in the earliest photographs was built to last, and although his readings of individual photographs tend to be over-egged and unconvincing his description of the images is unsurpassed. The long, slow exposure time penetrated the medium and produced the 'absolute continuum from brightest light to darkest shadow'.[17] The light struggled out of utter blackness, and this was what was banished with the arrival of faster lenses. Photographers then began to imitate the lost darknesses with re-touching and artificial highlights.

What I think Benjamin means regarding Atget's 'emancipation of object from aura' is that Atget strips photography of these 'fashionable twilights', eschews the picturesque and 'disinfects the stifling atmosphere generated by conventional portrait photography in an age of decline'. He 'pumps the aura out of reality like water from a sinking ship.'[18] His Paris lacks obvious romance; it is the known but overlooked, not the worn-out spectacle of landmarks and pretty touched-up scenes. The magic in these photographs is not uniqueness but the unexpected in the everyday, and this, though Benjamin doesn't spell it out, is

the consequence of his mastery of the new, more agile technology and equipment, and the complete resistance to fabrication. (It is interesting that a 'truth to materials' aspect of 1920s photography goes hand in hand with a new form of experimental manipulation.) What Atget, Sander and Blossfeldt have in common, moreover, is a complete lack of interest in making artistic photographs. Atget is recording Paris in the interests of a civic survey, Sander is making a scientific examination by direct observation of social types, Blossfeldt is taking hugely magnified close-ups of plant forms as a teaching aid for design students. Each therefore occupies an undefined position in the field of photography, belonging neither straightforwardly to science, nor to the arts, nor to the fairground 'where photography is at home to this day'.[19] The photographs of the late Victorian gardener Charles Jones, totally unknown at the time, were intended by him as documents, but similarly resonate with modernist photography (fig.2).

Benjamin makes an illuminating distinction between *photography as art* and *art as photography*. As he says, while there was fierce debate over the former, the 'far less questionable social fact of *art as photography* was given scarcely a glance'. He came back to one aspect of the notion of *art as photography* in the later essay, 'The Work of Art in the Age of Mechanical Reproduction' (1936), but in the 'Small History' he moves fast from the implications of the photographic reproduction of works of art to the phenomenon of artists newly turning to photography: Moholy-Nagy, Man Ray, Germaine Krull and others. They represent the 'present face' of photography.

Returning to the question of aura in 'The Work of Art in the Age of Mechanical Reproduction', Benjamin is less regretful of its 'loss'. He defines it in connection with the uniqueness of the work of art, its presence in time and space, either as cult or exhibition object, to be worshipped or contemplated. The photographic reproduction of works of art changed all that, altered the relationship between viewer and object, removed the latter's elite character together with the aura, and introduced an unresolved tension between photography and art. 'Much futile thought was devoted to the question of whether photography is an art.' The real question should be, 'whether the very invention of photography had not transformed the entire nature of art'.[20] This is what artists like Moholy-Nagy had understood.

Lucia Moholy also spends a good deal of time on the early history of photography, known in its beginnings as 'honest sun-pictures', explaining crucial technical developments such as reproducibility, the changes in exposure times and arrival of the instantaneous photograph. She is especially interested, however, in the technical and socio-political character of the new invention, noting the speed of its adoption by the public and its commercialisation, with a new class of technicians exploiting people's fascination, arguing that it quickly became the art of the middle classes. The photographer was artist, chemist and craftsman all in one, in a field where there was no tradition. Painters had their single princely patron; photographers appealed to a general public. But their status towards the end of the nineteenth century, she argues, was ambiguous and conflicted. On the one hand there was the view that they were professionals, not mechanics, and entitled to the same respect as a doctor or clergyman. On the other hand it was felt that since its heyday in the daguerreotype years, it had sunk to a mere craft, its practitioners occupying a social position somewhere between mechanics and jugglers.

What we tend to see as a dramatic change in its status, as modern artists turned to it in the 1920s, is discussed in the context of the long relationship between painting and photography, which Moholy argues was always close. She describes some of the most radical developments in the avant-garde somewhat cursorily, not least because the discoveries do not seem new to her:

> Photography has been adopted by a few abstract painters as a new medium by means of which they tried to give shape to their feelings of balance. They are Man Ray, living in France, and Moholy-Nagy, living in the USA. They took up the method of 'Photogenic drawing', discovered by Schulze in 1727 and familiar to Fox Talbot before 1834 and applied it in their own way. The results are abstract pictures called 'Rayographs' – 'Rayograms' – 'Photograms' – 'Shadowgrams' – 'Skiagrams' and other names. Some among the abstract artists claim to have discovered the veritable principles of photography. They have, indeed, rediscovered the principle from which photography was originally evolved, and adapted it to their purposes of abstract expression. The question whether photography has been subjected to any influence of the abstract arts does not, therefore, arise with regard to these pictures.[21]

Her primary interest is the technical potential of the medium. Scientific photography, she notes in a passage that makes a similar point to *Painting Photography Film* but in less polemical language, 'was able, in these first years already, to cover a field immeasurably wider than the human eye very much more quickly and more efficiently than any other tool'.[22] The only thing it lacked was colour. Despite her insistence that there was hardly any field covered by photography 'that was not foreshadowed within the first twenty years', Moholy's sense of its applications and potential was much closer to what has become the reality of the visual fields of communications opened up by photography in association with telegraphy, for example, than either Moholy-Nagy or Benjamin.

Photography has a close and complex relationship with a historical period from which we are now separated by eighty-odd years, but whose impact – politically, socially and culturally – remains profound. The decades in question can be defined in different ways according to one's priorities and prejudices: it can be described as the interwar period – that is, between the First World War of 1914-18, the so-called Great War, which transformed the geographical and political face of Europe, Russia and the Middle East, and the Second World War of 1939-45; it can be described in terms of the two great twentieth-century revolutions, in Mexico (1910-17) and Russia (1917), with their utopian ambitions, demands and beliefs, and then their failures; it can be described, in Europe, as the period of the rise of Fascism, in the rest of the world as the consolidation of colonial powers. Intellectually it was dominated by surrealism, as both Walter Benjamin and Jean-Paul Sartre admitted. It is a period, however differently it may be defined, that is given life now through the photographic images of this era - vastly increased in number with the massive rise in the circulation of daily newspapers and illustrated magazines: 'The numbers of these photographs reach astronomical figures and represent an immense power. Together with the printed word they have had a share in shaping public opinion for many years.'[23]

This period has also been described as the First Machine Age, from the perspective of a critical historian writing at the end of the 1950s, that is roughly at the end of a decade known variously as the 'Jet Age, the Detergent Decade, the Second Industrial Revolution', which marked the beginning of a Second Machine Age.[24] In *Theory and Design in the First Machine Age* Reyner Banham analysed the aesthetic theories that propelled modernist architects and designers in relation to a newly mechanised environment. The technical revolutions that justified the title of First Machine Age were, he argued, to do with the supply of energy (such as electricity) to the domestic sphere and electronic communications (such as the telephone), thus the reduction of machines to the human scale. The difference with the Second Machine Age is that access to the old status symbols like cars, and the new aids to living and entertainment like washing machines and televisions, were no longer just for the elite. He has curiously little to say about photography, despite giving a prominent place to Moholy-Nagy in recognition of the fundamental part he played at the Bauhaus. It seems to have a purely functional role in his book, although space is given to modern movements such as cubism and futurism and artists such as Duchamp, Paul Klee and Jean Arp, and this reflects a fairly common blinkered attitude to visual modernism, which had to be addressed in terms of style, abstraction and the constructive. Photography never fitted neatly into those primarily aesthetic categories, having its own basic laws, as spelt out by Moholy-Nagy in 'A New Instrument of Vision'. In a curious and paradoxical way photography was invisible (although everywhere) for some theorists of modernism (it was an old technology, commonplace, image-based, more document than art, compromised by its use in advertising and propaganda) at the same time that avant-garde artists were discovering it as the medium of the moment.

What is it that makes the photographs of Man Ray, Moholy-Nagy, Krull and Strand, among others, on the one hand the embodiments of a particular, difficult age, an already remote past, and on the other timeless examples of photography at its best? Is there a detectable relationship between the technique, its subjects and its product at the time that makes this so?

The following are some of the factors one could suggest: the black-and-white medium was also a metaphor that captured the spirit of the times; the camera opened onto an optical unconscious in the age of Freud; photography entered an alliance with fashion and became its glamorous face; it was a mechanical means of representation and reproduction in a machine age; it went into the street and the open air, at a time when everyone was stripping off as naturists, thanks to the portable camera; it is naturally open to experiment given its constantly evolving technical character.

Blessed, it seemed, with an inbuilt connection to the real, to be the register or trace of things, photography found the most devious and diverting ways to confound these expectations and to reveal all kinds of images invisible or surprising to the naked eye. It is therefore not unexpected that photography turned out to be one of the great forms of expression for the surrealists, and their encounters with the medium forms a thread that runs throughout this discussion. But at the same time photography gives the lie to one of the pieties of art historical accounts of the 1920s and 1930s – the opposition between the 'isms'; it cuts right across notional theoretical and stylistic divisions between dada, constructivism, surrealism, neo-plasticism and the Bauhaus, and fails to be contained by any of them.

BLACK AND WHITE

Salvador Dalí once worried his patron Edward James by claiming that the First World War happened in black and white, and wondering whether the next one (this was in 1939) would be in Technicolor. James took his views literally and informed him, having consulted veterans, that the First World War was not in black and white but khaki.[25] However, from the perspective of history it did take place in black and white: the photographs and films that recorded this violent convulsion of Europe constitute its memory in our imagination, just as computer screens highlighted with the flight paths of missiles constitute the public experience of the first Gulf War.

Moholy-Nagy observed that the modern world was experienced as though without colour, an effect allied to photography. 'The interplay of various facts has caused our age to shift almost imperceptibly towards colourlessness and grey: the grey of the big city, of the black and white newspaper, of the photographic and film services; the colour-eliminating tempo of our life today.'[26]

This was a time, moreover, when the black and white of the photograph was so intimately linked with its truth-telling that colour seemed to be an intrusion – we had become so accustomed to the specific tones of the photographic translation of the world into black, white and grey that it was difficult to accept chromatic reality in the photograph.

We take for granted this acquired ability to translate the hues of the objects, the faces, the landscapes and events of the world around us into the subtle tones of grey, partly because photographs were devoid of colour from the start, and also perhaps partly because we find it easy to subtract colour from light, for instance with the nightly example of moonlight. Moholy-Nagy's prediction was already coming into being: 'Organised grey-relationships, the living relationships of chiaroscuro, will of course emerge later on as a new aspect of the biological-optical experience of colour.'[27] This was an effect of modernity in which the photographic was deeply implicated, and Moholy-Nagy noted that there was a consequent need for painting - creation in colour – to prevent 'the atrophying of our optical organs'.

Some subjects carry with them undeniable and inbuilt colour, such as human skin, notoriously the most difficult to replicate in oil paint and the most miraculous when successfully rendered as in Giorgione's or Titian's portraits. In black-and-white photographs, as in Edward Weston's studies of nudes, the skin of the elegantly folded or fragmented bodies is subtly represented not just through the grey to light tones but also through the textural contrast with the background, with hair, and so on (pp.152, 153).

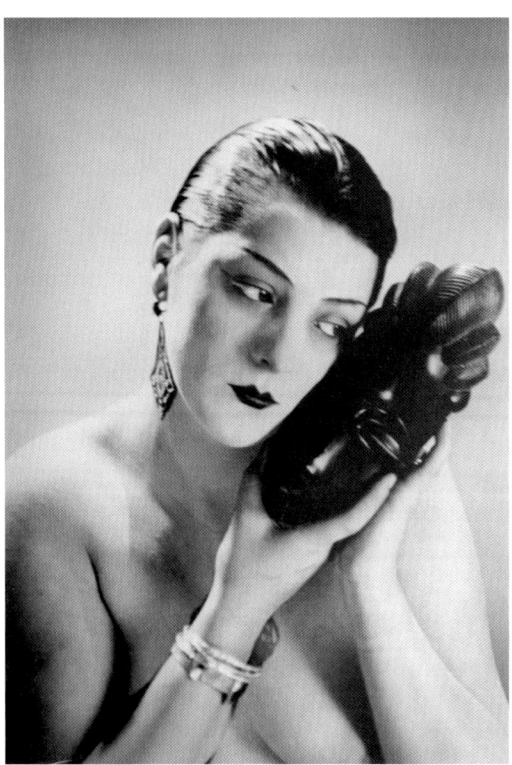

Photographers often chose subjects that played to the strengths of the medium, and were, for example, white in essence: like Josef Sudek's *Lily of the Valley* c.1954, where the white of the flower (its leaves removed) and the transparency of water and glass leave no room to regret the absence of colour, or Imogen Cunningham's still-life studies of flowers, such as her *Magnolia Blossom*, whose petals we assume are white, and whose wonderfully sensuous velvety surfaces float out from the densely seeded stamen like a ballerina's skirt (p.164).

Man Ray's *Ostrich Egg* (p.161) similarly is easy to accept as a true and complete image in that its subject is already white. But in other respects *Ostrich Egg* plays on deception. The size of the egg is impossible to tell: filling the print as it does there is no means of gauging the scale. Ambiguities of this kind, sometimes cutting across subjects so that whether it was a distant view or a still life was unclear, were popular. They were also to an extent dependent upon being in black and white. One illustration in *Painting Photography Film* is particularly deceptive: what appears to be a highly magnified close-up of a plant section, or possibly a machine tool, turns out to be a vertical view of pews and people in St Paul's Cathedral, seen distantly through the glass dome. The photographer may have been aware of some irony here: in the satirical magazine *Punch*

a drawing of the dome of St Paul's was titled 'Camera Obscura' with the note: 'We understand that, with the view to making the most of the Grand Ecclesiastical Exhibition Station, commonly called St Paul's Cathedral, the dome of that popular and attractive show is to be fitted up as a camera obscura.'[28]

Some commentators criticised a tendency in photography to regard tonal values more highly than the subject of the photograph; this was seen as analogous to theories of abstract art, which 'claimed that colours and tone values were expressive by themselves'. For Lucia Moholy, who had a socialist and a realist (not a 'socialist realist') approach to photography, this had led to an unnatural isolation of the object, and an 'over-consciousness of tone values and balance. Hence the great number of still-life and "pattern" photographs between 1920 and 1930, with a minimum of object and a maximum of lights and shades, rhythm and balance … Whether the object was an egg or a tea-cup, a score of pins or a pair of gloves, a piece of silk or a heap of sand, a row of corn sheaves or pebbles on a beach, was of no importance if the lights and shades were well arranged.'[29] The abstraction process generated by this emphasis on black-and-white tonal values in object photography was exclusively aesthetic, in her opinion, but the minimising of the object led to its isolation, and eventually to a counter-effect, to what she calls the 'self-assertiveness' of the object, ideologically dominant in the modern world in trade and industry. The result was modern pictorial photography, which found its 'most adequate sphere in modern advertising'.[30] The synergy between the close study of objects in tones of black, white and grey and advertising is undeniable, such as in Man Ray's *Glass Tears*, produced for a cosmetics advertisement (pp.16–17).

The black and white of photography was also a perfect metaphor for one of the most dynamic cultural drives of the 1920s: the craze for jazz, black culture and African art. Man Ray's *Noire et Blanche* is the iconic example of this, its metaphoricity emphasised by making the negative – with its reversed values of black and white – an equally important object (p.83).

Man Ray photographed his white lover Kiki – her face horizontal, eyes closed – holding upright a Baule mask in black ebony. It is an extraordinarily simple composition of apparent formal and cultural opposites, which has generated a very wide range of commentary from denunciation of its gender and racial stereotyping to celebration as a surrealist image. Its production, however, was extremely complex, from the original glass negative (now lost) to at least three internegatives, with retouching, to the roughly twenty-four prints now known, each of which is different.[31] The original title when it was first

4 ALFRED STIEGLITZ
Negro Art and *Brâncuşi* exhibitions
at the 291 gallery, New York, 1914
reproduced in *Camera Work*, no.48,
October 1916

published in Paris *Vogue* 7, no.5, May 1926, was 'Visage de nacre et Masque d'ébène' (Mother of Pearl Face and Ebony Mask), and on the facing page were photographs of another locally sourced exotic spectacle, 'Chinese Gladiators' at the Grand Music-Hall des Champs-Elysées. A variant of this subject, evidently taken at the same photo-shoot, shows Kiki awake and cradling the mask, which although charming entirely lacks the powerful, balanced contrasts of *Noire et Blanche* and turns the mask into a toy (fig.3). In *Noire et Blanche* the two heads enjoy a form of equality, which has also been criticised as equating women with savages. Both heads are highly wrought, the white as much as the black; the opposition between flesh and wood does not read as an opposition between nature and art.

The photograph was accompanied by an odd little primitivising text, certainly not written by either Man Ray or the owner of the mask, George Sakier, an assistant editor at Paris *Vogue* and friend of Man Ray's from earlier New York days (neither of whom had the requisite command of French), which adopts an uncomfortably social Darwinian tone:

> Face of a woman, calm transparent egg straining to shake off the thick head of hair through which she remains bound to primitive nature. It is through women that the evolution of the species to a place full of mystery will be accomplished. Sometimes plaintive, she returns with a feeling of curiosity and dread to one of the stages through which she has passed, perhaps before becoming today the evolved white creature.[32]

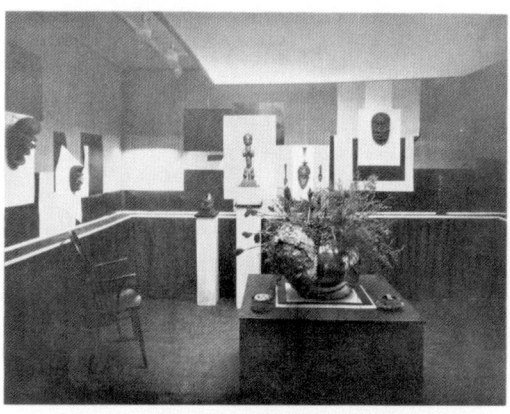

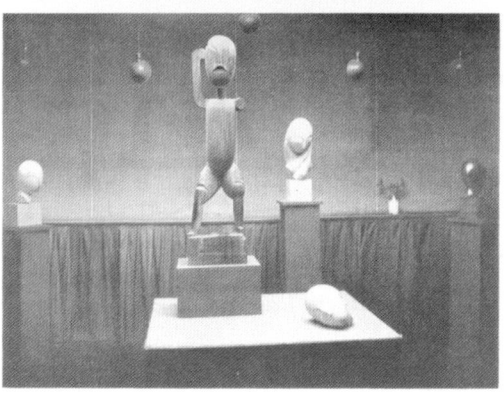

For *Vogue*, perhaps, the most striking thing about this photograph from a fashion point of view was Kiki's head – shorn, sleek and wholly representative of the New Woman, of whom Kiki was one the most famous and visible in Paris. The fabulous tight ridges of hair at the top of the mask are a perfect counterpart to Kiki's black helmet. Her hair could hardly be less like the 'primitive' thick head of hair of the accompanying text, which has been taken to conjure Baudelaire's poem 'La Chevelure', a homage to his mistress's mane of black hair and more generally to a non-European exotic world.[33] Baudelaire describes 'languorous Asia and burning Africa' as 'lointain, absent, presque défunt': distant, absent, almost extinct.[34]

But it seems that in a curious way *Noire et Blanche* is not primitivising in the sense of nostalgia for a distant or lost world. If the idea of the 'other' is being invoked, it is in a different sense. True, the fashion for African sculpture was seldom informed by an interest in its cultural meanings; it spoke more of 'the way in

which exotic artefacts were consumed by Western aficionados'.[35] Negrophilia in Paris conflated the exotic and the erotic. The catalogue of the Paris exhibition *Primitive Negro Sculpture* (1926, the same year as *Noire et Blanche*) claimed: 'the African fetish is an excuse for dreaming of deep mysterious forces, tom-toms and weird incantations, of dark warriors and women of the tropics'.[36] Man Ray would have seen a very different exhibition in *Negro Art* at Stieglitz's 291 gallery in New York in 1914 (fig.4): 'an exhibition of statuary in wood by African savages. This was the first time in the history of exhibitions, either in this country or elsewhere, that Negro statuary was shown solely from the point of view of art.'[37] What were the implications of this? To distance the sculpture further from any understanding of its meaning or to propose a universal idea of art that encompassed all cultural expression? Dreaming the heads in *Noire et Blanche* may be, but the mask has been transported from the ethnographic cases of museums or the walls of a curio shop not just into the world of art but also into the world of the living – an effect Man Ray also sought in *The Moon Rises over the Island of Nias*, the photograph

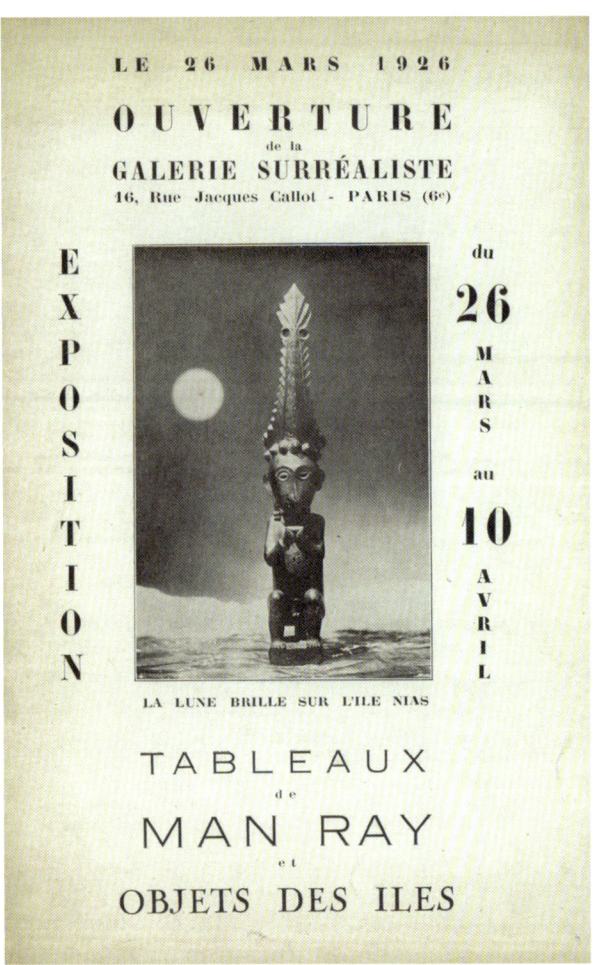

for the cover of the surrealist exhibition *Tableaux de Man Ray et objets des îles* (1926; fig.5). As anthropologist and curator Anthony Shelton wrote, 'Kiki, her face lacking all expression, has her eyes closed as in a dream, while the mask, upright and alert, might be attributed a wakeful state. Here has occurred transference of what surrealists considered to be the raw primordial essence of the mask into the Western subject.'[38] The two heads become the communicating vessels between dreaming and waking, the real and the imagined, and thus recall the core surrealist proposition: 'Everything tends to make us believe that there exists a certain point of the mind at which life and death, the real and imagined, past and future, the communicable and the incommunicable, high and low, cease to be perceived as contradictions.'[39]

Noire et Blanche might be a meditation on this enigma. The photograph is as complex as a poem. This is not to say it doesn't have meaning, but that meaning is embedded in the medium, not simply translatable into words, and can bear many interpretations. Talking about his relationship to painting, photography and film, in the same year he made *Noire et Blanche*, Man Ray said: 'We are touching here on the great struggle between beauty and poetry, aesthetics and ethics. I am resolutely on the side of poetry.'[40]

UNCONSCIOUS OPTICS

Recognition that the camera and the human eye were optically distinct added to the excitement generated by photography after the First World War. As Moholy-Nagy wrote, '*the photographic camera can either complete or supplement our optical instrument, the eye*'.[41] The fact that material things beyond the conscious scope of our eye could not just be made visible – as had been the case since the invention of the microscope – but also automatically recorded goes back to the beginnings of photography with, for example, microphotography. The invisible physical worlds increasingly captured by the camera were initially the domains of medicine and science (the first x-ray was made in 1895). For Moholy-Nagy the new vision was objective, a truth beyond the personal. For others its objectivity was more ambiguous.

The poet and future theorist of surrealism, André Breton, introduced his essay on the first Paris exhibition of fellow dadaist Max Ernst (1921) as follows: 'The invention of photography has dealt a mortal blow to the old modes of expression, in painting as well as in poetry, where automatic writing, which appeared at the end of the nineteenth century, is a true photography of thought.'[42] He goes on to marvel at the ability of film and photography to transcend the limitations of what the eye can see, for instance with slow motion and fast motion cameras. The collapse of our conventional experience of space and time was an aspect of the camera's ability to reveal a reality beyond what is immediately apparent to the human eye, a magical aspect of photography that appealed to Breton and the surrealists.

In describing automatic writing as the 'true photography of thought' Breton understood 'thought' in its widest implications, beyond the conscious and the rational, including the unconscious. The first proto-surrealist experiments in automatic writing had already been published in *Littérature*, and the debt to the nineteenth-century automatic writing of the spiritualist mediums was acknowledged. By the time Breton drew up the first *Manifeste du surréalisme* in 1924, automatism had been inscribed instead under the sign of Freud. This detached the exercises in automatism, whether visual or in writing, from the mediums, who claimed their writings were messages from

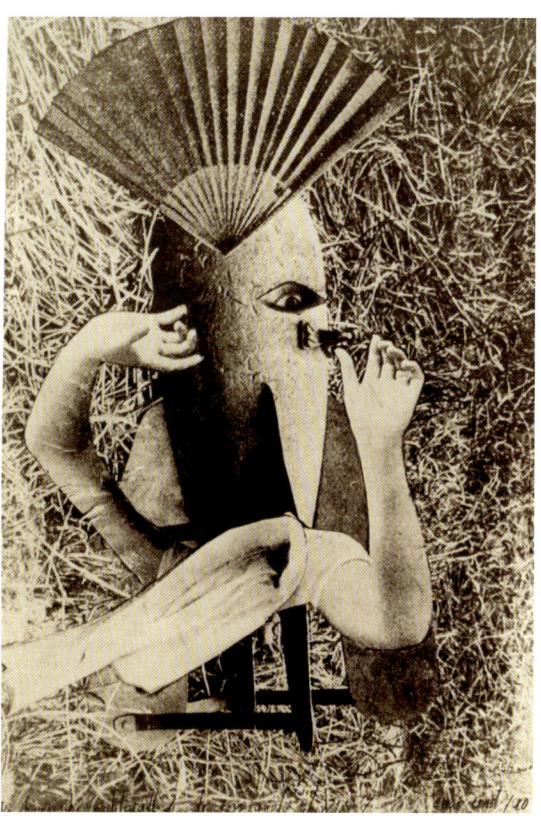

the beyond, and explained them instead as exploring 'the depths of our mind [which] contain within it strange forces capable of augmenting those on the surface, or of waging a victorious battle against them'.[43] Surrealism is defined as 'Pure psychic automatism, by which it is intended to express – verbally, in writing or in any other way – the true functioning of thought. The dictation of thought, in the absence of any control exerted by reason and outside any aesthetic or moral concerns.'[44] It is based on the belief in 'the omnipotence of dream and the disinterested play of thought'. It would seem that these were ideas inimical to photography, but the contrary proved to be the case. Ernst had drawn on photography for his early collages such as the *Chinese Nightingale*, producing startling juxtapositions analogous to the surrealist verbal image (fig.6). Man Ray, according to Breton, challenged photography's arrogant claim to represent the real by exploring that region which painting thought it had all to itself: that of the imagination, the dream and the unconscious, chance revelations and a certain kind of abstraction.[45] He had in mind the rayographs, published as *Champs délicieux* (1922) which were, like Moholy-Nagy's photograms or Christian Schad's schadographs, camera-less images made by exposing to light objects placed on photo-sensitive paper. The resulting images, inappropriately called abstract, were ghostly traces of the objects.

For Dalí, then a leader of a Catalan avant-garde interested in both dada and Neue Sachlichkeit (New Objectivity), the camera was 'the lens of authentic poetry', photography was 'the spiritual bird of thirty-six greys and forty new types of inspiration', sliding 'with continual imagination over new events'. Deeply fascinated by *Painting Photography Film*, even stealing one of its photographs to illustrate an article in the Catalan avant-garde journal *L'Amic de les arts*, Dalí revelled in the pure inventiveness and poetic imagination of photography which 'can caress the cold delicacy of white toilets, follow the languid slowness of aquaria; analyze the most subtle articulations of electrical apparatuses with all the unreal precision of its own magic'.[46] It was not just special effects, such as close-up, that he admired but the concentration on the object. He was familiar with a wide range of modernist photography and film – the examples he gives call to mind Edward Weston, Albert Renger-Patzsch and the films of Jean Painlevé. Dalí's language wonderfully draws on but diverts the streamlined precision of the machine age by piling on adjectives and enthusing over poetry. He makes a comparison, significantly, between photography and the unconscious, but favours the former whose 'brain waves are faster and more agile than the murky processes of the subconscious'.[47]

The analogy between photography and another kind of science, that of psychoanalysis, was drawn most explicitly by Benjamin, in terms that borrow from the earlier arguments of Moholy-Nagy and Breton. Like Breton, Benjamin recognised that 'it is another nature that speaks to the camera than to the eye: other in the sense that a space informed by the human consciousness gives way to a space informed by the unconscious ... Photography, with its devices of slow motion and enlargement, reveals the secret. It is through photography that we first discover the existence of this optical unconscious, just as we discover the instinctual unconscious through psychoanalysis.'[48]

THE HUMAN FIGURE: PORTRAITS AND HANDS
The portrait is, and has been since its earliest days, photography's commonist currency. Those affected most acutely, in economic terms, by its invention were not landscape or scene painters but portrait miniaturists, according to Benjamin, and already by 1840 innumerable miniaturists had become professional photographers. Everyone is fascinated by faces, not least their own, as the ubiquity of the selfie demonstrates. The use of photo-portraits as identity documents goes back to the nineteenth century. In 1855 a prison governor proposed establishing a portrait gallery of criminals in every prison in England. The magazine *Punch* remarked at the time that 'The idea may have some value, but we must confess that we never saw any photographic portrait yet, which did not give the idea of the

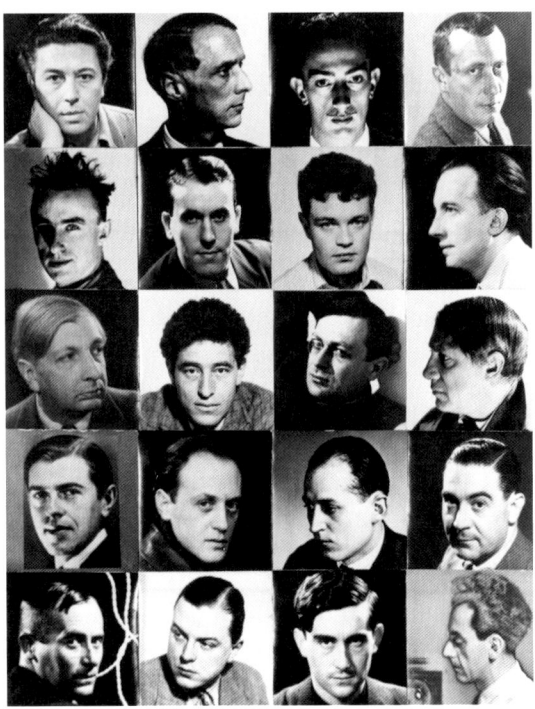

criminal', a perception Duchamp played on in his *Wanted* poster. W.H. Auden grumbled at the inability of the camera to record the actual experience of looking at someone:

> We never look at two people
> or one person twice
> in the same way.[49]

One could retort that the camera sees in a different way from us and thus reveals another reality in the person.

In her *Hundred Years* Lucia Moholy devotes considerable attention to portraiture in photography, both in the amateur and professional contexts. She mentions her own work as a photographer in connection with what she describes as the more realistic form of portrait photography, which she contrasts with the 'soft-focused, smooth and lovely portraiture', in the style of Joshua Reynolds and Thomas Gainsborough, of Cecil Beaton or Dorothy Wilding. The two final images in the modest plate section of the book illustrate this difference, contrasting a photographic portrait by Beaton of the Princess Paley (whether taken in the studio or outdoors is unclear), softly haloed in a leafy garden, hand clasped to her breast, with her own portrait of the Countess of Asquith and Oxford, a tightly cropped image of a formidable head, her profile dark against a neutral ground.

In the 1920s and 1930s there was a close relationship between celebrity portraits and fashion, evident in the work of Man Ray, George Platt Lynes, Edward Steichen, Peter Rose Pulham and many others. A principled opposition to the commercialisation of photography was felt by some more than others. Platt Lynes, who like Rose Pulham did fashion shoots as well as portraits,

destroyed all his fashion negatives at the end of his life.

Man Ray more than anyone made the photograph – whether of high fashion, or of his surrealist friends, or in his experimental mode – the visual currency of the era. His portrait of *André Breton* was placed top left in his photomontage *Surrealist Chessboard* (fig.7), with his own self-portrait in profile at bottom right, holding his camera. This was in a tradition of collective portraits of the group, dating from the first issue of the journal *La Révolution surréaliste* (1924) in which its members, augmented with photographs of admired figures such as Freud and Picasso, surround the photograph of the anarchist Germaine Berton. The final issue echoed this with another collective portrait, this time using snapshots taken in automatic photo booths of the surrealists with closed eyes surrounding René Magritte's painting *I Do Not See the [Woman] Hidden in the Woods* 1929. In 1931 Max Ernst dramatised the characters and their relationships in a photomontage reproduced in *Le Surréalisme au service de la révolution*, no.4 (1931), which he entitled *Au Rendez-vous des amis* (A Friends' Reunion) in memory of his painting of that title of 1922 with which he had celebrated his arrival in Paris. Each of these collective photo-portraits announces in its own way a collaborative ideal, with Breton usually occupying a dominant position. For *Surrealist Chessboard* Man Ray has cropped the photographs to focus on the head – Breton alone has a hand visible. Showing only the head eliminates the need for consideration of setting, context, accoutrements, attributes, hands, arms and body.

Remote from Man Ray's seductive portraits of friends, artists, celebrities and high society are his more informal, sometimes game-playing, self-portraits, such as the one in which he wears a white towelling dressing-gown (p.58). Man Ray, in cahoots with his friend Duchamp, was expert at using photography to question, play with or create identity, thereby emphasising its contingencies and fragility. Duchamp's female alter ego, Rrose Sélavy, embodied in Man Ray's photographs, is the most famous example but Man Ray also photographed himself *en femme*.

Photographs of the photographer are especially interesting. Tina Modotti's portrait, *Edward Weston with his Camera, Mexico* (p.63), juxtaposes Weston's head with the imposing camera lens. Head and lens turn their regard up and away to the left, as though Modotti is comparing the mechanical with the organic eye. She may be giving a heroic tilt to the human, but it is the camera that dominates. (Weston's portrait of Modotti [p.65] shows her not as photographer, but apparently reciting.) Weegee's *Self-Portrait (Distortion)* (fig.8) seems to use distorting mirrors for comic effect, the kind of optical joke identified by

8 Weegee (Arthur Fellig)
Self-Portrait (Distortion)
c.1955

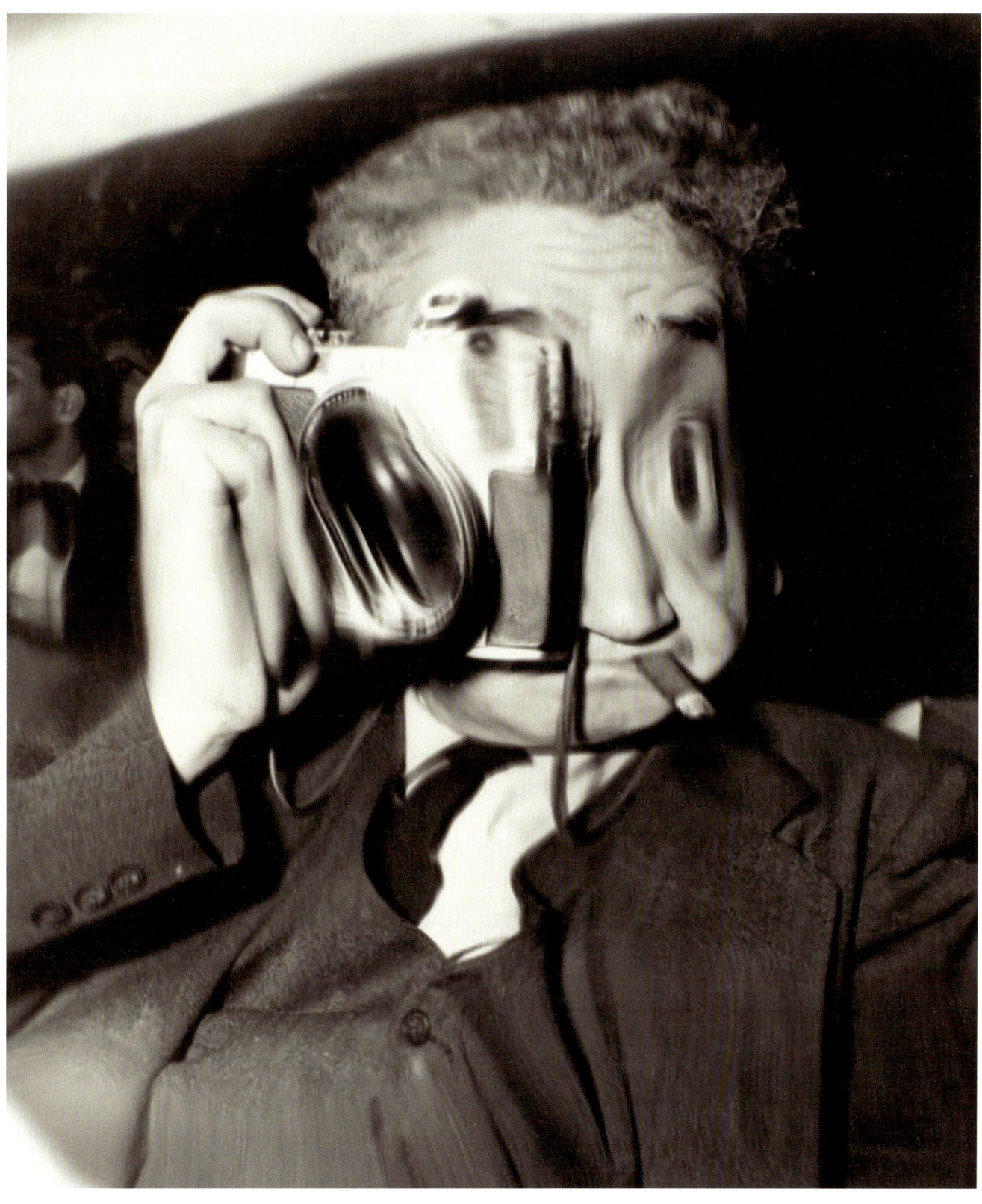

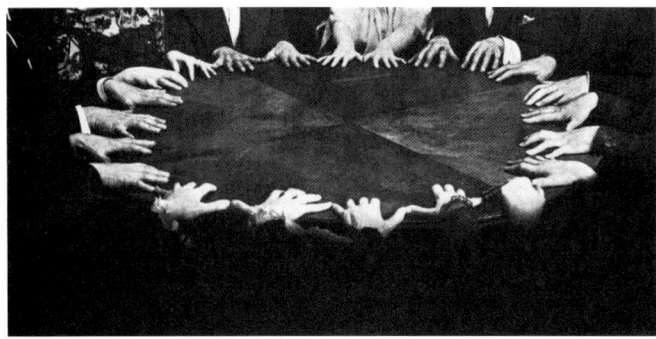

Moholy-Nagy as one of the inbuilt elements of photography.
More emphatically than in Modotti's portrait of Weston, camera
and eye are brought together, though in this case not only is
each askew, but also the 'eye' appears as a camera lens.

What is a portrait? Deriving from the French *pourtraire*
(delineate), which comes from the Latin *protrahere* (draw forth),
it is defined as representing some object, now almost always
the likeness of a person. We tend to assume the subject of the
portrait is not only a person, but also an individual, and named.

The Depression-era photographs by Walker Evans and
Dorothea Lange are very far from the celebrity studio portrait.
With minimal but telling background detail – rough wooden
fence, dilapidated wall – they capture the grim poverty of rural
life. Evans always names his subjects and where they live
(*Allie Mae Burroughs, Hale County, Alabama*; p.117). Lange, by
contrast, although photographing with a similarly sharp eye,
gives her photographs emotive or generic titles: *The Damage
is Already Done, Shacktown, Elm Grove, Oklahoma* (p.112), or
Migrant Mother (p.24). The latter, or the similarly unidentified
One of the Homeless Wandering Boys (p.121), are not, however,
like Sander's studies of individuals representing class, work and
profession. These are objective, scientific images purporting to
be permanent documents of social types. Lange's photographs
may be documentary but they are also evidently protests at
inhuman conditions, which, as the images imply, should change.
There is even, despite the fact they are clearly individual people,
a hint of allegory about these figures, as if they stand for
abstract ills like poverty, misery and fear.

And then there are the portraits without the subject, whose
presence and identity are indicated by objects, as with André
Kertész's *Ady's Poem* or *Mondrian's Eyeglasses and Pipe, Paris*
(pp.172, 173). These are portraits masquerading as still lifes,
and the objects are personal and specific rather than symbolic
of the subject's way of life or career.

Hands have been a traditional concern of the portraitist
throughout history, whether painter or photographer, as a
means of supplementing, reinforcing or contradicting the
character of the sitter. Alma Lavenson photographs her own

hands holding the camera in a mirror, reflected in the lens
(p.189). Herbert Bayer's *Lonely Metropolitan* (p.103) plays on
the idea of hands as portrait, montaging the eyes onto them.

Moholy-Nagy was not entirely having fun when he reproduced
an image of table-turning (fig.9) from the film *Dr Mabuse* in
Painting Photography Film, commenting:

> The psychological problem of hands – the objective
> of many painters from Leonardo onwards – caught in
> a fraction of a second.[50]

Hands can be as potent in terms of revealing identity and
character as any part of the body. For artists and criminals they
have received attention only second to the head. The publication
Unit One (1934) presented the work of eleven artists associated
with modernism in Britain. Each was introduced with two
photographs: 'Portrait and Hands', of equal size and significance.
They are excellent photographs but never acknowledged in their
own right – simply listed among the acknowledgements of the
photographs of the 'works of art' by a variety of photographers.
(Francis Bruguière, it turned out, took the head and hands of
Paul Nash.) This was not uncharacteristic practice in Britain
where, unlike Germany, France, the Soviet Union or the United
States, photography, unless it was celebrity/fashion, had little
or no foothold in contemporary culture.

PHOTOGRAPHY IN THE MACHINE AGE: THE GIRL BORN WITHOUT A MOTHER

Photography as visual technology was the clearest marker of the
possibilities of reproduction and representation of modernity
in the machine age. But its social, political and aesthetic potential
was seen in different ways and for different purposes by the artists
and writers who embraced it. These differences are particularly
striking between the practitioners and theorists in the Soviet
Union, and at the Bauhaus in Germany and the United States.

Paul Haviland, in the magazine *291*, which temporarily
interrupted the publication of Alfred Stieglitz's *Camera Work*
in 1915, wrote:

> We are living in the age of the machine. Man made the machine
> in his own image ... The machine is his 'daughter born without
> a mother'. That is why he loves her. He has made the machine
> superior to himself. Photography is one of the fine fruits of
> this union. The photographic print is one element of this new
> trinity: Man the creator, with thought and will: the machine
> mother-action: and their product the work accomplished.[51]

10 FRANCIS PICABIA
Here, This is Stieglitz / Faith and Love 1915
reproduced in *291*, no.5/6, July/August 1915

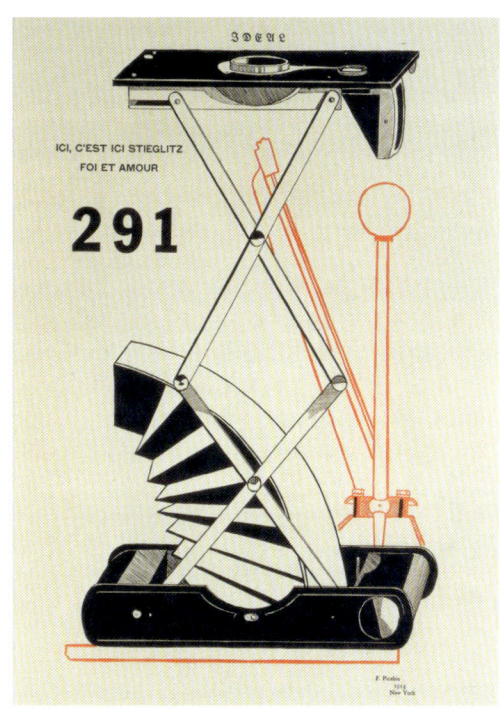

The question of modernity in relation to photography had not really posed itself in these terms before, and photography had certainly not been seen as its aesthetic justification. However, there were contradictory attitudes to the relationship between photography, mechanical reproduction and the work of art in the New York avant-garde, and these were exemplified in *291* – an experimental magazine 'dedicated to the most modern art and satire'.[52] Paul B. Haviland's faintly futurist celebration of man and machine took its metaphor from Francis Picabia's drawing *Girl Born without a Mother*, which had been reproduced in *291*, but ignored Picabia's ironic eroticisation of the 'machine-nude'. Rather than Picabia's caricatural object-portraits such as *Here, This is Stieglitz/Faith and Love* (fig.10), a machine-style drawing of Stieglitz as a camera, which appeared in the previous issue of *291*, Haviland's essay was accompanied by Stieglitz's famous photograph, *The Steerage* 1907. Picabia soon absorbed photography into his proto-dada provocations – the photographic equivalents of his machine drawings and paintings appeared in his own magazine *391* in 1917, the same year that Stieglitz photographed *Fountain* for Marcel Duchamp (fig.11).

The attitude of Duchamp and Picabia to the machine was doubly ironic, in that their machine-style drawing and painting was an affront to art, while their representations of machines were no celebration of technology, and photography was drawn into their sceptical scenarios. There was no such taunting in the work and ideas of Aleksandr Rodchenko in the Soviet Union and Moholy-Nagy at the Bauhaus in Germany. For them the technological side of photography was one of its greatest strengths, even if they understood its social and political applications differently.

The Bauhaus was the most influential school of art and design in the interwar period, and its impact was felt far beyond Germany's borders, following the scattering of its teachers after its closure by the Nazis. The photography course at the Bauhaus was more concerned with experiment, such as close-up and photomontage, than with the documentary side of photography (though it did feed into this, too).[53] Umbo (Otto Umbehr) and Paul Citroën studied there, as did Bayer who taught typography, advertising and exhibition design from 1925 to 1928. The cross-fertilisation of the courses encouraged the exploration of the photographic medium in different contexts. Bayer, for example, carried his interest in photomontage into his advertising work. Moholy-Nagy, who taught painting, sculpture and graphics, published *Painting Photography Film* at the Bauhaus.

11 ALFRED STIEGLITZ
Photograph of Marcel Duchamp's *Fountain*
reproduced in *The Blind Man* 1917

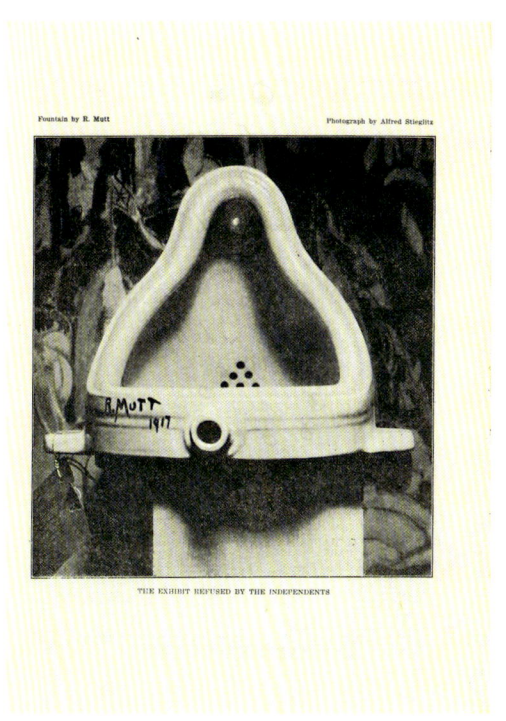

12 Aleksandr Rodchenko
Note-Pad and Leica c.1925

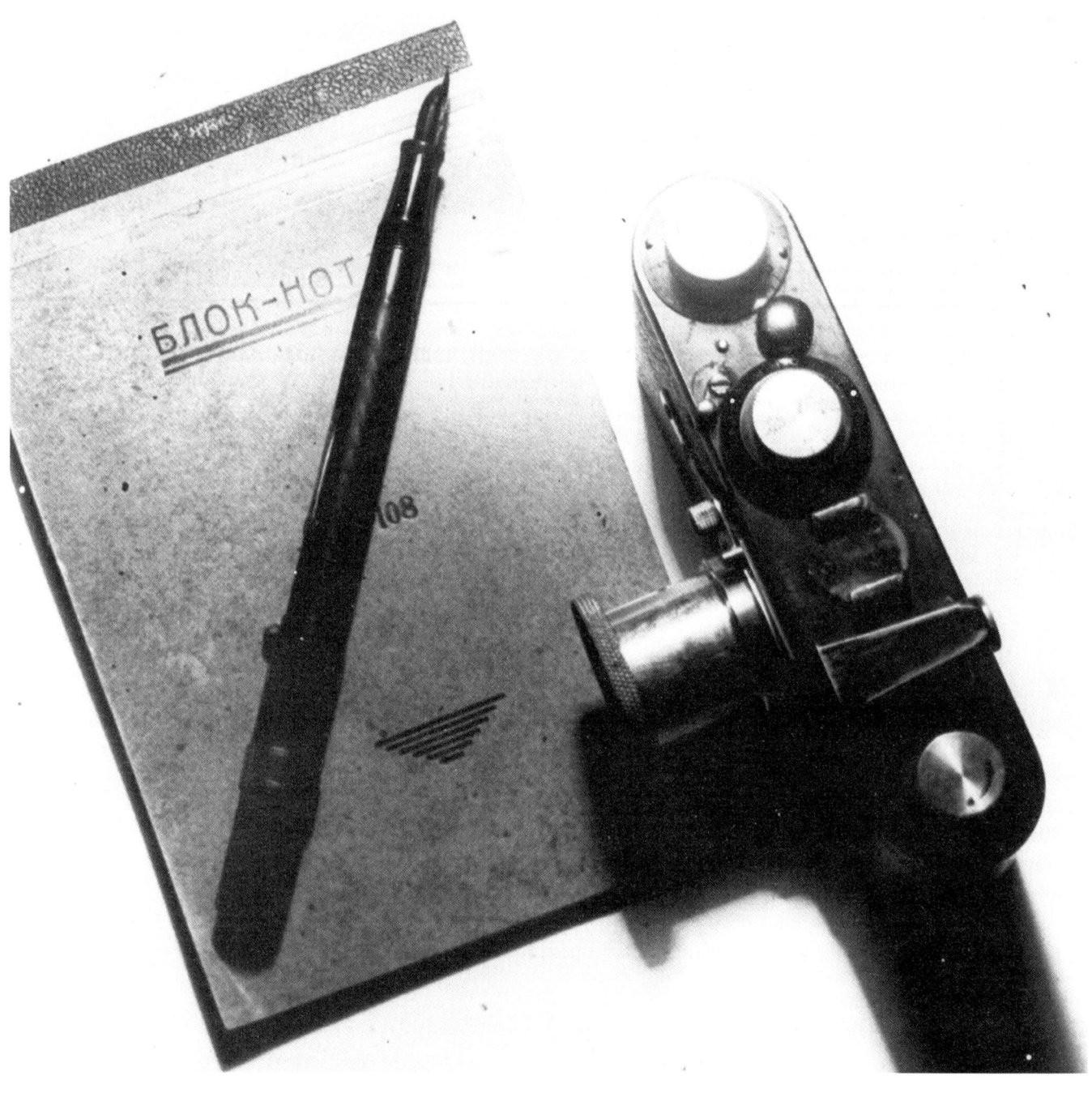

REVOLUTIONS

The Bauhaus had a radical programme of education, which was geared to greater involvement of art and design with industry, from craft-based to stream-lined. For Moholy-Nagy 'Everyone is equal before the machine … there is no tradition in technology, no class-consciousness.'[54] But for Rodchenko the Bauhaus was dependent on a capitalist system of production. Technology may be without class-consciousness, but all depends on how it is used. The constructivists in Russia, like Rodchenko, sought to put their ideas and their skills at the service of modernisation in the interests of all. Among the constructivist slogans was 'Down with art, long live technical science'. Technological ambitions were expressed in general theoretical terms: the Productivist Manifesto, which Rodchenko wrote with his partner Varvara Stepanova (1921), was intended to direct studio work to practical activity: 'The specific elements involved in the work of this [constructivist] group, that is "Tektonika", construction and "Faktura", provide ideological, theoretical and practical justification for the transposition of the material elements of industrial culture into volume, plane, colour, space and light'.[55] The call for technology, not art, preceded his interest in photography but was answered by it. He came to photography through his revolutionary photomontages, such as those for Vladimir Mayakovsky's poem 'Pro Eto'. 'Working on photomontage I began to be interested in photography … I bought myself two cameras – one 134 × 18 with a triple extension and a Dagor lens and the second a camera for reproductions and a pocket size Kodak.'[56] (fig.12)

As with Moholy-Nagy and many other photographers of the time, the acquisition of a light and portable camera brought entirely new possibilities that spoke to a new sense of modernity. The steeply angled viewpoint could eliminate perspective and produce almost abstract compositions, such as Moholy-Nagy's *View from the Berlin Radio Tower* (p.8), or exaggerate it as with Rodchenko's *Shukhov Tower* (p.192).

Rodchenko explored modern industrial structures from dramatic angles, but he ran into trouble later in the 1920s as attitudes in the Soviet Union hardened against constructivism and modernist experiments. In the Moscow-based periodical *Sovetskoe foto* his photographs were accused of being over-aesthetic, not realistic, and moreover of plagiarising the work of foreign photographers like Moholy-Nagy and Renger-Patzsch.[57] Rodchenko mounted a defence that led to a series of exchanges in the journal *Novyi Lef* (1928). He argued that the similarity between his and Moholy-Nagy's photographs was due not to plagiarism but to the search for a new viewpoint common to modernist photographers:

In photography there are old points of view, for instance the angle of vision, the view of a person standing on the ground looking straight ahead, or as I call it belly shots, with the camera held to the stomach. I am fighting against this viewpoint and shall fight it just as my comrades in the new photography are doing. Take shots from all angles except the navel until all these points of view are recognised. The interesting angles of the present are those from above down and from below up.[58]

Criticism also came from fellow-constructivist Boris Kusner, who retorted that the angled viewpoint hampered the informative value of a photograph. 'To show a 150-metre high radio tower looking like a bread basket made of wire, that is not paying attention to reality but ridiculing facts.' Rodchenko retaliated by describing how he had at first disliked the Eiffel Tower but then 'one day I passed nearby in a bus, and when I saw through the window the iron girder rising up and narrowing from left to right I had a real impression of mass and construction'.[59]

In the Soviet Union, after the Communist Revolution of 1917, photography was fought over, as we have seen, with conflicting views of its revolutionary applicability. All were agreed that it should educate rather than charm, and that in a still largely illiterate population it was a medium accessible to all.[60] But for *Sovetskoe foto* and the socialist realists, its documentary value should be allied as far as possible with a basically straight, 'realistic' viewpoint (a viewpoint slightly angled upwards, although a hangover from the constructivists, was acceptable as symbolising a forward-looking optimism). For the constructivists and modernists, by contrast, the camera introduced a new viewpoint that was valued for its optical and for its political and social implications. For Rodchenko, it was necessarily experimental because the old tropes that the camera had copied from painting had to be destroyed. 'A worker photographed as if he were Christ or an aristocrat, a working girl as if a Madonna are eloquent examples of what not to do. To state it more clearly, we must find a new aesthetic.'[61]

For Soviet photographers of whatever aesthetic persuasion, and however experimental, the attitude to the image was positive. If not today, the promise goes, then tomorrow. But from a different perspective, photography had either become increasingly compromised by its co-option by advertising – 'the posture of a photography that can endow any soup can with cosmic significance but cannot grasp a single one of the human connexions in which it exists' – or was incapable of revealing the truth about the relations between human beings and their world:

13 JOHN HEARTFIELD
*The Finest Products of Capitalism
(Spitzenprodukte des Kapitalismus)* 1932
Ilustration to M. Iljin, *Fünf Jahre, die Welt
verändern*, 1932

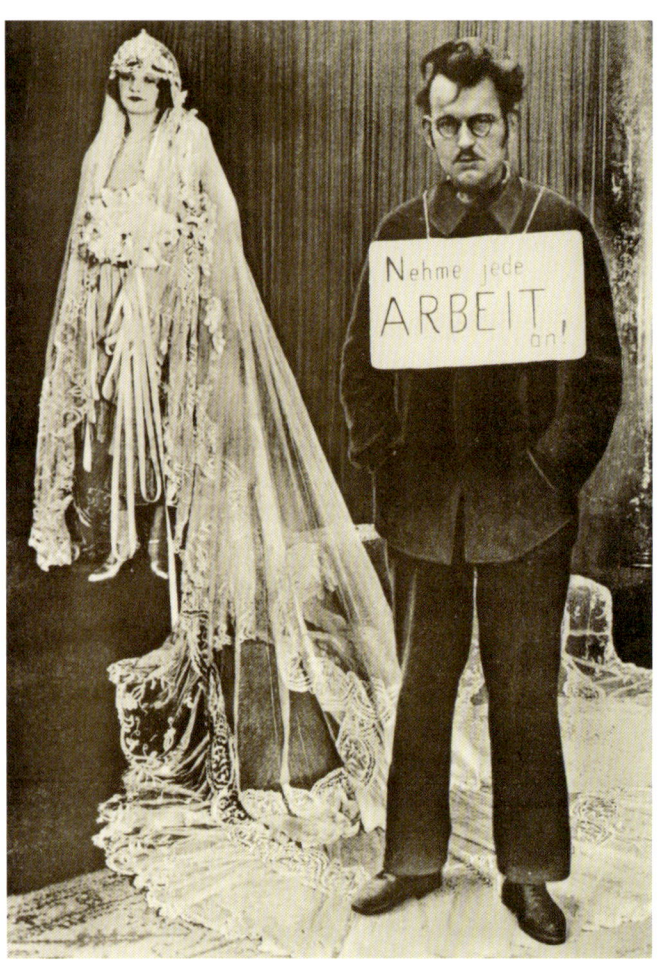

although it was the muralist painters such as Diego Rivera who gained most prominence in visualising them. However, the ideological aims were not as clear as in Russia, or at least did not take shape in terms of a totalising modernism. A nationalist agenda emerged, especially in culture, which had an ambiguous relationship with modernism. This nationalist agenda was strongly inflected by one of the effects of the Revolution – recognition of the 'Indian' past and the persistent presence of the indigenous population. The indigenism that followed, favouring 'folk art' and Native American culture (while the state was simultaneously trying to modernise, for example, through literacy programmes only in Spanish), spread into many aspects of life. Carmen Mondragón was given the name Nahui Olín, a Nahuatl term from the Aztec calendar, by her lover, the artist Dr Atl, whose name was also an adopted Nahuatl term. A painter and poet herself, she was photographed by both Weston (pp.73, 74) and Modotti.

Photography represented the more modernist face of Mexican culture, but could also allude imaginatively to the absence of modernity. Modotti's *Bandolier, Corn and Sickle* (p.185) is a brilliant instance of this. She has taken the symbol of the Russian Revolution, the hammer and sickle, which stood for the alliance of peasant and industrial worker, and transformed it into a symbolic portrait of the Mexican revolutionary, but photographed close-up like a still life. The hammer is eliminated, as there was virtually no industry in Mexico; the trinity of sickle, corn (the staple diet but also in legend the material from which Man is made) and bandolier stands for the alliance of peasant and soldier in the land.

Less than ever does the mere reflection of reality reveal anything about reality. A photograph of the Krupp works or the A.E.G. tells us next to nothing about these institutions. Actual reality has slipped into the functional. The reification of human relations – the factory, say – means that they are no longer explicit. So something must be *built up*, something artificial, posed.[62]

Bertolt Brecht's critique exactly explains the photomontage tradition started by Berlin dada and continued by John Heartfield (fig.13), in which by cutting up the photographic document – the newspaper image, for example – and recombining it, an underlying truth of relationships, a political-economic system, can be uncovered, as in Heartfield's juxtaposition of the jobless and luxury goods. (No change there.) Photomontage in the Soviet Union, by contrast, tended to celebrate the coming Utopia.

In Mexico photography was also prominent in the revisions of cultural and artistic ambition after the Revolution of 1910-17,

CONCLUSION

Photography has a privileged relationship to modernity, but not in the terms that modernism in art established for itself. The history of one was written from a quite different perspective to that of the other. Cross-referencing photography to painting and vice versa helped neither to reach a better understanding of their respective ambitions, strengths and weaknesses nor a definition of art. Photography's interconnection with the visual culture and social habits of an era is constantly changing. But during the period covered by the works in this exhibition, photography in all its variety – documentary, glamorous, realist, surrealist, idealist – came into its own, experiencing for the first time since its invention an exact congruence between technique and subject.

NOTES

1 László Moholy-Nagy [1936], in Kostelanetz 1970, p.53.
2 Moholy-Nagy [1925] 1969, p.28.
3 Benjamin [1931] 1979, p.254.
4 Man Ray, 'Apparences trompeuses' [1926], in Man Ray 2016, p.88.
5 Benjamin [1931] 1979, p.241.
6 Naumann and Obalk 2000, p.109.
7 Duchamp to Man Ray, April or May 1922, ibid., p.106. (I'm thrilled to know that you are having a good time and above all that you've abandoned painting.)
8 *Camera Work*, XLVIII, October 1916, p.11.
9 *The Steerage* was reproduced in the experimental (proto-dada) magazine *291* (1915), which temporarily took the place of *Camera Work*.
10 [Unsigned, but probably by Stieglitz], 'Is Photography a New Art?', *Camera Work*, XXI, January 1908.
11 Ibid.
12 Paul Strand, 'Photography', *Camera Work*, XLIX/L, June 1917, p.3.
13 Moholy 1939, p.15.
14 Moholy-Nagy [1925] 1969, p.15. The emphasis is as in the original.
15 'A Small History of Photography', in Benjamin [1931] 1979, p.250.
16 Ibid., p.248.
17 Ibid., p.247.
18 Ibid., p.250.
19 Ibid., p.240.
20 'The Work of Art in the Age of Mechanical Reproduction' [1936], in Benjamin 1968, p.229.
21 Moholy 1939, p.162.
22 Ibid., p.97.
23 Ibid., pp.175-6.
24 Peter Reyner Banham, *Theory and Design in the First Machine Age*, London 1960.
25 Edward James, 'Wars I haven't known', undated ms., Edward James Archive, West Dean.
26 Moholy-Nagy [1925] 1969, footnote p.15.
27 Ibid.
28 Cited in Moholy 1939, p.51.
29 Ibid., p.163.
30 Ibid., p.165.
31 See Wendy A. Grossman and Steven Manford, 'Unmasking Man Ray's Noire et blanche', *American Art*, Summer 2006, p.142.
32 Paris *Vogue* 7, no.5, May 1926, p.37. Translated in Wendy A. Grossman, *Man Ray, African Art and the Modernist Lens*, Washington DC 2009, p.130.
33 Ibid.
34 Charles Baudelaire, 'La Chevelure' from 'Spleen et idéal', *Les Fleurs du mal* [1861], Paris 1964, p.37.

35 James Clifford, 'On Ethnographic Surrealism', quoted in Whitney Chadwick, 'Fetishizing Fashion/Fetishizing Culture: Man Ray's Noire et blanche', *Oxford Art Journal*, vol.18, no.2, 1995, p.8.
36 Paul Guillaume and Thomas Munro, *Primitive Negro Sculpture* [1926], quoted in Chadwick 1995, p.13.
37 *Negro Art* [291 exhibition, 1914-16], *Camera Work*, XLVIII, October 1916, p.7. Man Ray was part of Stieglitz's circle in New York before he went to Paris, and frequented his 291 gallery: 'The grey walls of the little gallery are always pregnant', he noted in 'Impressions of 291', *Camera Work*, XLVII, July 1914, p.72.
38 Anthony Shelton, Foreword, in Grossman 2009, p.ix.
39 André Breton, *Second manifeste du surréalisme* [1930], in Breton, *Manifestoes of Surrealism*, trans. Richard Seaver and Helen R. Lane, Ann Arbor 1969, p.123.
40 Man Ray, 'Apparences trompeuses', *Paris-Soir*, 23 March 1926, quoted in Man Ray 2016, p.89.
41 Moholy-Nagy [1925] 1969, p.28. The emphasis is as in the original.
42 André Breton, 'Max Ernst' [1921], in Max Ernst, *Beyond Painting*, New York 1948, p.177 (where it is erroneously dated 1920).
43 André Breton, *Manifeste du surréalisme* [1924], in Breton 1969, p.10.
44 Ibid., p.26. Translation modified by the author.
45 See Dawn Ades, 'Camera Creation', in Jennifer Mundy (ed.), *Duchamp Man Ray Picabia*, exh. cat., Tate 2008, pp.88-113.
46 Salvador Dalí, 'Photography: Pure Creation of the Mind' ('La fotografia, pura creació de l'esperit', *L'Amic de les arts*, no.18, September 1927), in Salvador Dalí, *Salvador Dalí: Oui, the Paranoid-Critical Revolution: Writings 1927-1933*, ed. Robert Descharnes, trans. Yvonne Shafir, Boston 1998, p.13.
47 Ibid.
48 Benjamin [1931] 1979, p.243. Benjamin returned to this theme in 'The Work of Art in the Age of Mechanical Reproduction' [1936], in Benjamin 1968, p.239: 'The camera introduces us to unconscious optics as does psychoanalysis to unconscious impulses'. Rosalind Krauss picked up the idea for her study of surrealism, psychoanalysis and optics (Krauss 1993).
49 W.H. Auden, 'I am not a Camera', *Collected Poems*, London 2007, p.841.
50 Moholy-Nagy [1925] 1969, p.68.
51 Paul B. Haviland, 'We are living in the age of the machine', *291*, no.7/8, September/October 1915. Stieglitz's famous photograph

The Steerage was reprinted in the same issue of *291*.
52 Marius de Zayas, Paul B. Haviland and Agnes Ernst Meyer proposed the idea to Stieglitz of a fixed-period journal to be published by his 291 gallery. *291* was published for one year, 1915, during which *Camera Work* was suspended.
53 Robert Frank, for example, studied with Michael Wolgensinger who had trained at the Bauhaus.
54 Moholy-Nagy, quoted in Stephen Bayley, *Bauhaus+BMW*, London 2006, n.p.
55 Aleksandr Rodchenko and Varvara Stepanova, 'Productivist Manifesto' [1921], in Elliott 1979, p.130.
56 Aleksandr Rodchenko, 'Working with Mayakovsky' [1940], in ibid., p.103. See also Lavrentiev, Rodchenko and Stepanova 1982, p.30 (Rodchenko's Leica with accessories).
57 *Sovetskoe foto*, April 1928.
58 From *Novyi Lef*, 1928, translated in *Creative Camera* 1978.
59 See Dawn Ades, Introduction, in Ades and Francis 1979-80.
60 Benjamin commented that the achievements of the Russian film directors were only possible 'in a country where photography does not set out to charm or persuade, but to experiment and instruct'. Benjamin [1931] 1979, p.255.
61 Rodchenko, quoted in Burgin 1982, p.178.
62 Bertolt Brecht, quoted in Benjamin [1931] 1979, p.255. Benjamin oddly credits the surrealists with the invention of photomontage: 'We owe it to the surrealists that they trained the pioneers of such a constructivist photography.' But constructivists, such as Gustavs Klutsis, invented photomontage in the Soviet Union simultaneously with the dadaists in Berlin, such as Raoul Hausmann and John Heartfield, and in Cologne Max Ernst (who brought photomontage to the surrealists in Paris). For the surrealists photomontage was a different form of critique of reality.

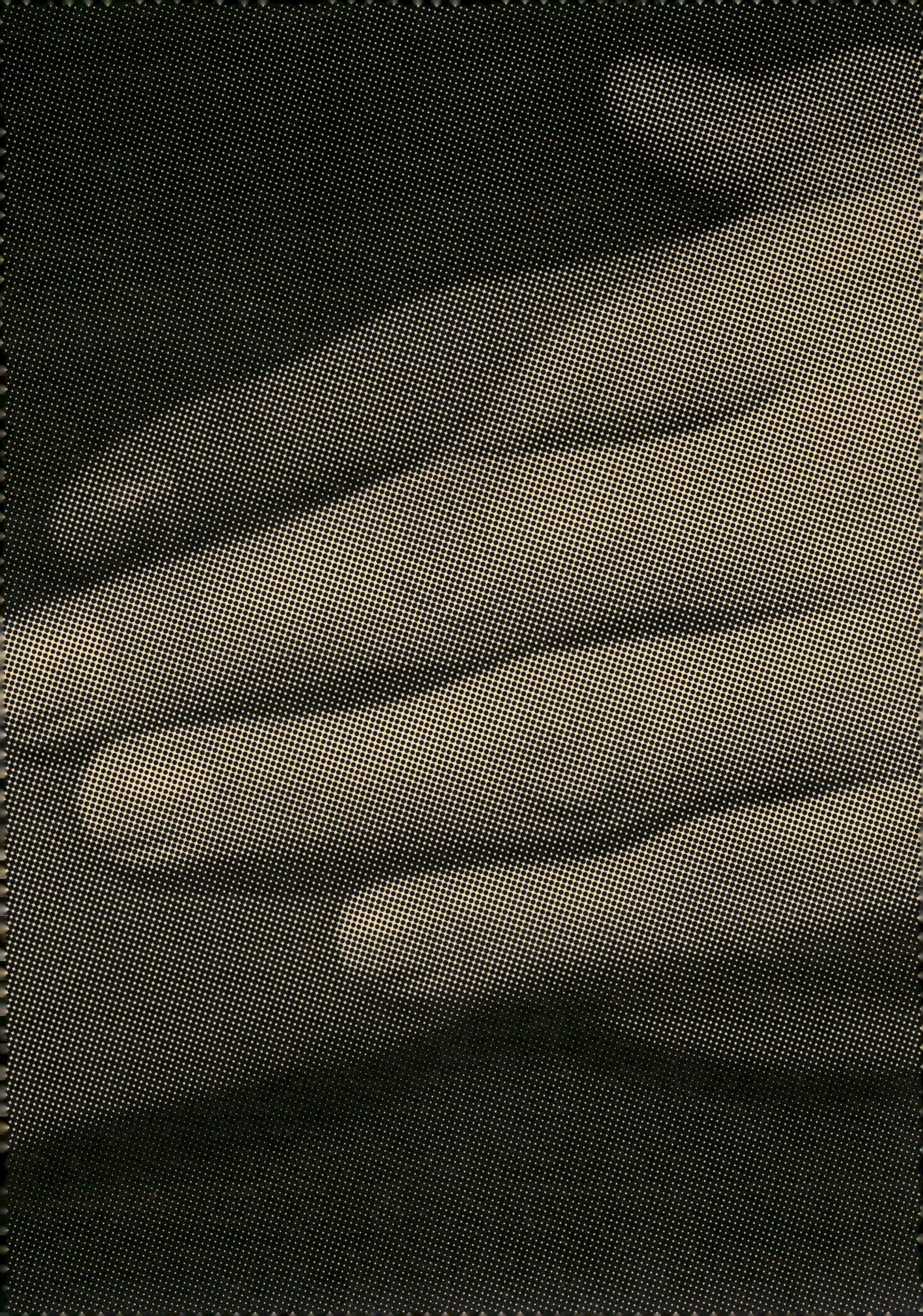

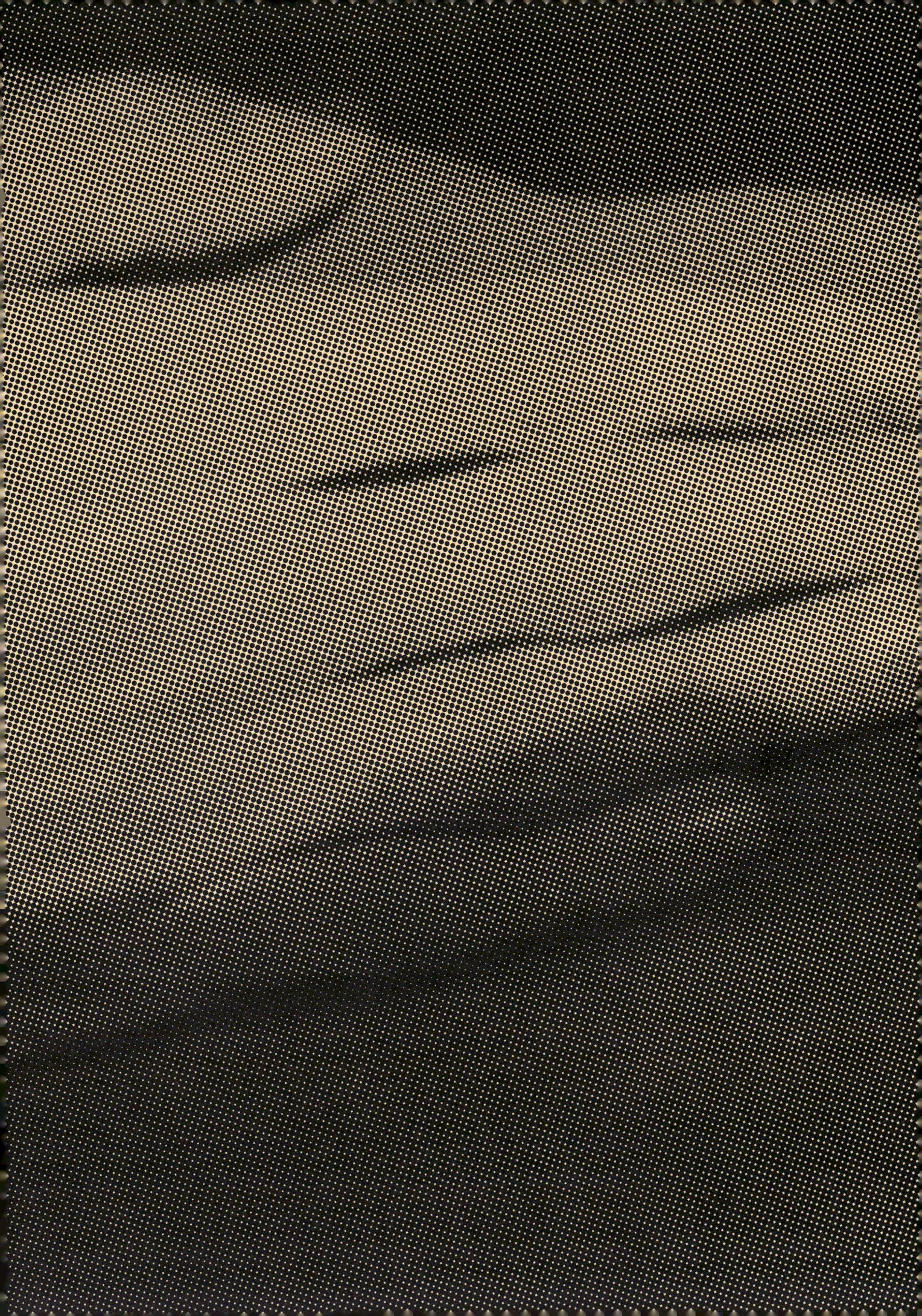

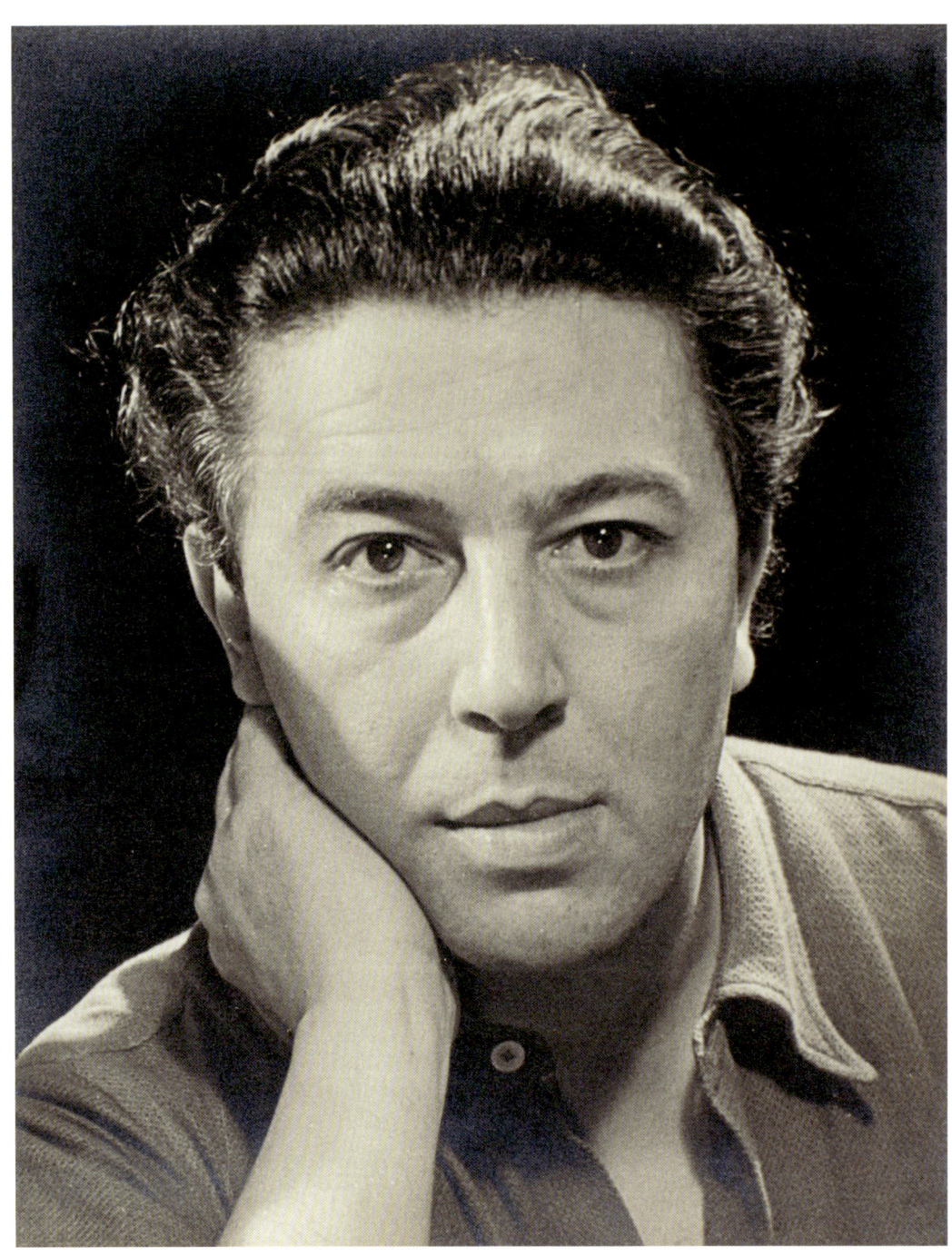

Man Ray
André Breton 1930
23.2 × 18.1 cm

PORTRAITS

From its outset, photography was seized upon by the middle and upper classes as a fashionable means of capturing their 'likeness'. By the end of the nineteenth century, as many photographers were seeking to establish the medium's status as more than just a documentary tool, others began to explore the portrait as a site for artistic expression. Then, in the years following the First World War, as avant-garde movements flourished and photography gained a foothold in popular magazines, the portrait was once again subject to scrutiny by photographers who wanted to find ways of representing character and individuality as much as physical appearance. By harnessing qualities unique to their medium, they established what it meant to make a truly 'photographic' portrait.

Whereas formal portraiture had traditionally conveyed the sitter's occupation and status, modern portraits now assumed that knowledge from the viewer. This allowed a greater level of compositional freedom via close-ups, tight crops and experimentations with large areas of negative (empty) space. Meanwhile, those working at the vanguard of experimental photographic practice employed abstraction as a means of destabilising identity, utilising the innumerable means available to them – through camera, darkroom and print techniques – to represent the juncture between outer and inner self.

One of the most important channels for the new approach to portraiture was the illustrated press, which enjoyed a boom during the 1920s. Establishing a model that would continue into the twenty-first century, high-end magazines such as *Vogue, Vanity Fair* and *Harper's Bazaar* reproduced the best examples of modern photography. Together with weeklies such as *Vu*, these publications fuelled public appetite for portraits of the well-known figures of the day. Under progressive editorship, this extended beyond figures from high society, fashion and theatre to include leading members of the artistic and literary avant-garde, who now relied on the portrait photographer to help craft their public persona.

The idea of 'persona' derived from new psychological theories about the self, the term referencing its Latin meaning, literally a mask, or character played by an actor. A preoccupation with the psyche is evident in surrealist photography, in which masks make a frequent appearance as a means of giving form to something abstract. Funerary masks were among the many manifestations of an obsession with death, while in the context of fashion and beauty editorials, African – most frequently Ivorian – masks represented the ideal of feminine beauty. Echoed in the heart-shaped face, bow-shaped lips and high, arched eyebrows of the models and muses, the mask reflected the surrealist inclinations of many leading photographers, who worked in both an artistic and commercial capacity, throughout the period. EL

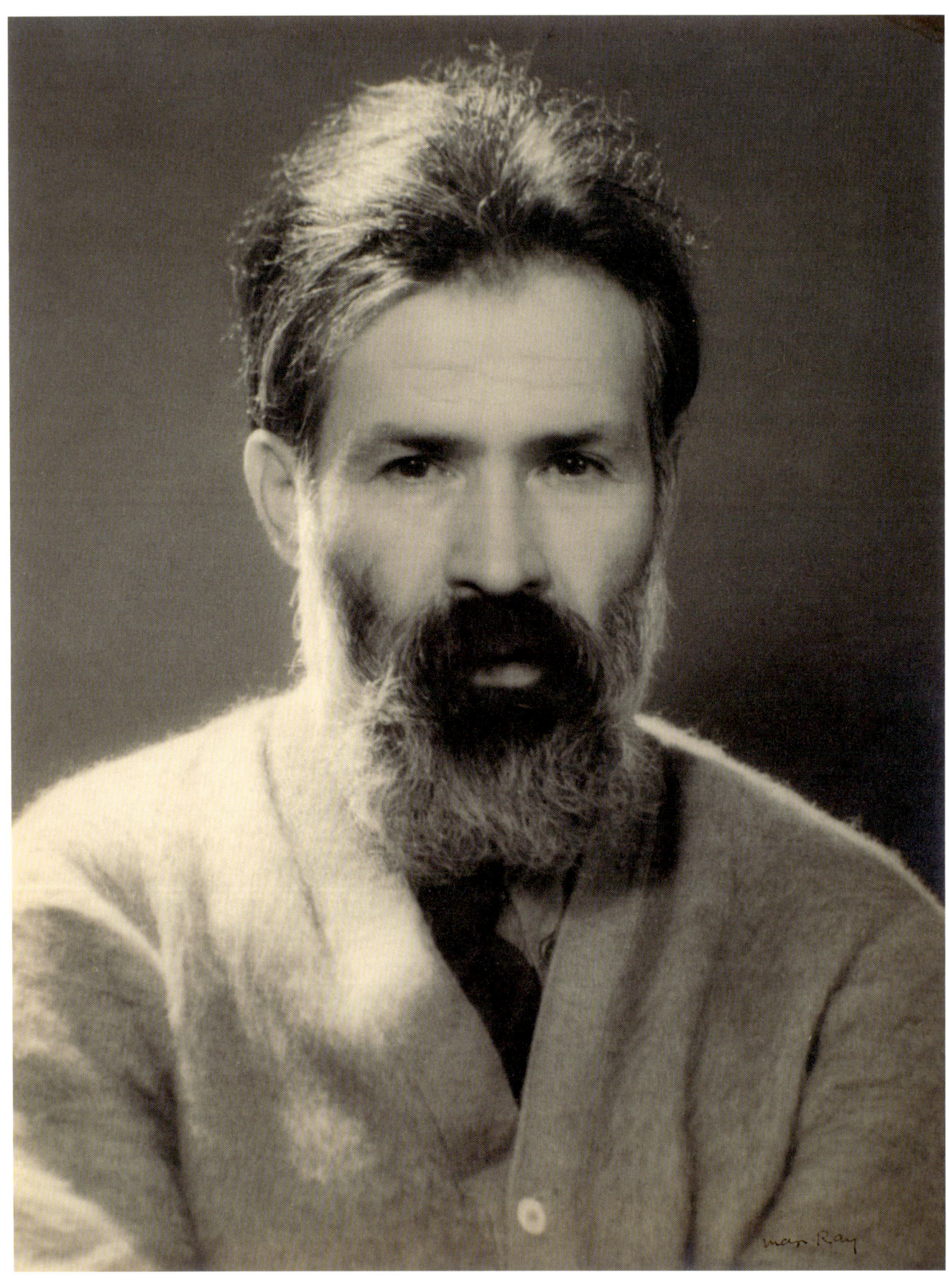

MAN RAY *Constantin Brâncuşi* 1930, 23.2 × 17.8 cm

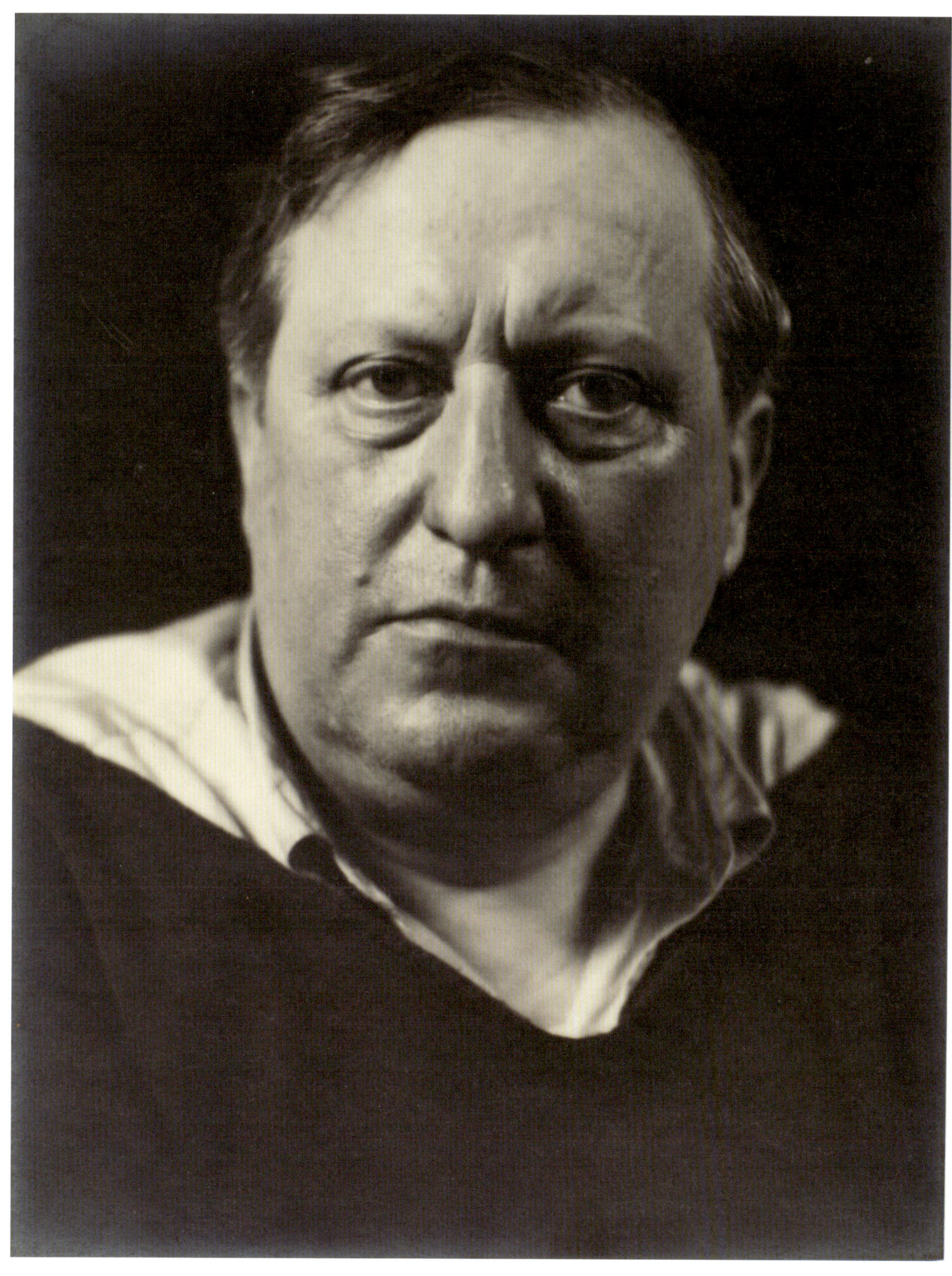

MAN RAY *André Derain* c.1924, 23.5 × 17.8 cm

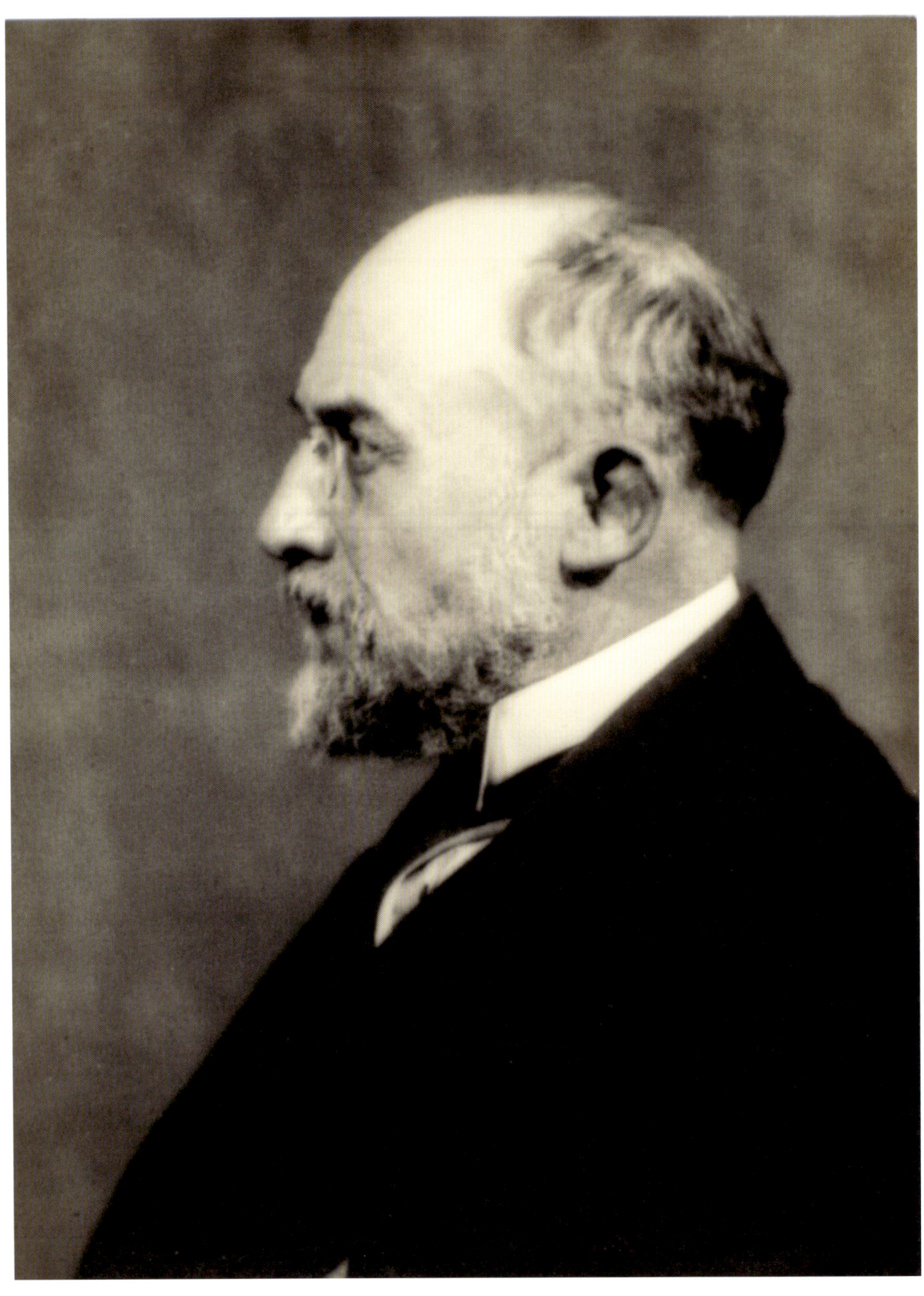

Man Ray *Erik Satie* 1922, 22.9 × 17.1 cm

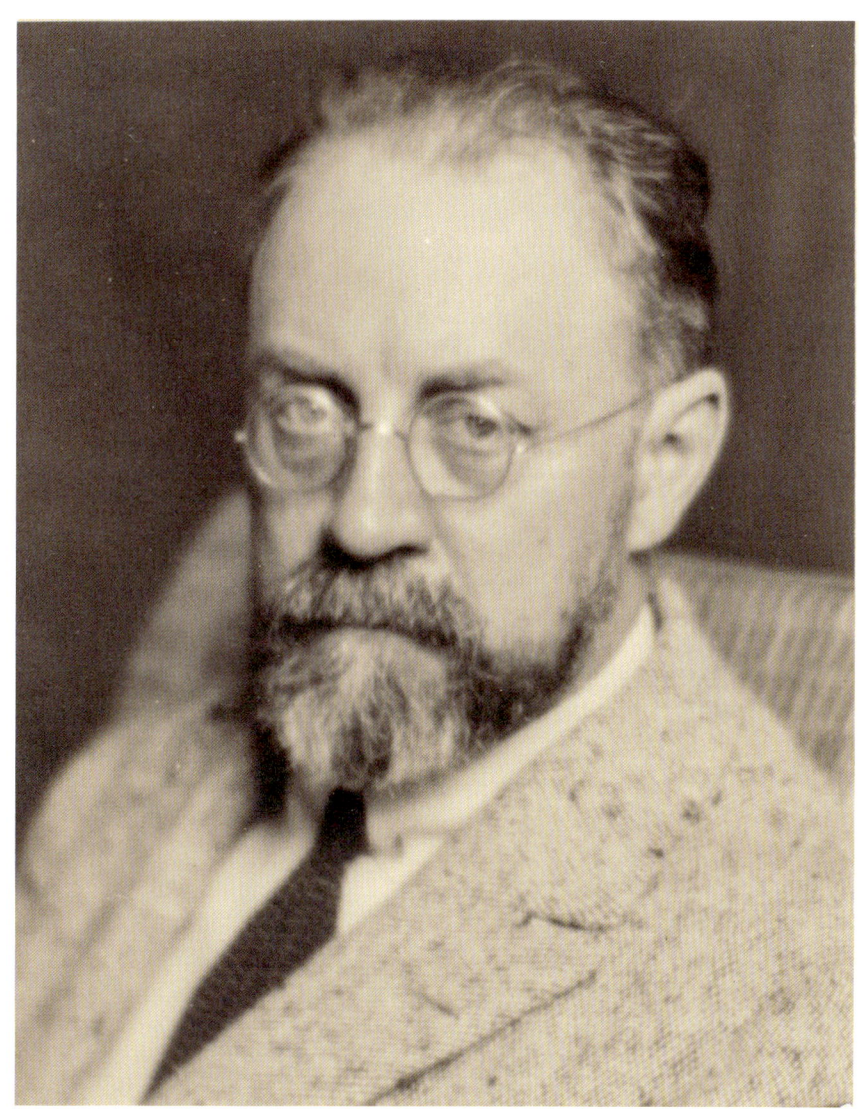

Man Ray *Henri Matisse* 1923, 12.5 × 10 cm

Manuel Álvarez Bravo *Isabel Villaseñor* 1936, 20.3 × 17.1 cm

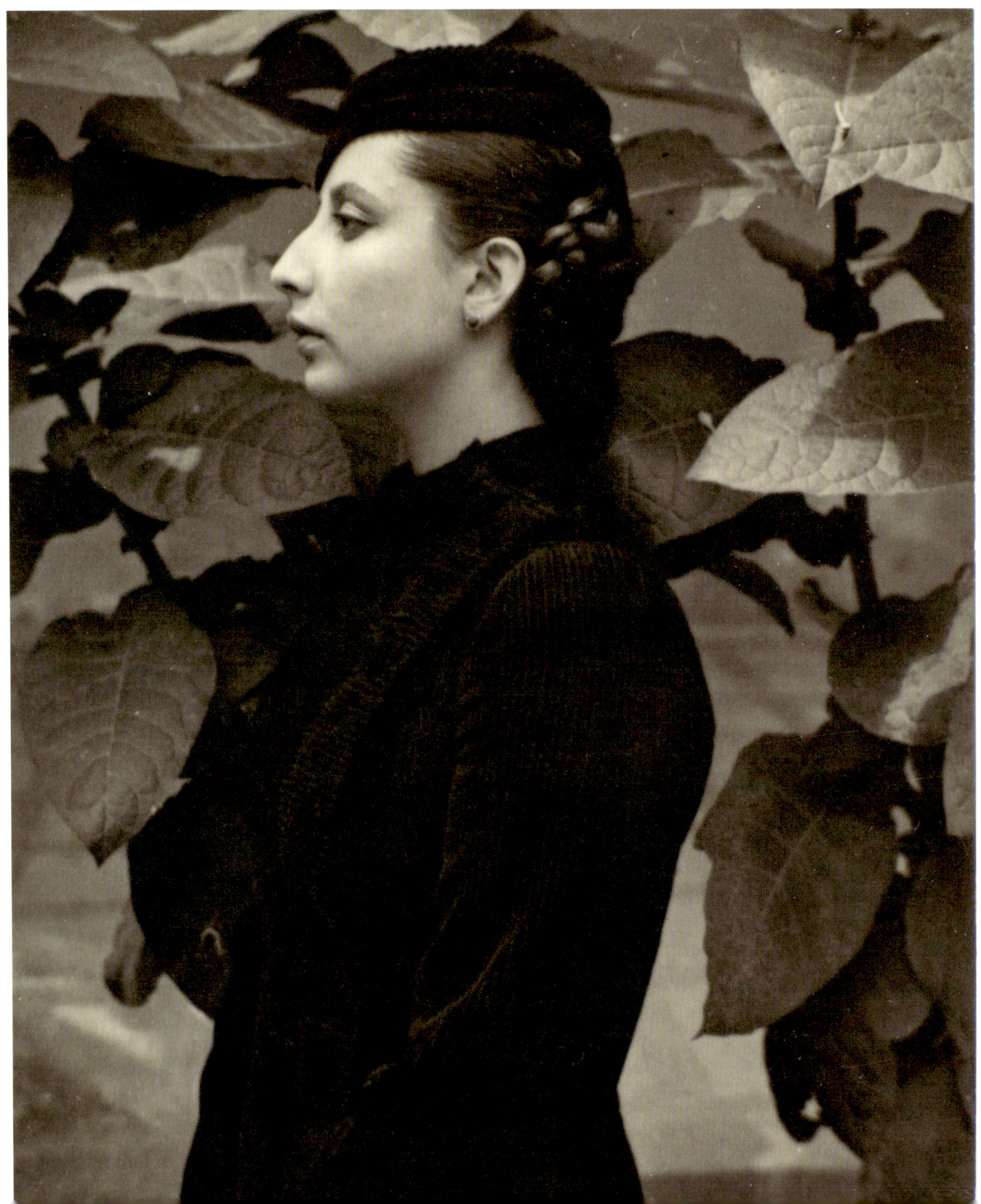

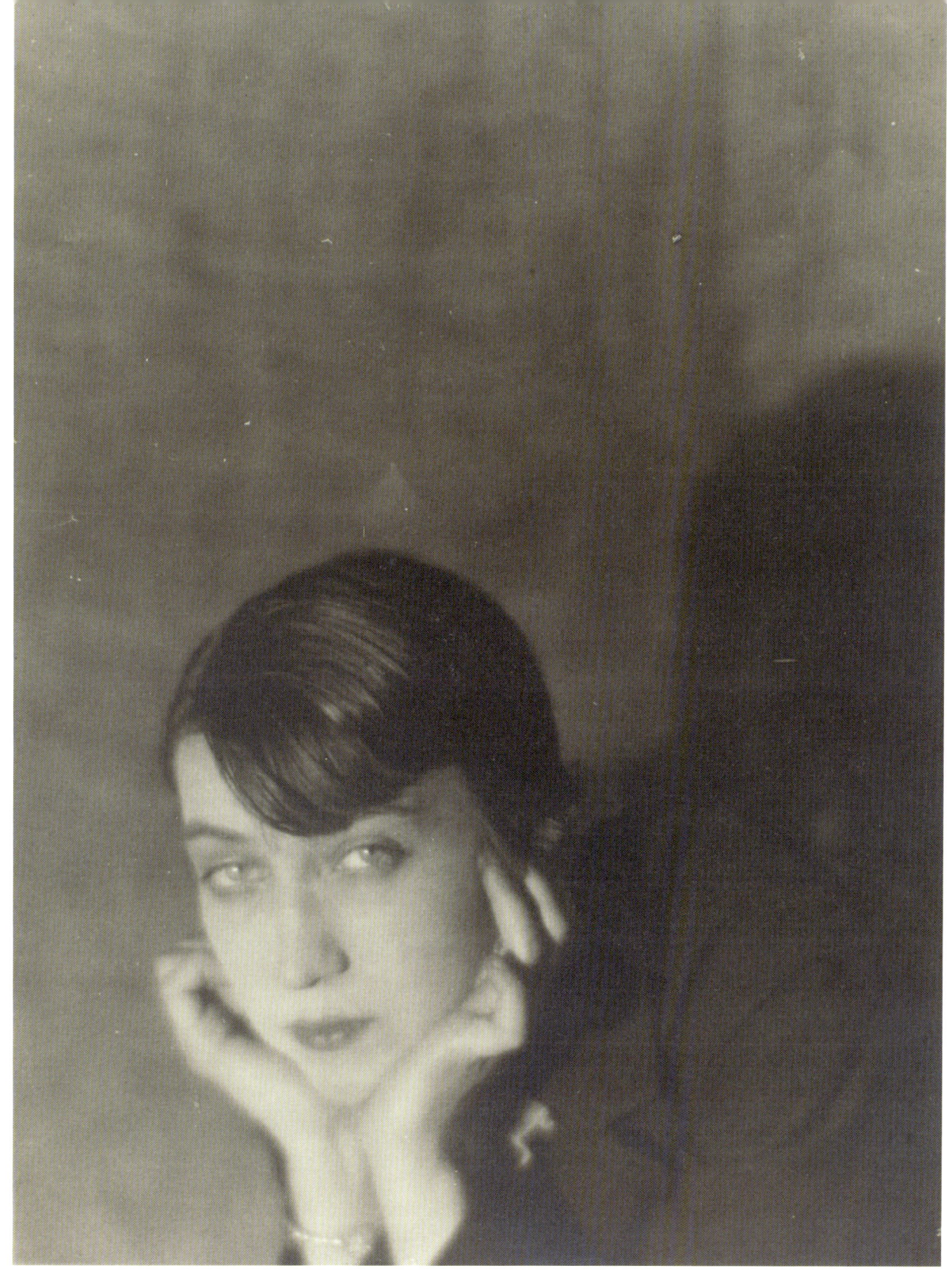

MAN RAY *Berenice Abbott* 1921, 18.1 × 15.6 cm

Johan Hagemeyer *Salvador Dalí* 1944, 9.2 × 11.7 cm

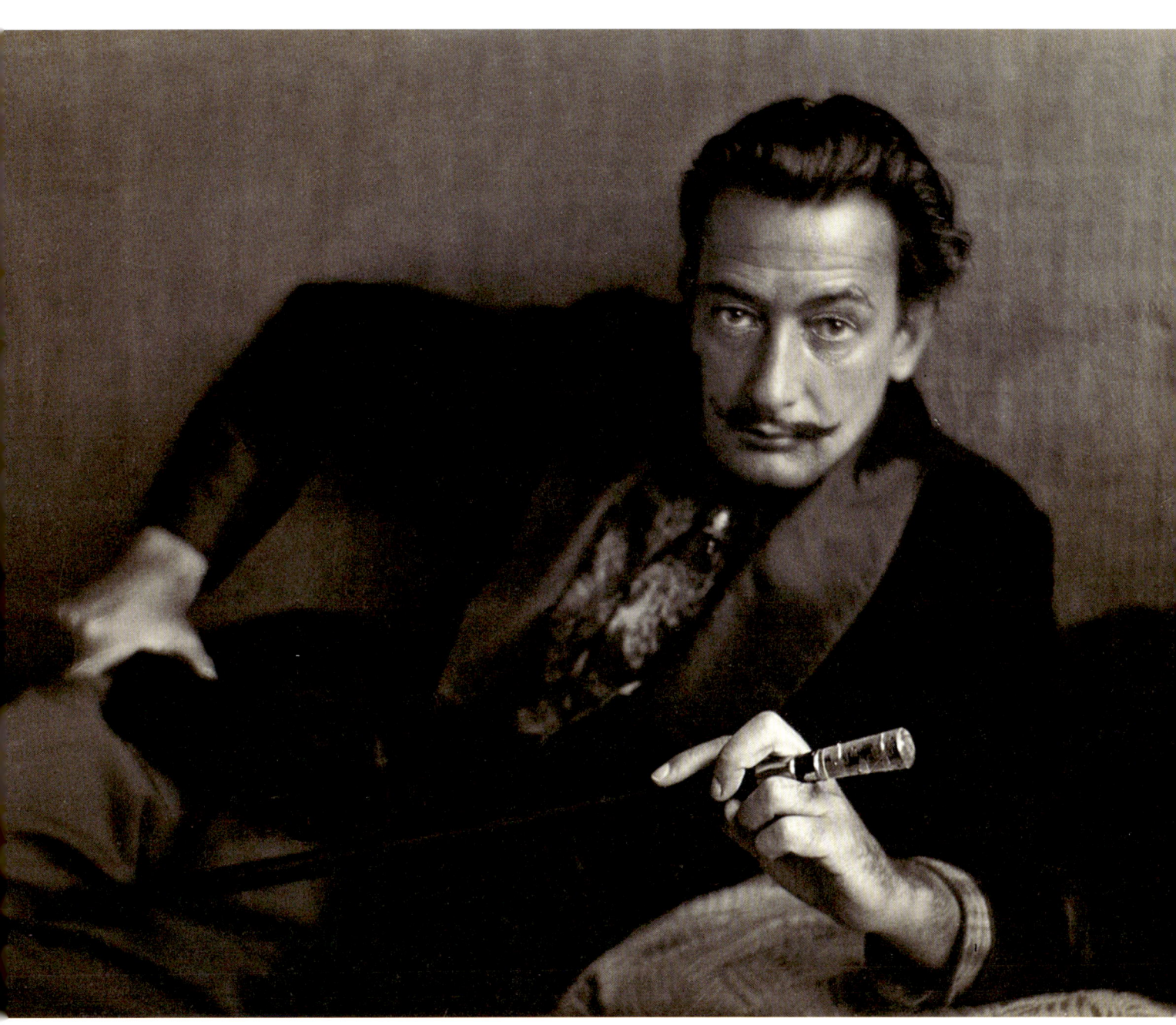

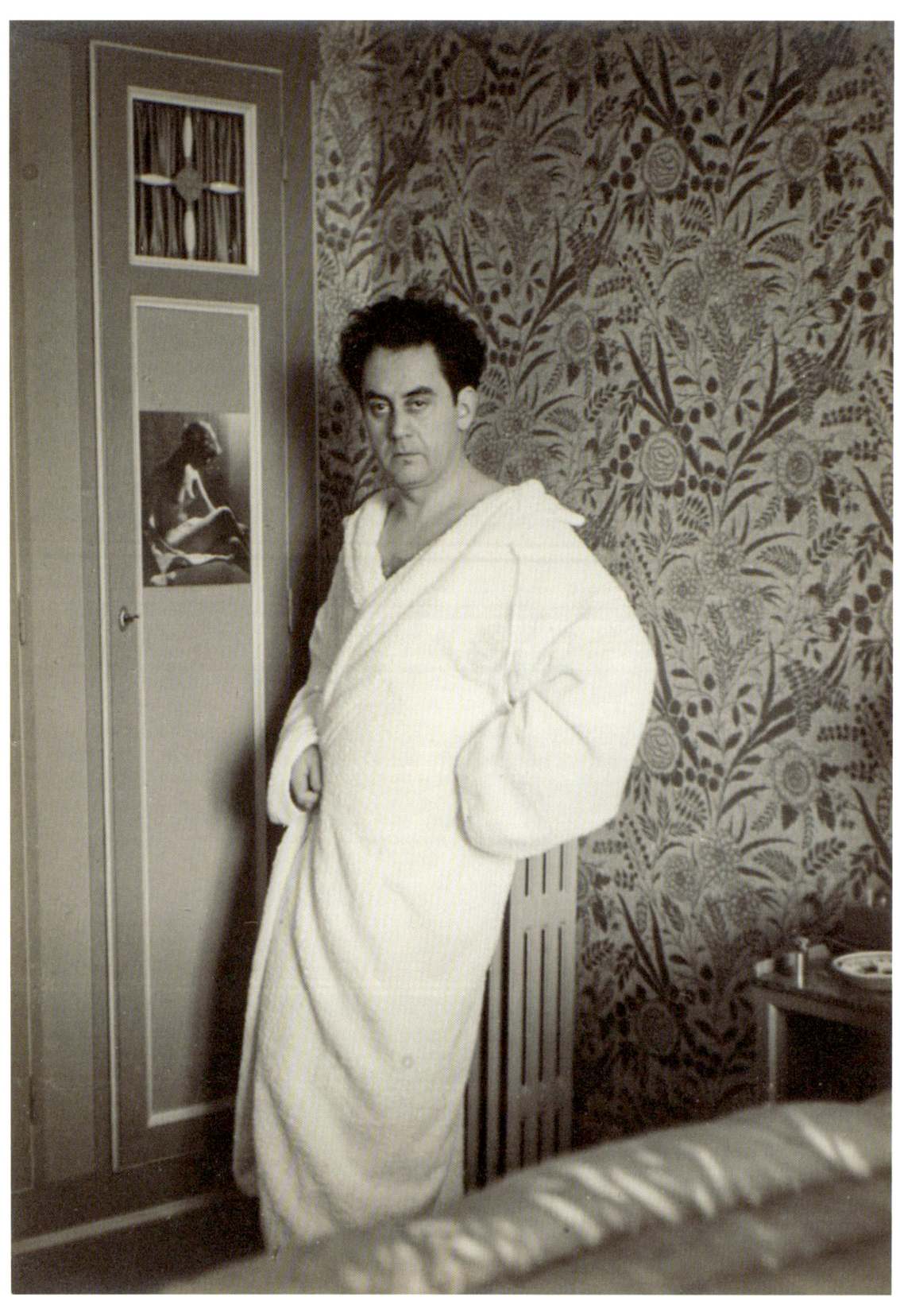

MAN RAY *Self-Portrait in Bathrobe, Paris 1929*, 11.4 × 8.3 cm

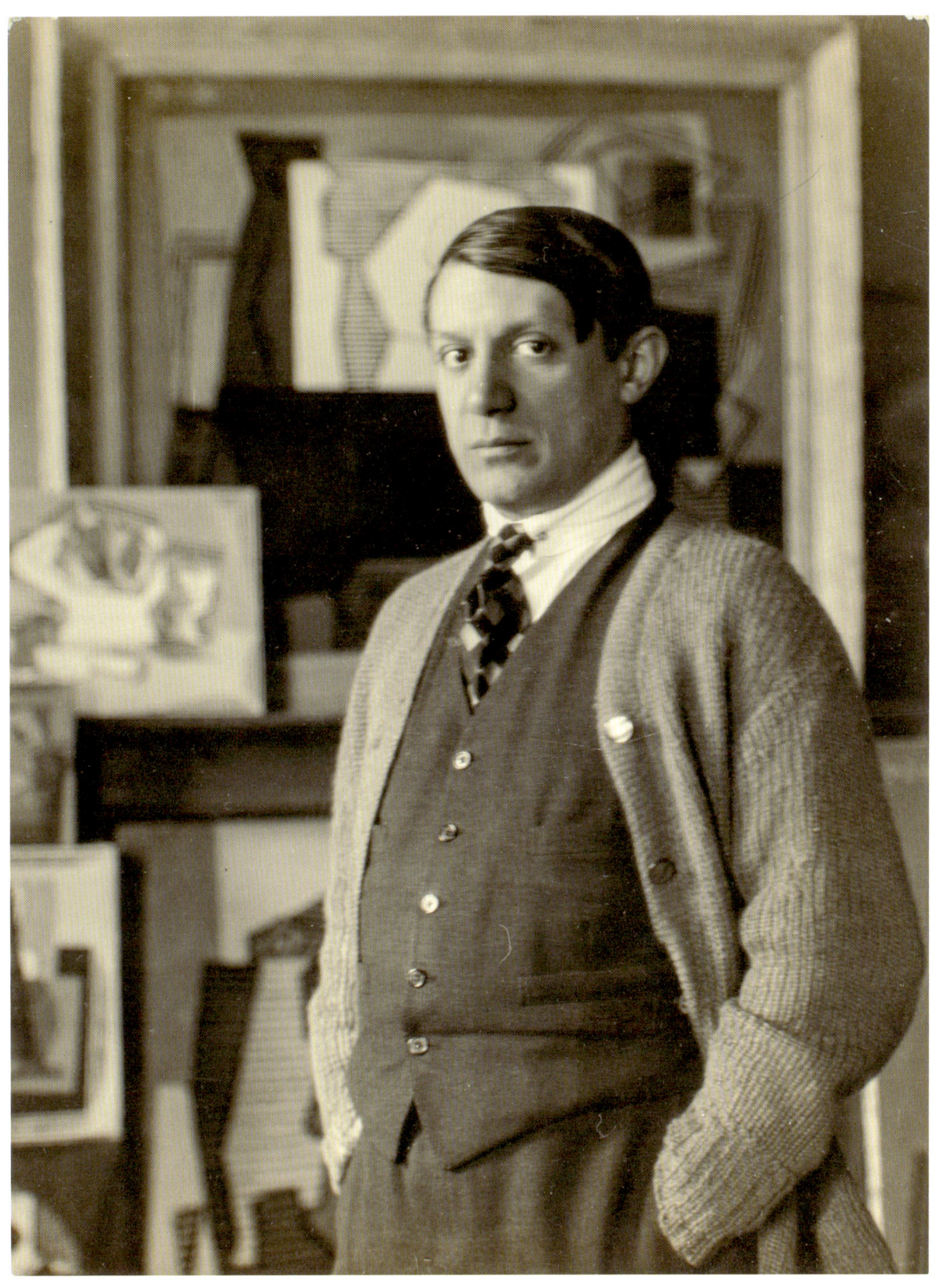

Man Ray *Pablo Picasso* 1922, 17.8 × 12.7 cm

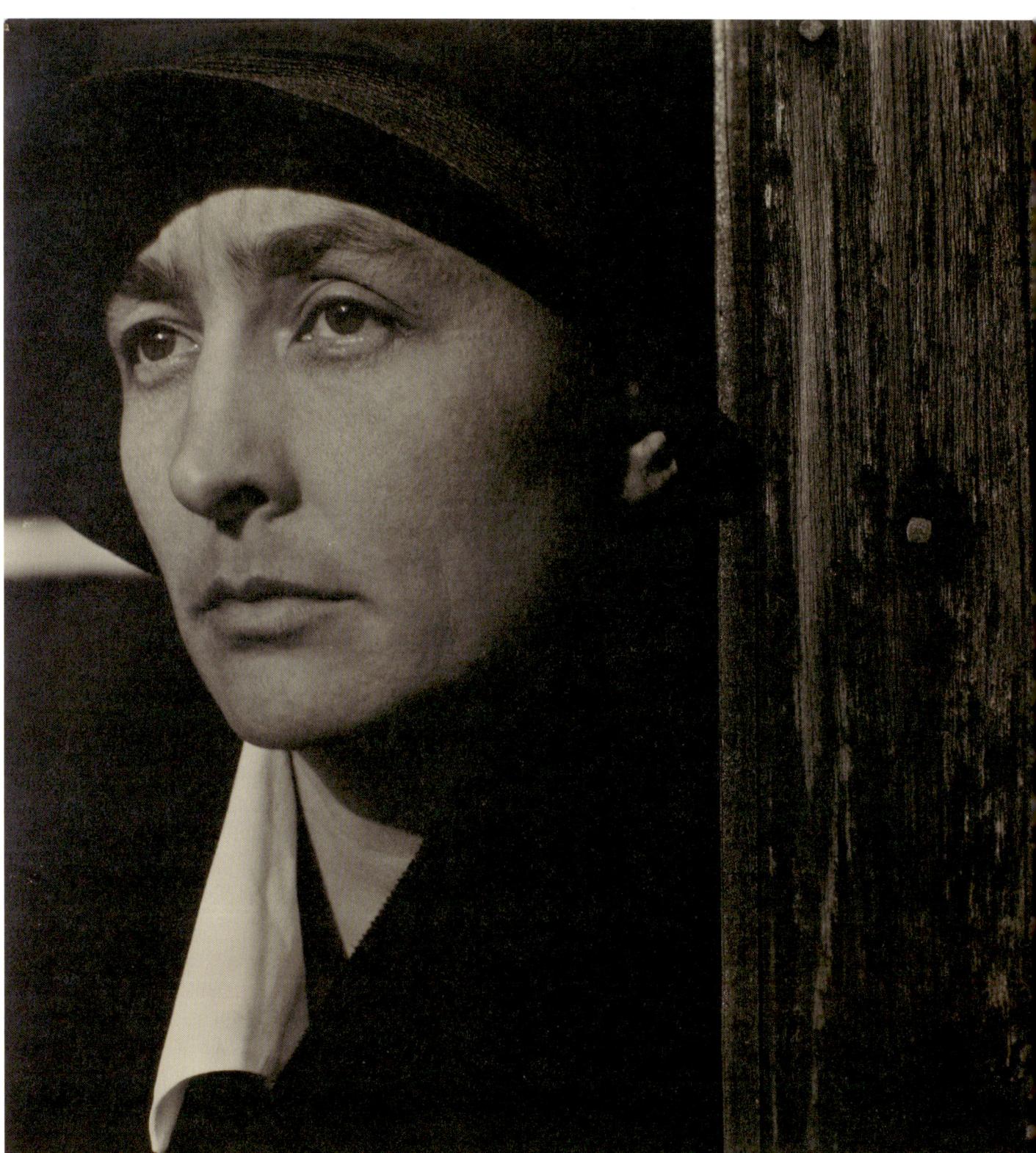

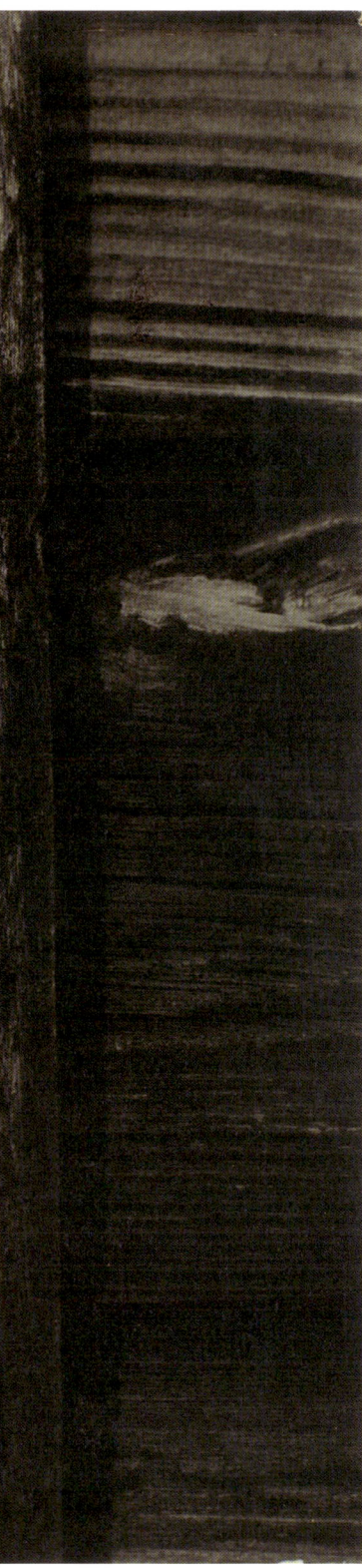

ALFRED STIEGLITZ
Georgia O'Keeffe 1922
19.1 × 23.8 cm

Below: **DOROTHY NORMAN**
*An American Place – Alfred Stieglitz
in Full-Length Cape* 1934
8.9 × 4.8 cm

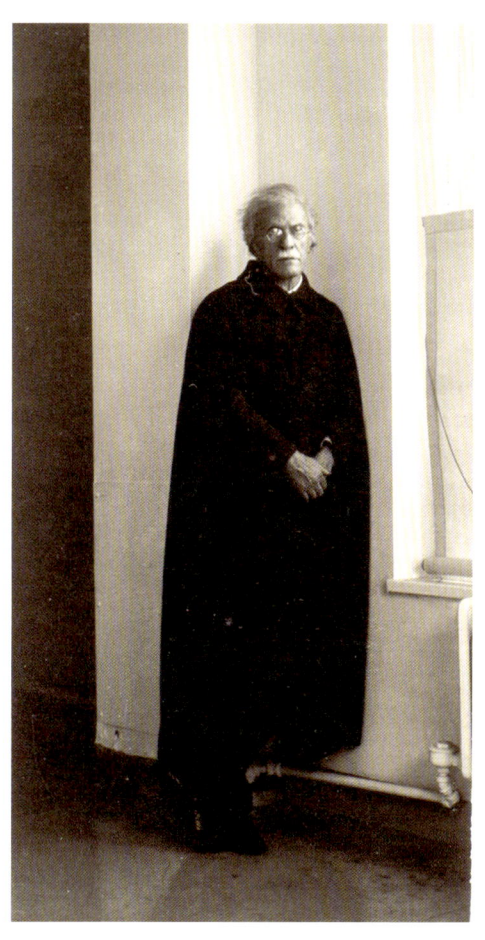

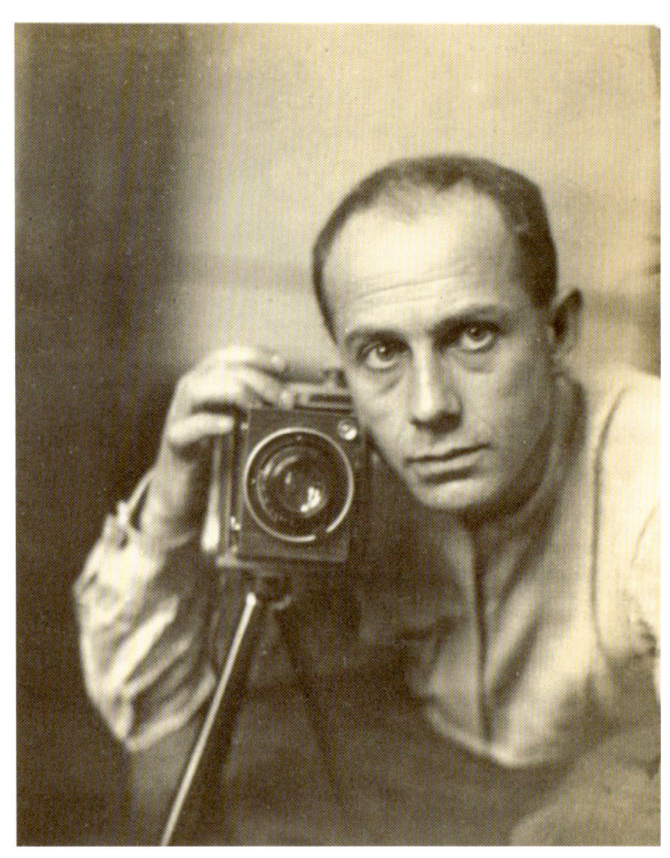

Paul Citroën *Self-Portrait* 1930, 5.4 × 4.4 cm

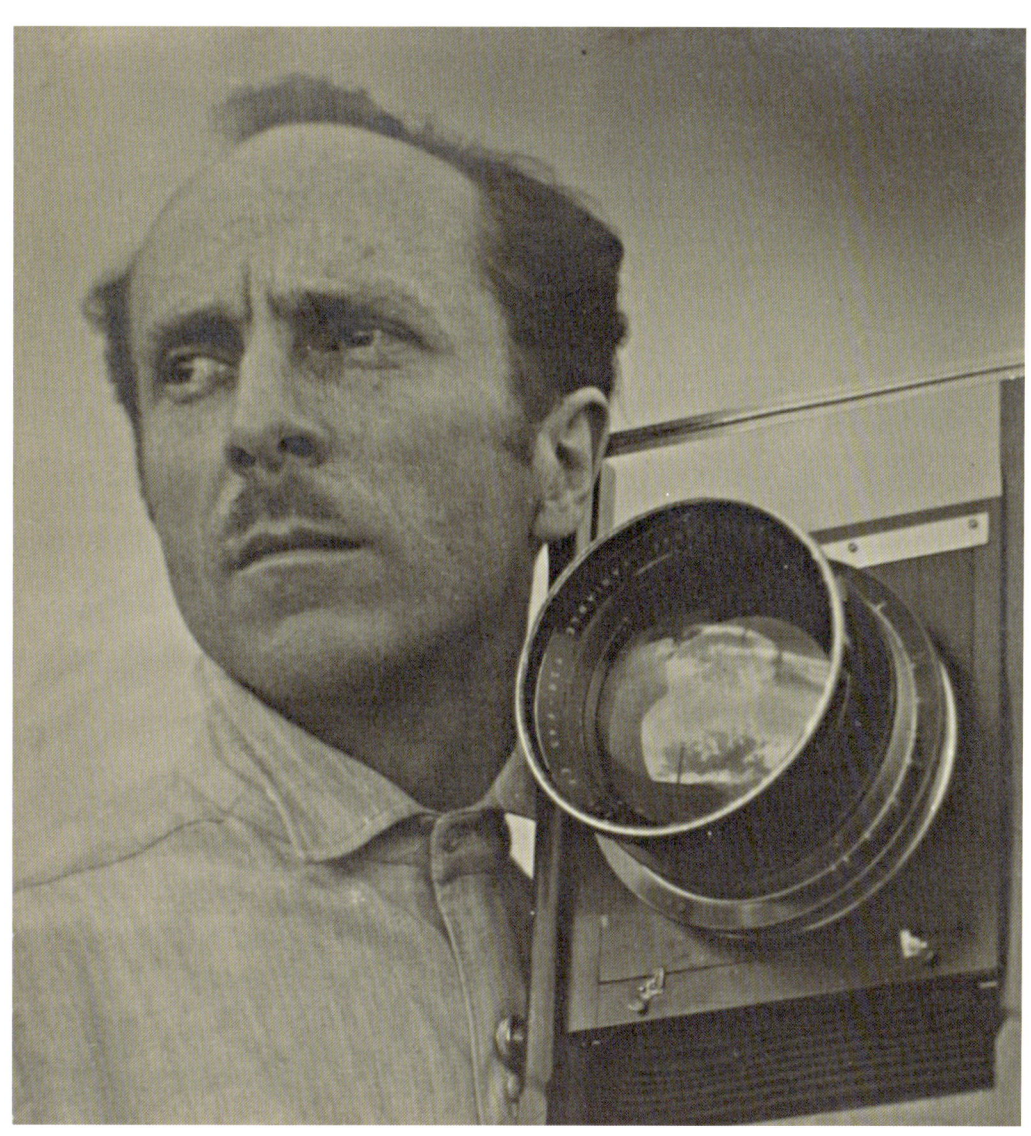

Tina Modotti *Edward Weston with his Camera, Mexico* c.1923, 7.6 × 7.3 cm

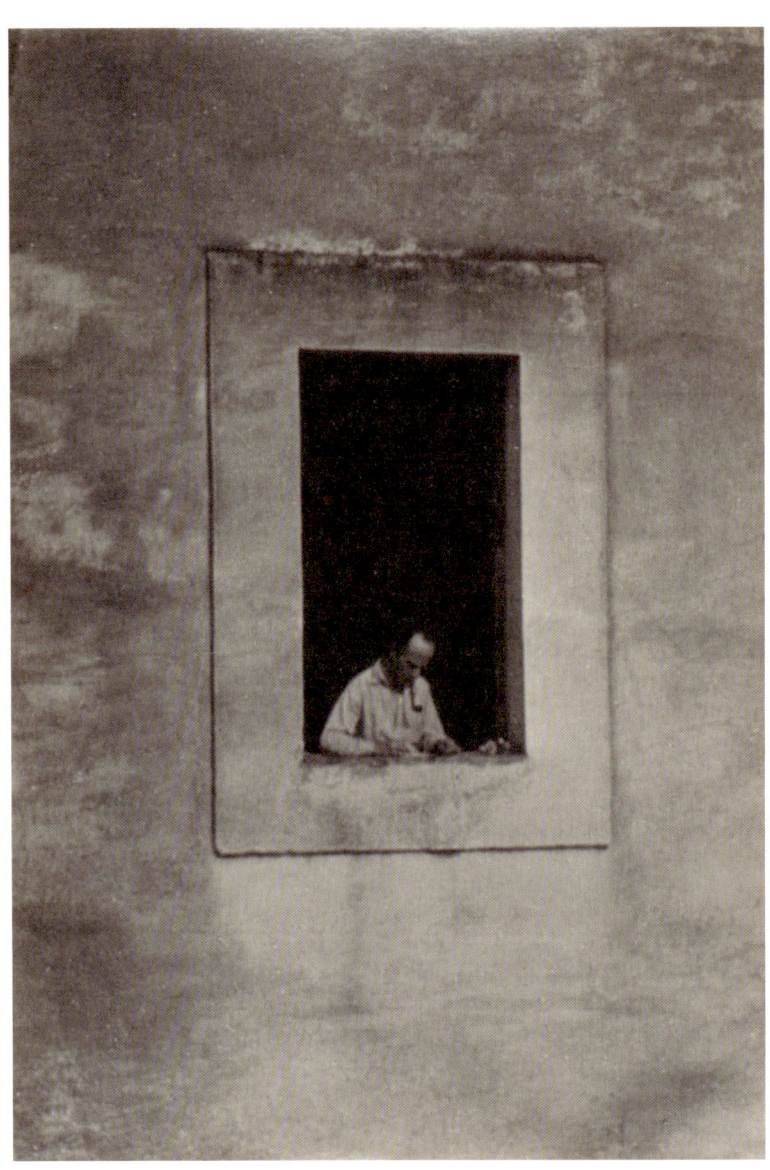

Tina Modotti *Weston in a Window, Tepotzotlán, Mexico* 1924, 8.3 × 5.7 cm

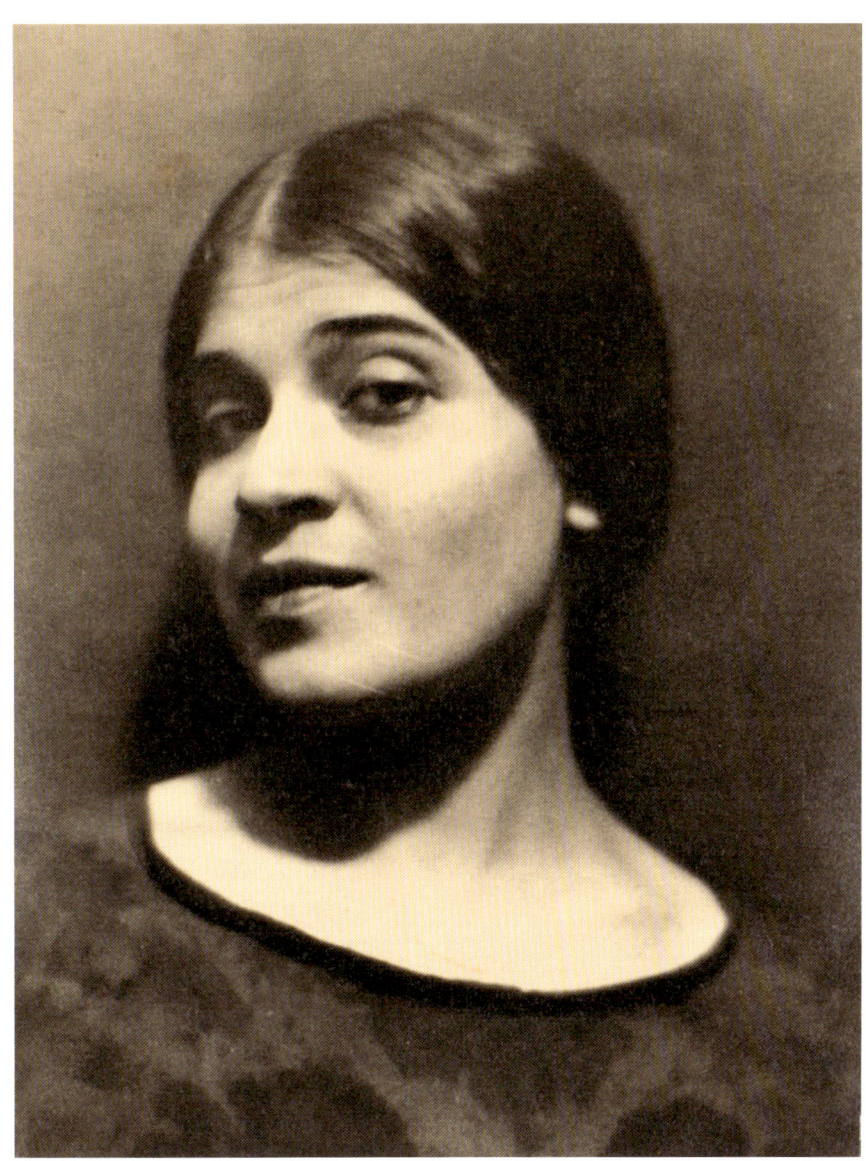

EDWARD WESTON *Tina Reciting* 1924, 9.2 × 6 cm

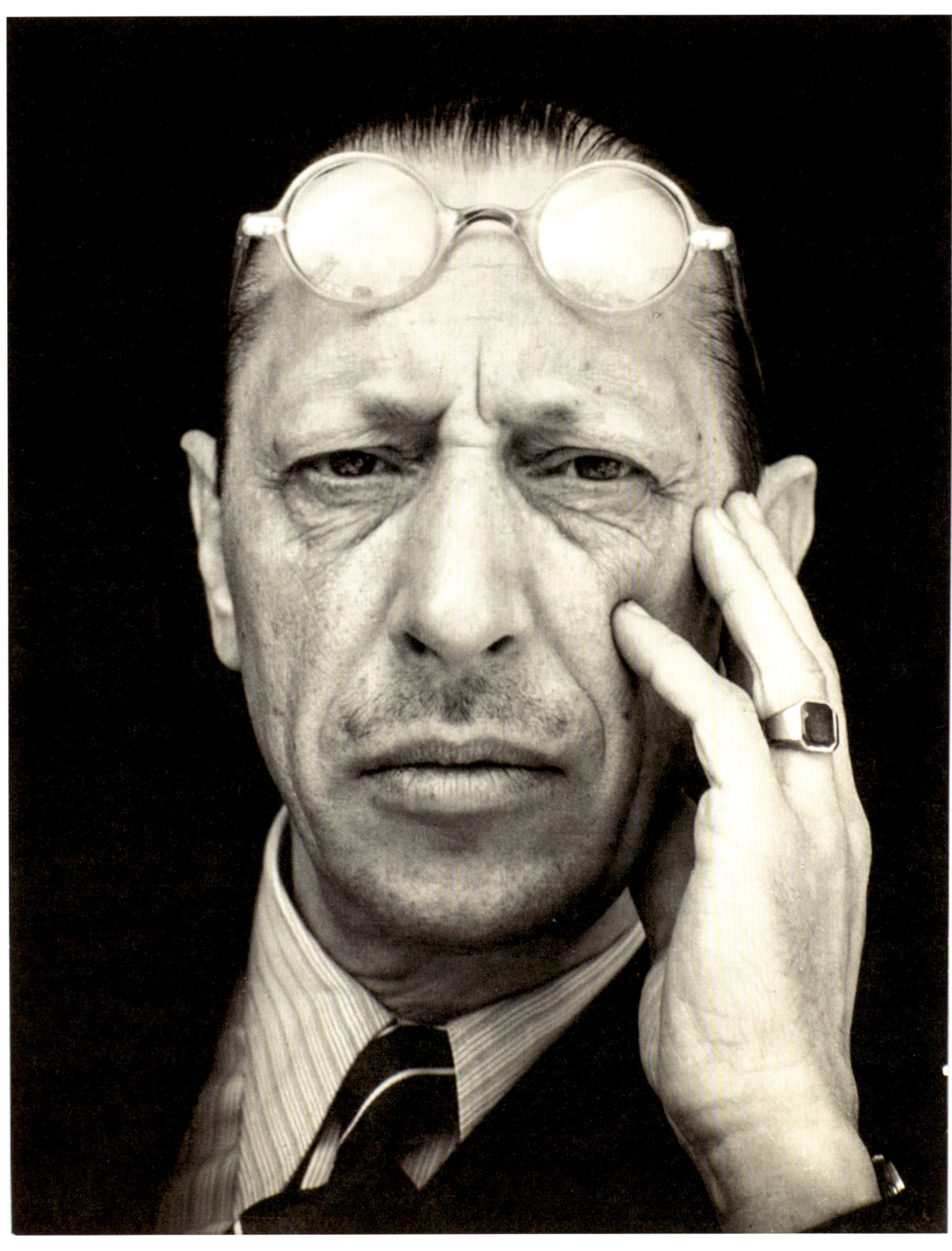

Edward Weston *Igor Stravinsky* 1935, 11.7 × 9.2 cm

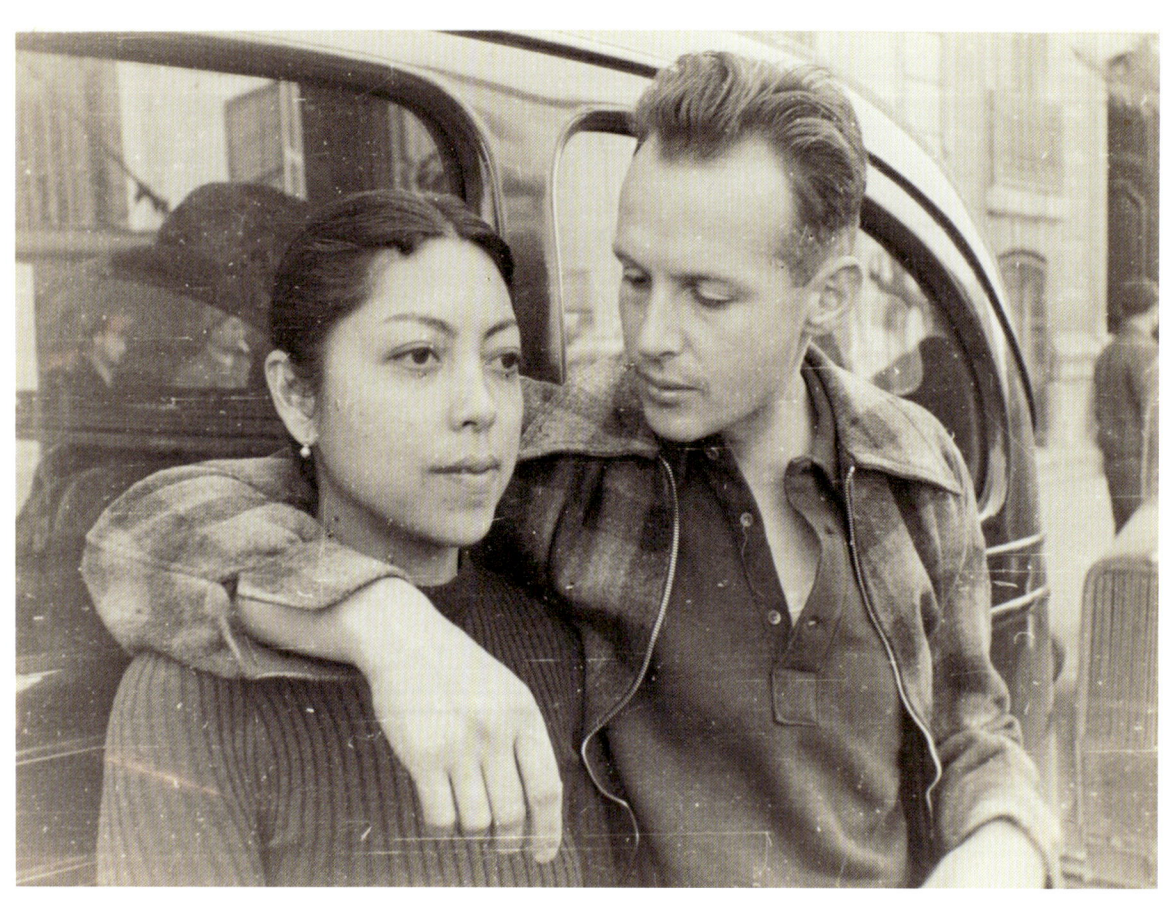

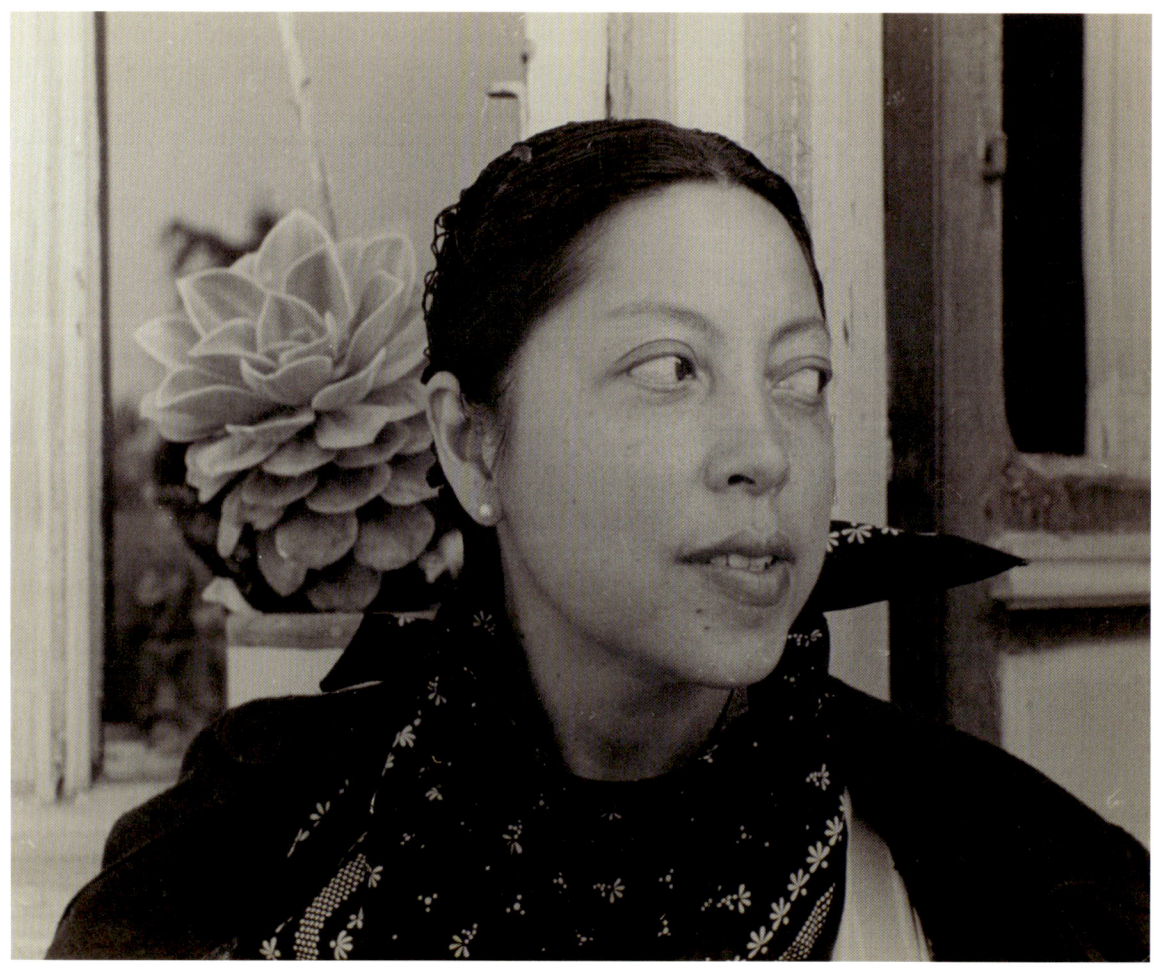

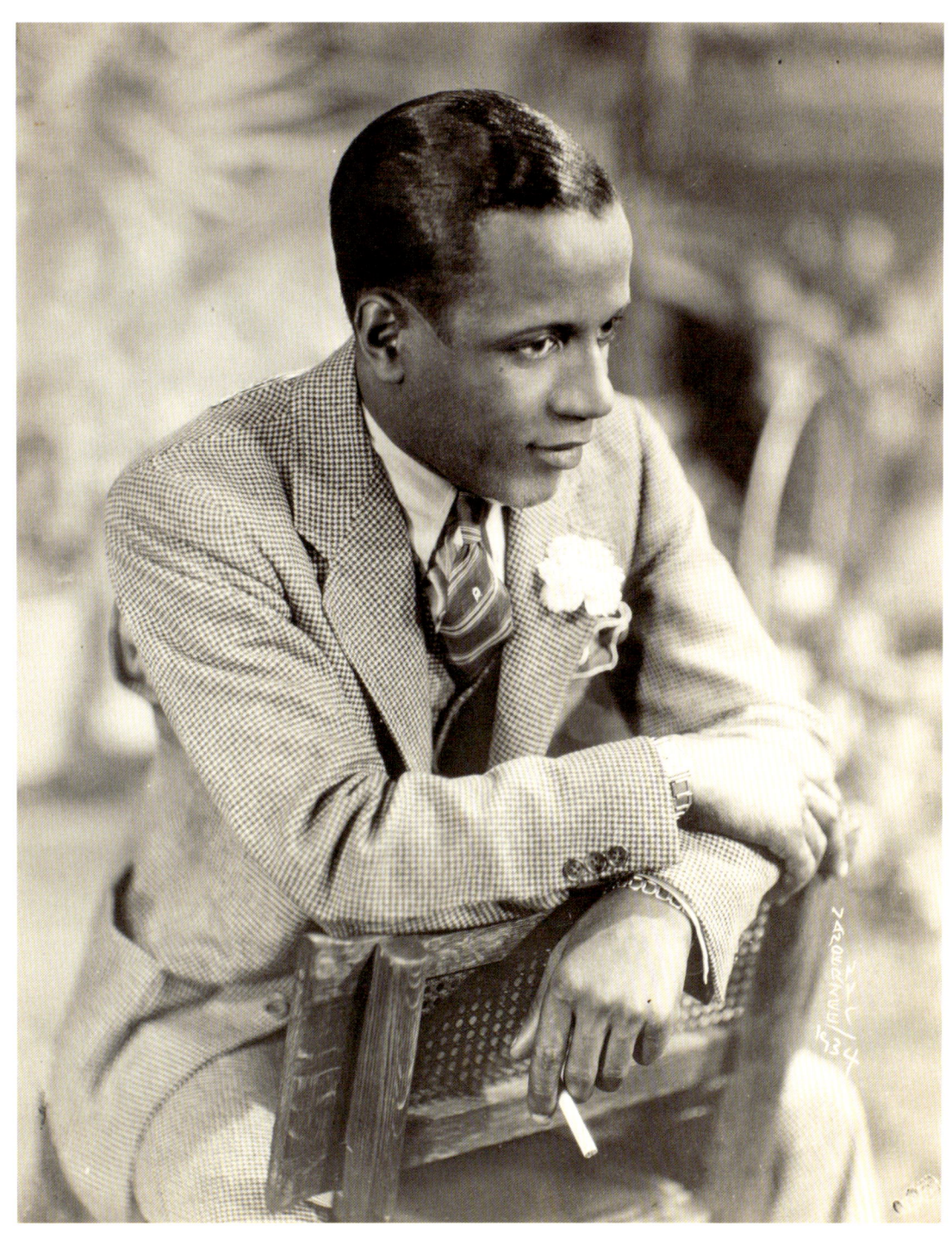

Top left: **HENRI CARTIER-BRESSON**
Henri Cartier-Bresson with his Wife
Ratna Mohini, Madrid, Spain 1936
12.7 × 17.5 cm

Bottom left: **HENRI CARTIER-BRESSON**
Ratna Mohini, Wife of Henri Cartier-
Bresson c.1936, 17.1 × 22.2 cm   Above: **JAMES VAN DER ZEE** *Portrait, Harlem 1934, 23.5 × 19.4 cm*

Brassaï *A Costume for Two, Magic-City Ball, Paris* 1931, 28.3 × 21.3 cm

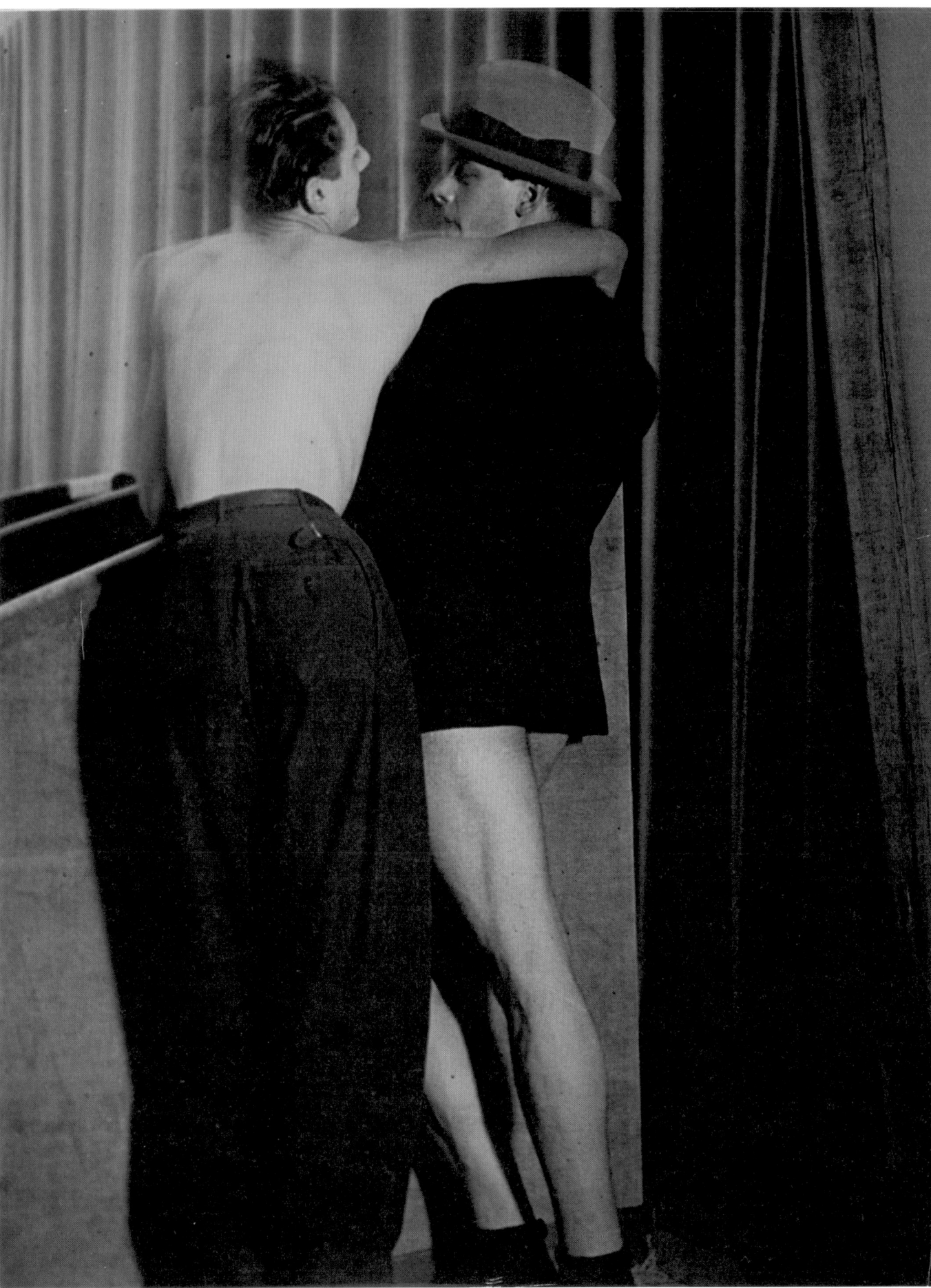

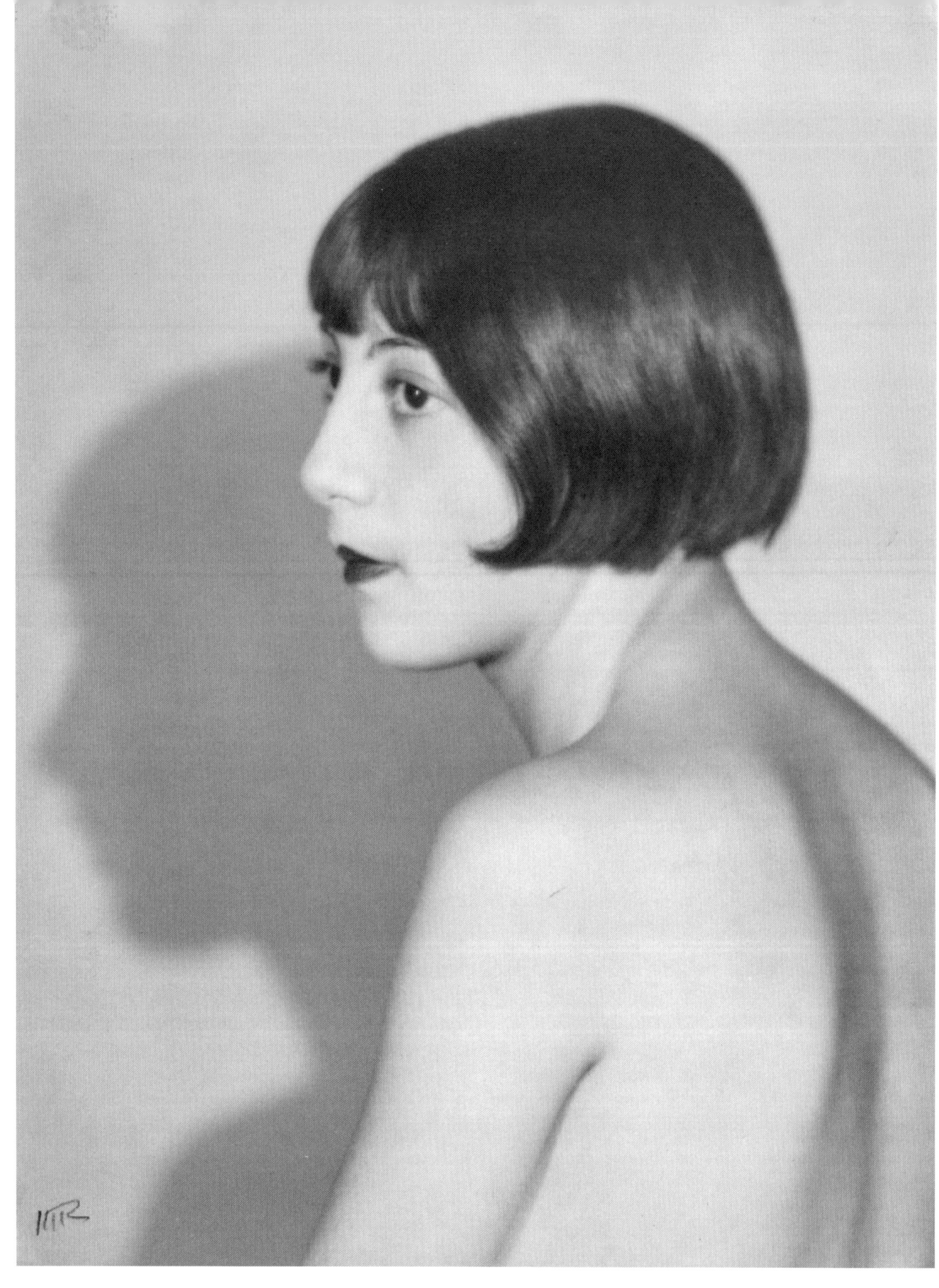

Man Ray *Dominique (Kiki's Younger Sister) c.1926, 22.9 × 17.5 cm*

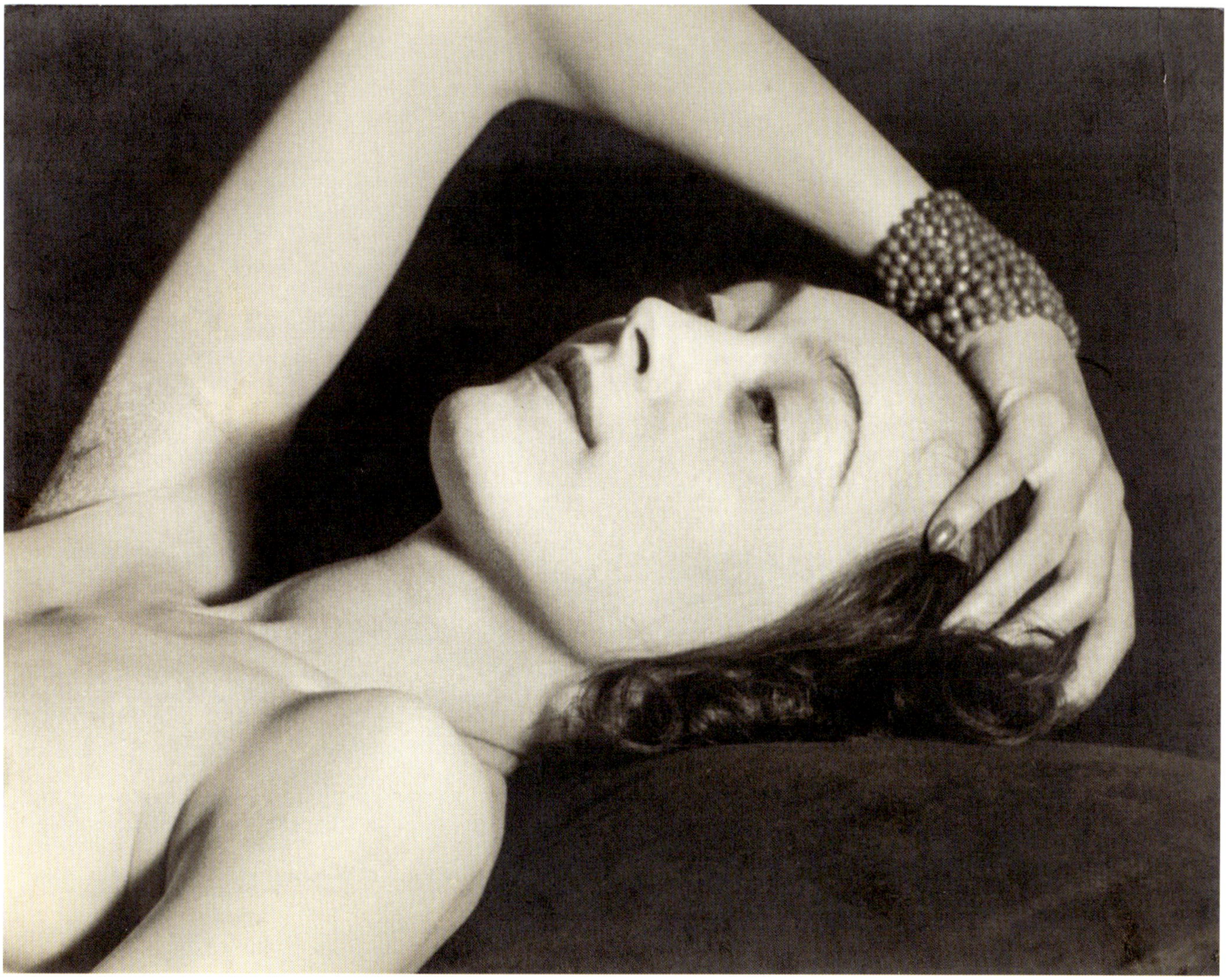

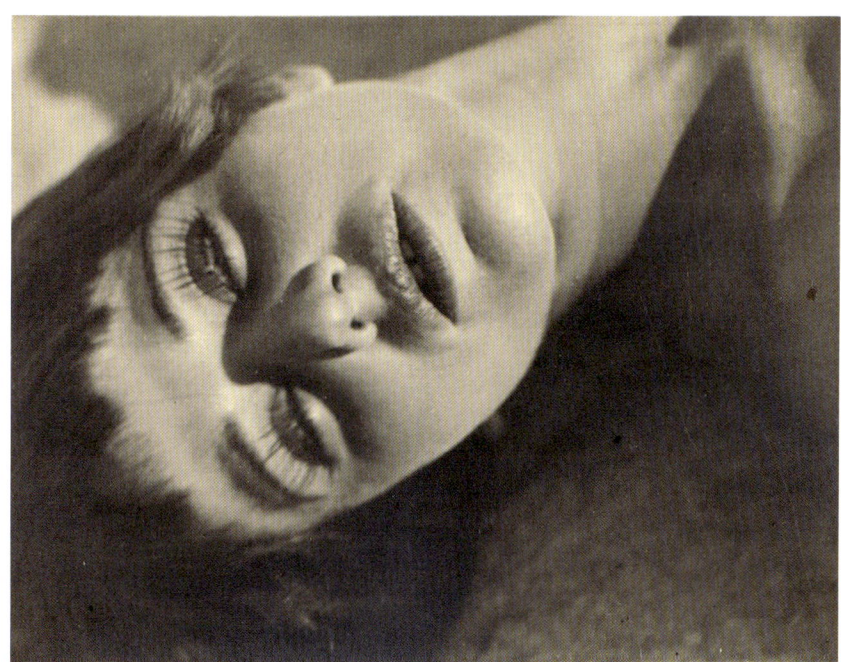

Top:
MAN RAY
Nusch Eluard 1928
17.5 × 22.5 cm

Right:
EDWARD WESTON
Nahui Olín c.1923
7.3 × 9.8 cm

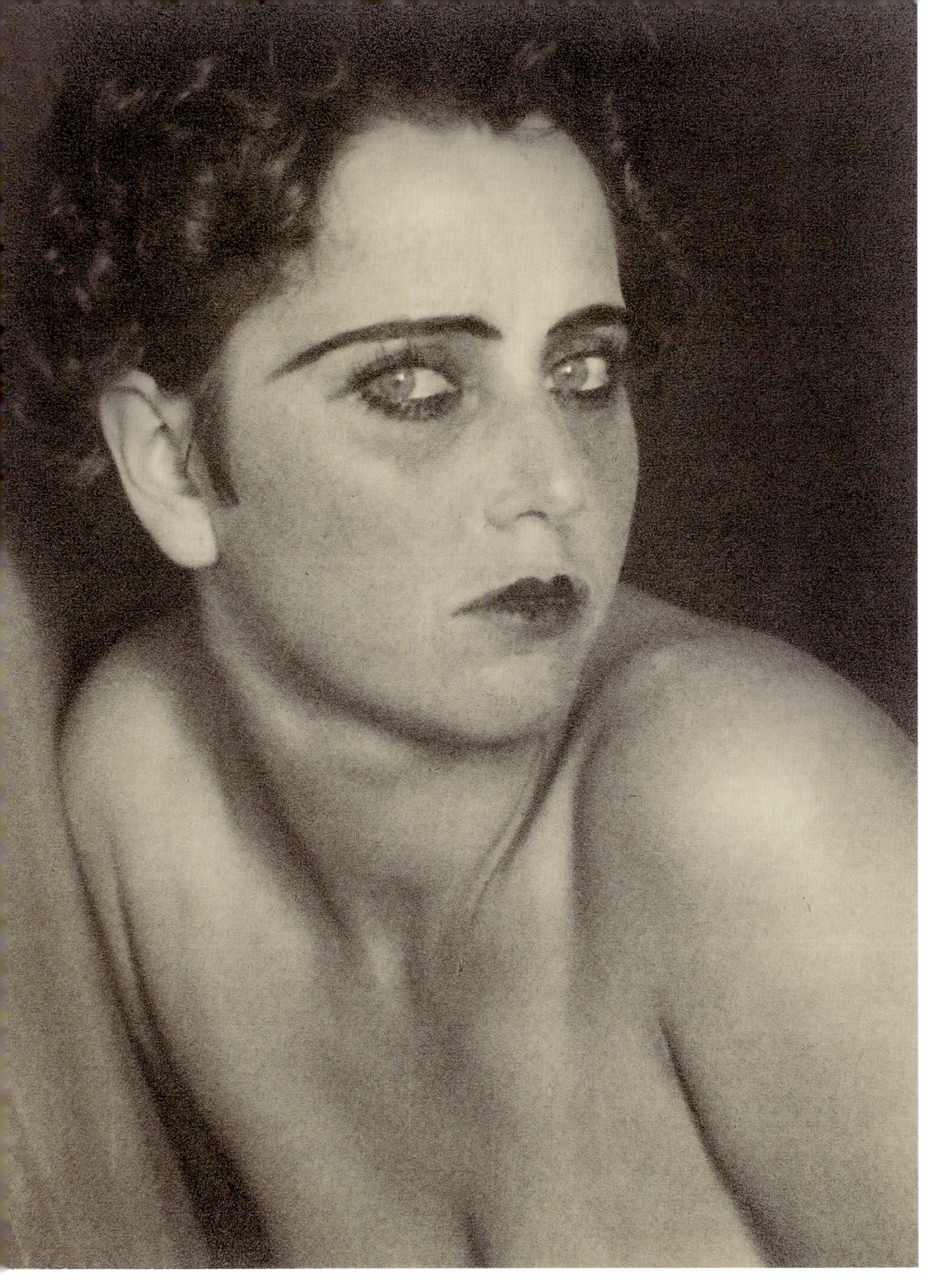

EDWARD WESTON *Nahui Olín* 1924, 21.6 × 16.5 cm

Jaroslav Fabinger *Head of a Woman* c.1930, 12.1 × 16.5 cm

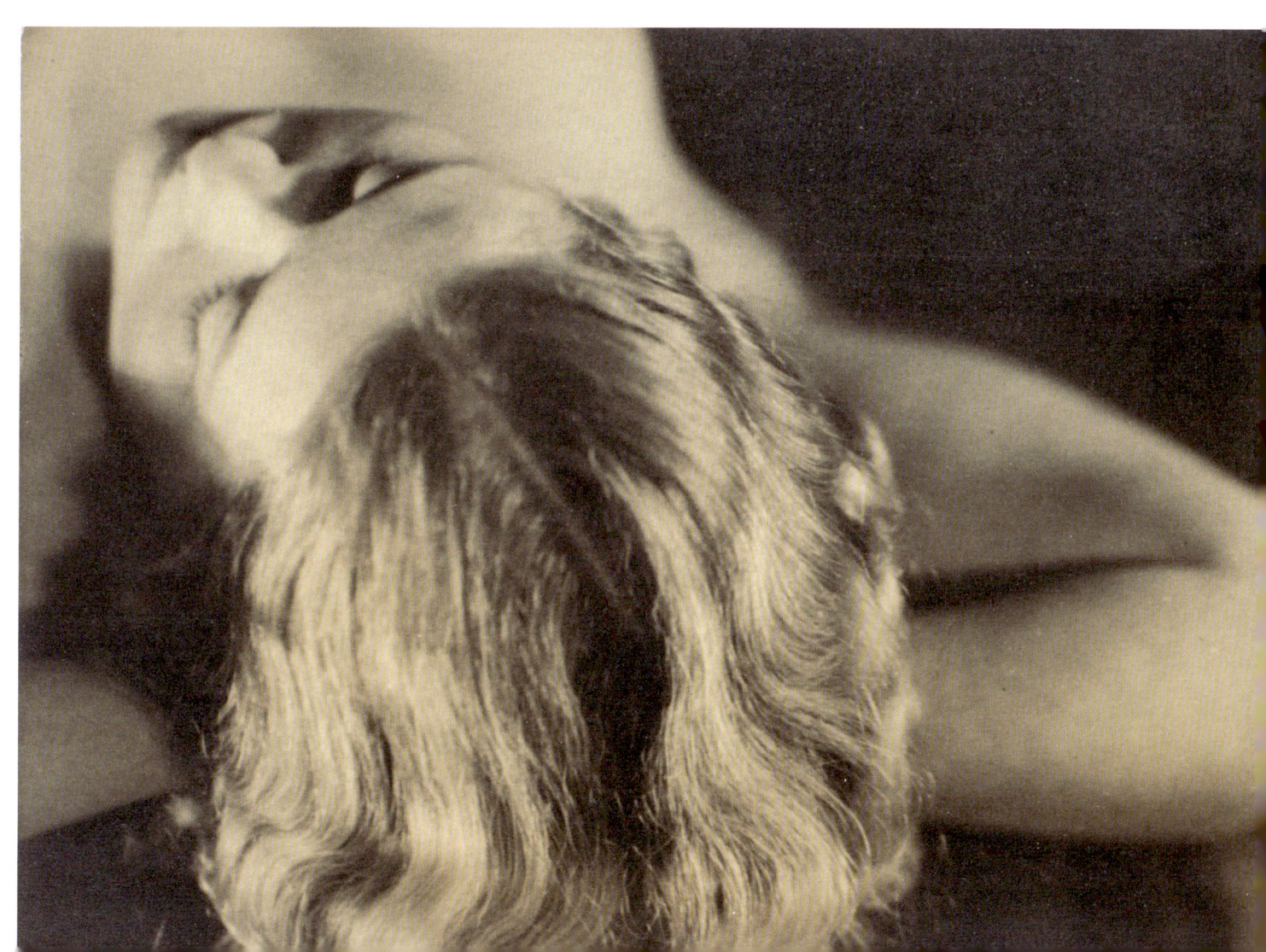

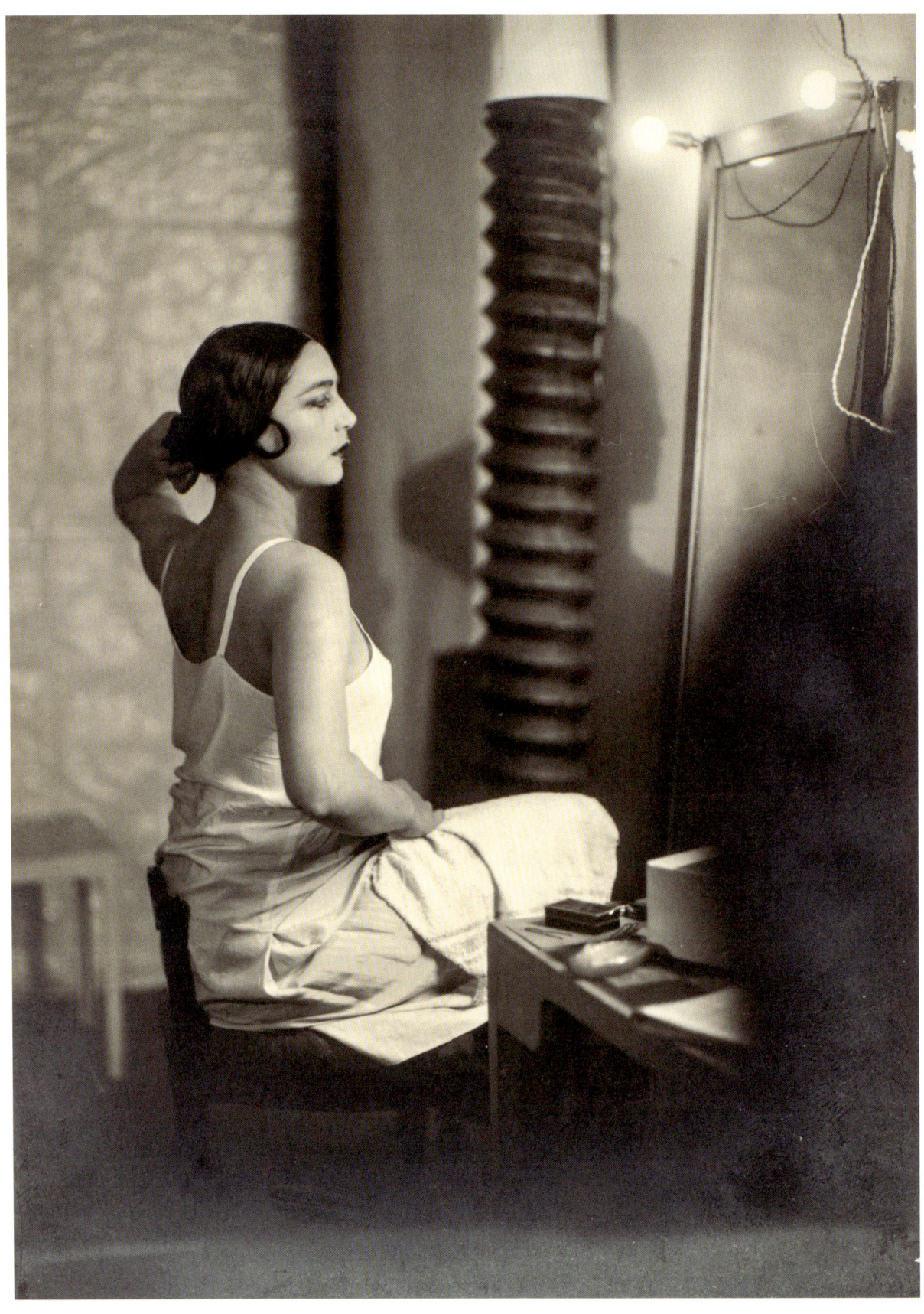

MAN RAY *Rosa Covarrubias* 1928, 16.5 × 12.1 cm

MAN RAY *Portrait of a Woman* c.1930, 22.2 × 18.1 cm

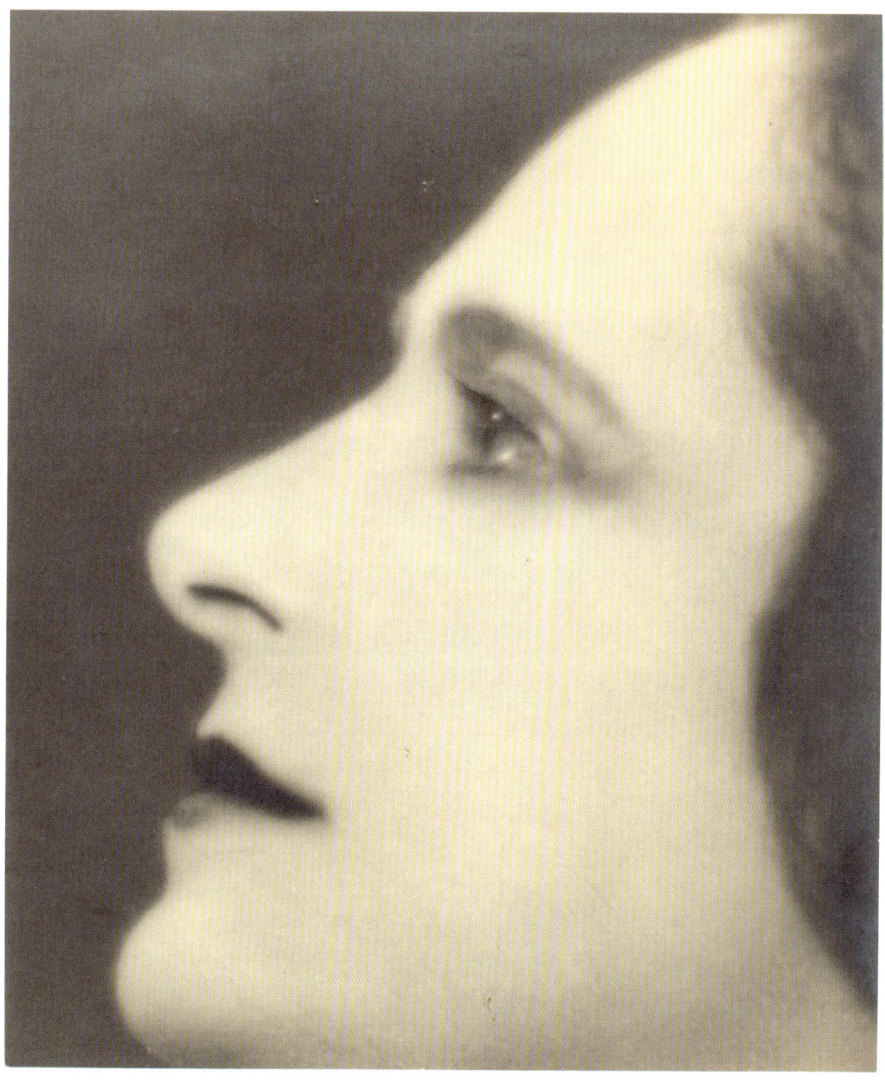

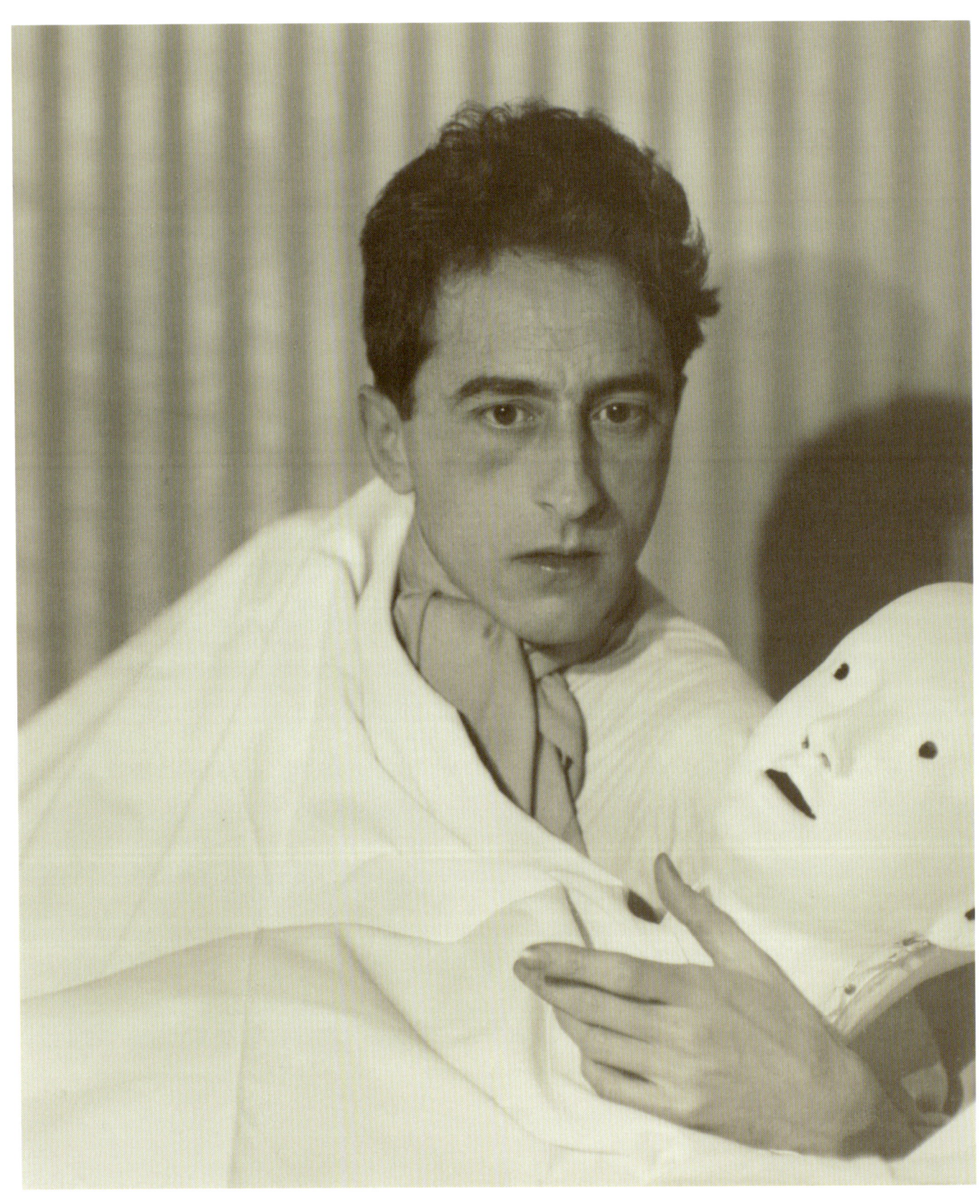

BERENICE ABBOTT *Cocteau with Mask of Antigone, Paris 1927, 23.5 × 20 cm*

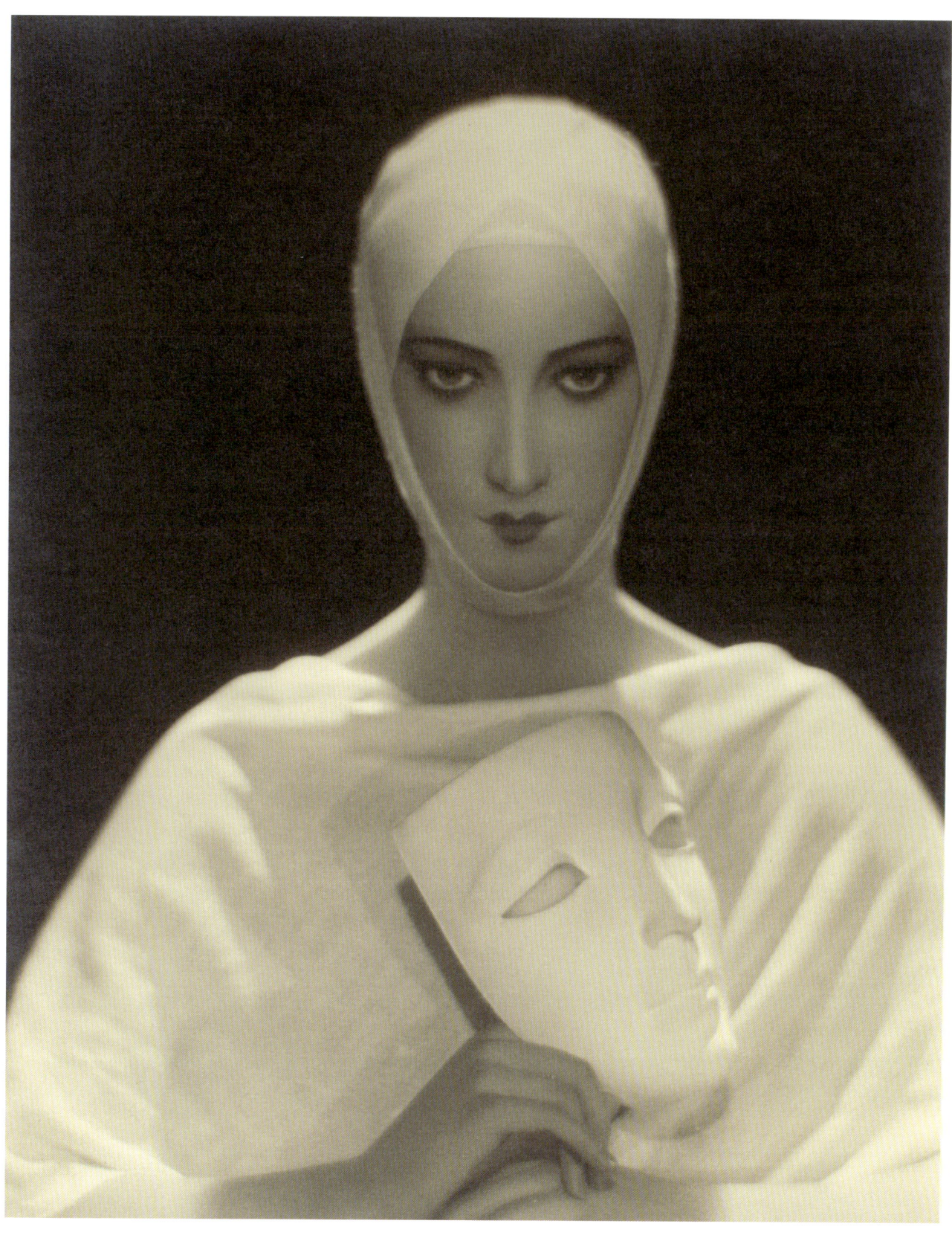

ADOLF DE MEYER *Advertising Photograph for Elizabeth Arden, November 1931*
bromoil gelatin silver print, 35.6 × 27.6 cm

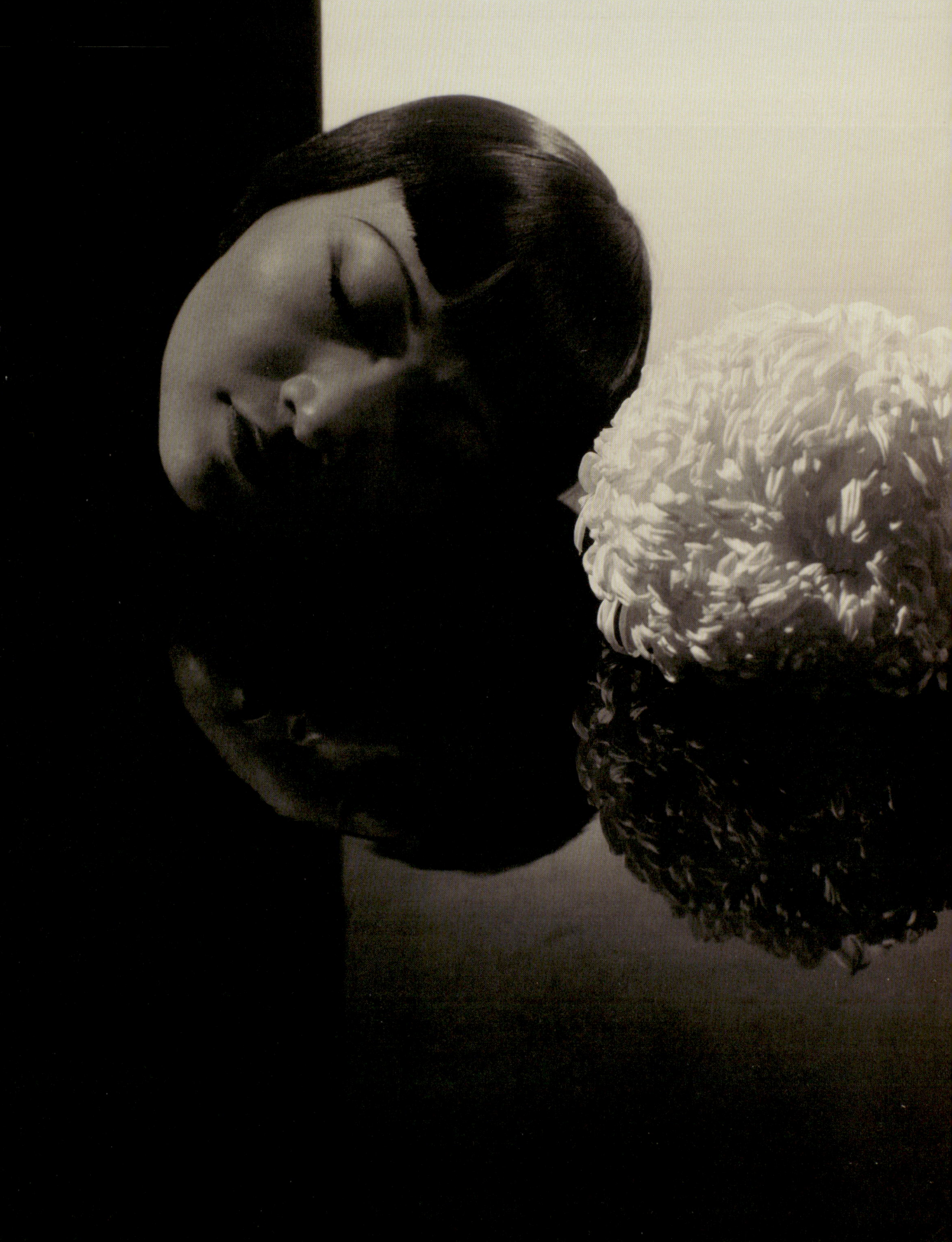

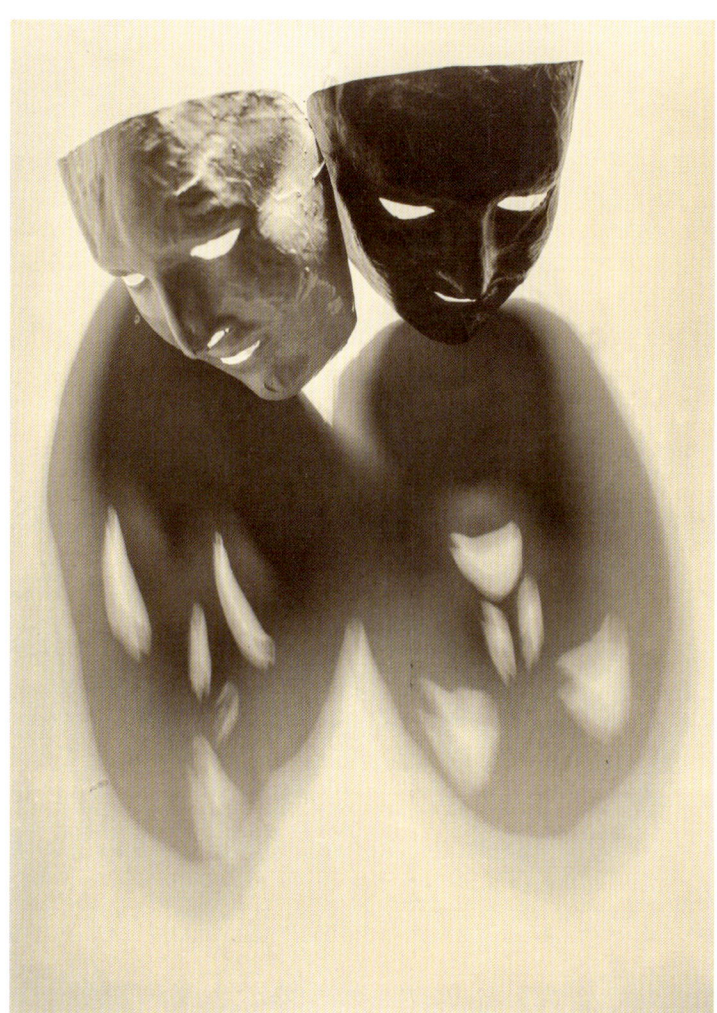

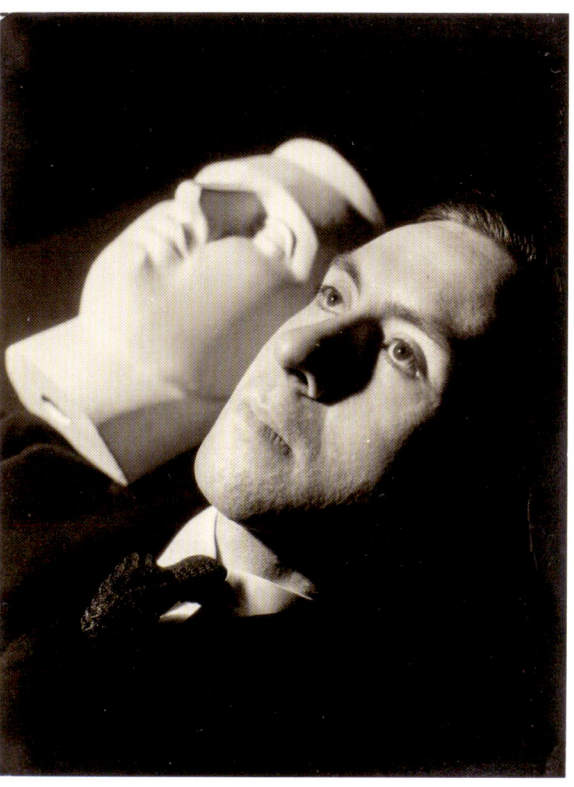

Left: **Emmanuel Sougez**
Carnival is Dead – Two Masks with their Shadows 1930
36.2 × 26.7 cm

Below: **Edward Quigley**
Self–Portrait with Classical Bust 1933
14 × 10.8 cm

Opposite:
Edward Steichen
*Anna May Wong,
New York* 1930
23.8 × 19.4 cm

Right:
Norman Parkinson
*Edward James with
his Death Mask of
Napoleon, Painted
by Magritte* 1938
19.1 × 26 cm

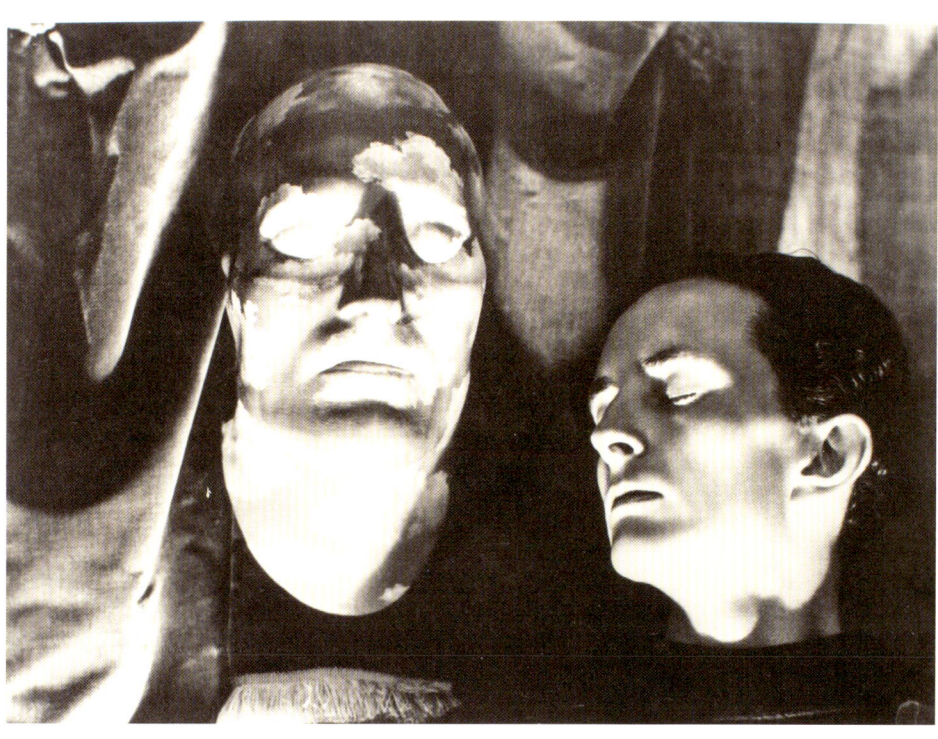

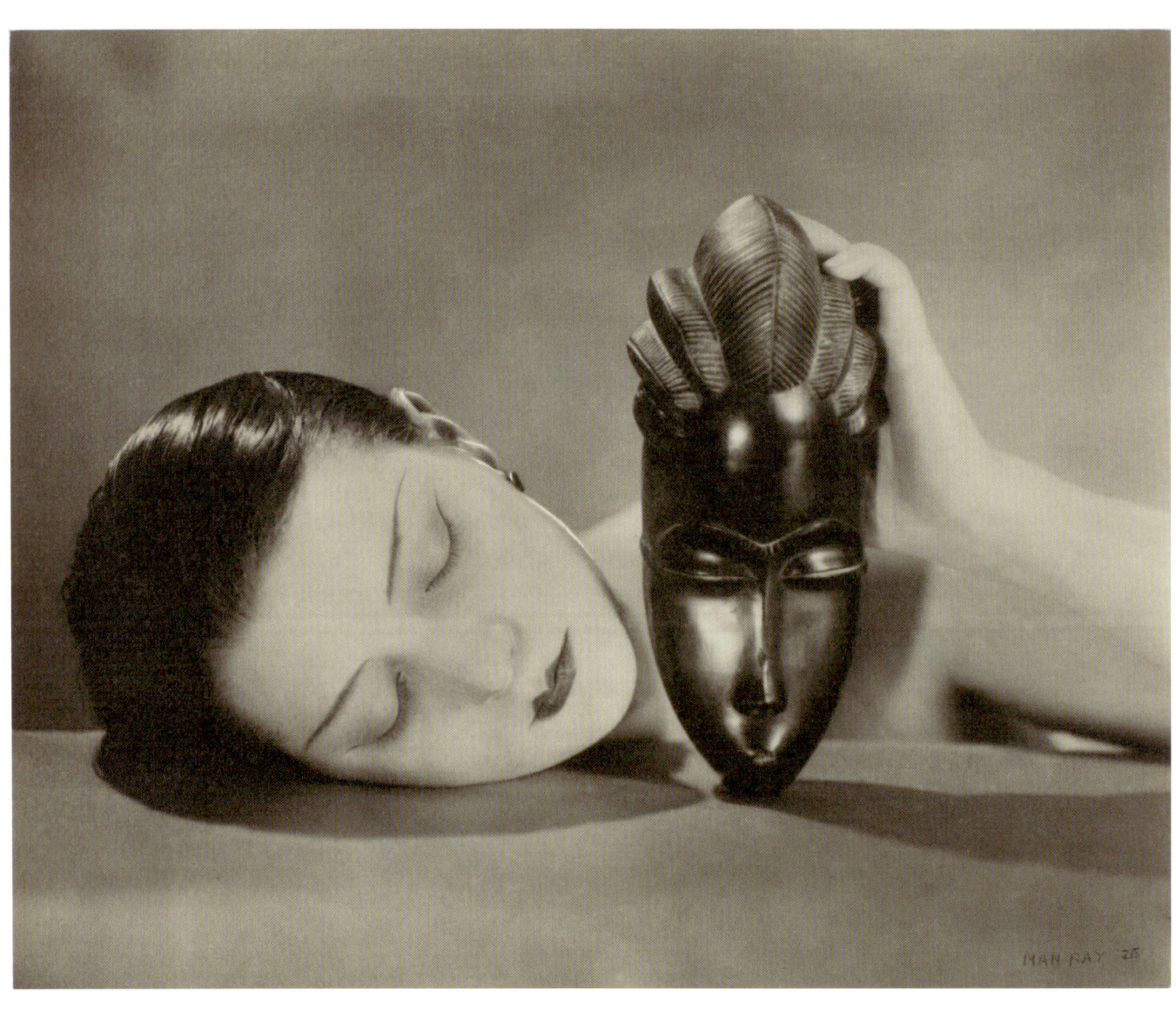

MAN RAY *Noire et Blanche (Positive)* 1926, 21.9 × 27.3 cm

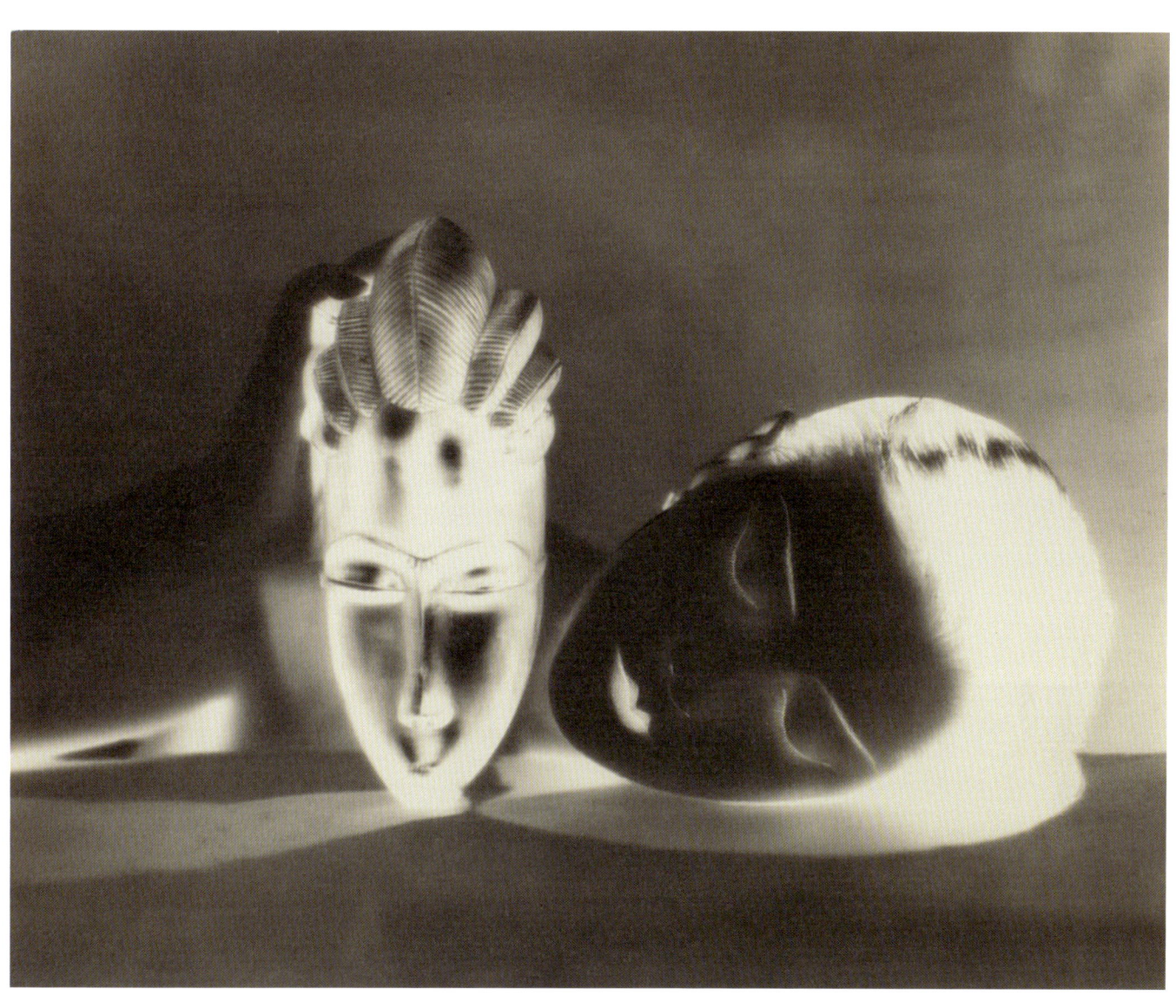

MAN RAY *Noire et Blanche (Negative)* 1926, 22.5 × 27.9 cm

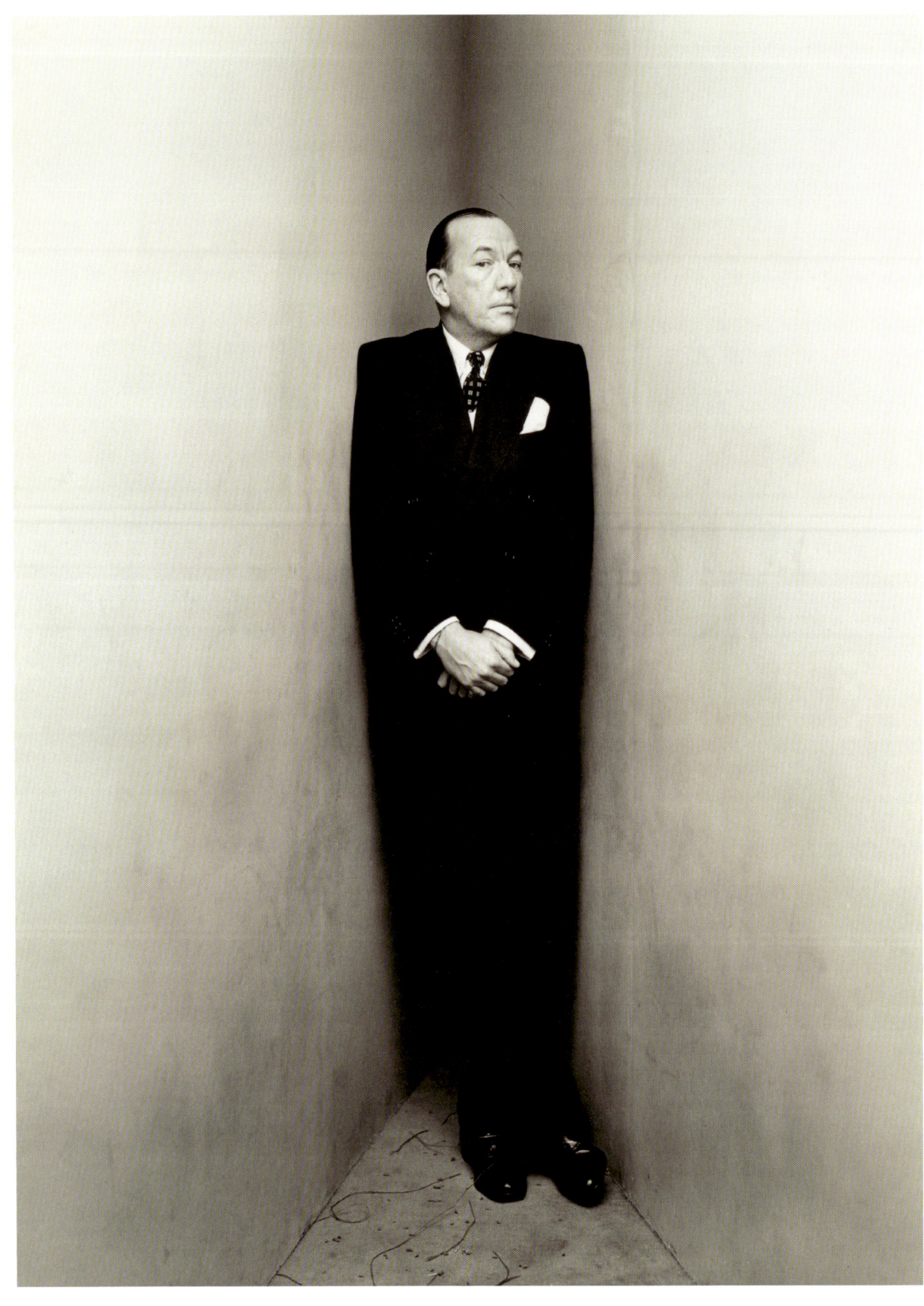

IRVING PENN *Noël Coward, New York (2 of 3)* 1948, 22.5 × 15.9 cm

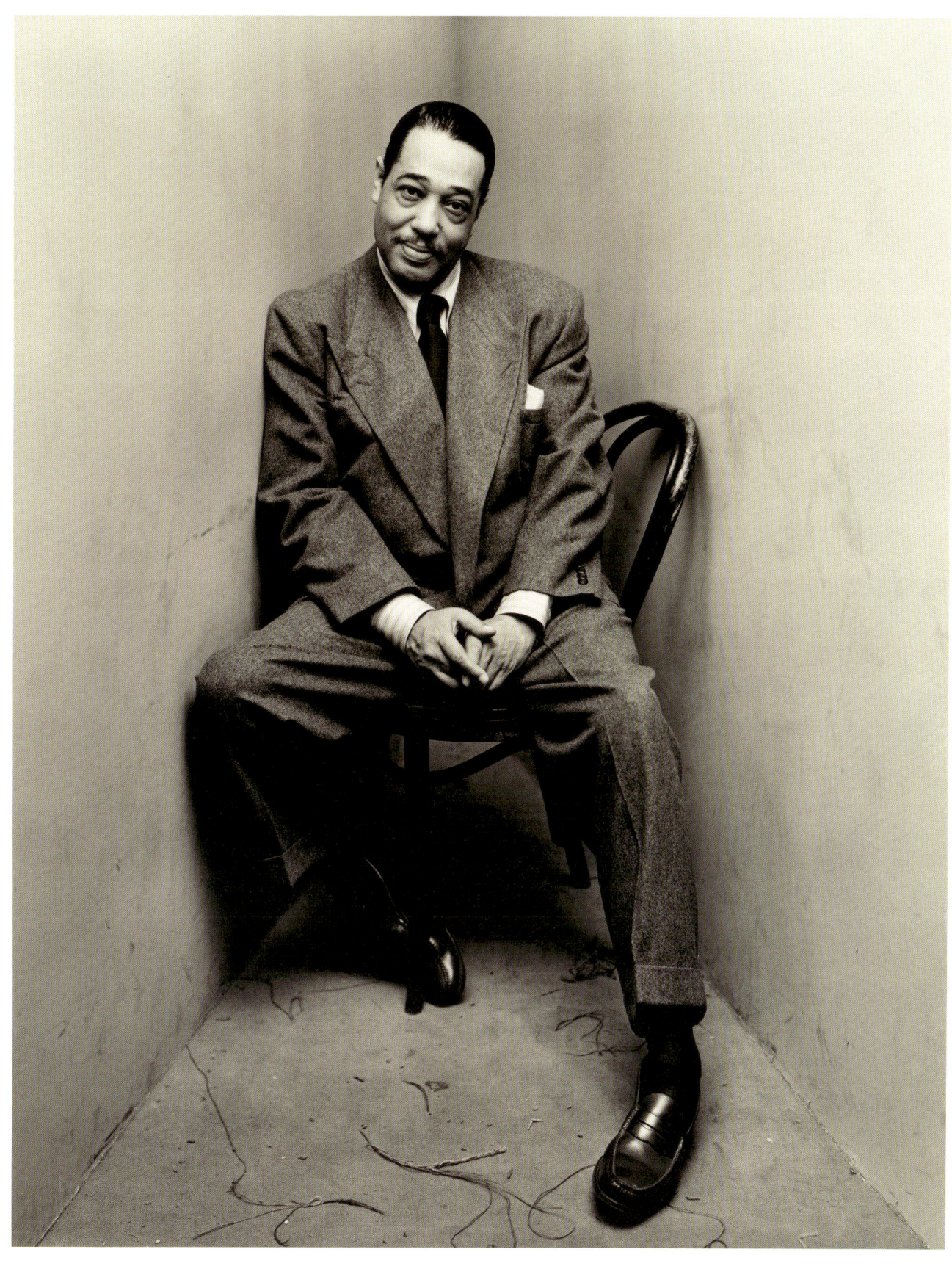

IRVING PENN *Duke Ellington, New York* (3 of 3) 1948, 23.5 × 18.4 cm

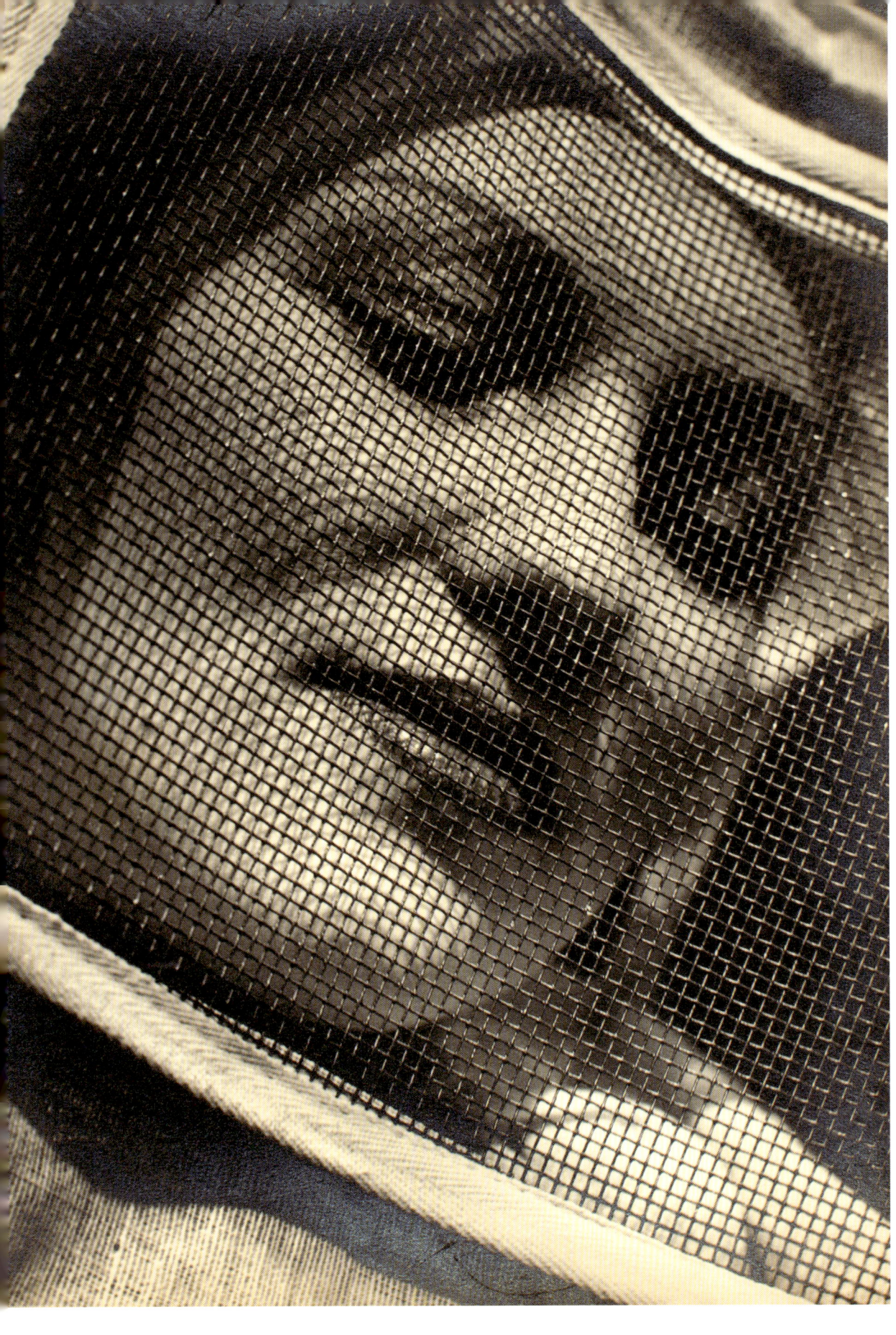

NORMAN PARKINSON *The Beekeeper* 1939, 36.8 × 26.7 cm

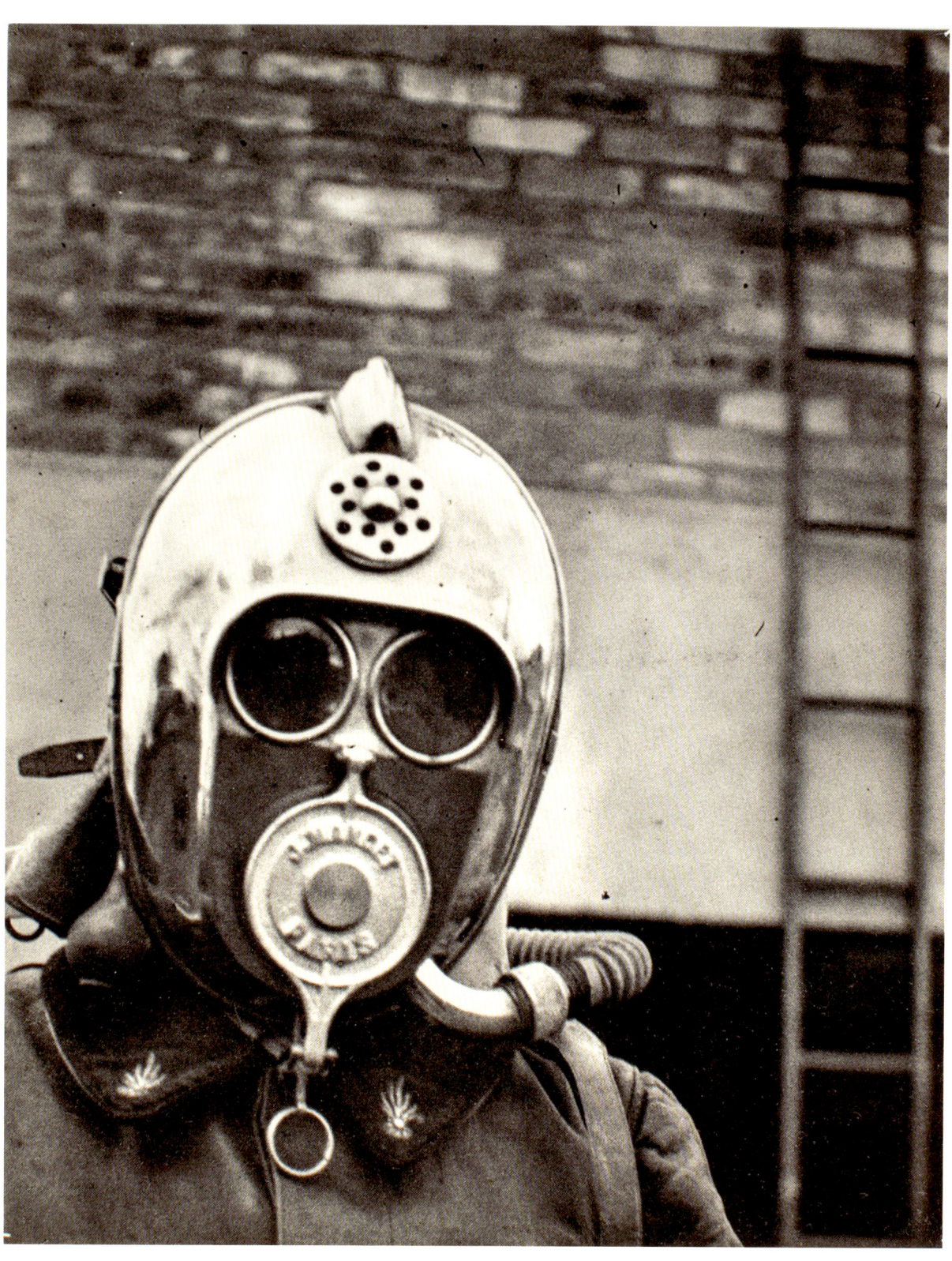

Josef Breitenbach *Fireman, Paris* c.1935, 29.5 × 23.8 cm

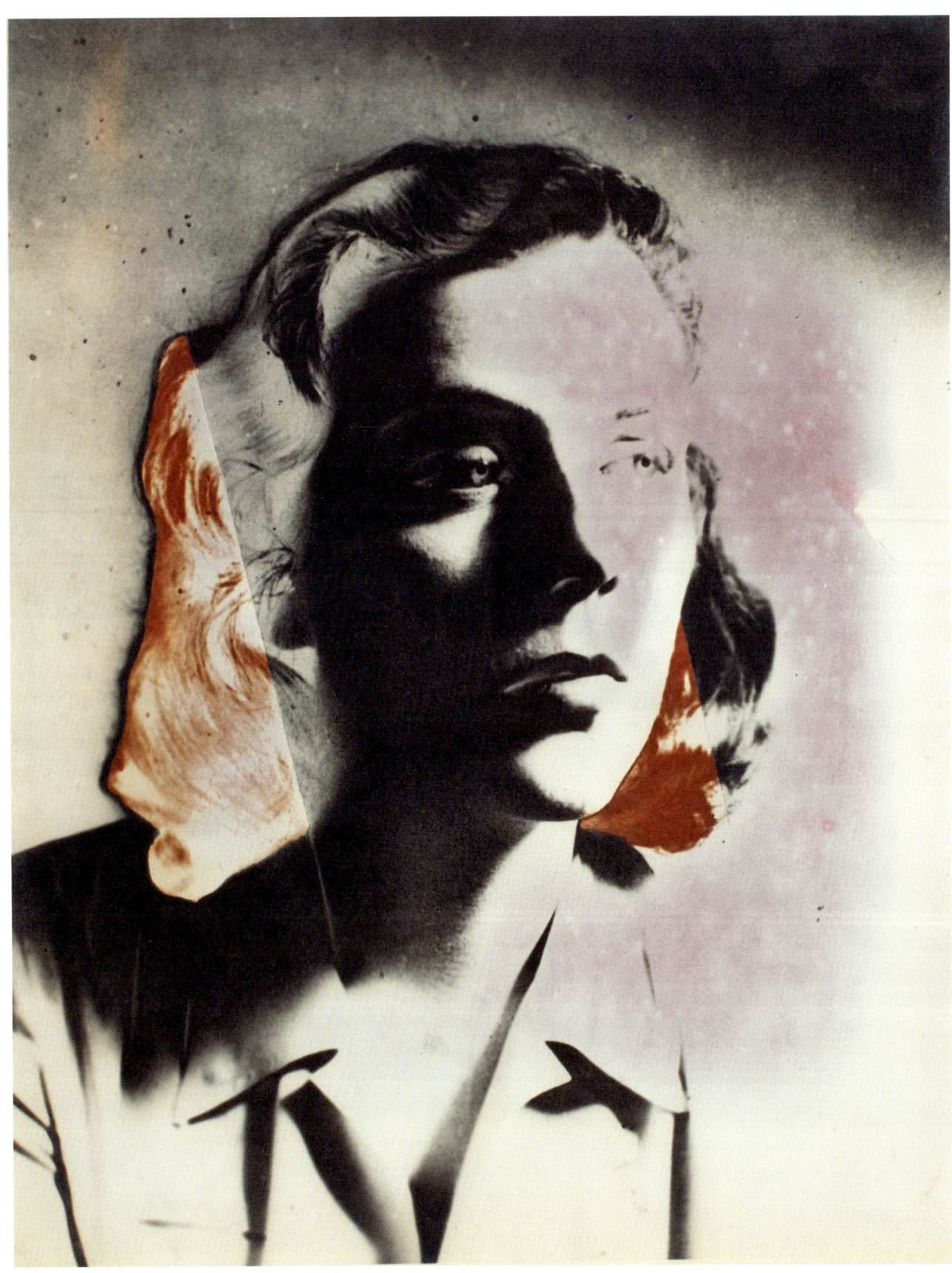

JOSEF BREITENBACH
Patricia, New York c.1942
bromoil transfer print onto
gelatin silver paper
34.3 × 25.7 cm

EXPERIMENTS

The single defining quality that helped photography to establish itself was its ability to make records that were more faithful to reality than drawing or painting could ever be. Yet it was precisely this attribute that would be scrutinised by the photographers, designers and critics who wanted to create a new role for the photograph within modern society.

The concept of the 'photographic' stimulated curiosity and each stage of the process was opened up to experimentation: from capturing the image to making interventions on the surface of the print. Different lenses and perspectives, cropping, overlaying and enlargement were all used to abstract meaning and distort perception. Testing the innumerable possibilities of light on sensitised paper expanded an understanding of how the photograph can represent three dimensions in two, while *brûlage* (a kind of burning technique) and solarisation (reversing tones by over-exposing the negative) were among the many techniques used to distort the image. What the nineteenth-century photographer might have discarded, the modernist often celebrated.

László Moholy-Nagy's essays *Production-Reproduction* (1922) and his polemic *Painting Photography Film* (1925) functioned as early blueprints for this new, experimental approach. He argued that a century after its invention, photography's creative possibilities were only just beginning to be discovered. To realise its potential, he explained, meant approaching the photograph not as a tool for replicating reality, but as a way to create *new* realities. Many felt this sentiment ignored the artistry and experimentation – not to mention the determination – that had enabled the medium to progress thus far. Nonetheless, his voice rallied a generation to experiment and innovate.

The breadth and depth of this new approach was represented most fully in the international group exhibition *Film and Photo* in Stuttgart (1929). In its wake, debate about the purpose of photography continued with renewed zeal. Some of the most animated discussions centred around photomontage. The combining of different images to create new meanings was seen as the ultimate expression of the imagination and an exciting way of constructing an alternative reality – a 'super-reality', as Moholy-Nagy described it. For teacher and designer Jan Tschichold, writing in his influential essay *Photography and Typography* (1928), the photomontage constituted 'a truly free, human creation that is independent of nature'. Reflecting their wider goal to integrate photography into mass culture, both Moholy-Nagy and Tschichold were vocal advocates for its use in the graphic arts.

This re-consideration of the print as a material object was also expressed in the application of colour to the surface. Photographers reinvigorated the early traditions of tinting and transfer with a determinedly non-realistic and subjective aesthetic. From the early 1930s, the introduction of viable techniques for producing colour prints uncovered a whole new arena of possibilities that would be contested, and eventually embraced, in the following decades. EL

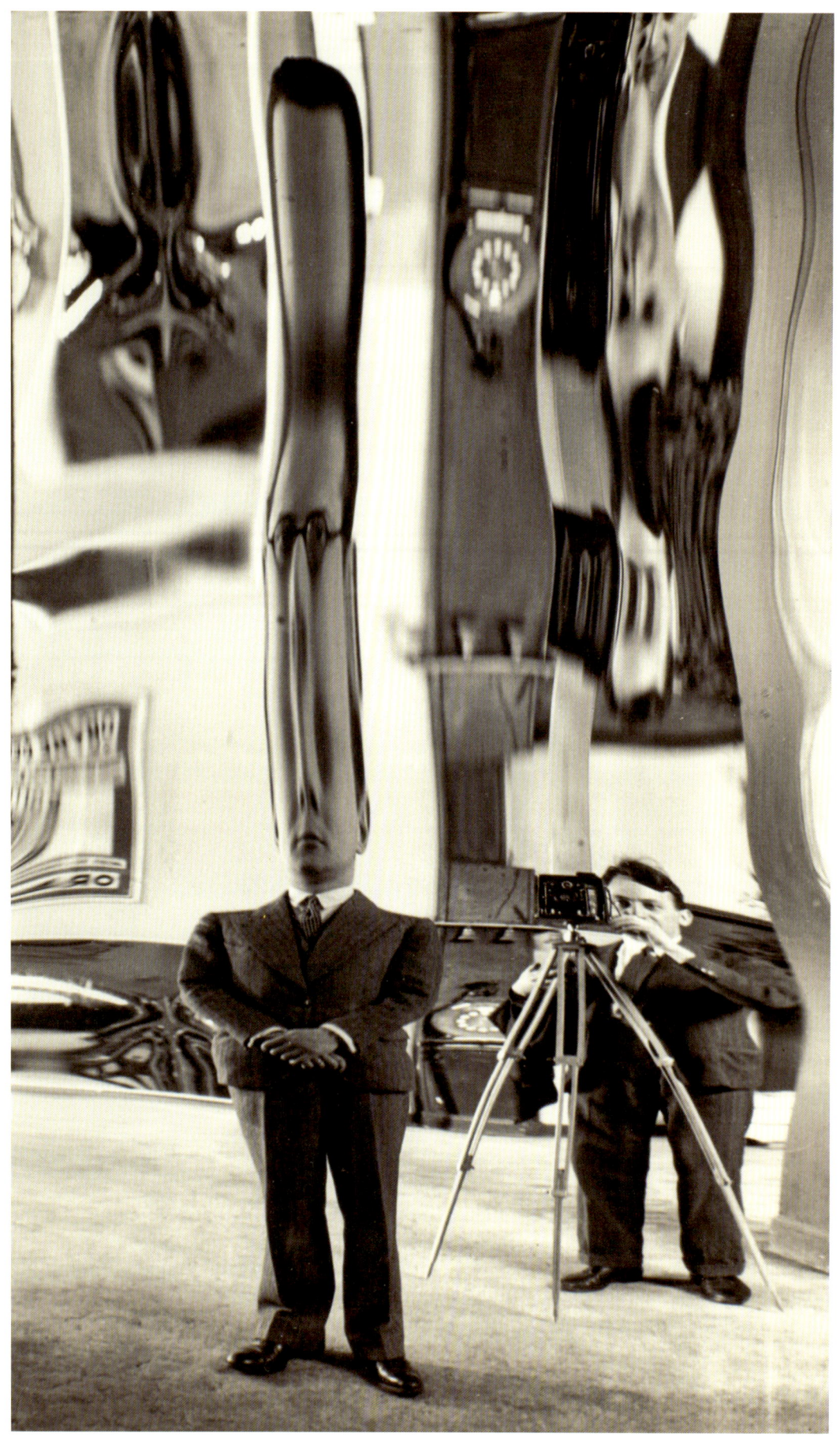

André Kertész *Self-Portrait with Carlo Rim, Luna Park 1930, 22.5 × 14.6 cm*

BERENICE ABBOTT *Portrait of the Artist as a Young Woman* c.1940s, 18.4 × 15.9 cm

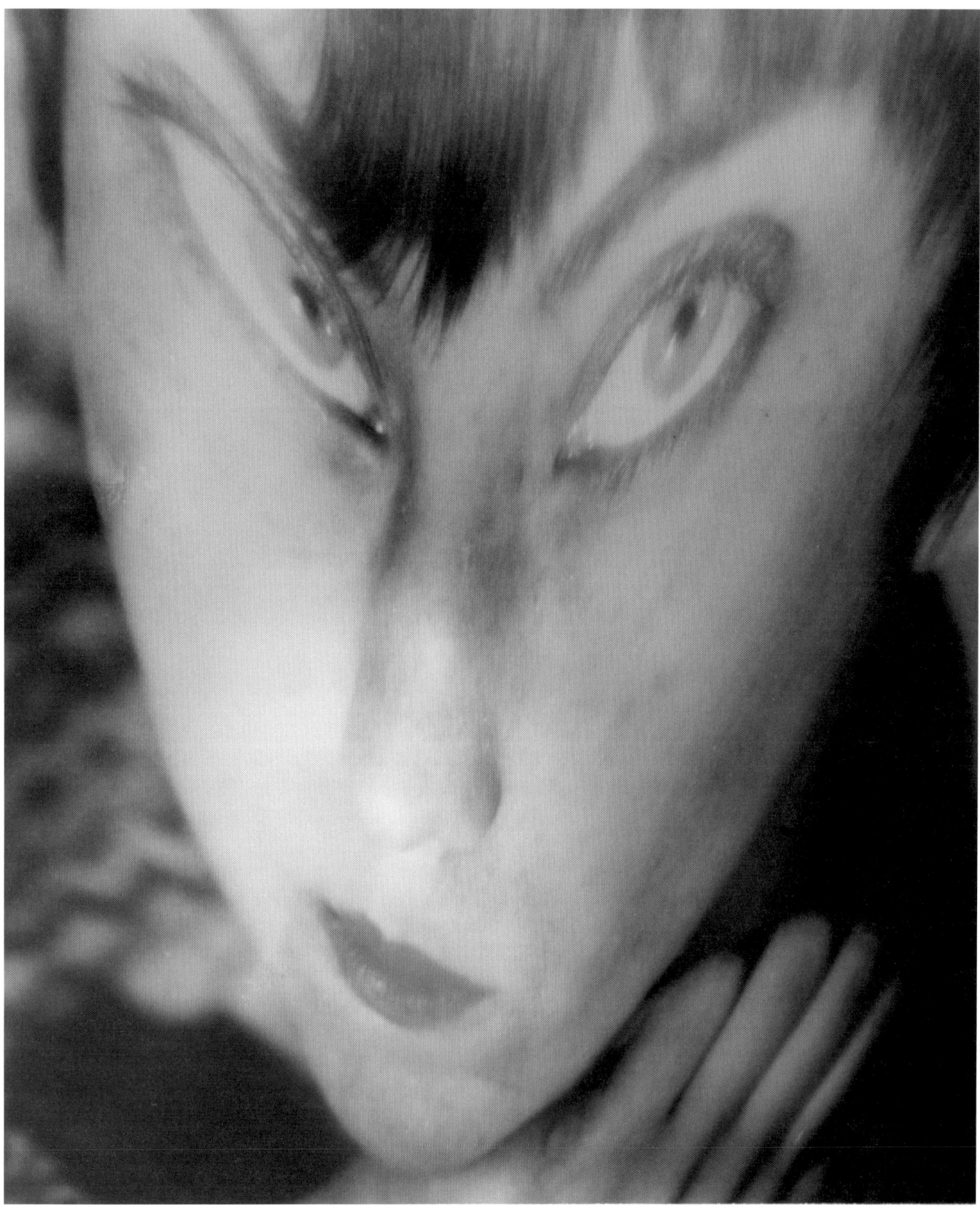

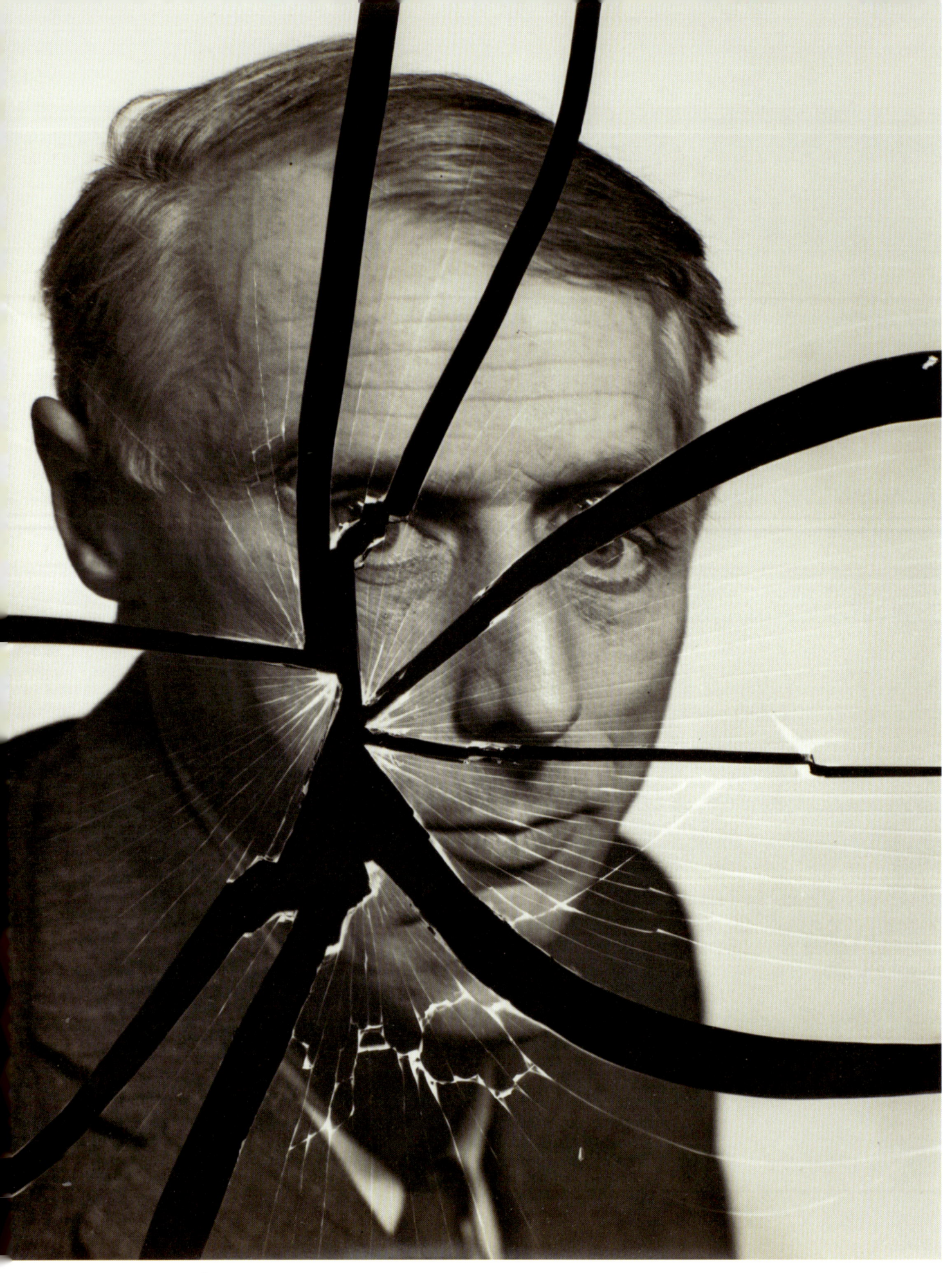

MAN RAY *Max Ernst* 1938, 22.9 × 17.5 cm

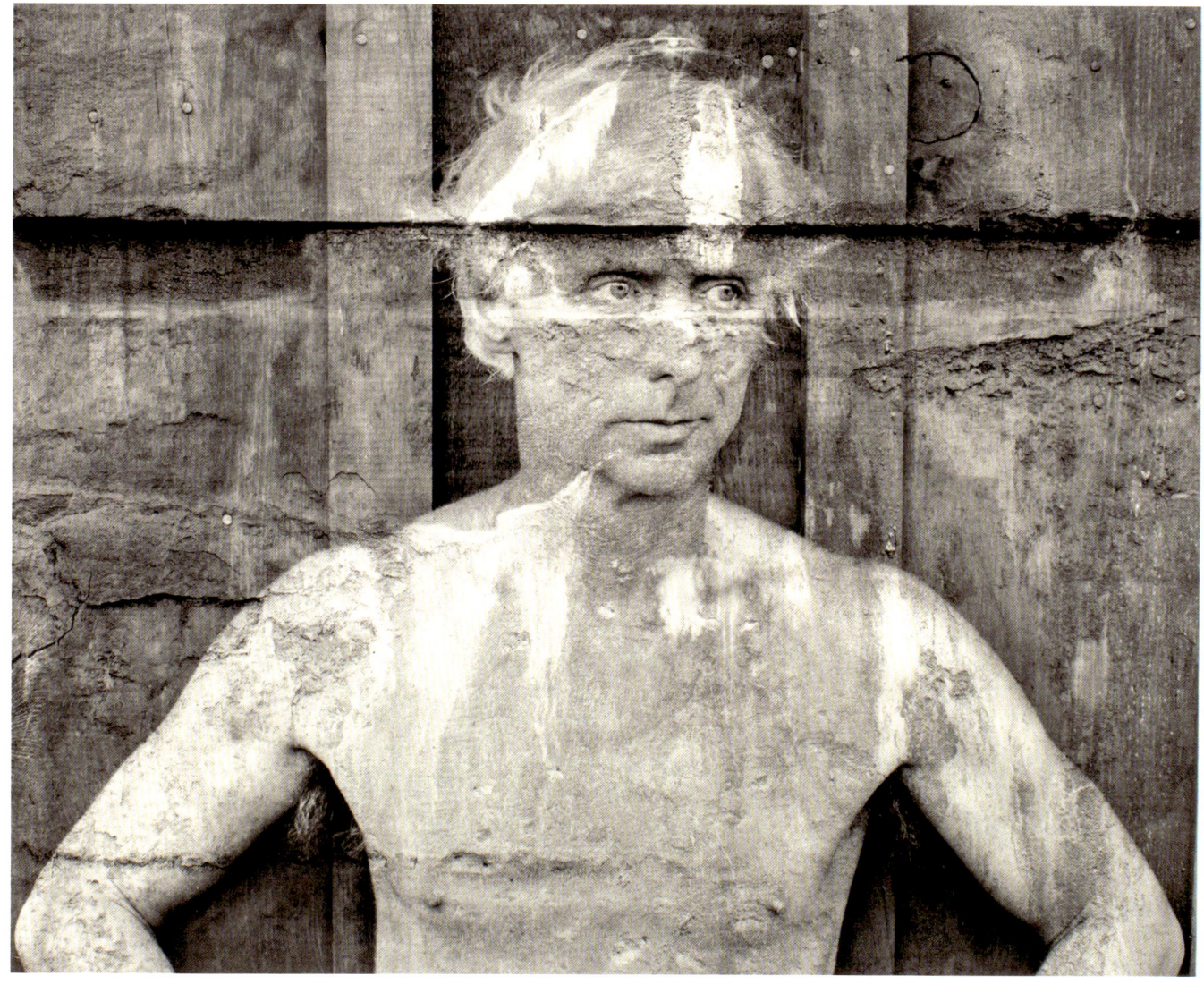

FREDERICK SOMMER *Max Ernst* 1946, printed later, 20.3 × 25.4 cm

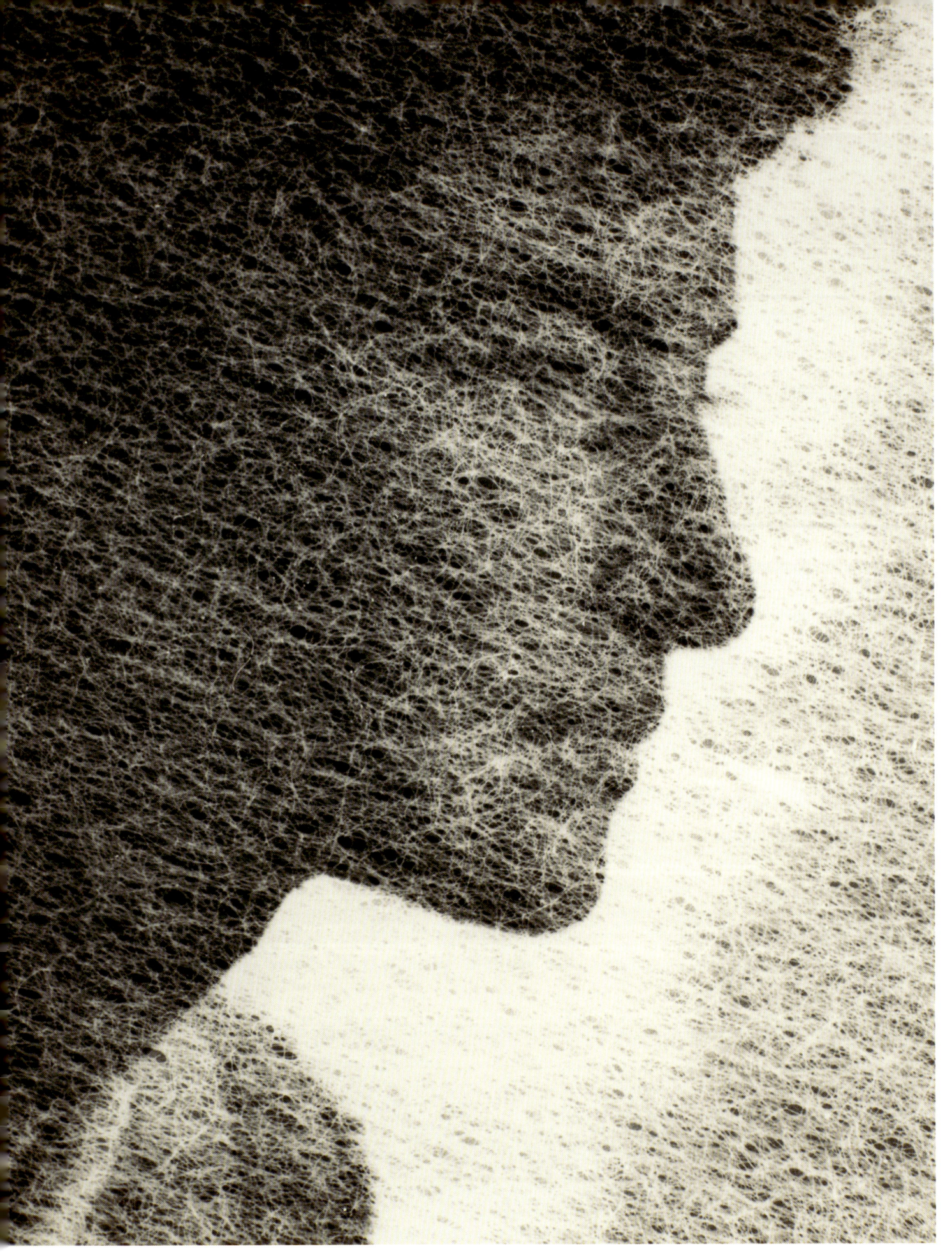

MAN RAY *Juliet in Profile* c.1945, 25.4 × 20 cm

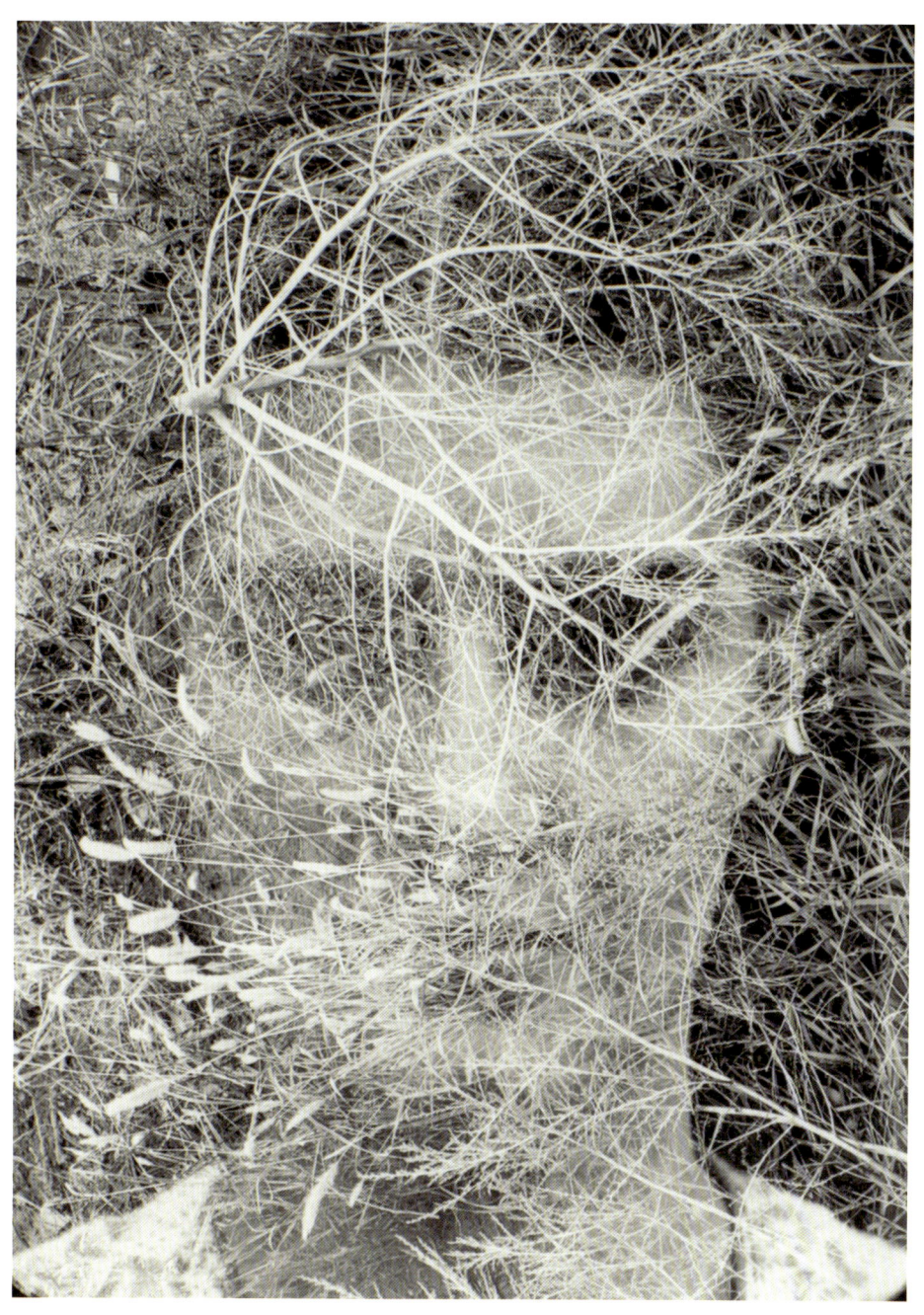

Harry Callahan *Detroit* c.1942, 11.4 × 8.3 cm

MAN RAY *Dora Maar* 1936, 21.5 × 16.5 cm

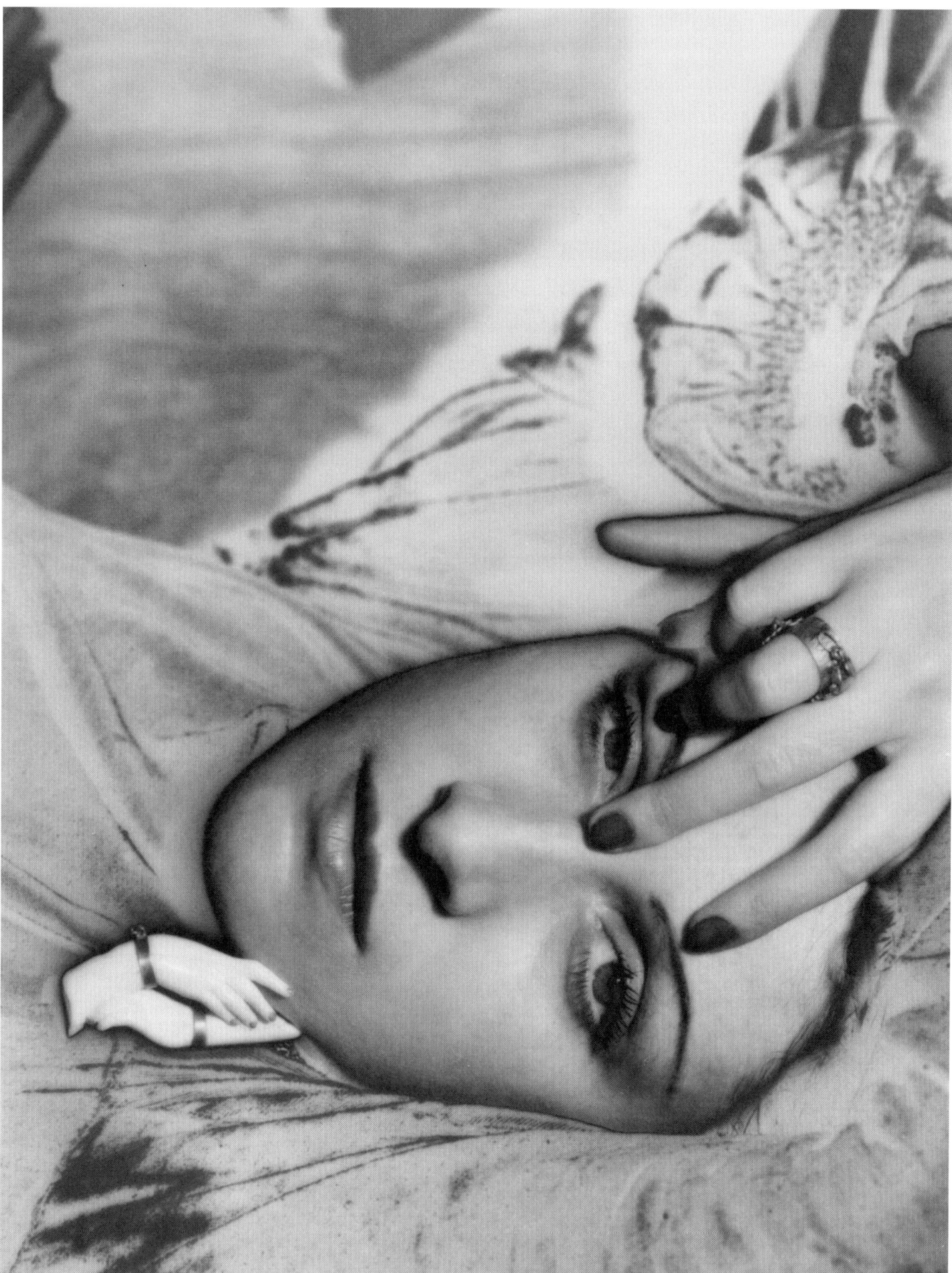

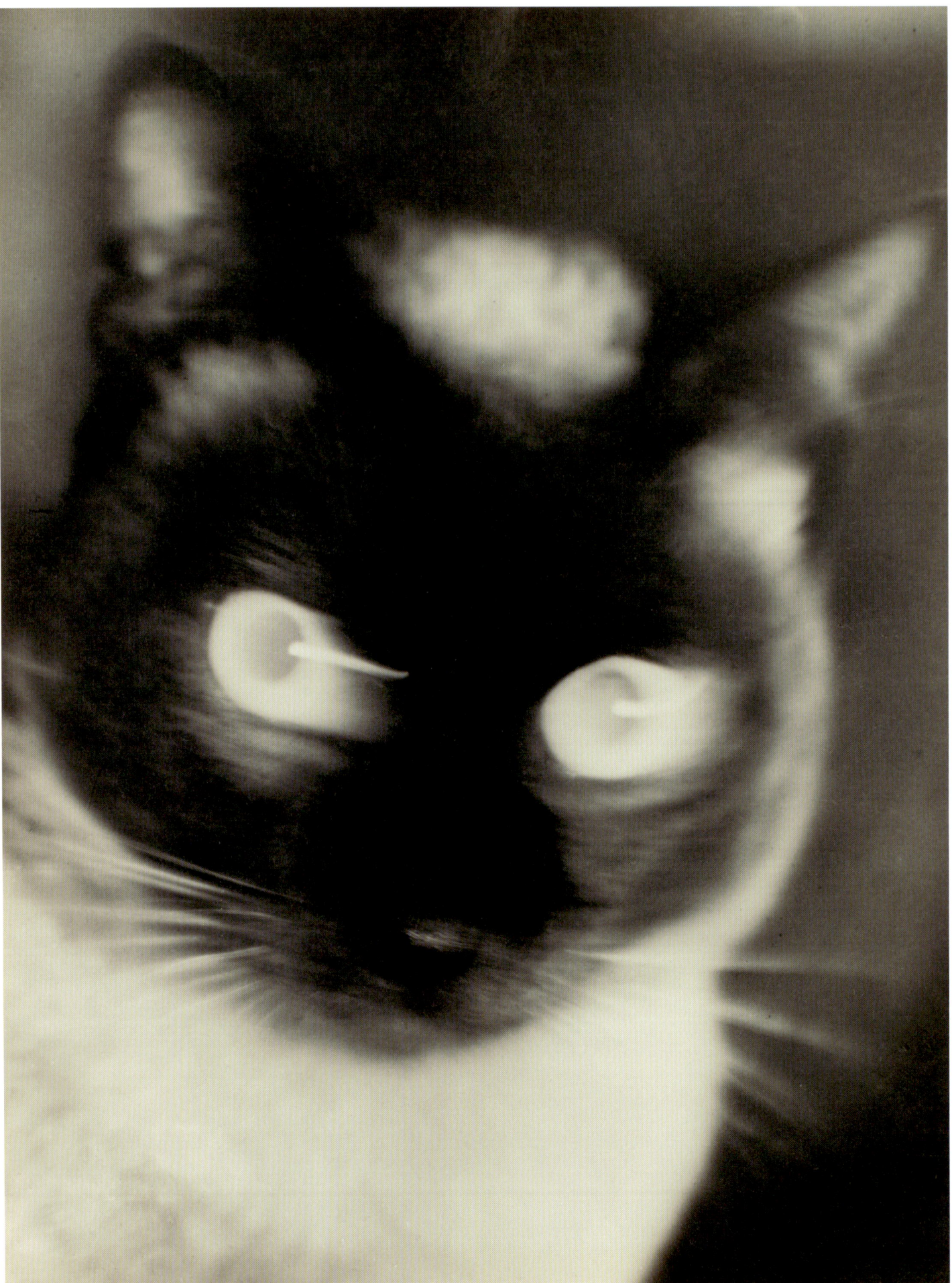

Umbo (Otto Umbehr) *Cat* 1927, 29.2 × 22.5 cm

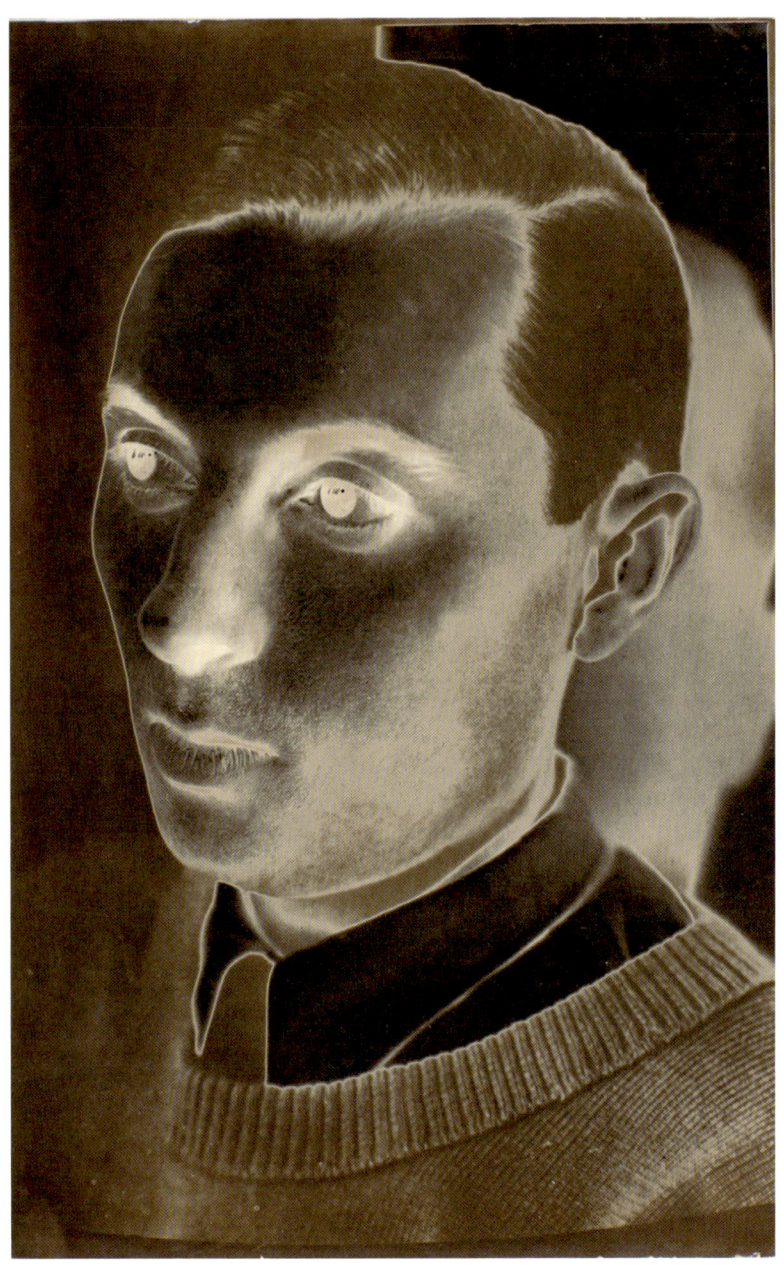

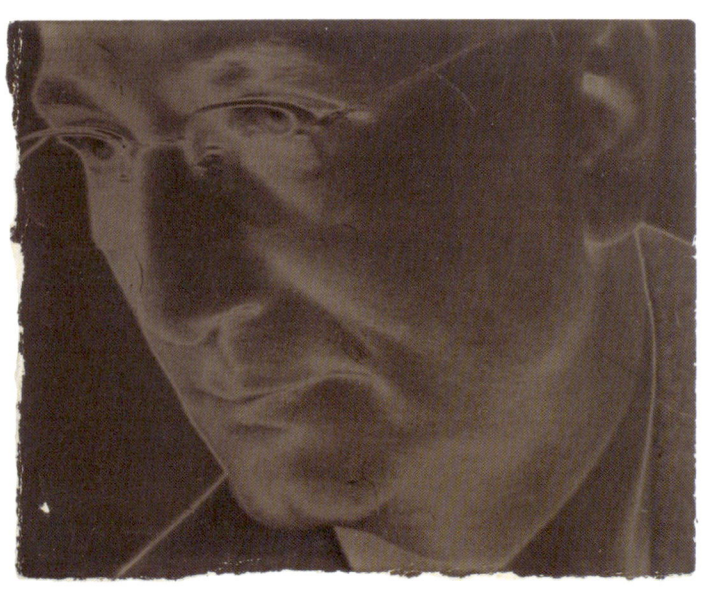

Above: **MAURICE TABARD**
Solarised Man 1930
24.8 × 16.5 cm

Left: **JOSEF BREITENBACH**
Solarised Man, Paris
c.1935, 8.6 × 12.7 cm

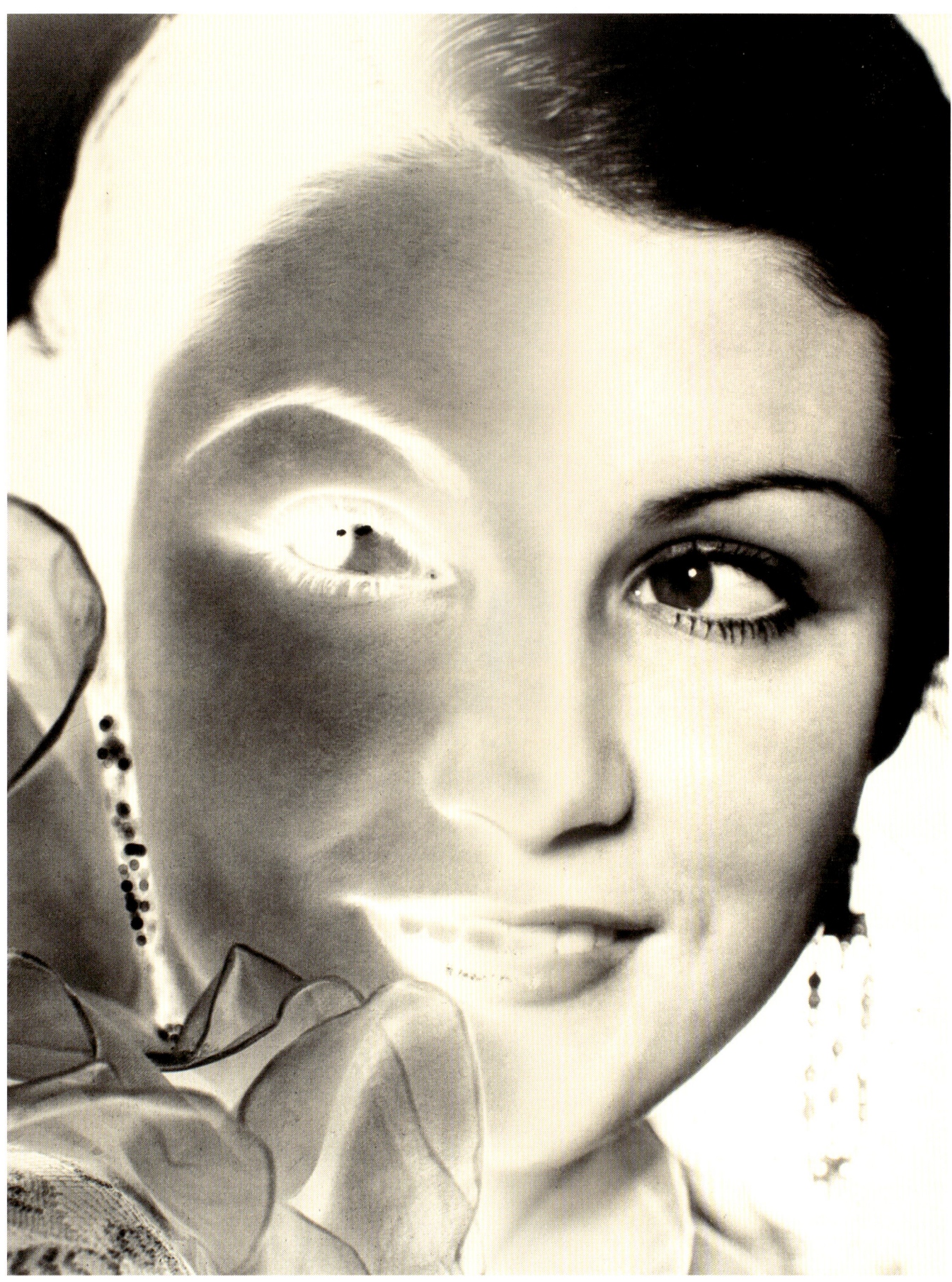

GORDON COSTER *Experimental Photograph (Reversal of Image
from Positive to Negative)* 1934, 43.2 × 33.7 cm

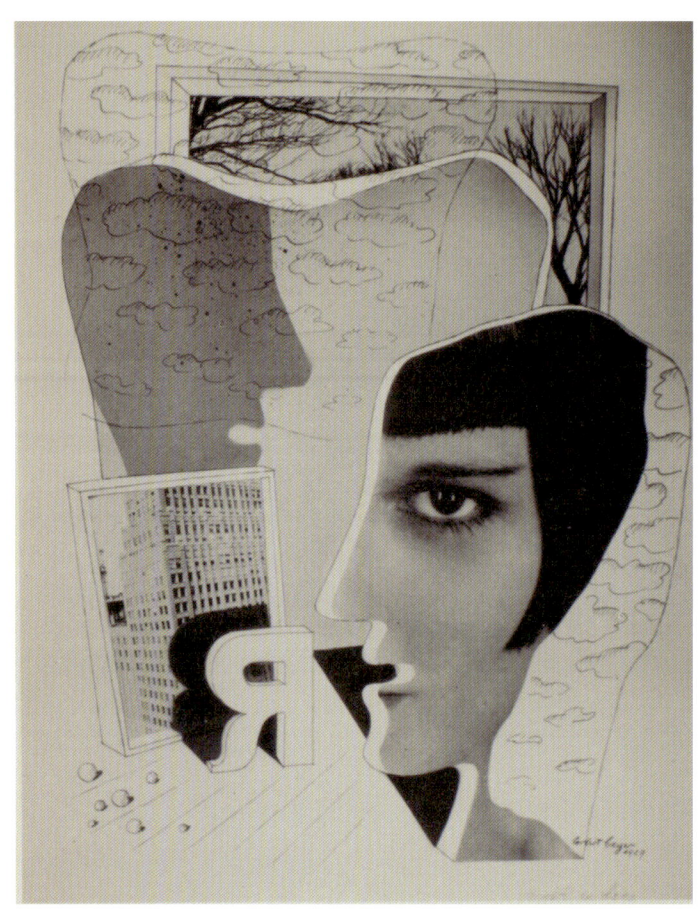

Herbert Bayer *Frontal Profile* 1929, 9.5 × 7.6 cm

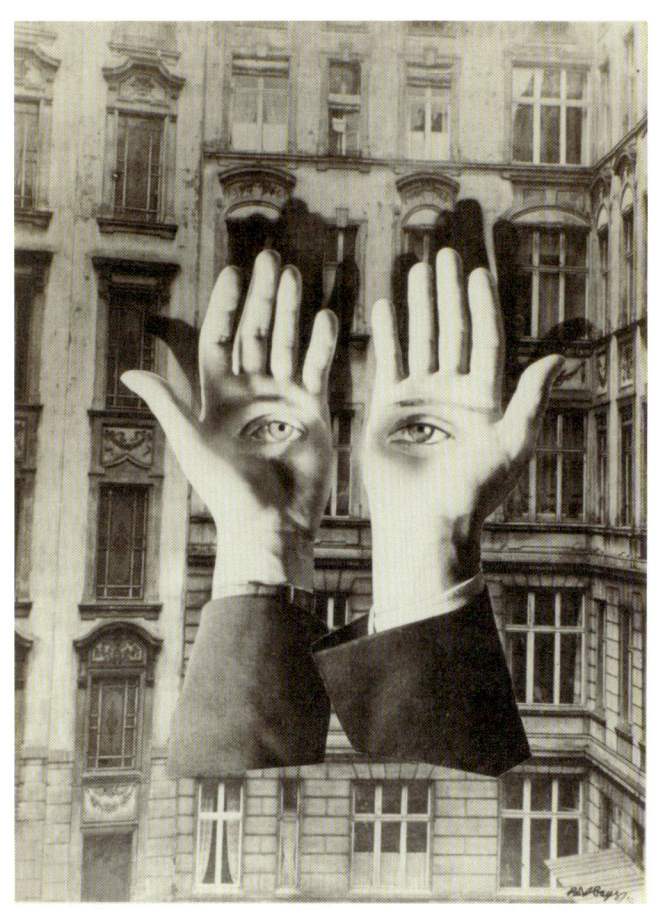

HERBERT BAYER *Lonely Metropolitan* 1932, 10.2 × 7.6 cm

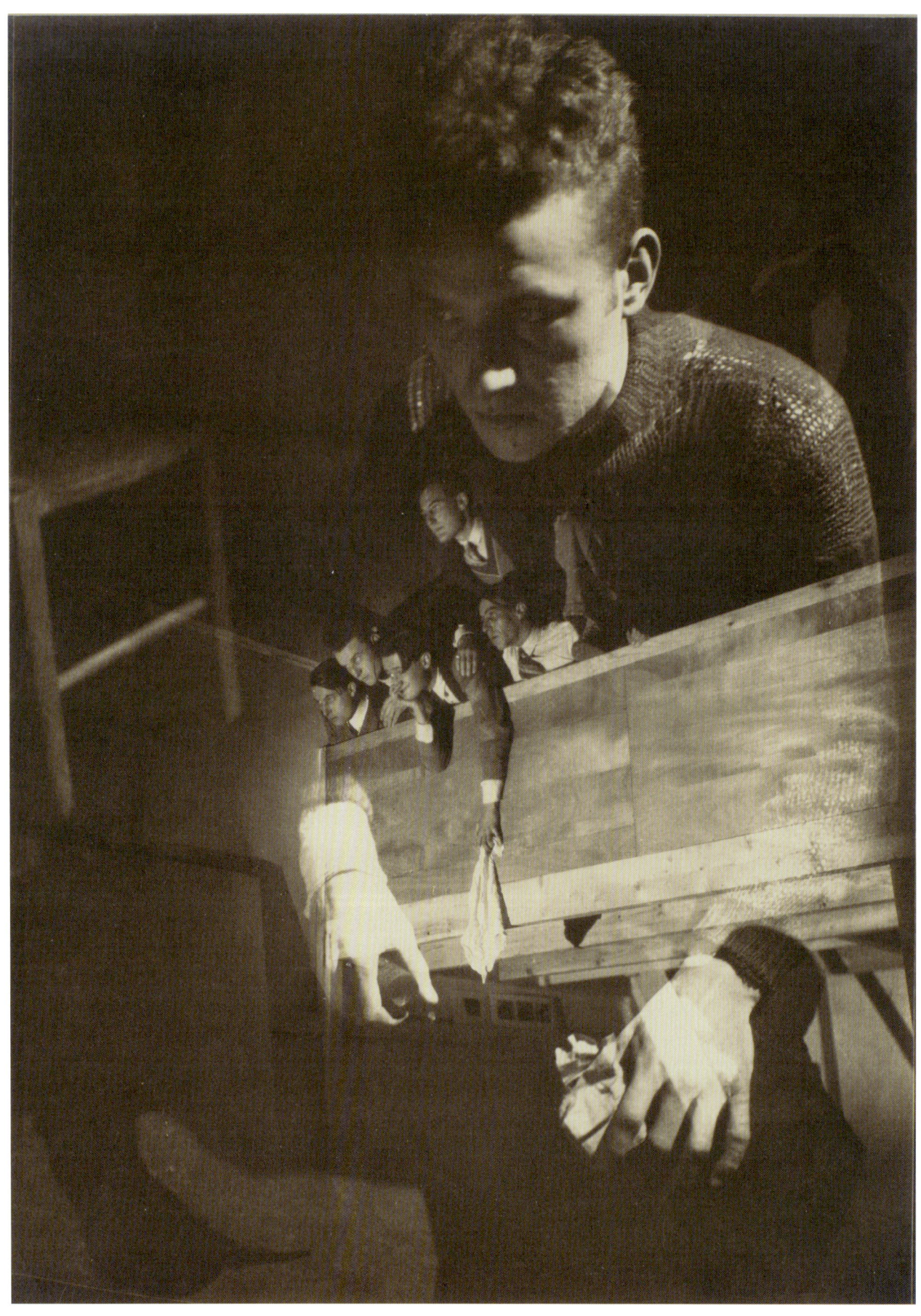

MAURICE TABARD *Fabian Loris with Box of Men* 1927, 22.9 × 17.1 cm

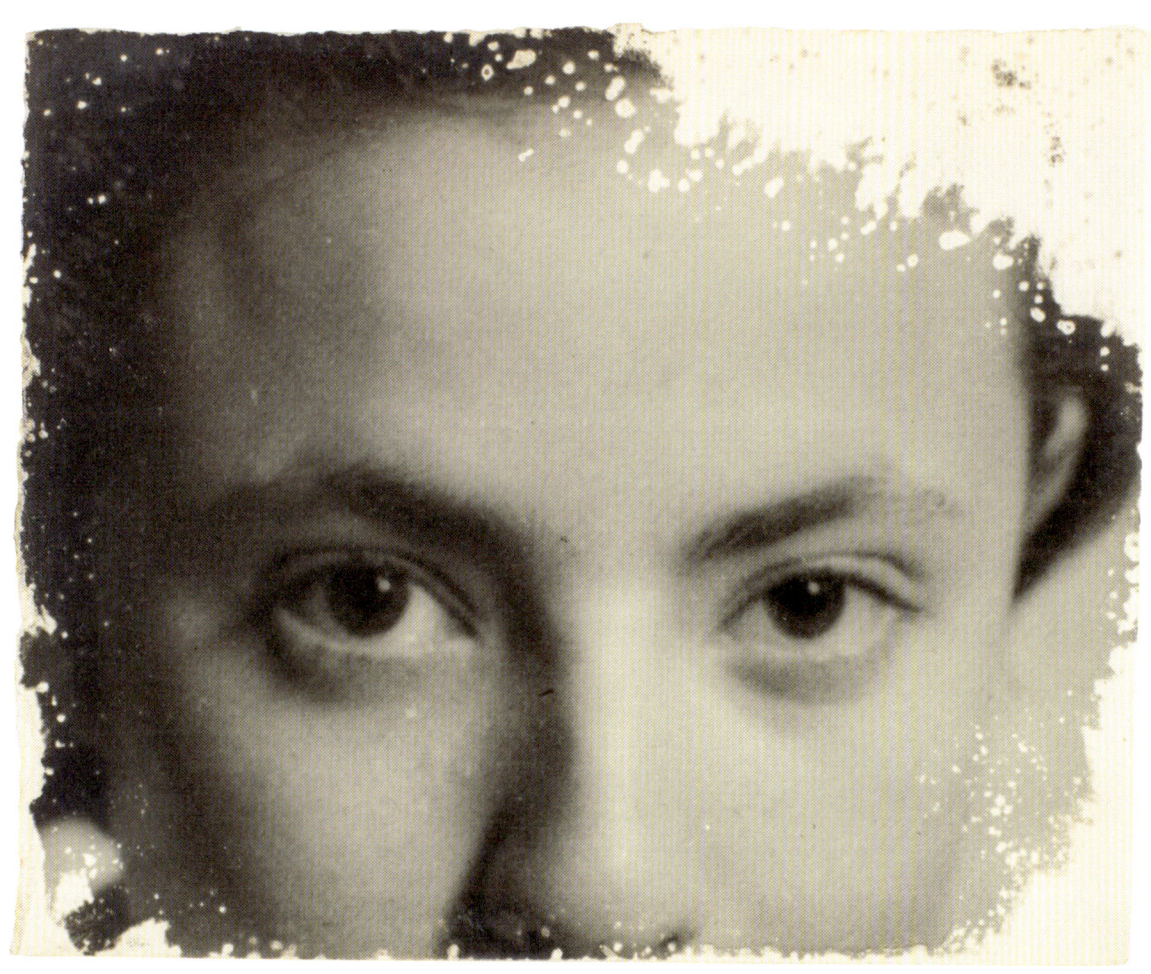

JOSEF BREITENBACH *Child's World, Paris* c.1935, 11.7 × 14.9 cm

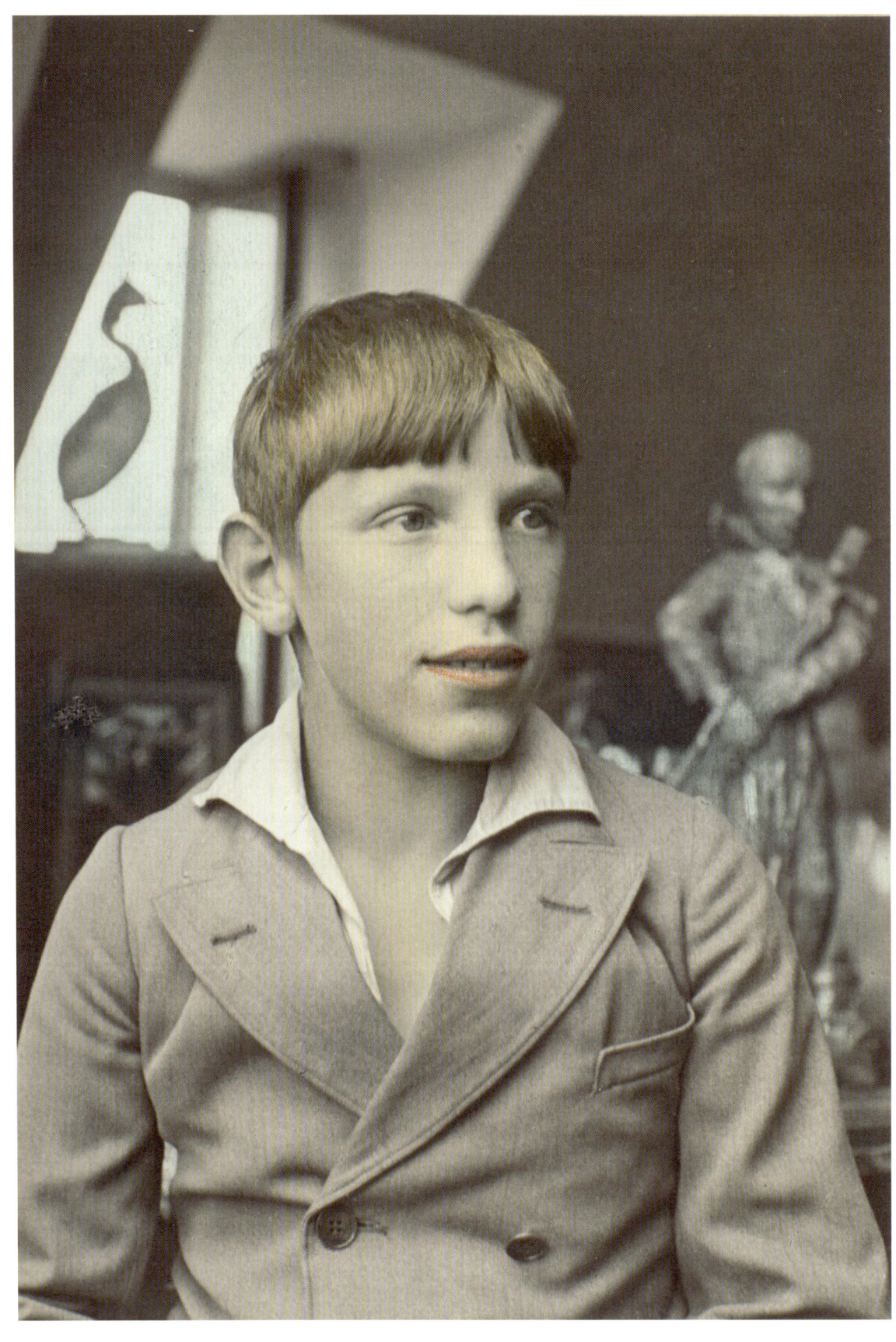

JOSEF BREITENBACH *Hans Wolf Breitenbach, Munich* 1931
hand-tinted gelatin silver print, 17.8 × 12.4 cm

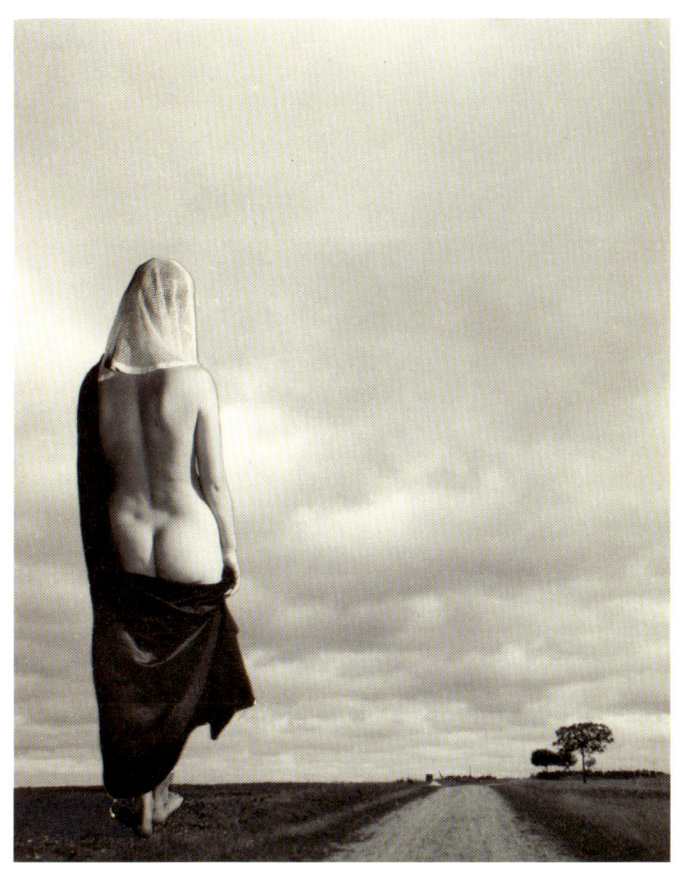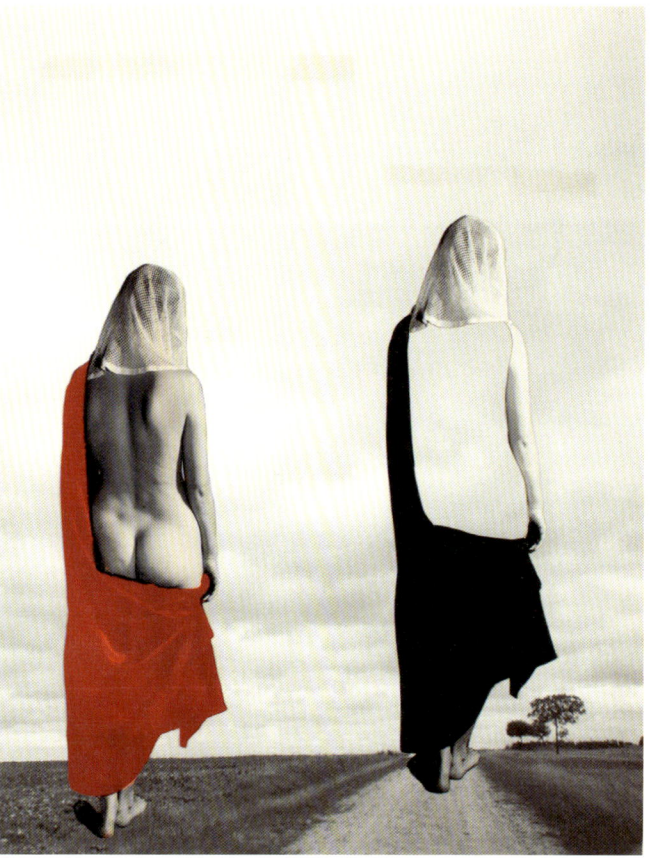

JOSEF BREITENBACH *Forever and Ever, Paris* 1938
collage, gelatin silver print, acrylic paint
each 29.8 × 23.8 cm

JOSEF BREITENBACH *Coloured Bust, Paris* 1935
bromoil transfer print onto gelatin silver paper, 29.5 × 23.8 cm

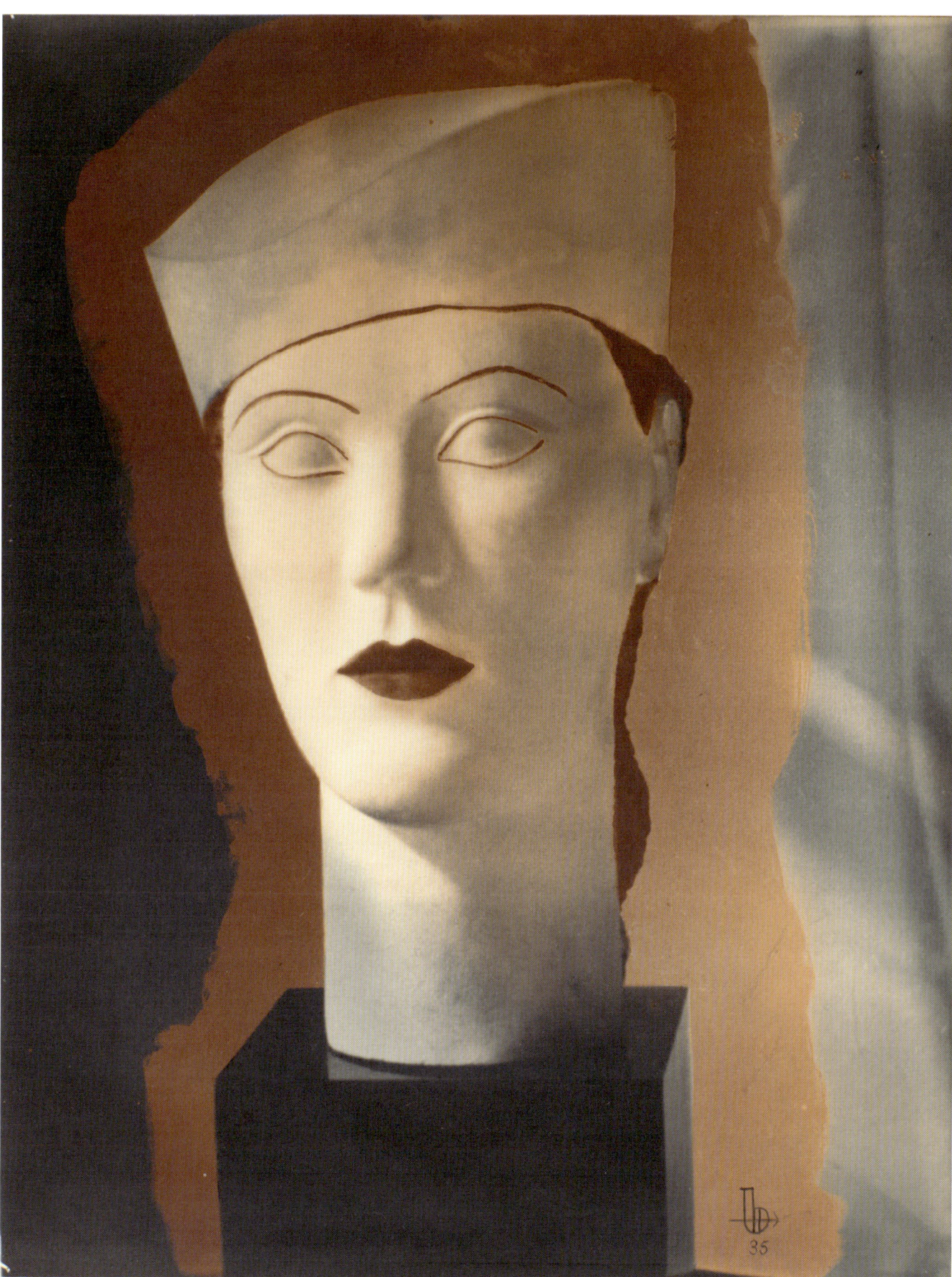

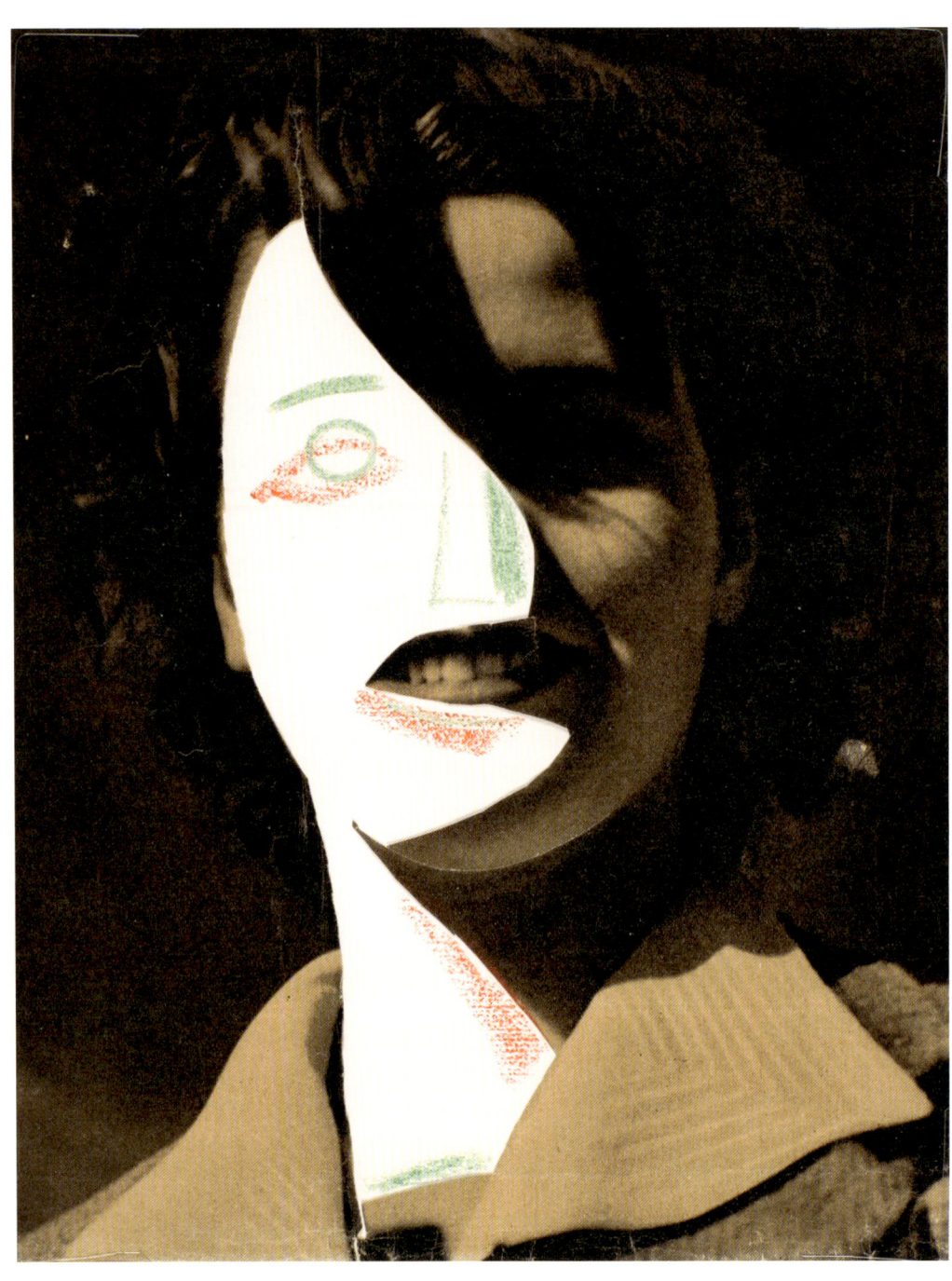

Marcello Nizzoli *Portrait of a Woman* 1936
collage, gelatin silver print, paper, crayon, 19.1 × 14.9 cm

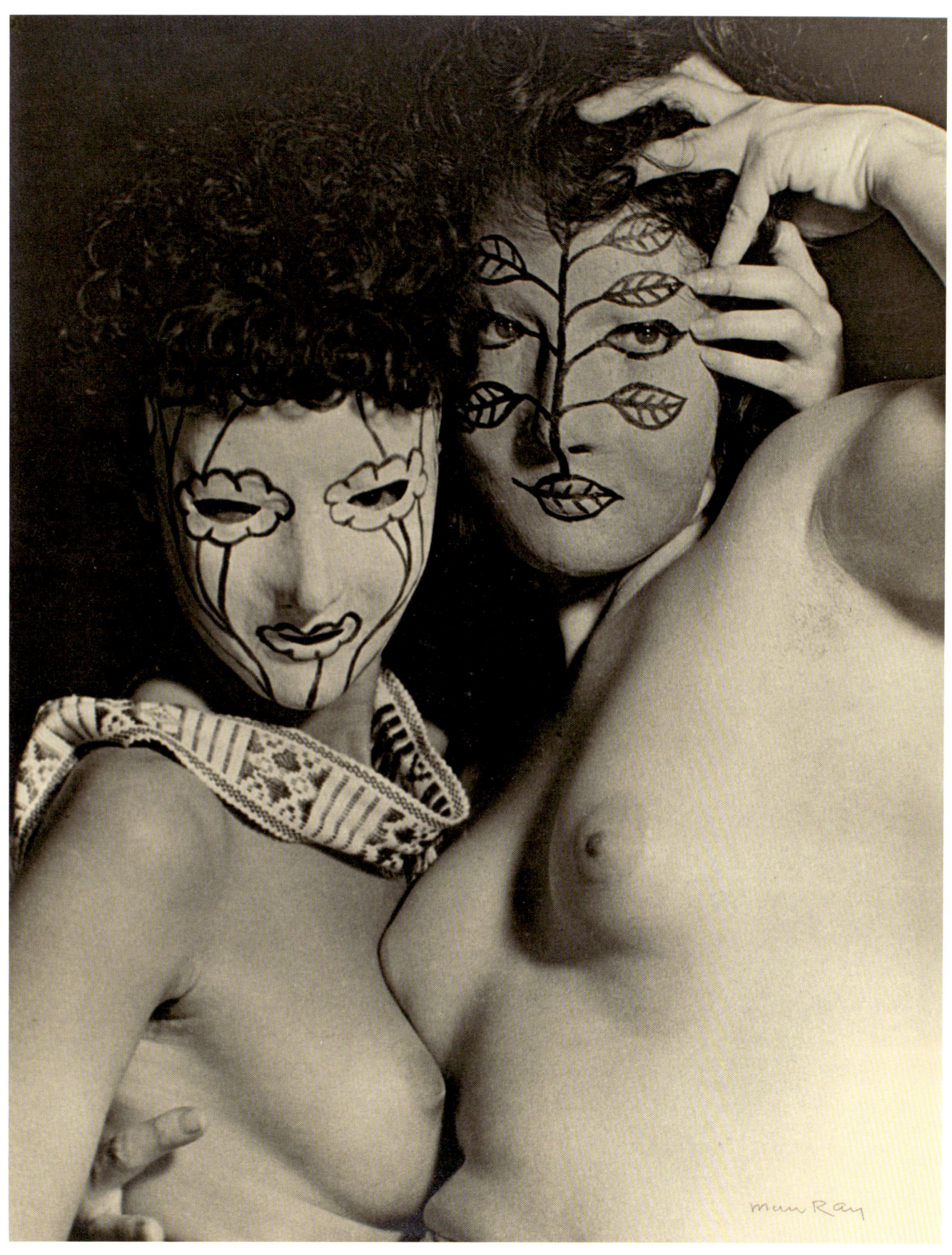

MAN RAY *Juliet and Margaret Nieman in Papier-Mâché Masks c.1945, 34.9 × 27.3 cm*

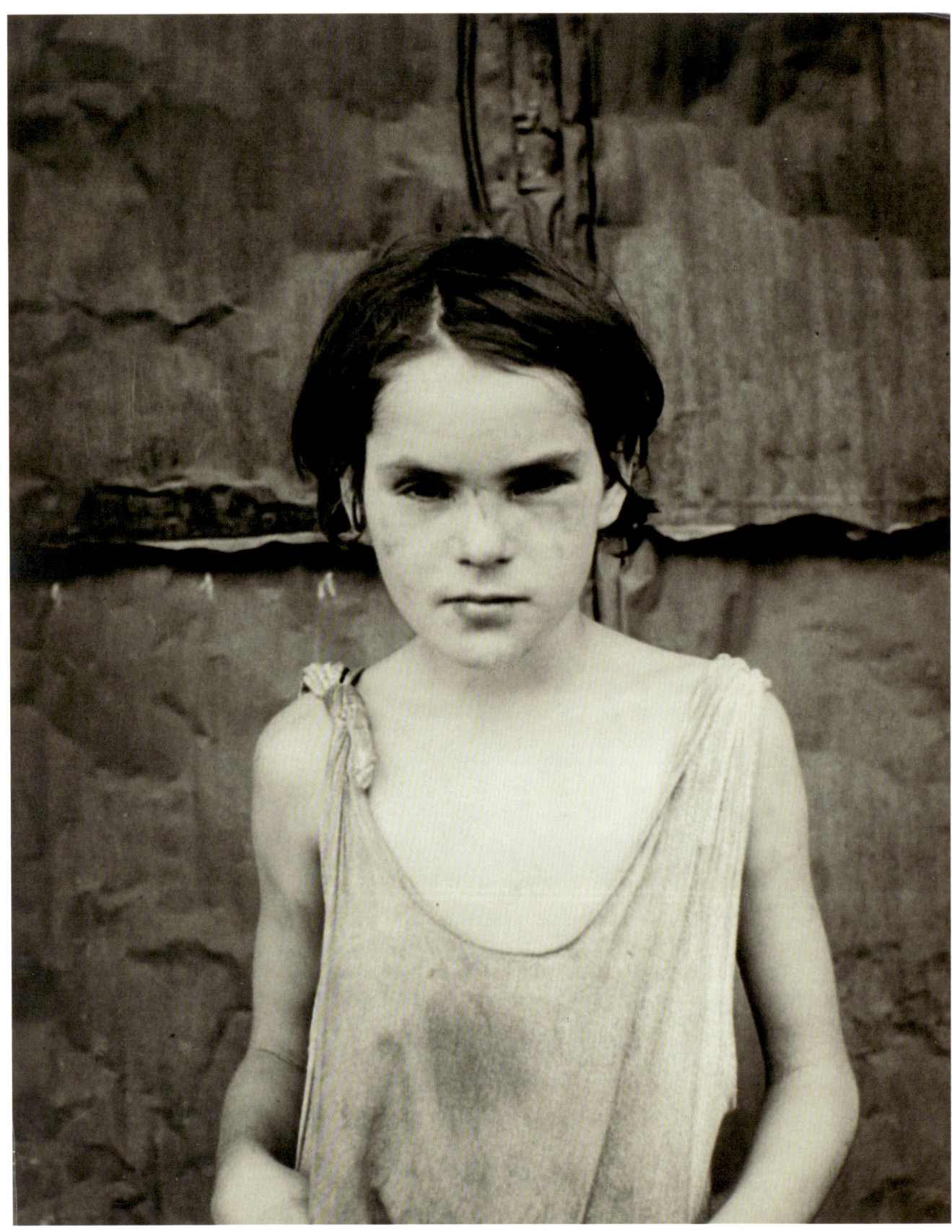

DOROTHEA LANGE
The Damage is Already Done,
Shacktown, Elm Grove, Oklahoma 1936
23.8 × 19.1 cm

DOCUMENTS

Photography's capacity as a tool for social reform was first championed from the last decades of the nineteenth century by photographers who worked on assignment for charities or government agencies, or who were compelled to publish their own studies of people enduring poor living and working conditions. But it was not until the 1930s that the documentary category, as we understand it today, was fully established. It was during this decade that writers, photographers and filmmakers refined the formula for what was, for a time, called the 'human document': factual information presented in a moving way, in order to maximise its impact.

In photography, this approach was formulated by those working both in an official and unofficial capacity, who chronicled the effects of the Great Depression in the United States. Walker Evans and Dorothea Lange were among the dozens of photographers who, at various stages between 1935 and 1943, were commissioned to visit rural and small-town communities in order to document the consequences of the Depression and the relief work of the Resettlement (later, the Farm Security) Administration. Roy Stryker, as head of the FSA's Historical Section, was responsible for ensuring that its activities were recorded for posterity. He also supplied these images to the press and, on occasion, for public exhibition.

To coordinate the types of photographs taken, and to help create an overarching narrative, Stryker often issued his charges with 'shooting scripts'. His direction, together with his responsibility for selecting specific images from contact sheets, and combined with the powerful, often poetic captions the photographers themselves supplied, helped transform images of everyday moments into a powerful social document. What the viewer saw was not only a portrayal of a particular individual, but also that of many thousands of others who shared their plight. Cumulatively, the FSA programme resulted in some 175,000 negatives and colour transparencies, and over 100,000 prints – in both impact and scale of operation the most substantial contribution to the documentary genre during the twentieth century.

Stryker would later say the images 'introduced America to Americans'. But they also highlighted the almost impossible position the documentary photograph occupies: that of historical evidence, instrument of propaganda and, more latterly, as work of art. Subsequent American government programmes, including the New York-based Photo League, continued to commission documentary surveys during this era, but some of the most notable examples of such images were published by photographers acting independently. These include Margaret Bourke-White's *You Have Seen Their Faces* (1937), Dorothea Lange and Paul Taylor's *An American Exodus* (1939) as well as writer James Agee's *Let Us Now Praise Famous Men* (1941), which included works by Evans. The images produced by these photographers and their peers anticipated the emergence of the photo-essay in magazines such as *Life*, which launched in 1936, as well as the raw and emotive style of street photography that flourished in the aftermath of the Second World War. EL

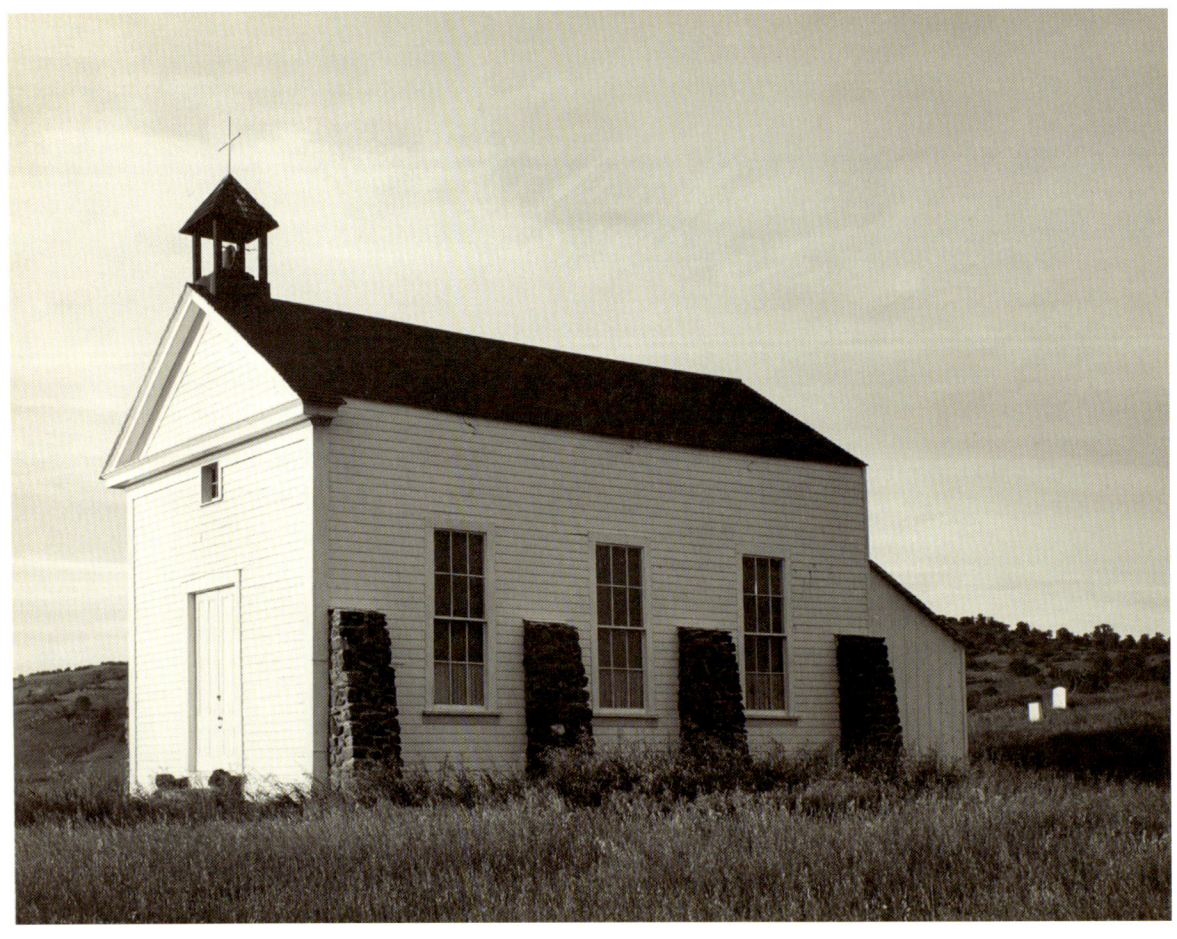

Ansel Adams *Church – Hornitos* c.1940, 16.5 × 21.6 cm

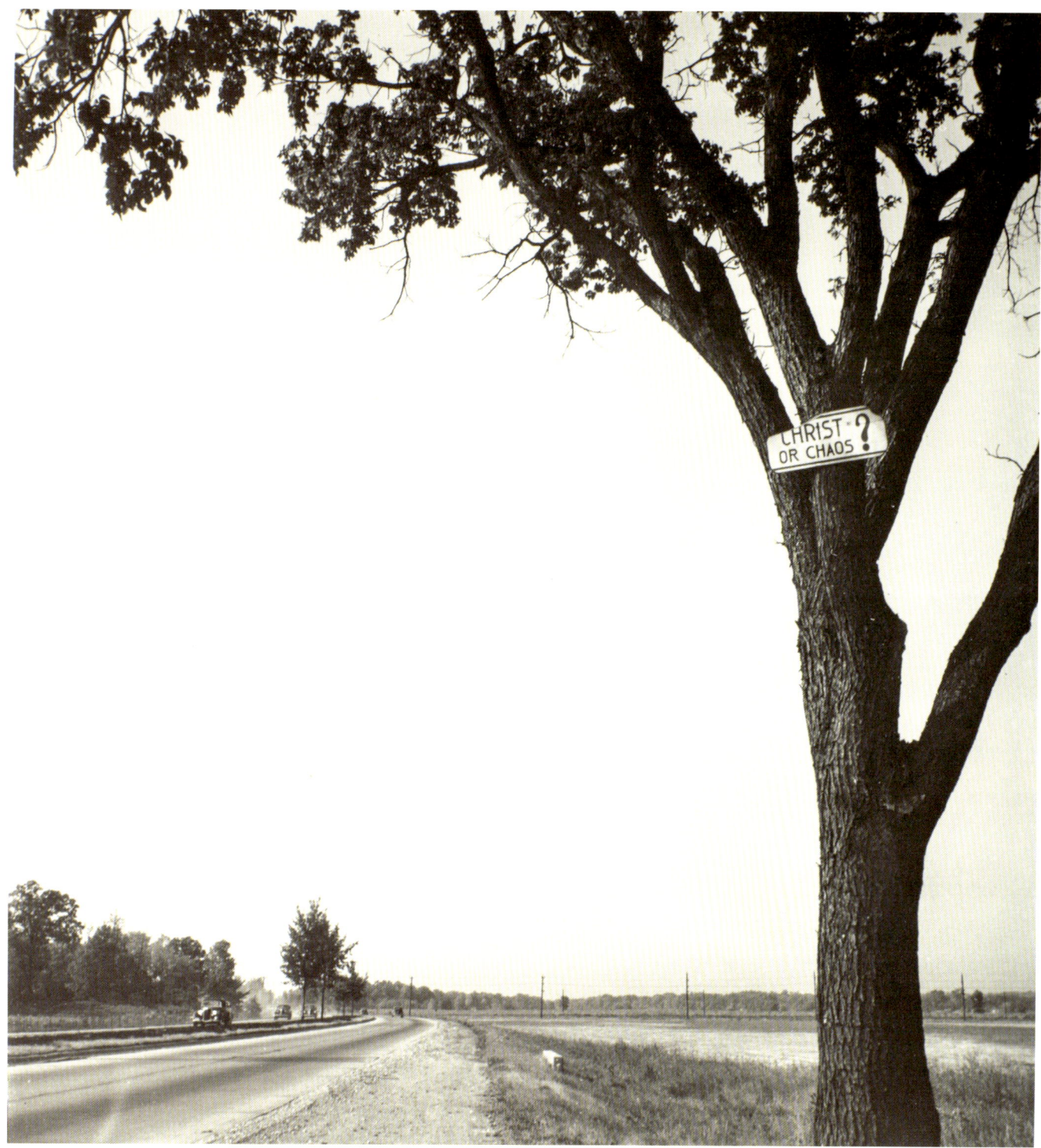

WALKER EVANS *Christ or Chaos?* 1946, 22.2 × 20.3 cm

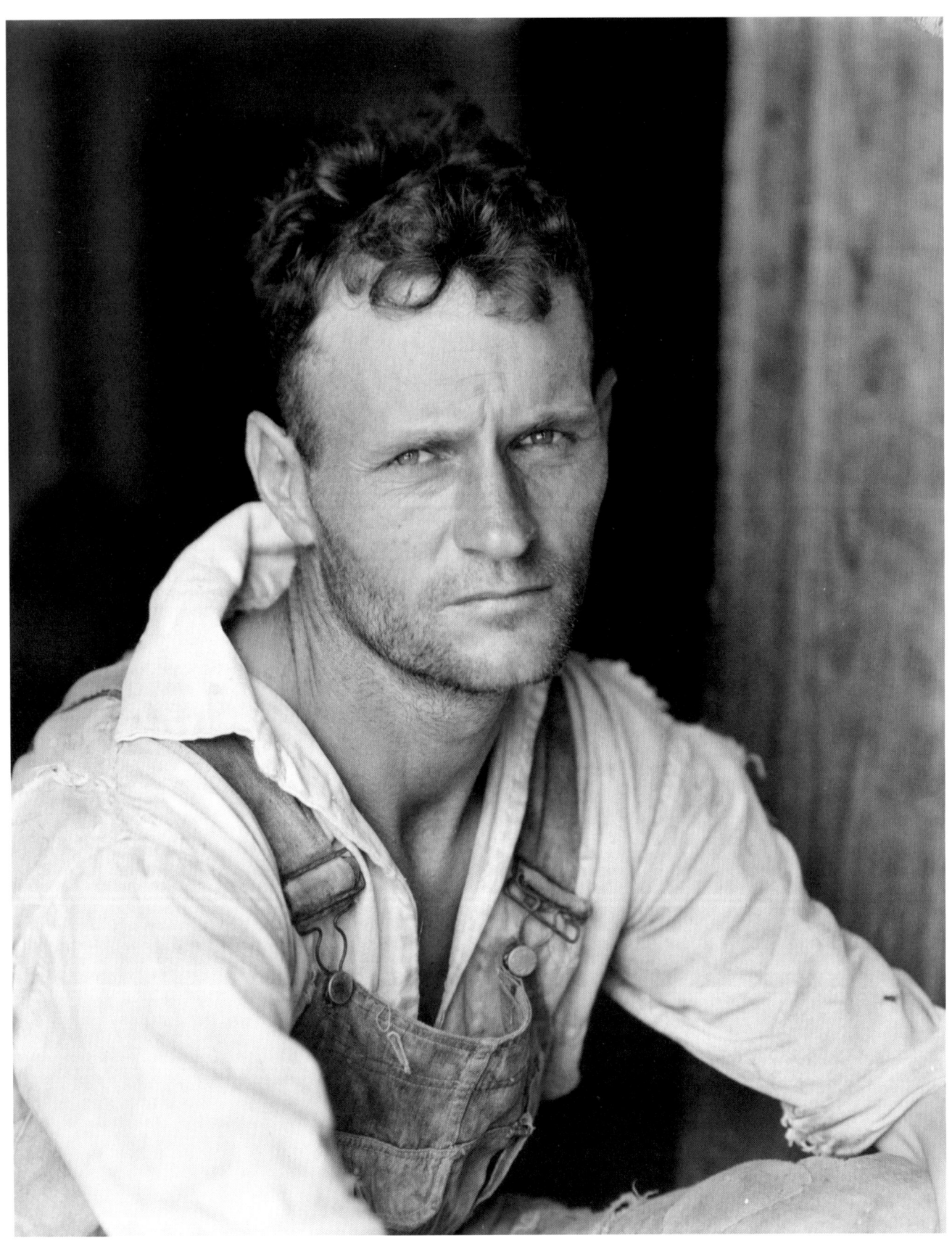

WALKER EVANS *Floyd Burroughs, Hale County, Alabama* 1936, printed 1950s, 24.1 × 19.1 cm

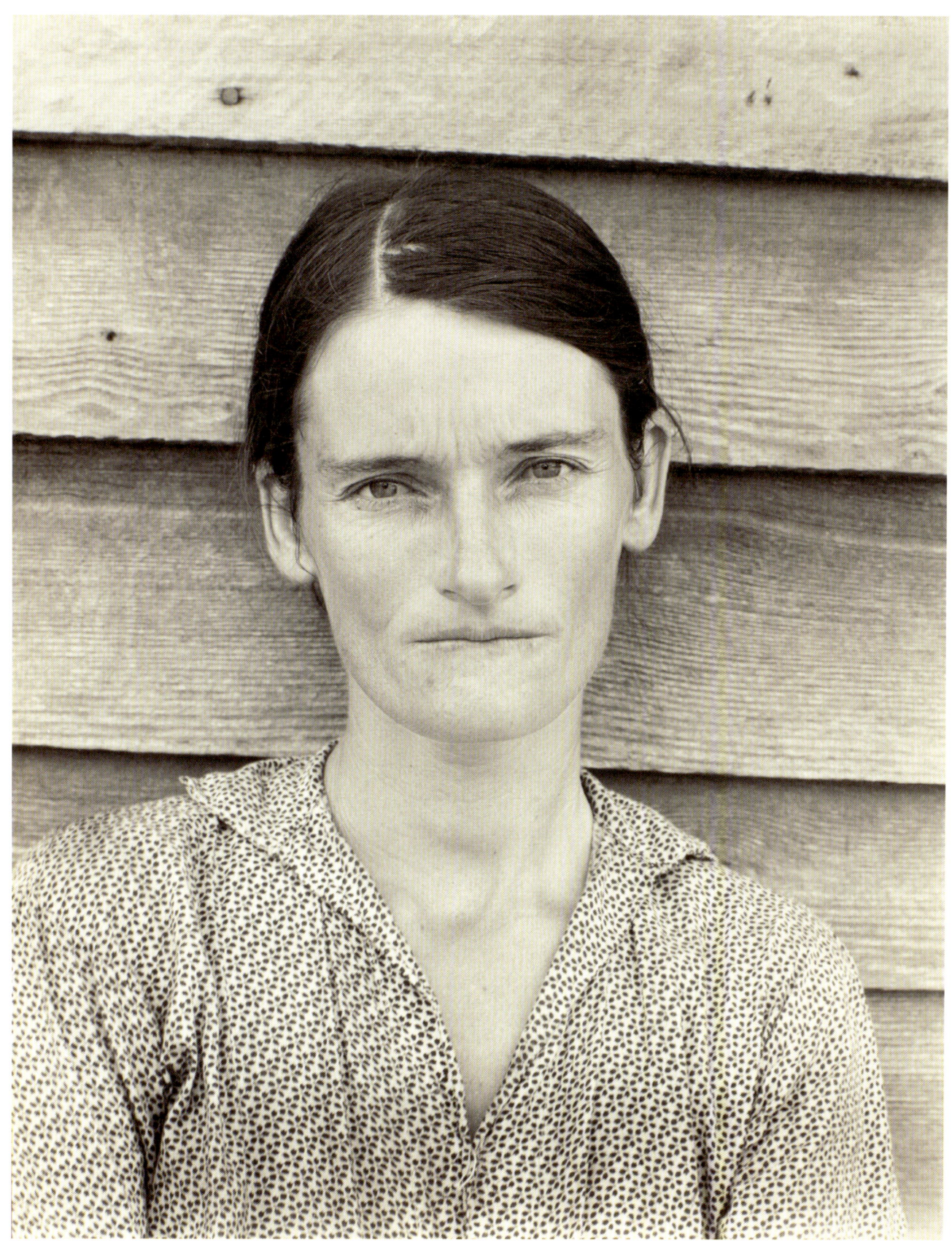

WALKER EVANS *Allie Mae Burroughs, Hale County, Alabama 1936, 24.4 × 19.1 cm*

Walker Evans *Bud Fields, Alabama Tenant Farmer* 1936, 13.7 × 12.1 cm

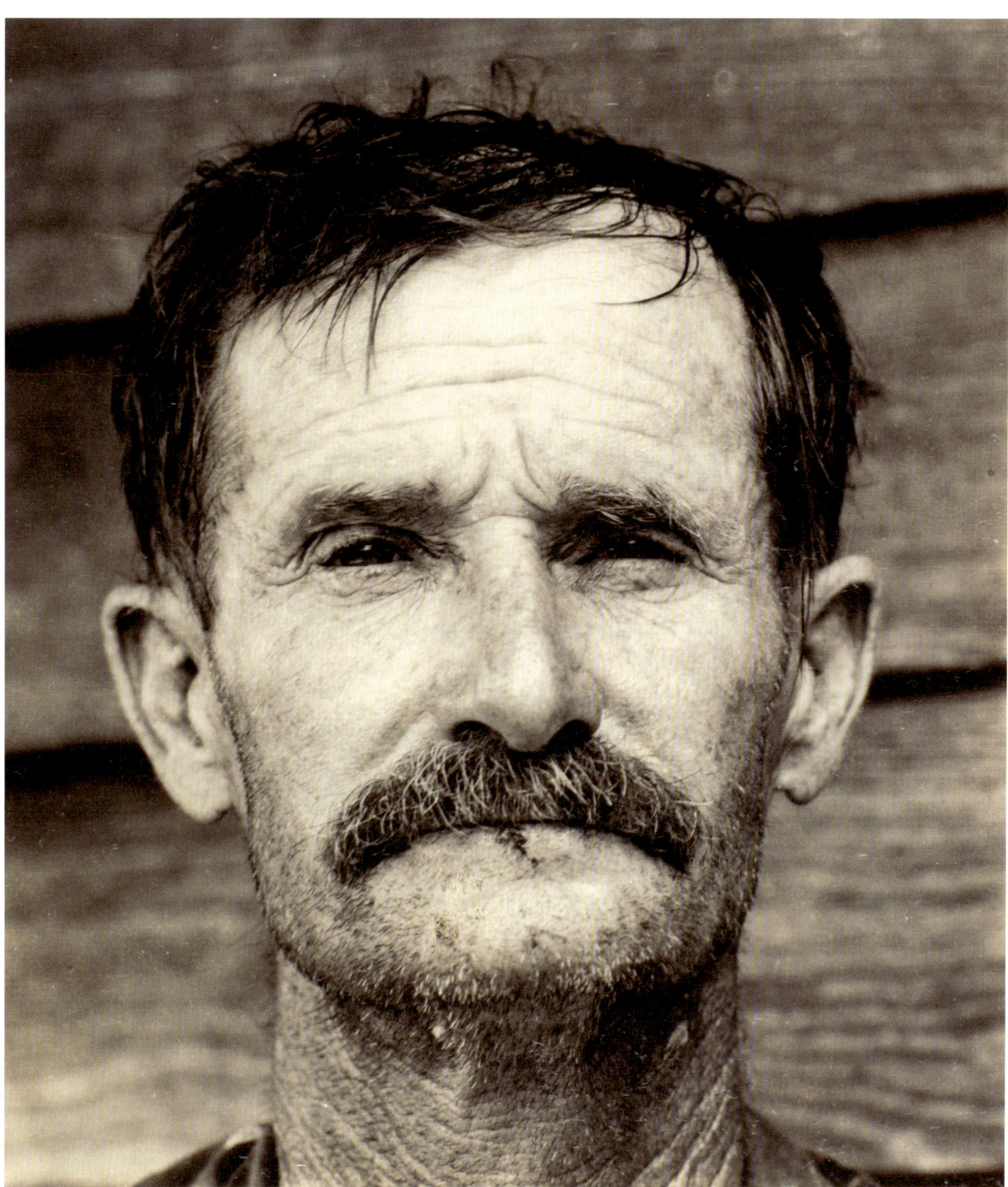

Dorothea Lange *One of the Homeless Wandering Boys* 1934, 24.1 × 18.4 cm

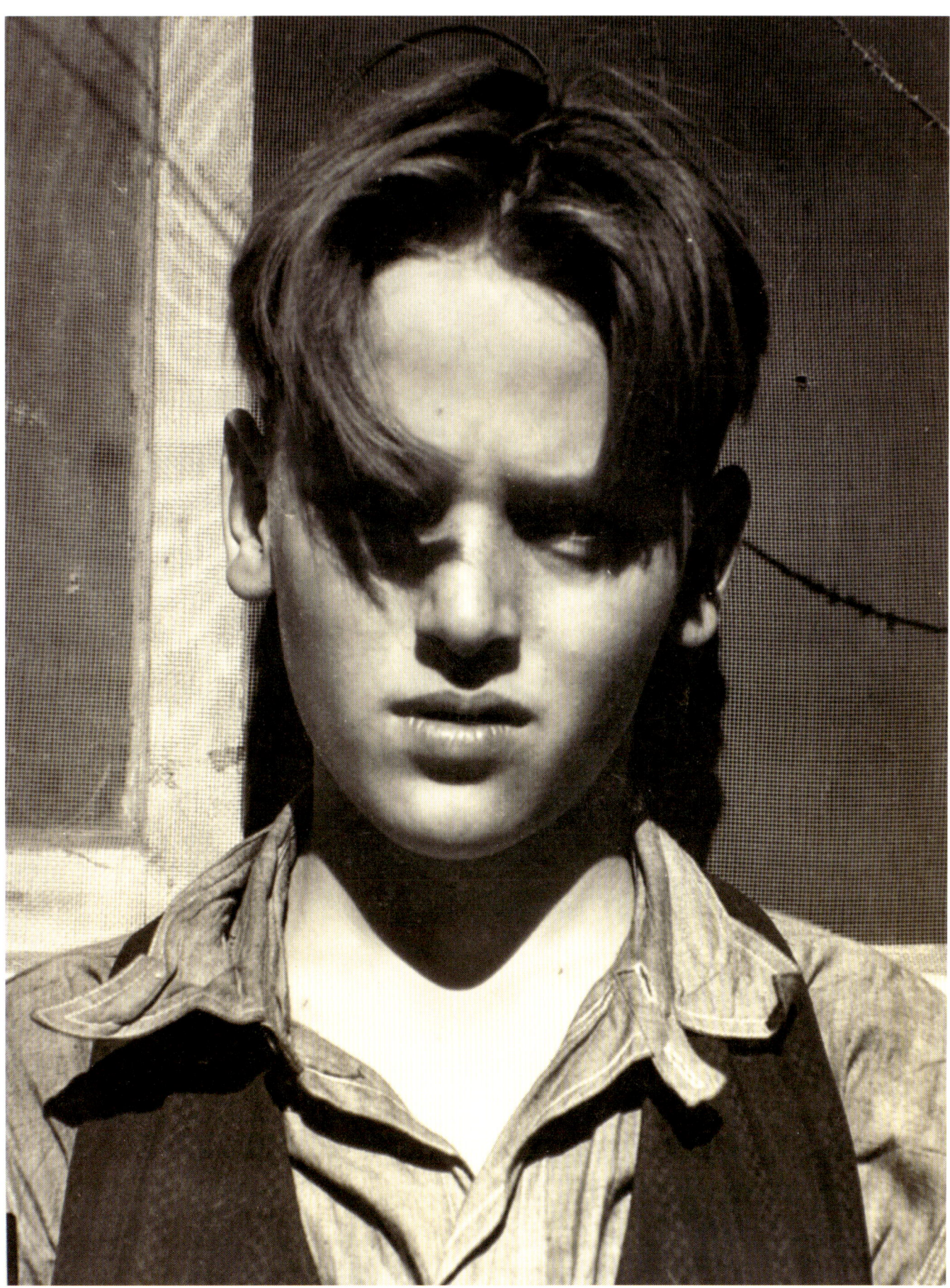

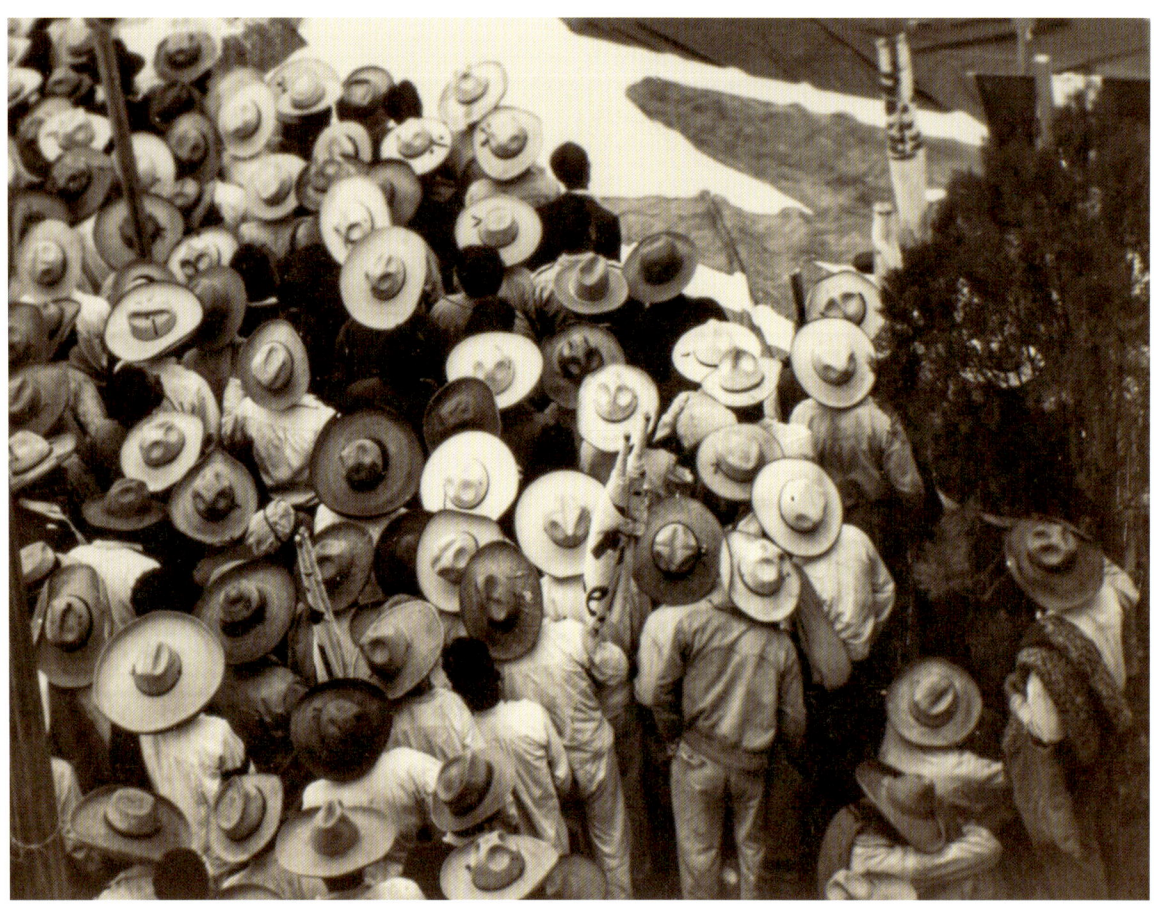

Tina Modotti *Untitled* 1929, 8.3 × 10.8 cm

Dorothea Lange *White Angel Bread Line, San Francisco* 1933, 19.1 × 15.9 cm

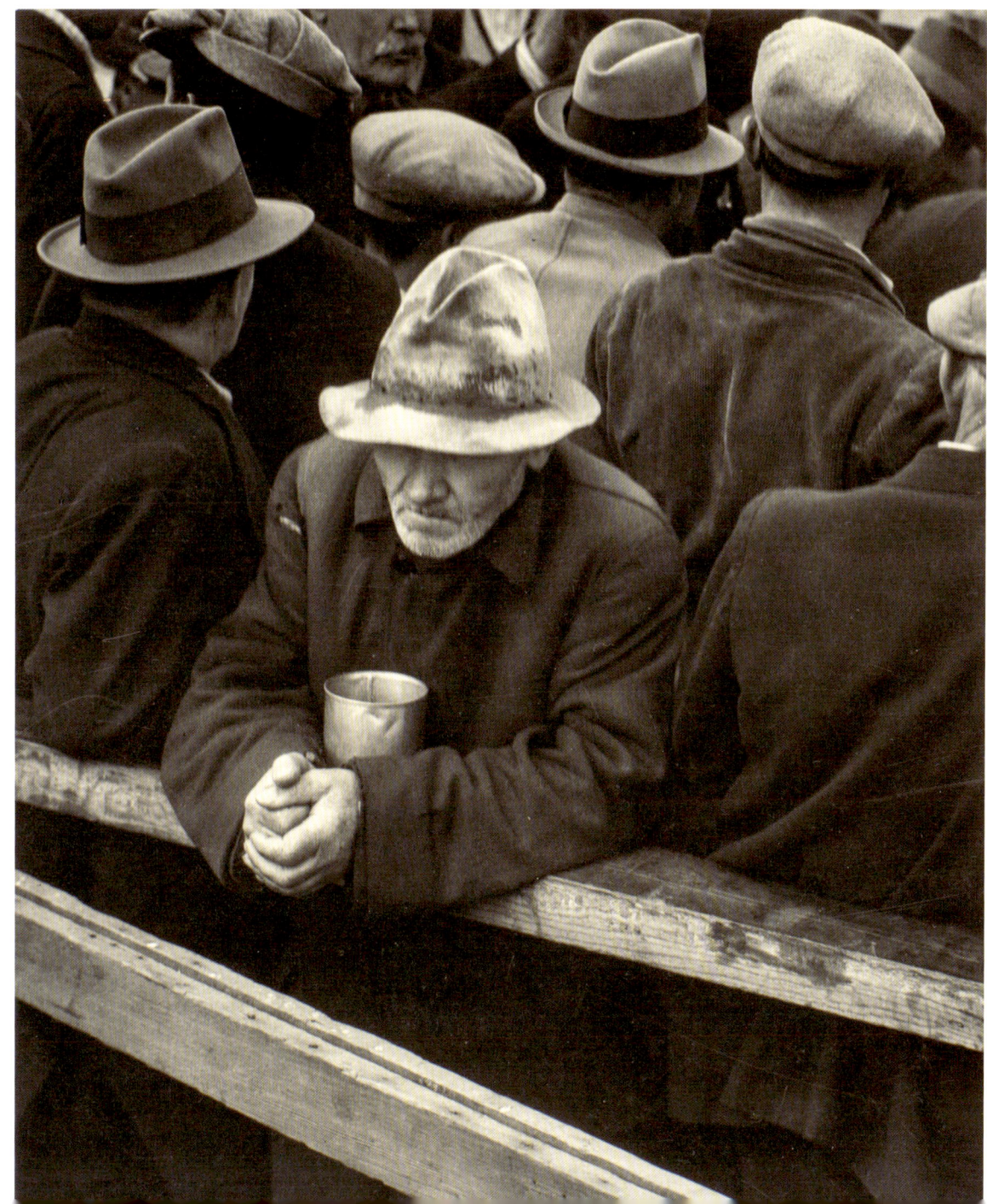

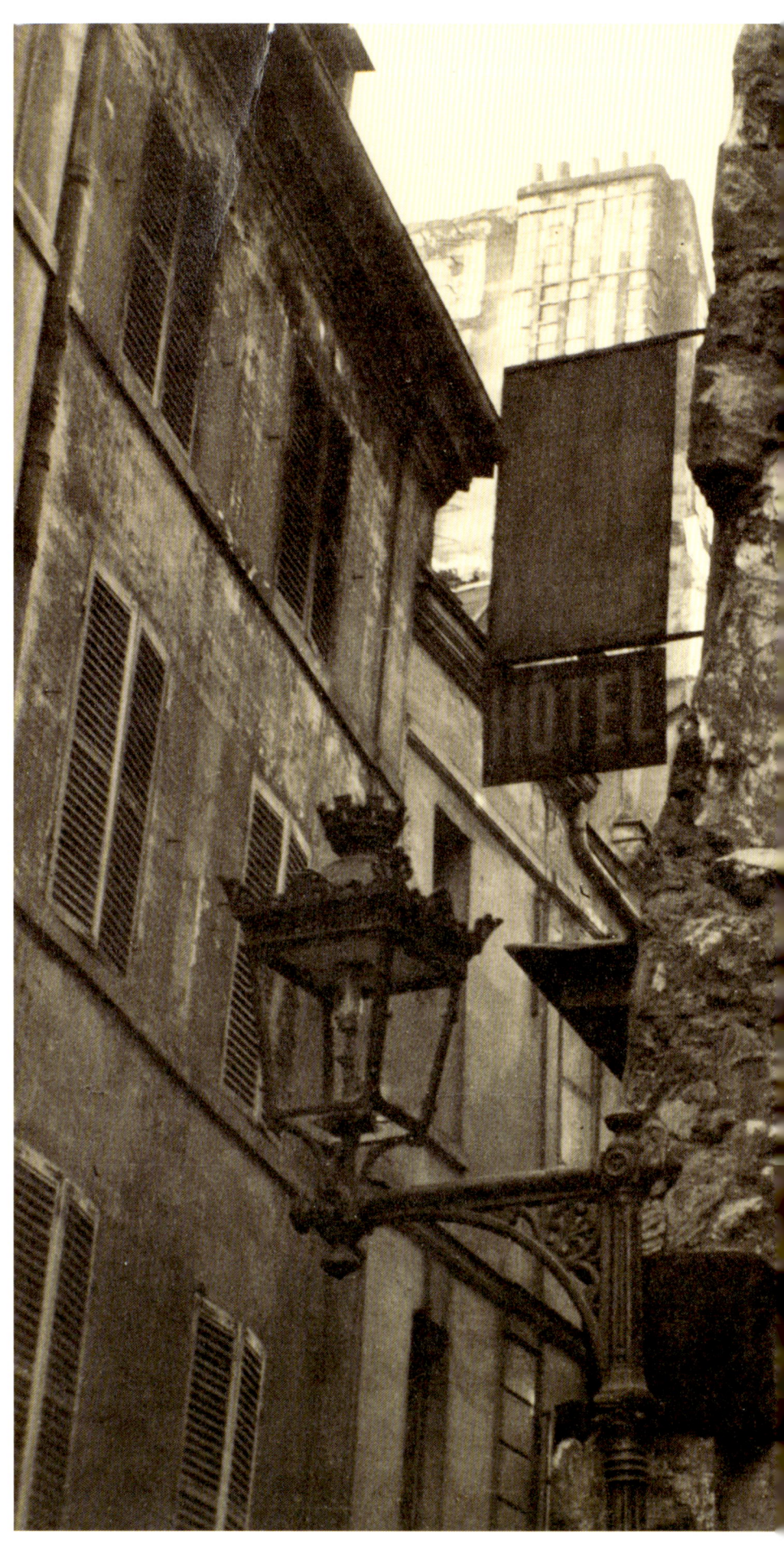

ILSE BING *Greta Garbo Poster,*
Paris 1932, 22.2 × 27.9 cm

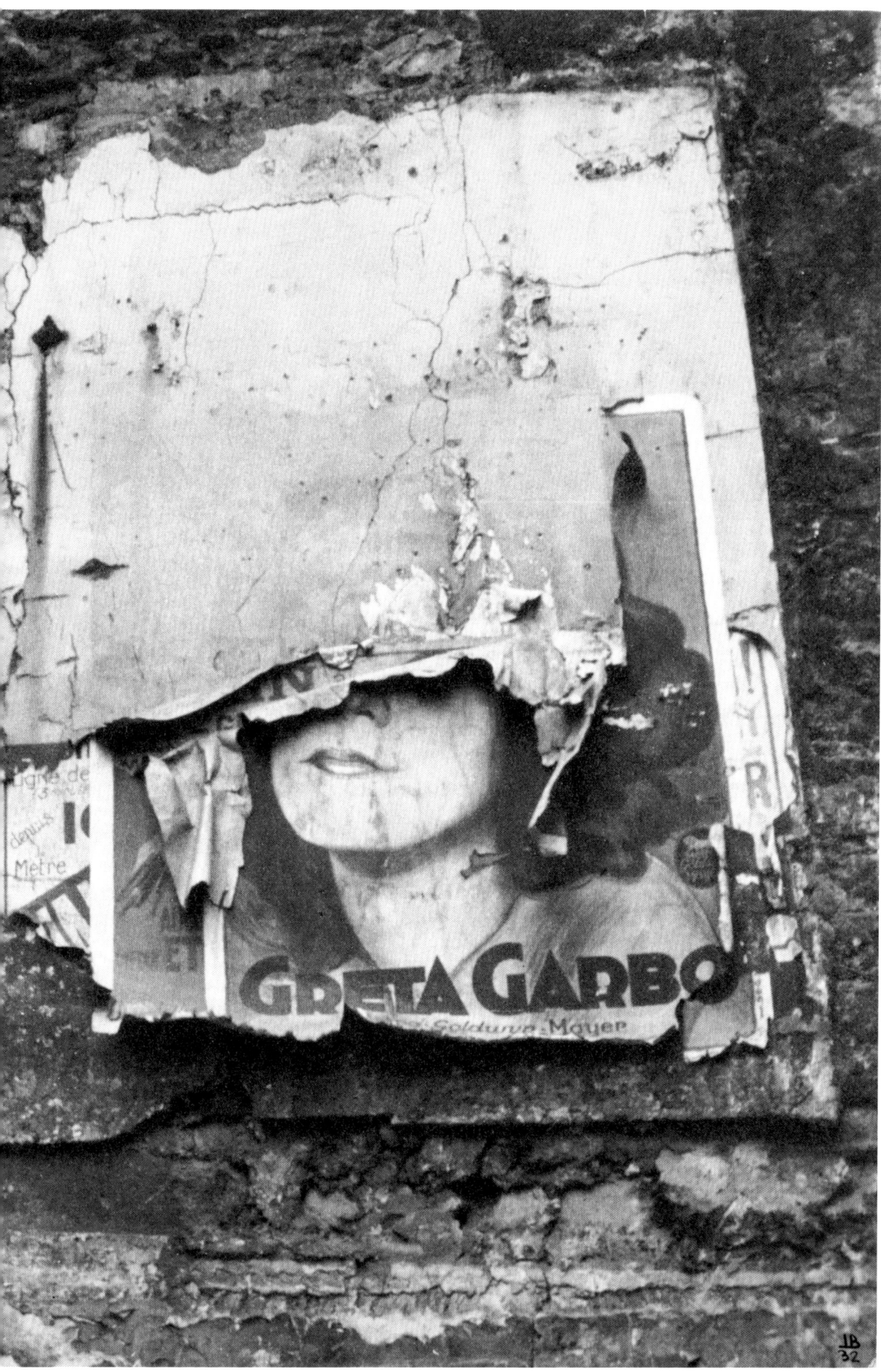

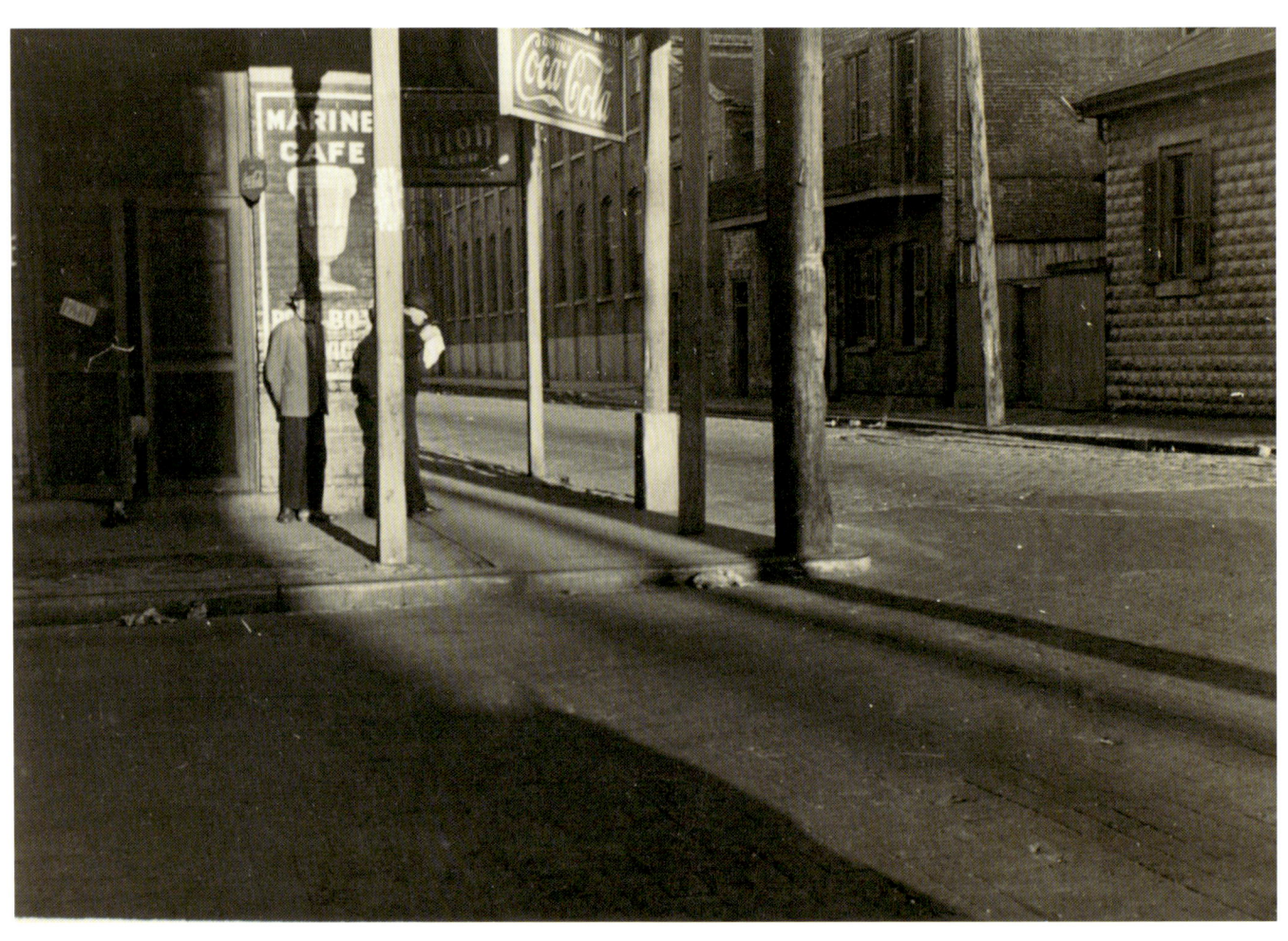

Walker Evans *New Orleans, Louisiana (Street Corner)* c.1936, 11.4 × 17.1 cm

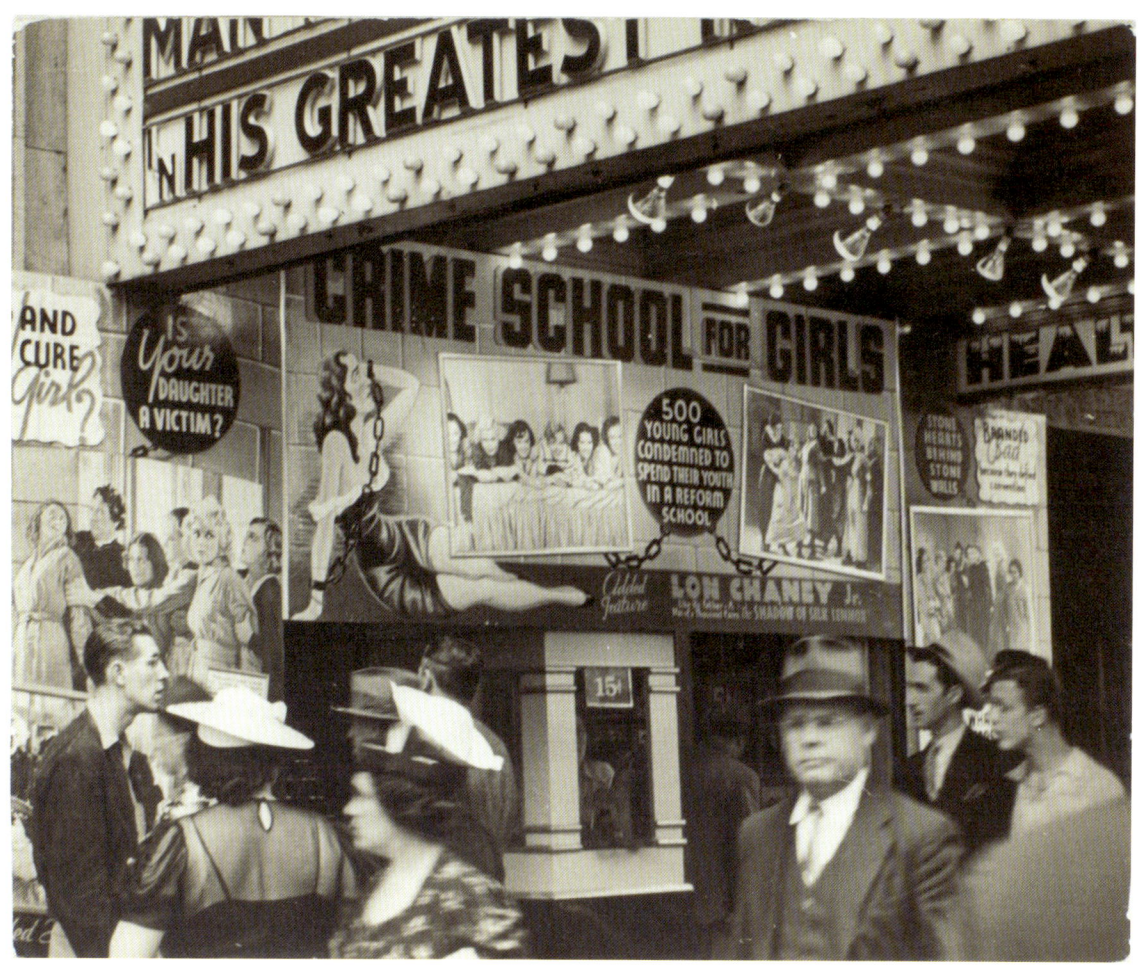

André Kertész *Crime School for Girls* 1938, 9.8 × 12.1 cm

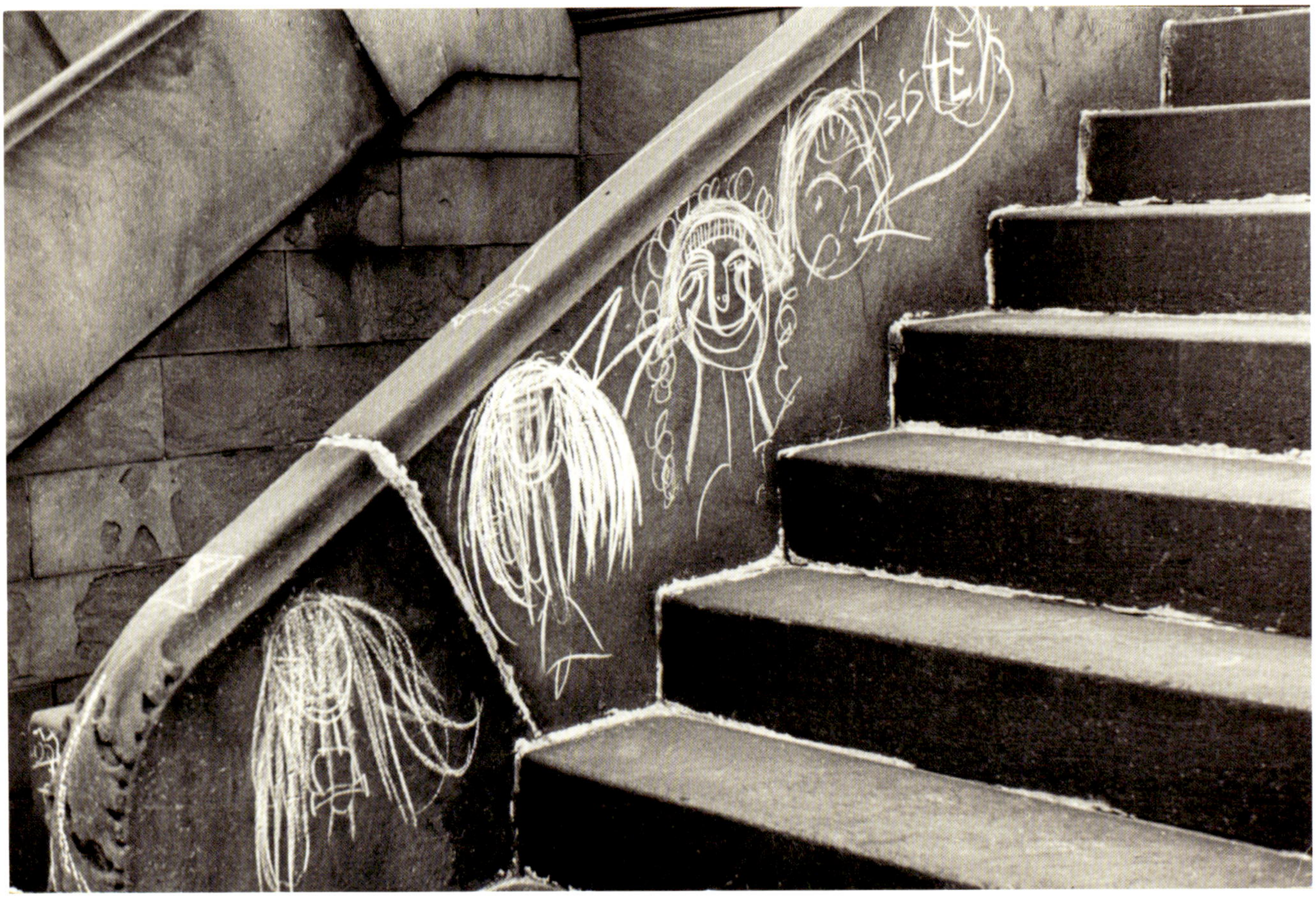

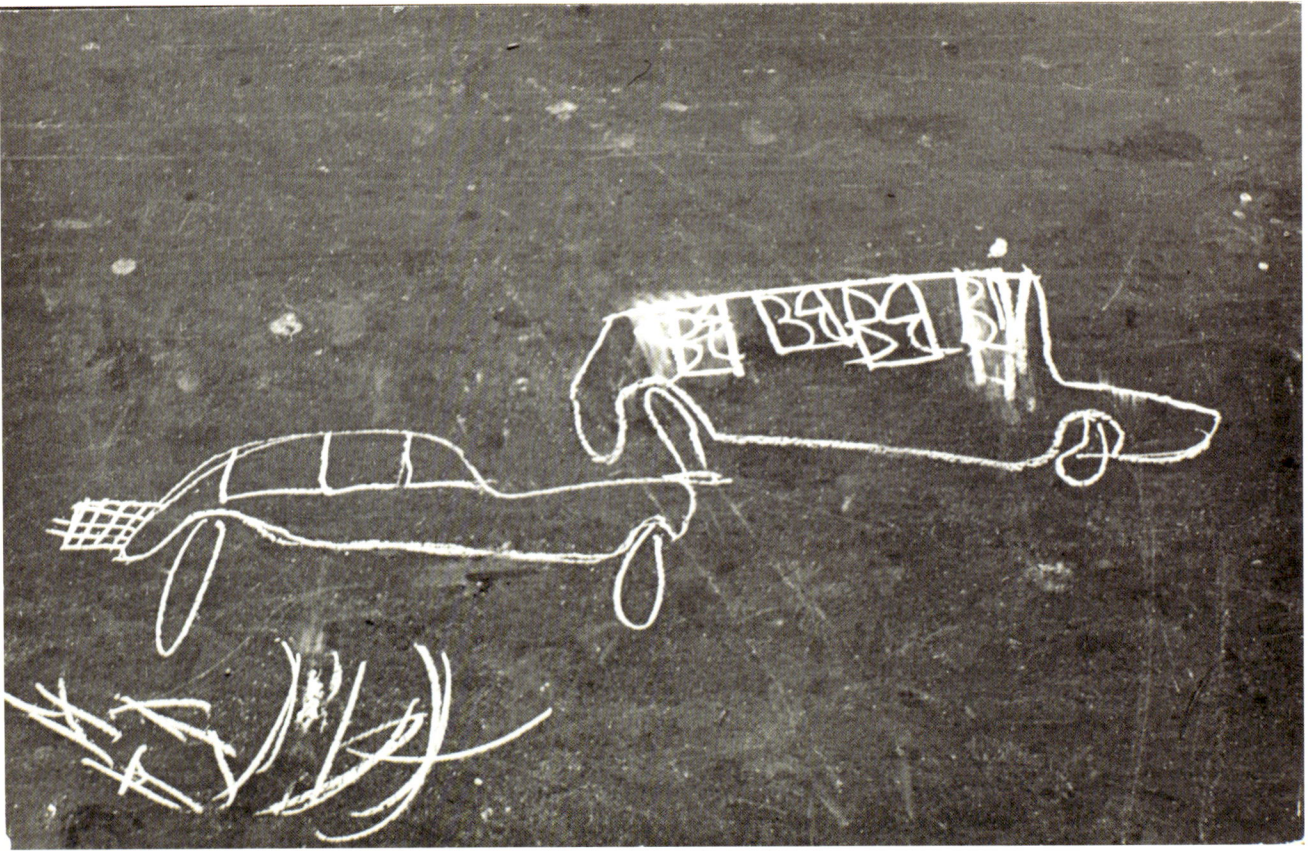

Top: **HELEN LEVITT** *New York* c.1938, 15.6 × 23.8 cm   Above: **HELEN LEVITT** *New York* c.1939, 17.1 × 27.3 cm

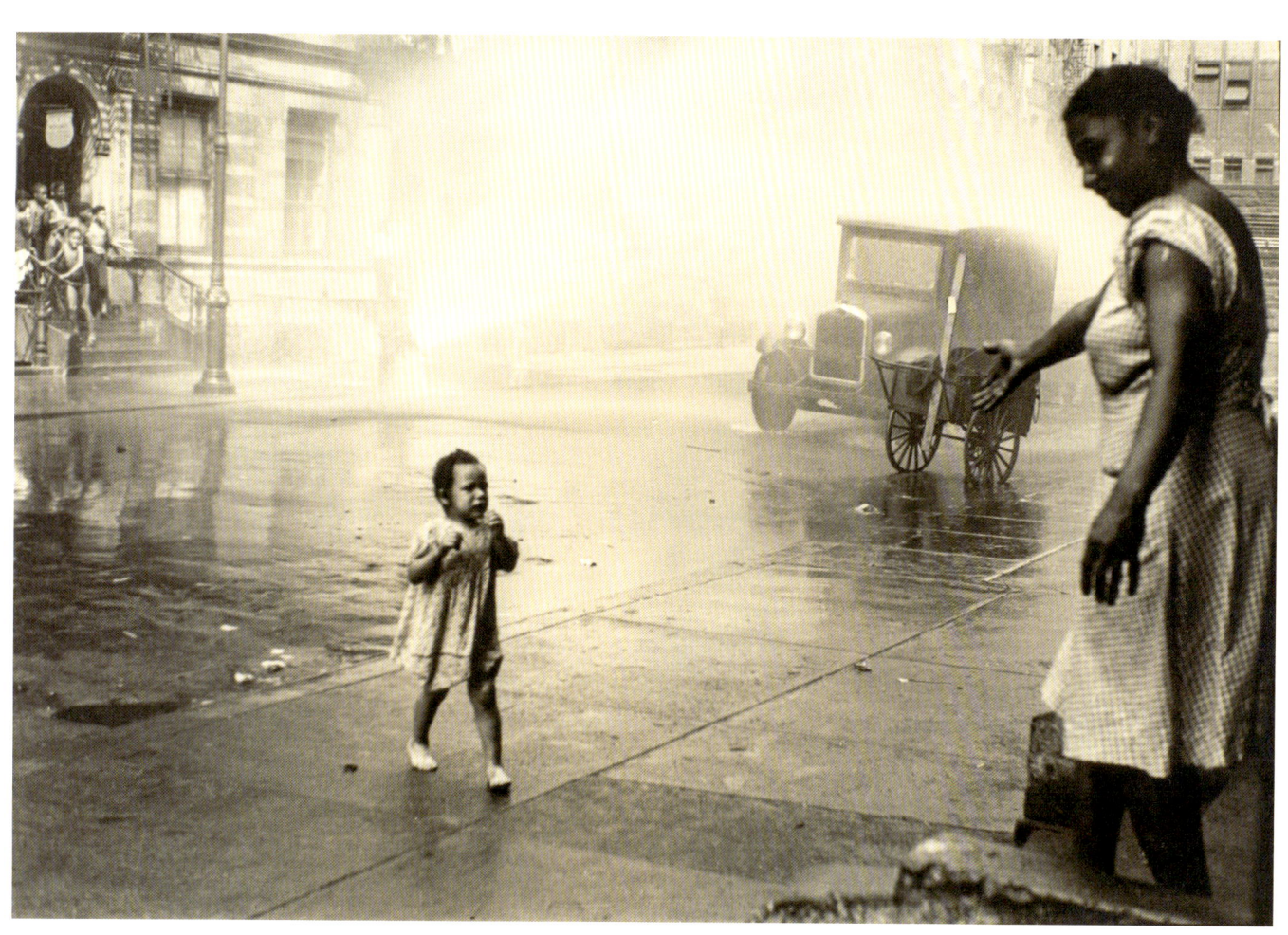

HELEN LEVITT *New York* 1939, 14.9 × 22.2 cm

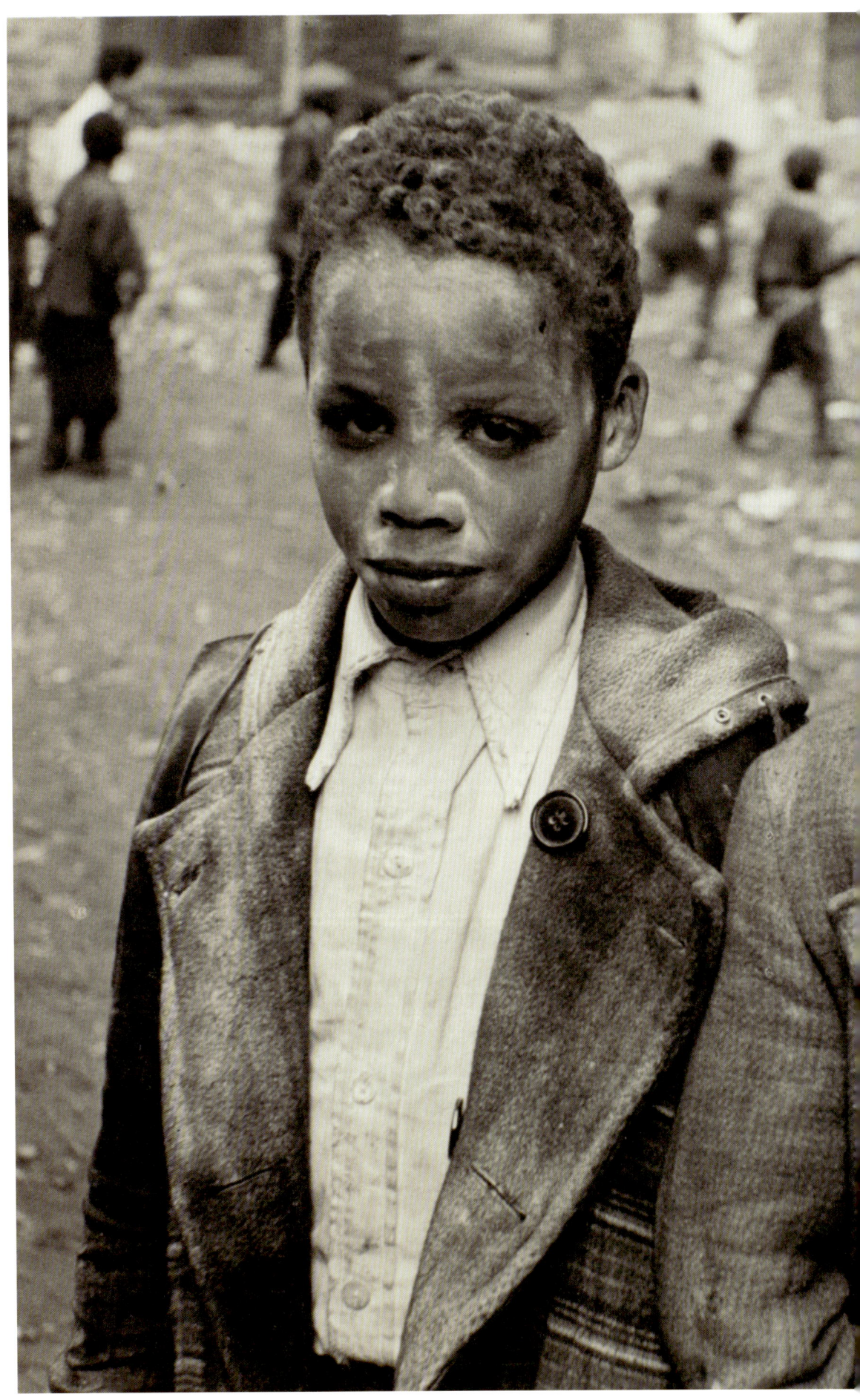

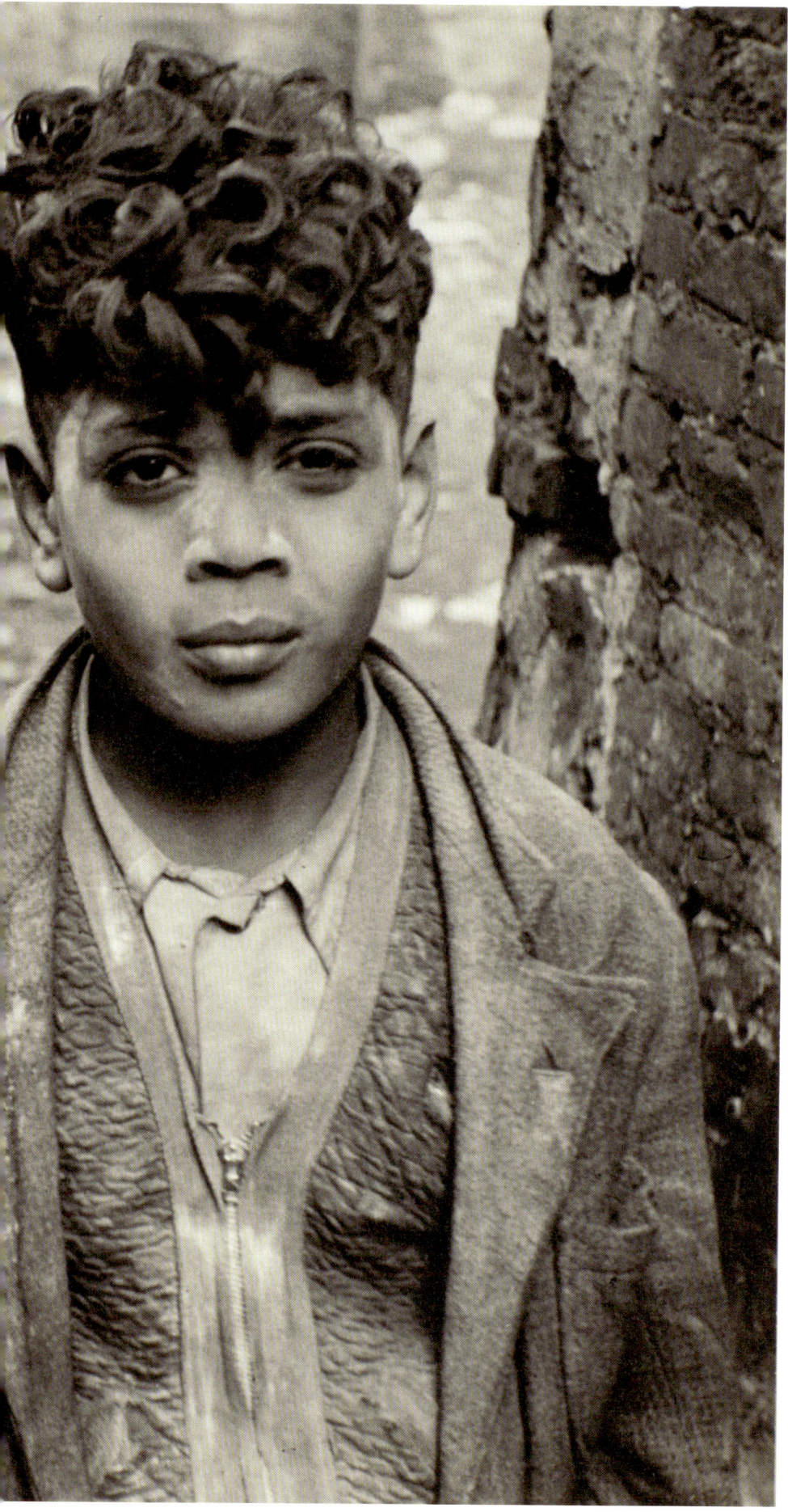

ROBERT FRANK
Paris 1949
34 × 21.9 cm

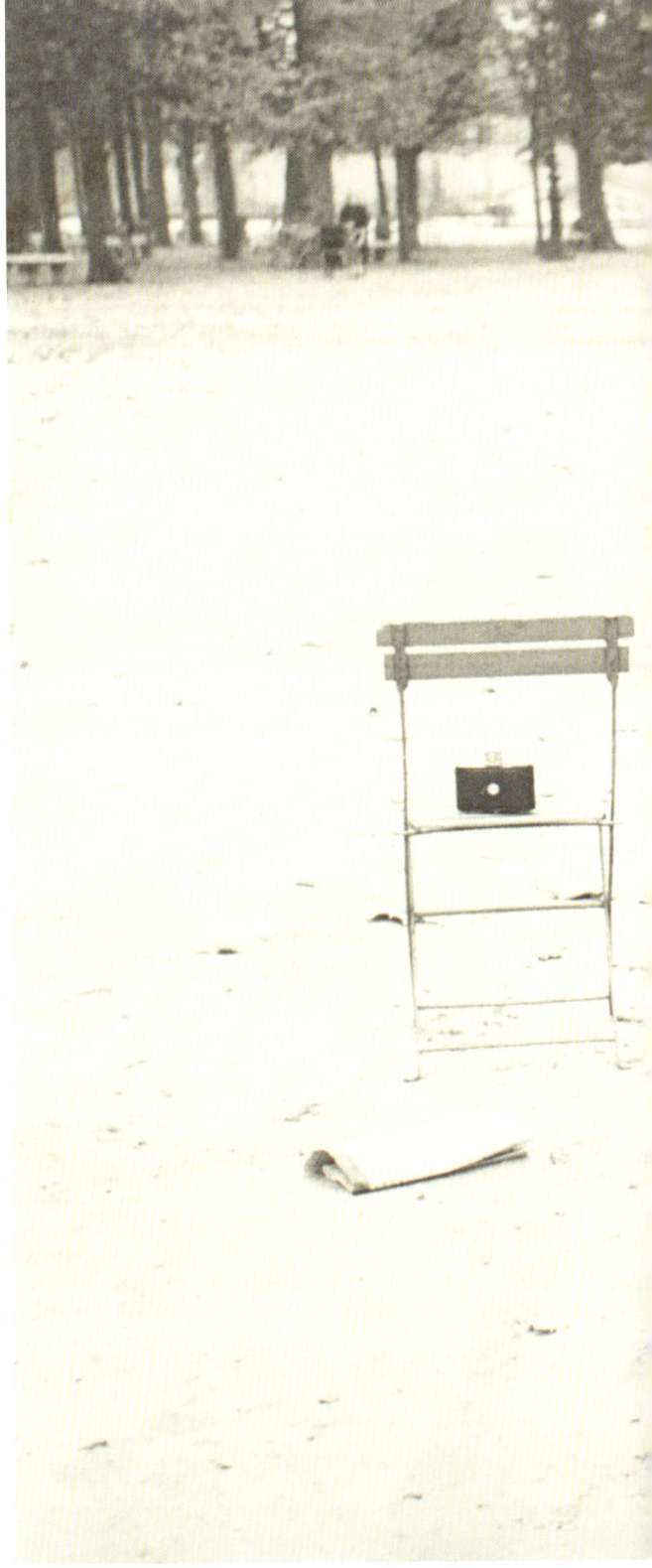

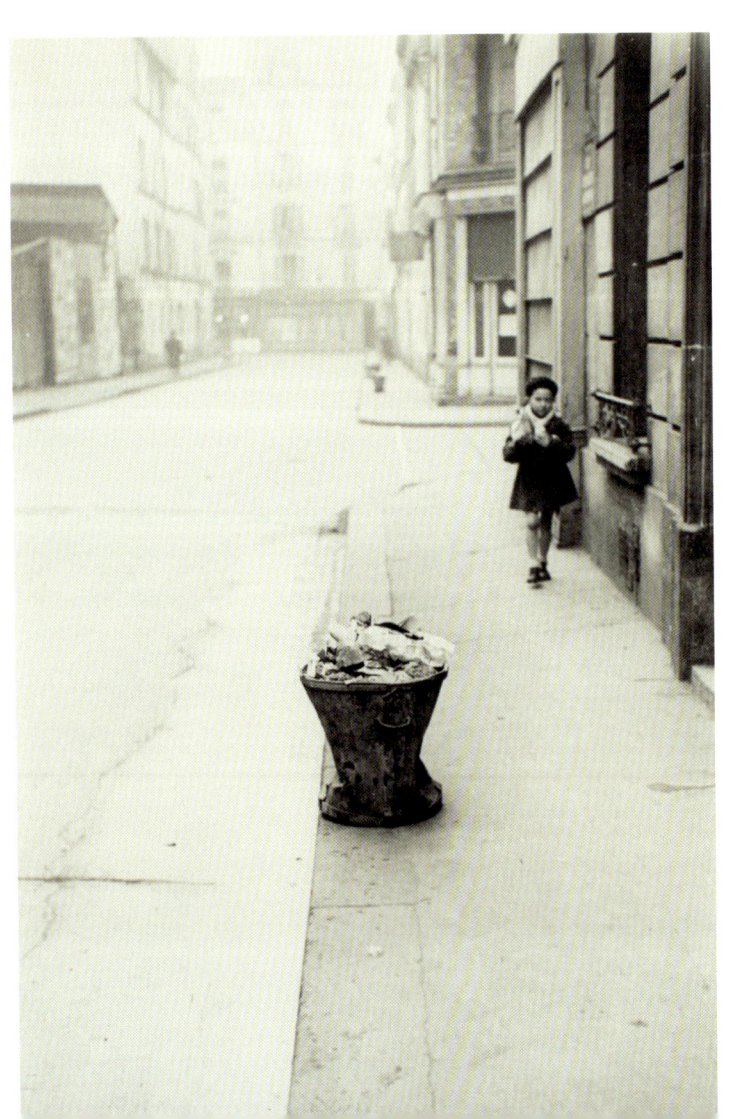

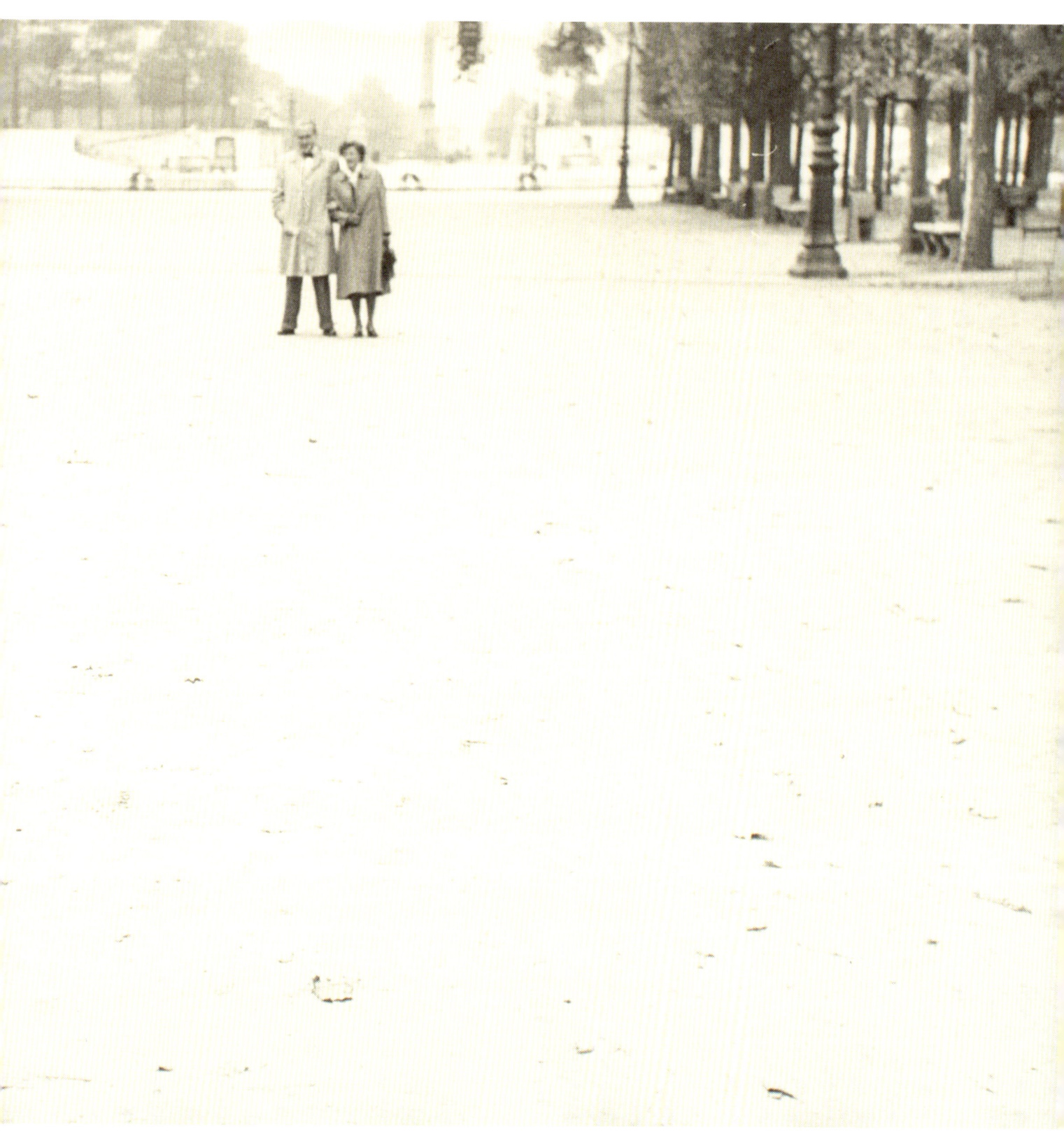

ROBERT FRANK *Paris* 1949, 18.7 × 28.6 cm

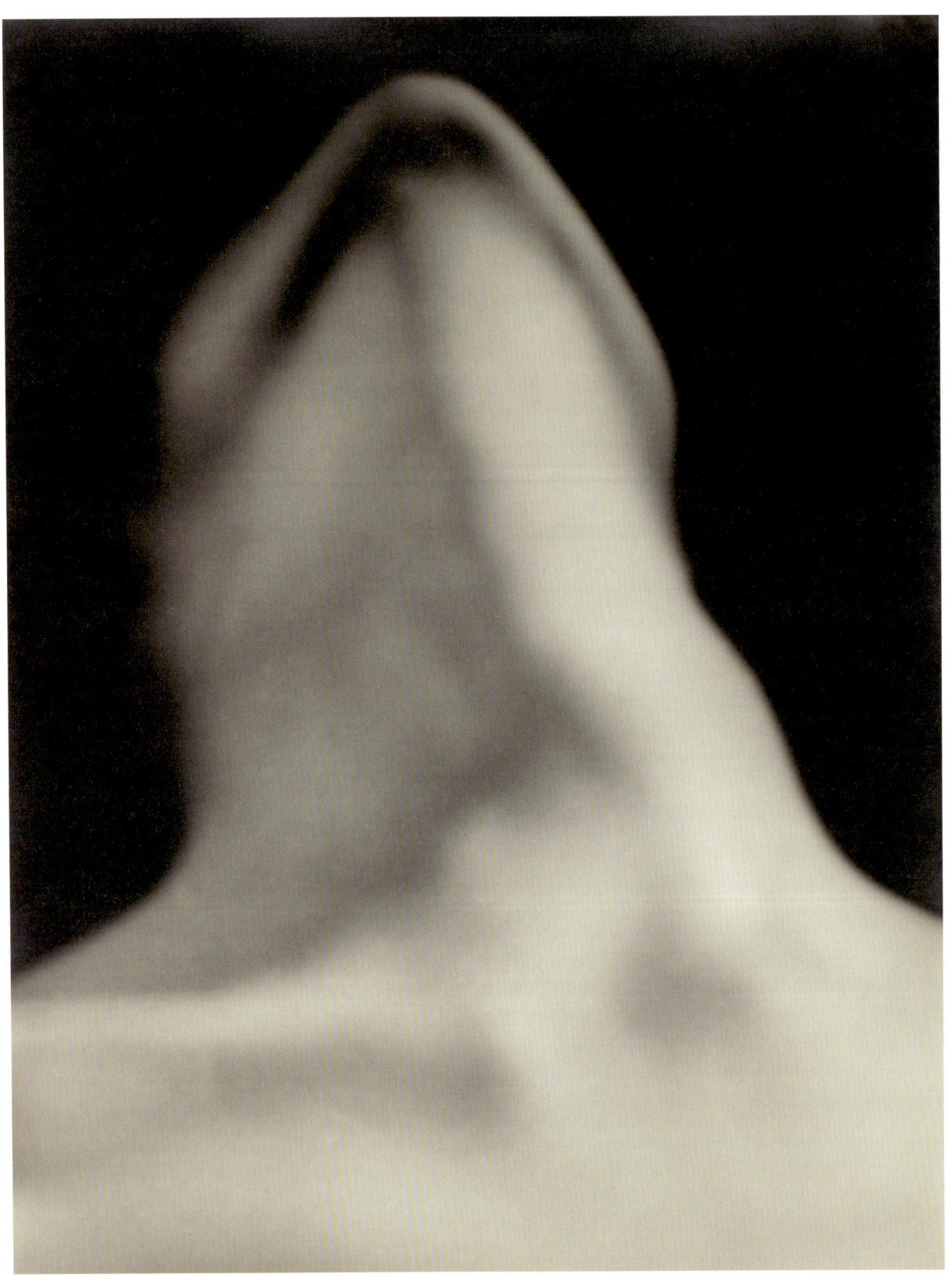

Man Ray
Anatomies 1930
28.9 × 22.5 cm

BODIES

The cataclysmic effects of the First World War provoked dramatic changes in attitudes towards the body and human psychology, and this was reflected in the new ways in which artists and photographers began to represent the human form. Various schools associated with the twentieth-century avant-garde used photographic abstraction to depict – or, as was often the case, to distort – the body in order to convey their own artistic or political agenda. Other photographers used improved camera technologies to record, precisely and often systematically, the physical form.

These approaches offered a radically different view of the body. Apart from medicine and the social sciences (and excluding the market for erotica), photographic depictions of the human form had largely been limited to two categories. One was the academic study, used as a reference by painters and draughtsmen; the other was the pictorialist composition, in which the female body would typically be presented in allegorical guise, or otherwise heavily aestheticised by the photographer using soft-focus lenses, or processes that enabled painterly effects to be created directly on the print surface. The male nude was deemed too explicit altogether.

One of the ways in which the physical form was now re-presented was through a reimagining of the studio setting. Photographers experimented on the one hand with distinctly modern stage sets to convey energy and dynamism, or conversely borrowed from the classical or pastoral traditions in painting and sculpture, in order to introduce the male nude as a subject for scrutiny.

Access to new, sharp-focus camera lenses and the popularity of gelatin silver printing techniques enabled the contours of form and the tones of flesh to be revealed with greater precision. 'The camera should be used for a recording of *life*,' wrote Edward Weston in 1924, 'for rendering the very substance and quintessence of the *thing itself*, whether it be polished steel or palpitating flesh'. In 1936, the philosopher Walter Benjamin would compare the camera to the surgeon's knife, able to permeate the body by splicing it into fragments. Indeed, like many photographers, Weston often focused on one part of the body. This invited a deeper understanding of the physical; it also drew attention to the abstract nature of form, accenting curves and angles, the body now as depersonalised as a plant or landscape.

Developments in camera technology during this period were also responsible for one of the most dramatic advances in photography of the body during this period – that of capturing movement. Previously, motion had only been suggested by the blurring effect of a long exposure accompanied by flash (a favoured technique of the futurists), or conveyed through sequences of static frames. Now, for the first time, thanks to faster shutter speeds and roll film, photographers were able to freeze the body in action, to show what it looked like running, or suspended in mid-air. Shorter exposure times opened up new avenues to the photographer, as models were required to hold a pose for seconds rather than minutes. Figures were now seen jumping, twirling and leaping into the photographic frame, demonstrating a new freedom of personal expression and a radical shift away from old notions of propriety. EL

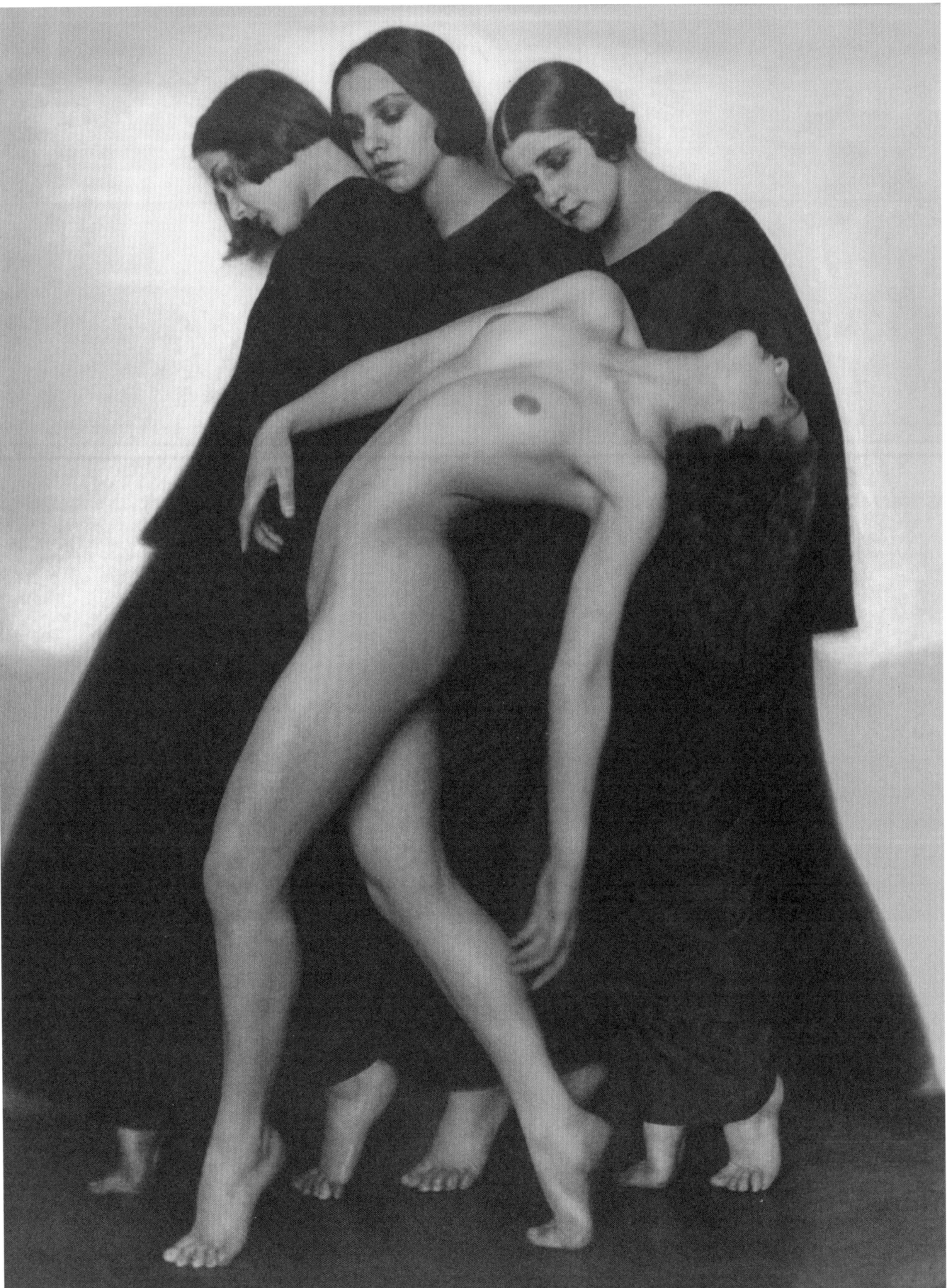

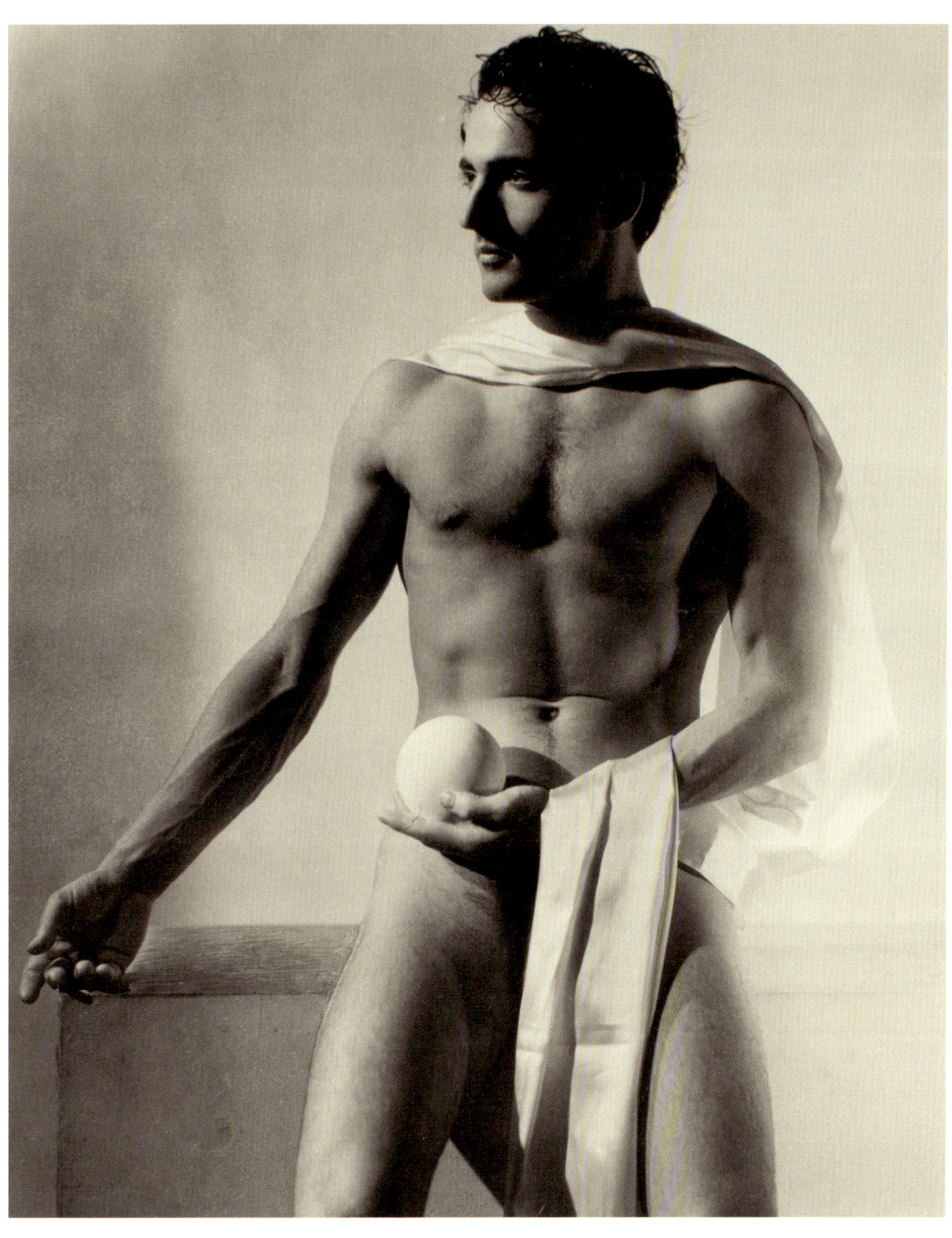

Left: **RUDOLF KOPPITZ** *Movement Study*
1925, carbon print, 36.8 × 27.6 cm

Above: **DORA MAAR** *The Dancer Alberto Spadolini*
1935, 37.5 × 26.7 cm

Man Ray *Male Nude* 1933, 25.4 × 19.7 cm

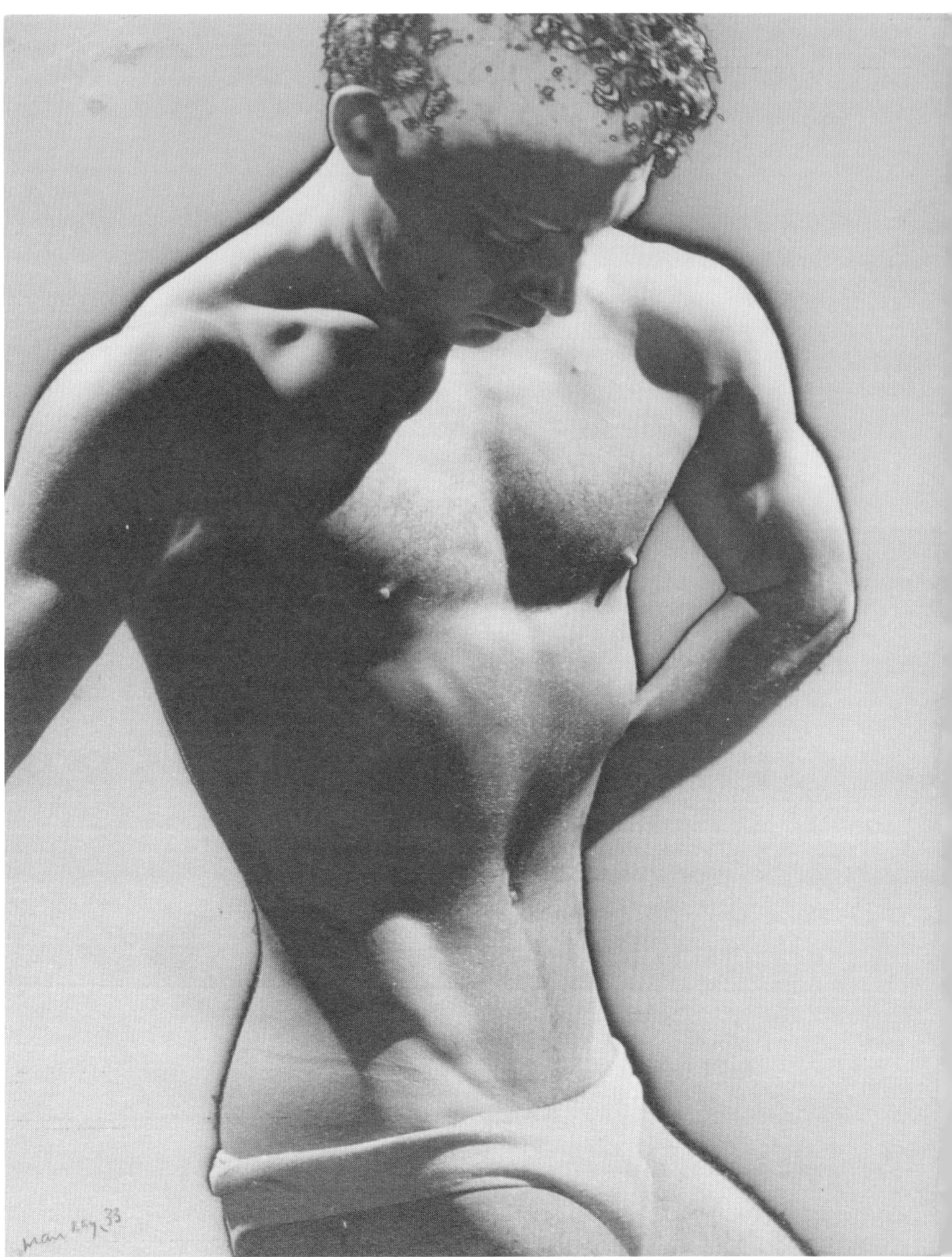

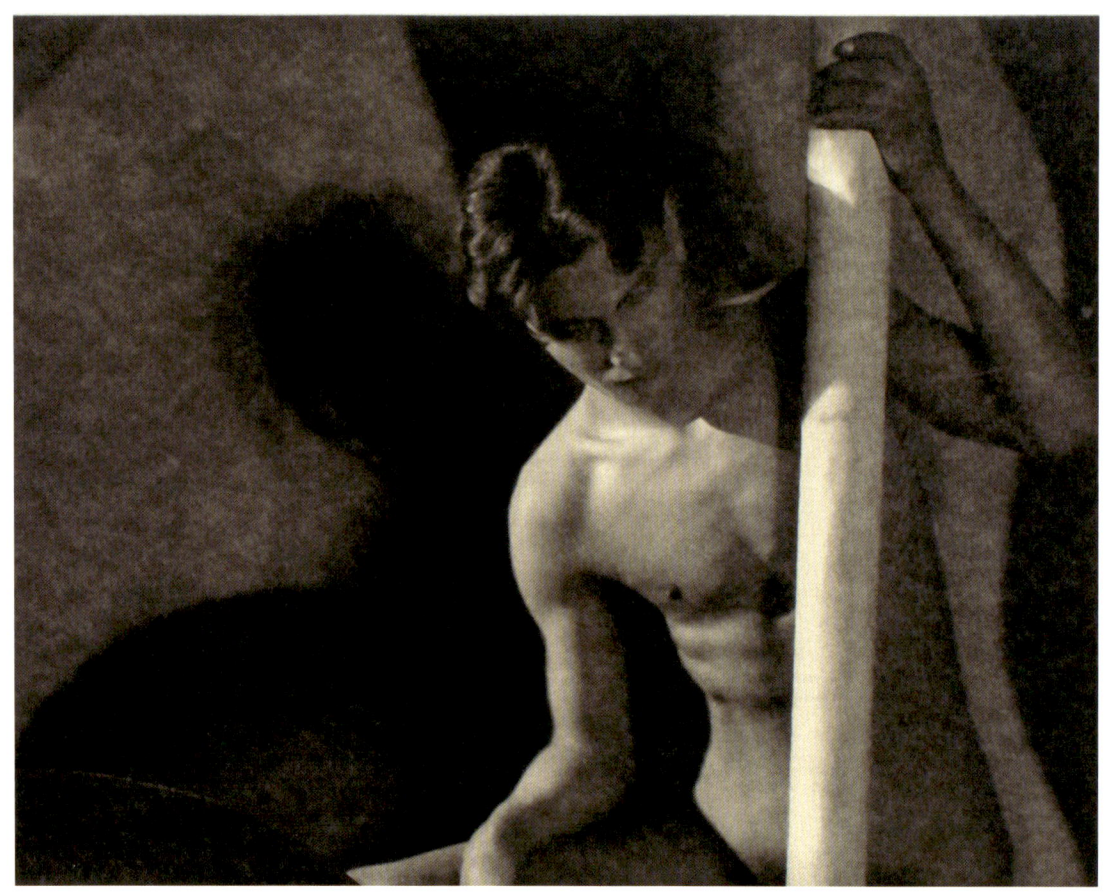

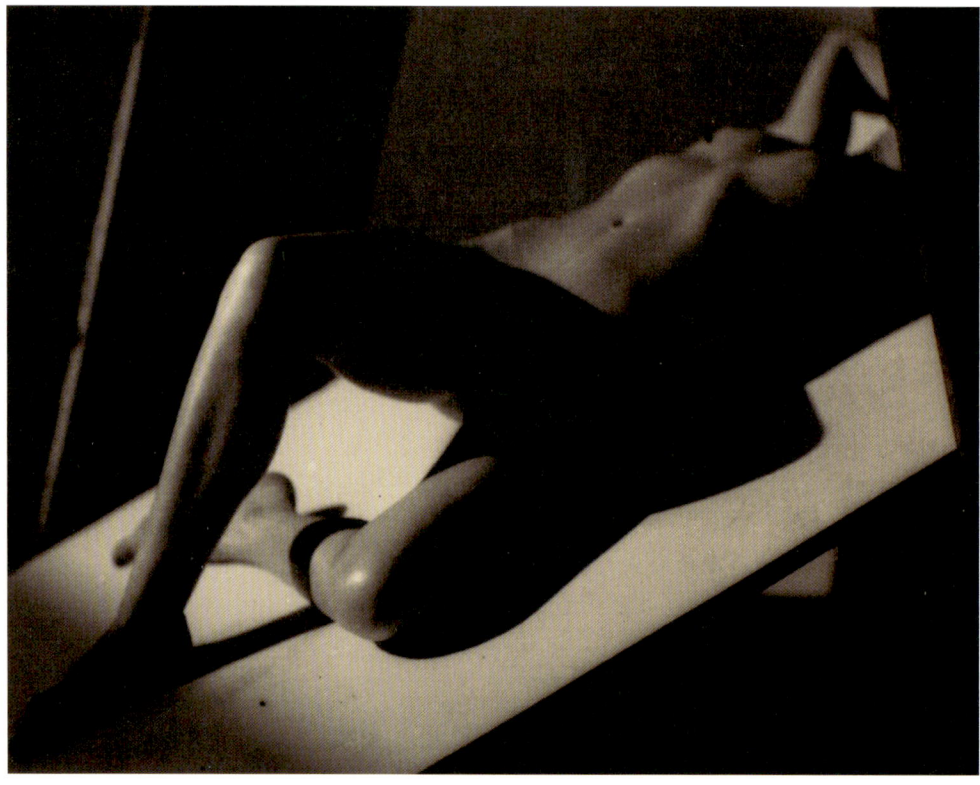

Top: **František Drtikol** *Male Nude* c.1925, pigment print, 21.9 × 28.6 cm
Above: **František Drtikol** *Composition* 1929, pigment print, 9.8 × 12.4 cm

František Drtikol *Untitled (Nude with Wave Construction)* 1925, pigment print, 22.2 × 27.3 cm

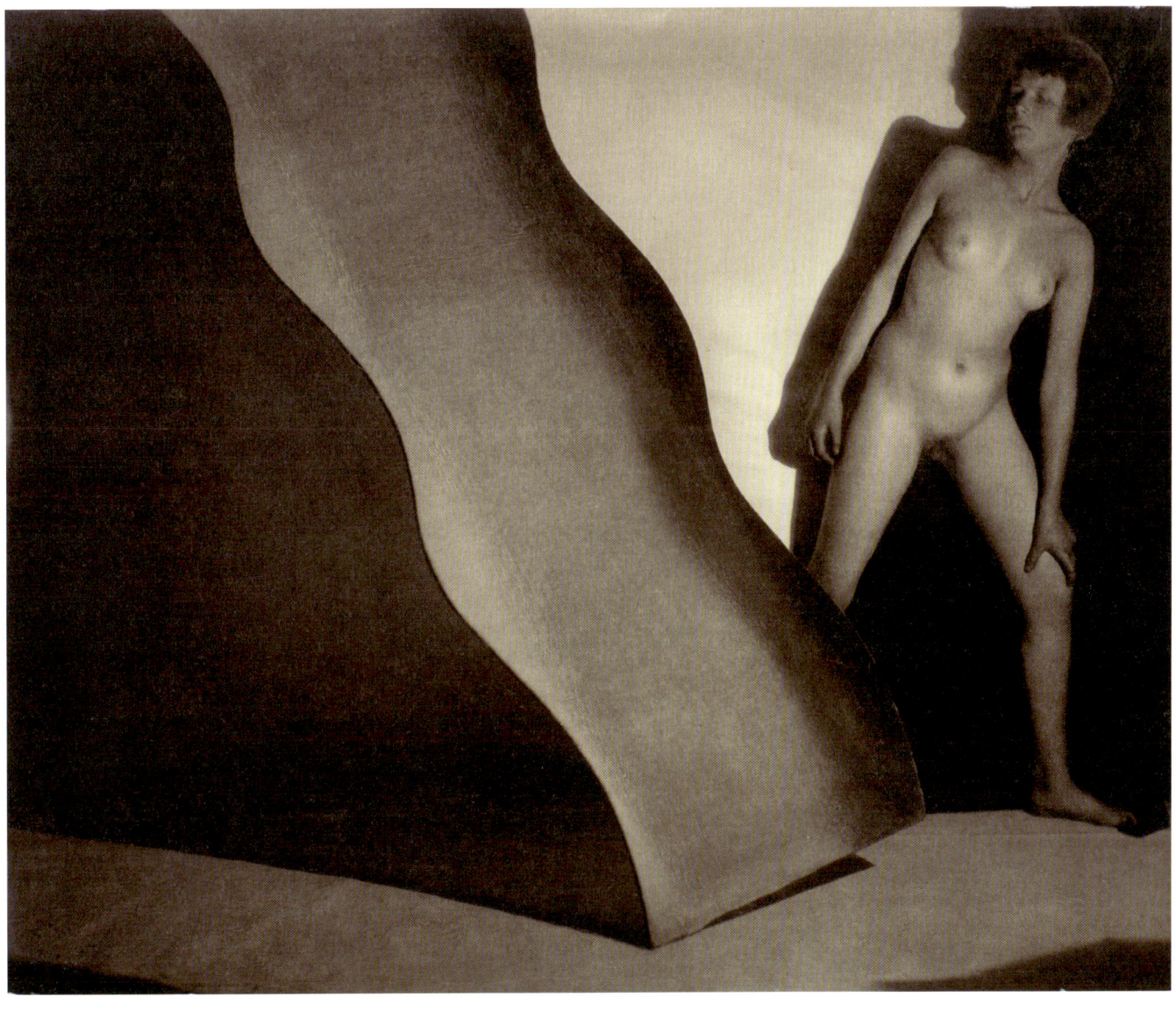

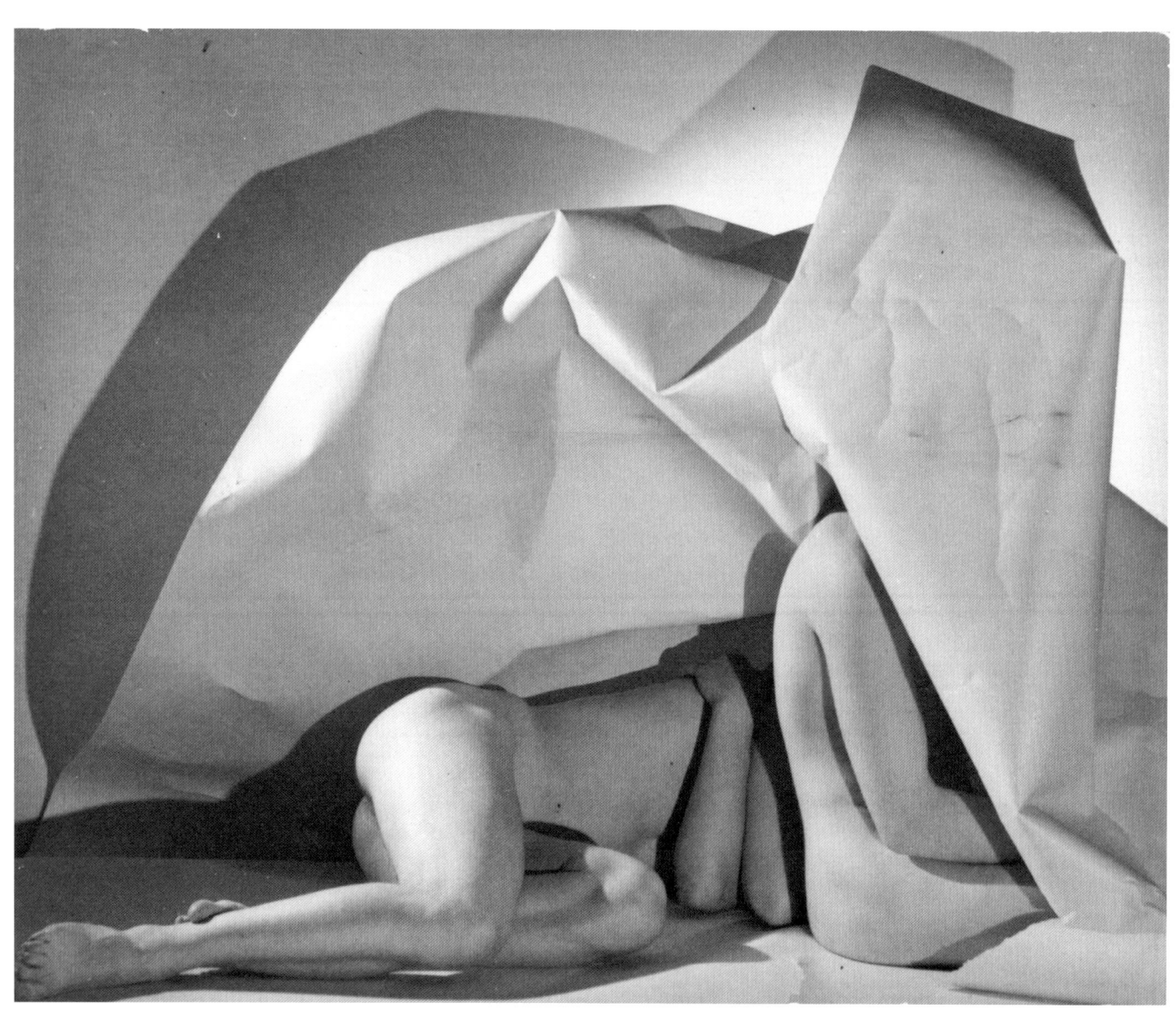

George Platt Lynes *Tex Smutney and Friend with Paper* 1943, 19.4 × 23.5 cm

142

Below: **GEORGE PLATT LYNES** *A Forgotten Model* c.1937, 17.1 × 21 cm
Bottom: **MINOR WHITE** *Tom Murphy, San Francisco* 1948, 6.1 × 11.4 cm

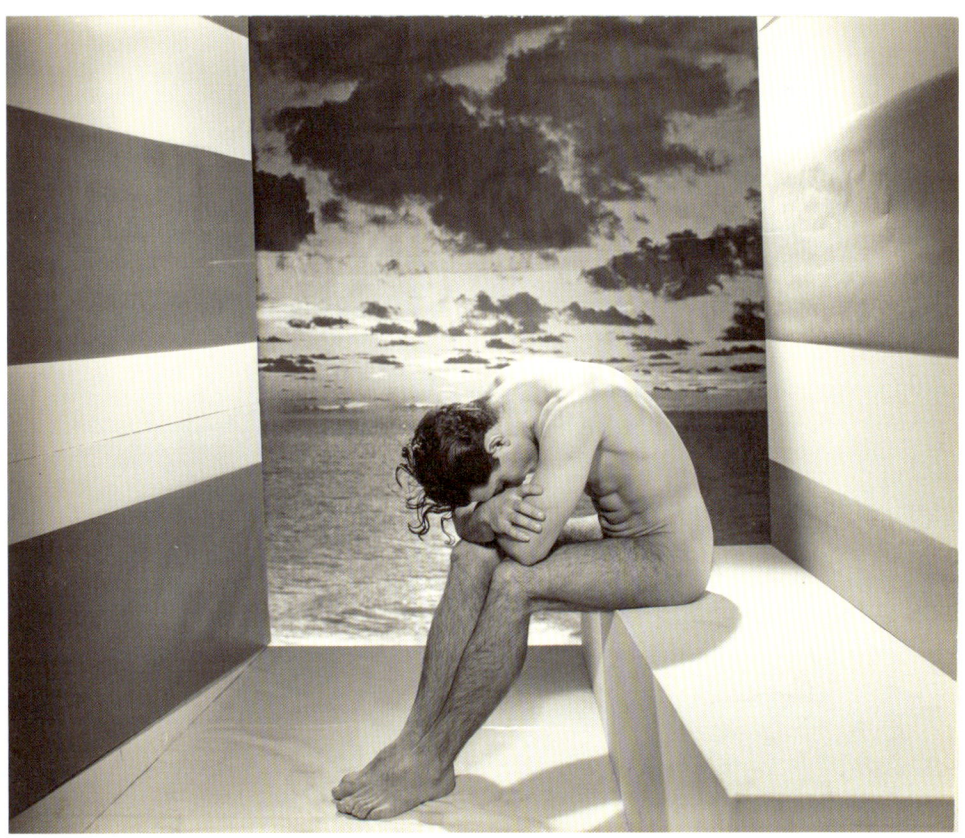

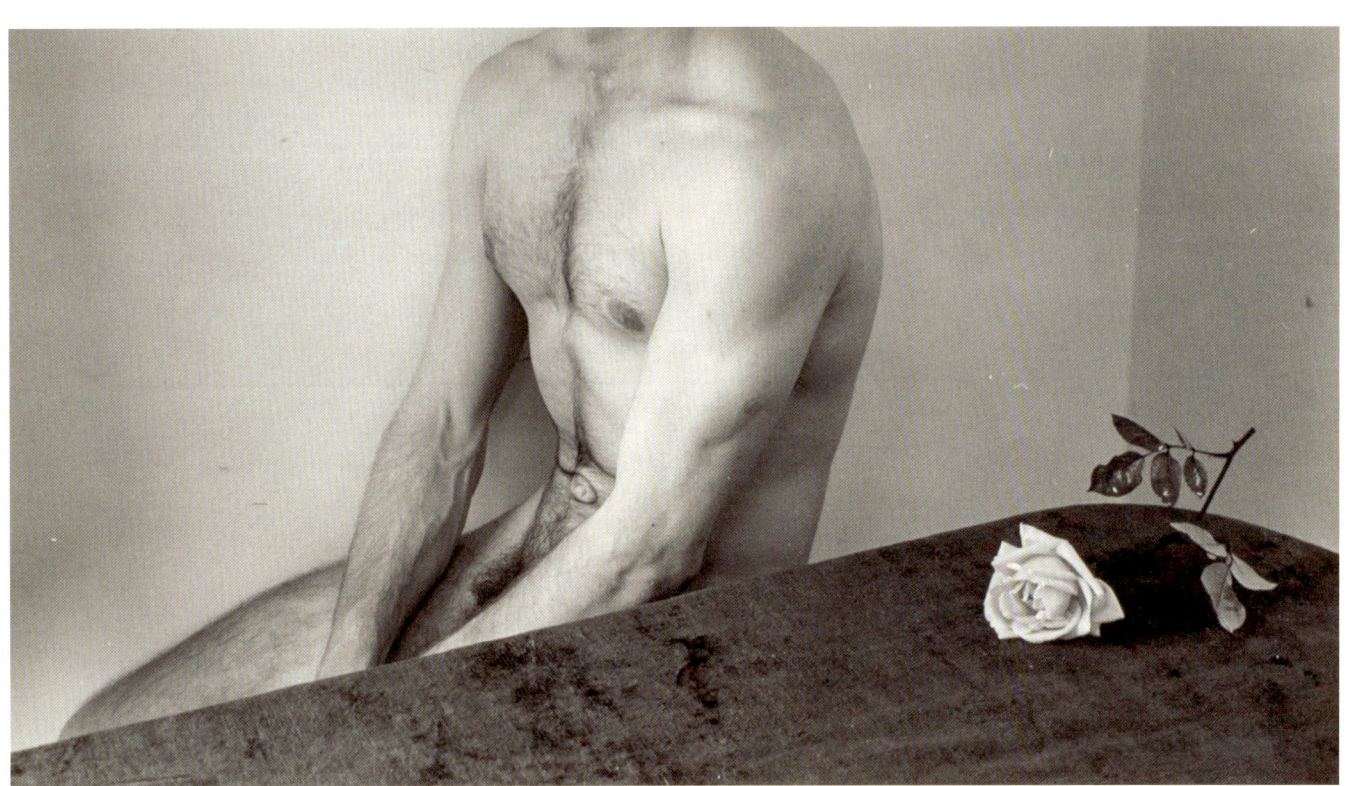

143

Carl Van Vechten *Leo Coleman as Toby in 'The Medium', 18 May 1946, 16.5 × 24 cm*

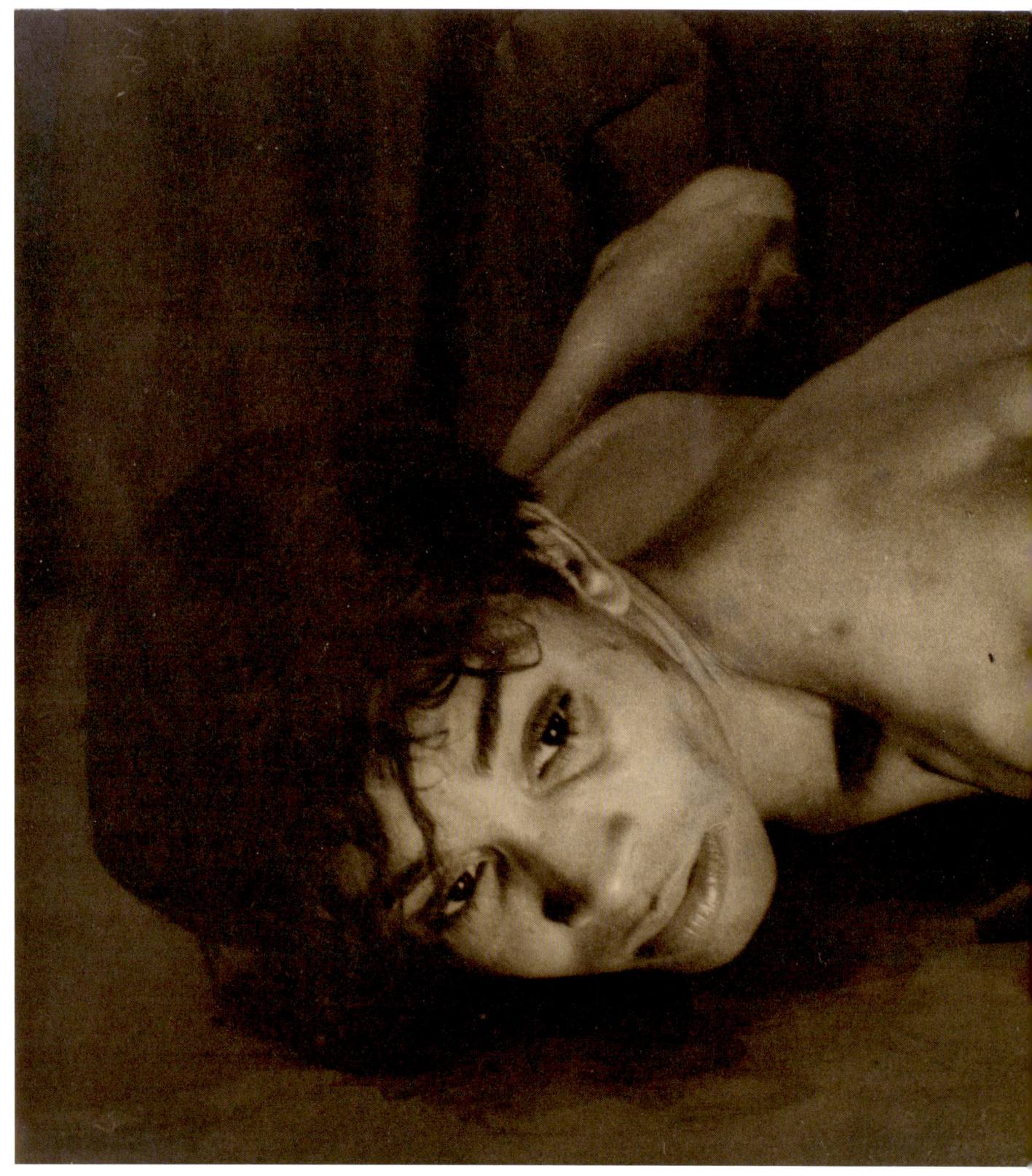

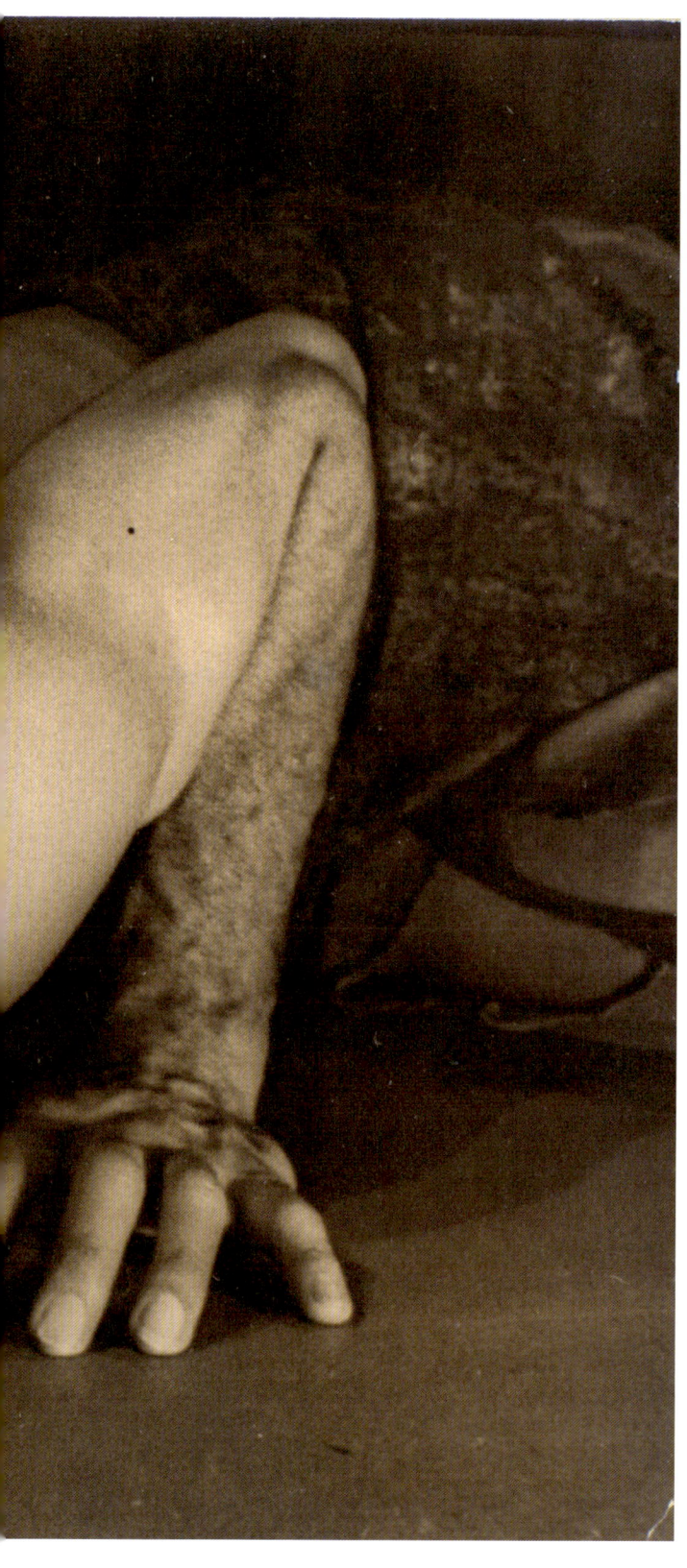

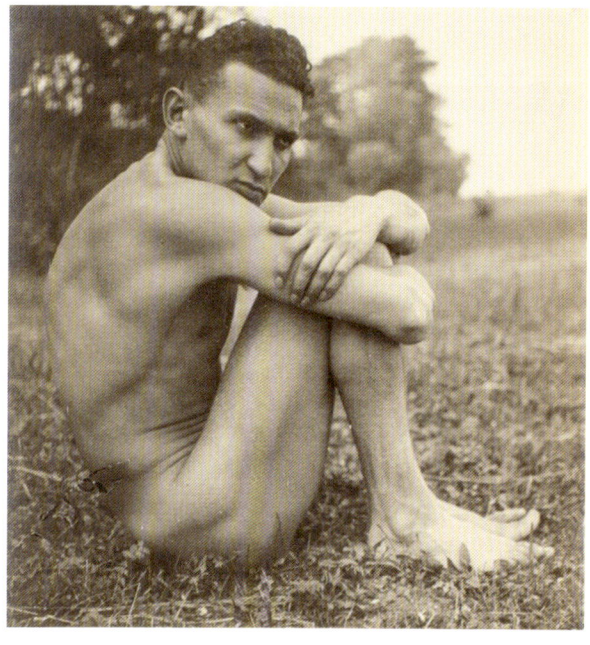

André Kertész *My Brother Eugene* 1919, 7 × 7 cm

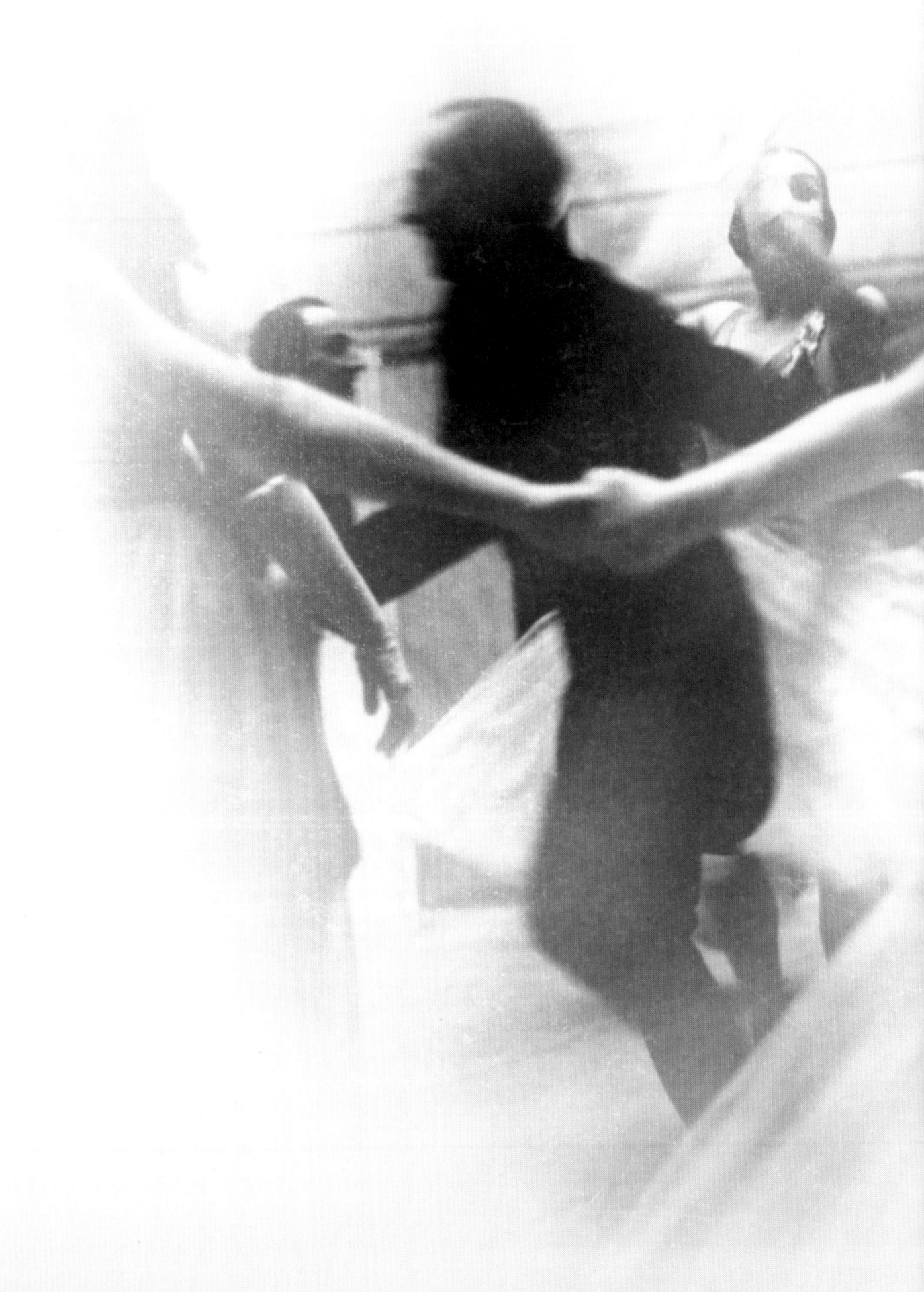

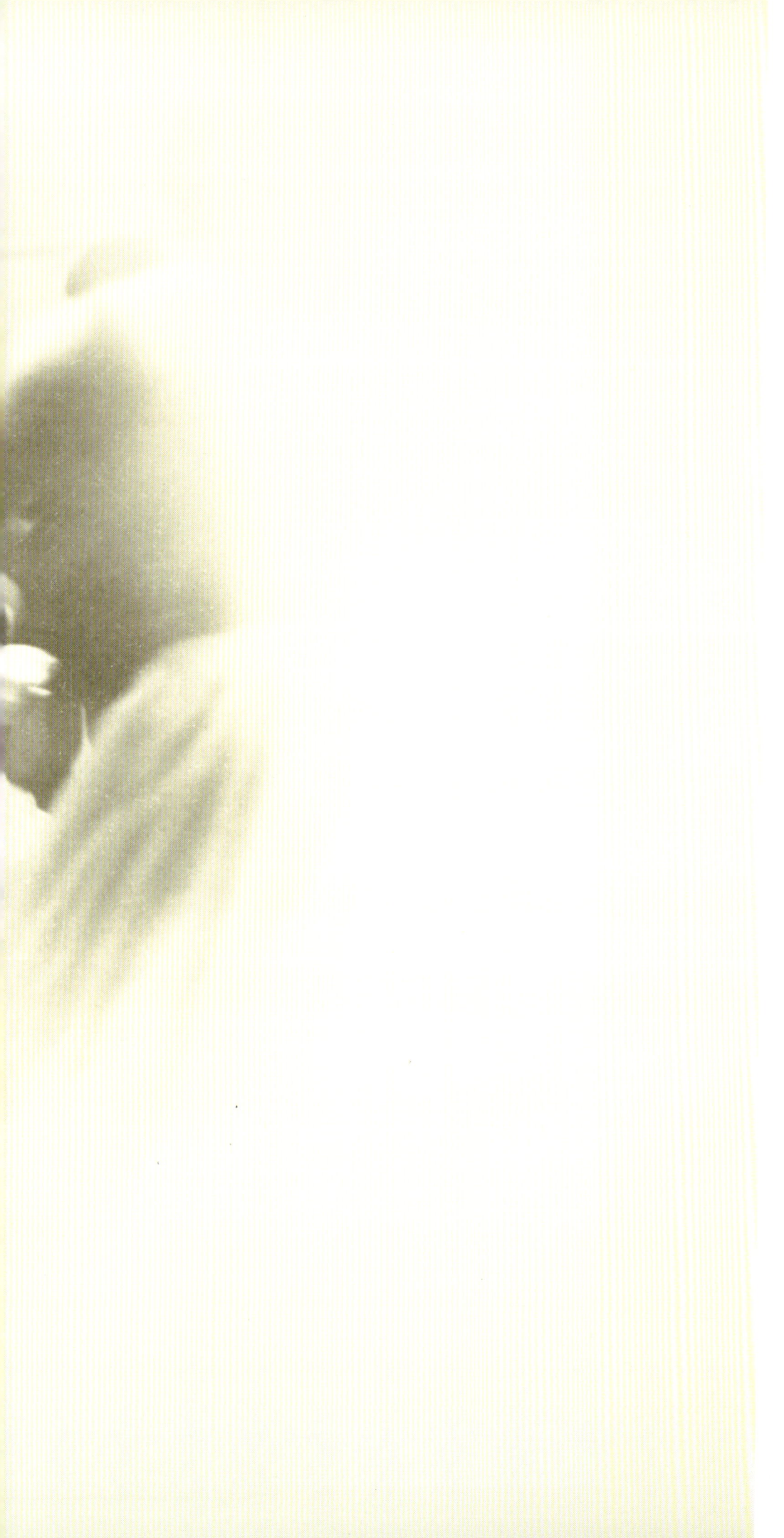

ALEXEY BRODOVITCH
Cotillion c.1935
23.8 × 34 cm

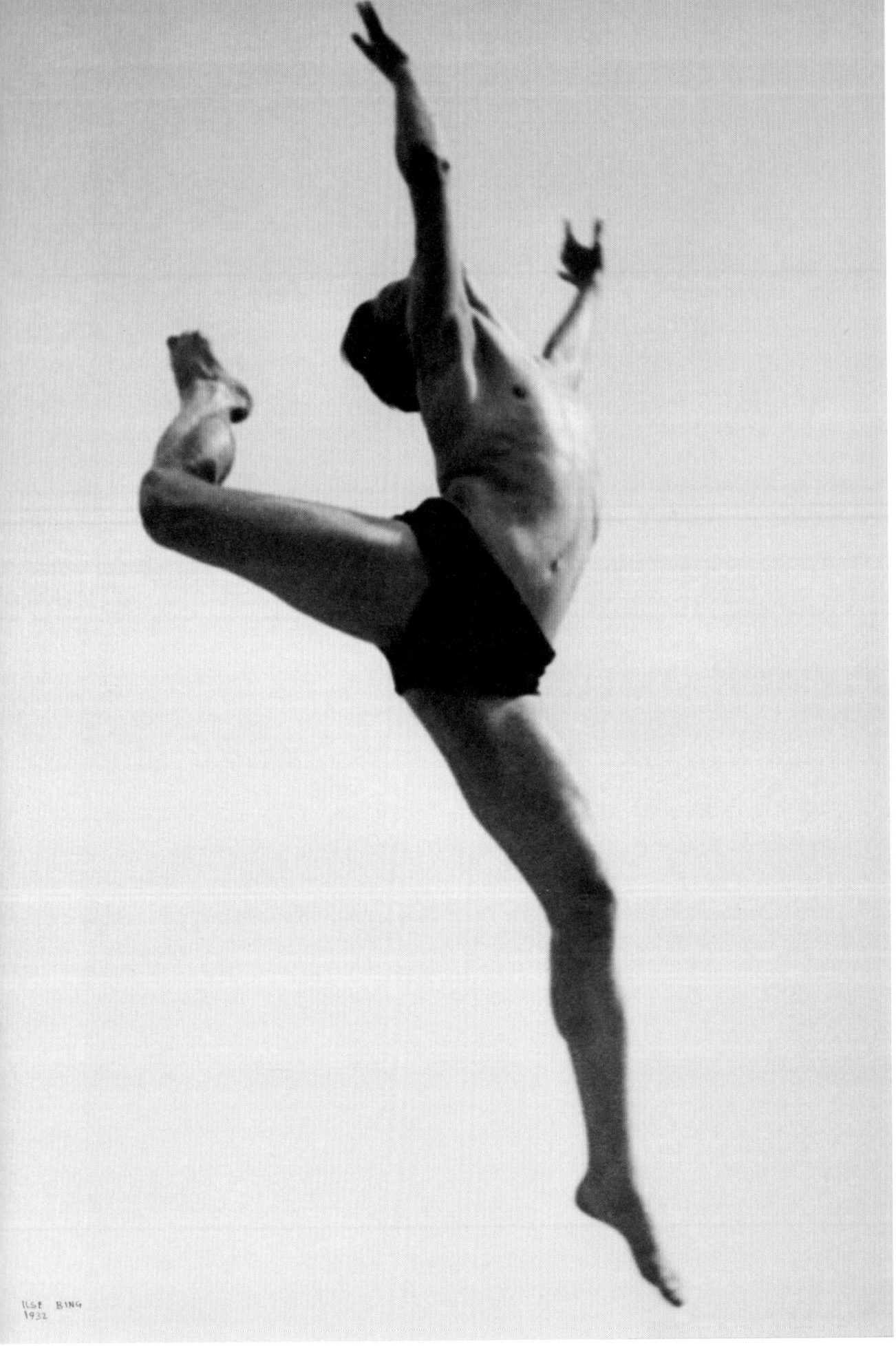

ILSE BING
1932

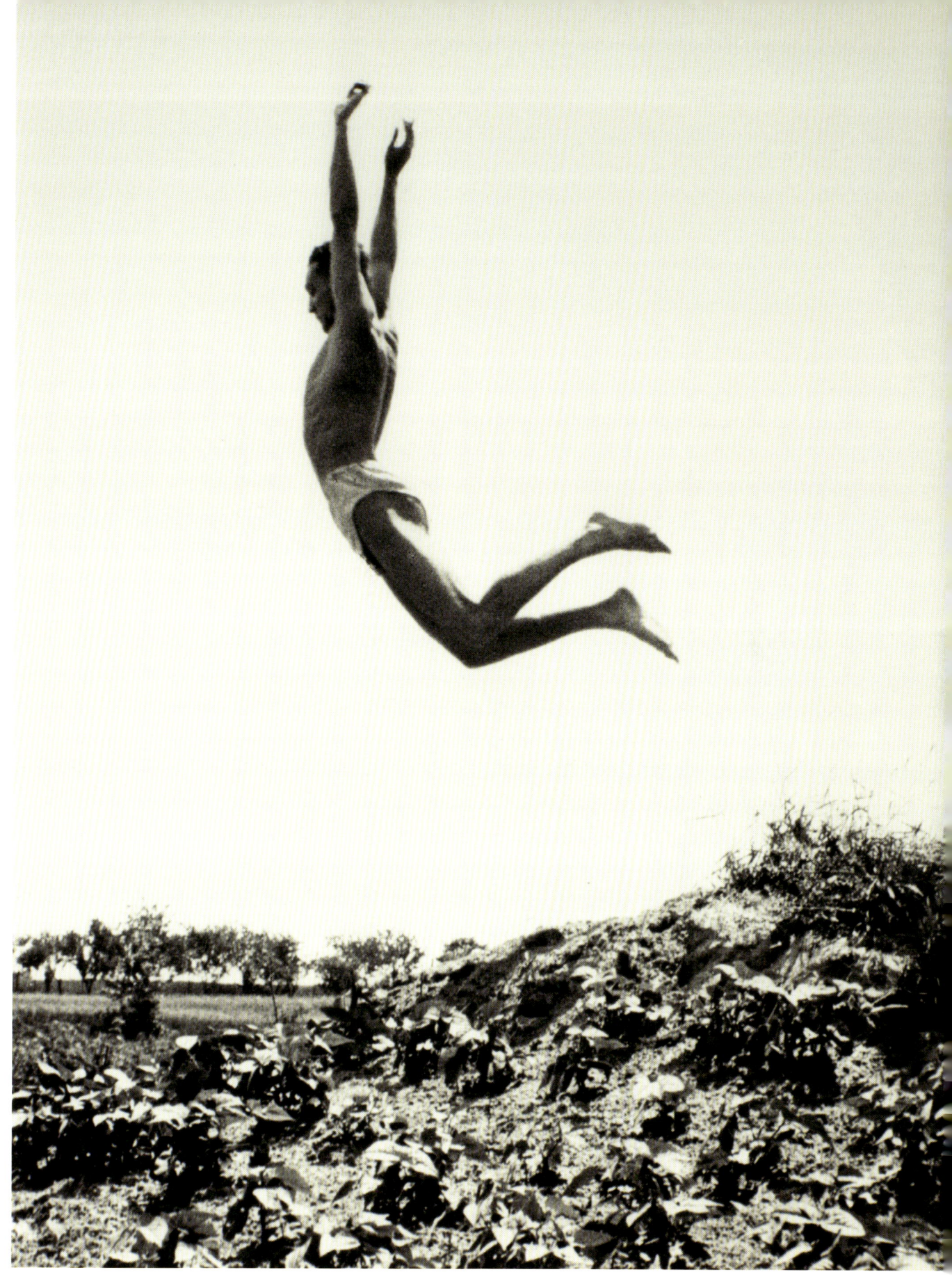

Above: **ANDRÉ KERTÉSZ** *My Brother as Icarus, June 1919, 23.5 × 18.4 cm*
Left: **ILSE BING** *Dancer, Willem van Loon, Paris 1932, 27.6 × 18.4 cm*

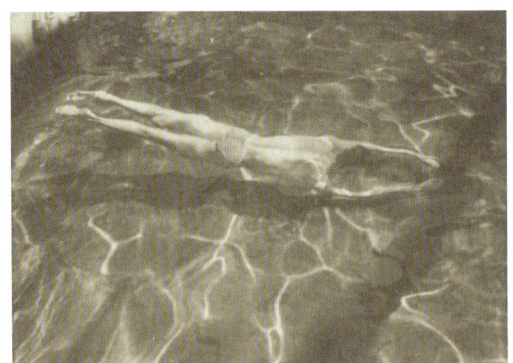

André Kertész *Underwater Swimmer, Esztergom,*
Hungary, 30 June 1917, 3.2 × 4.5 cm

Ferenc Csík *Diver 1936, 48.3 × 41.3 cm*

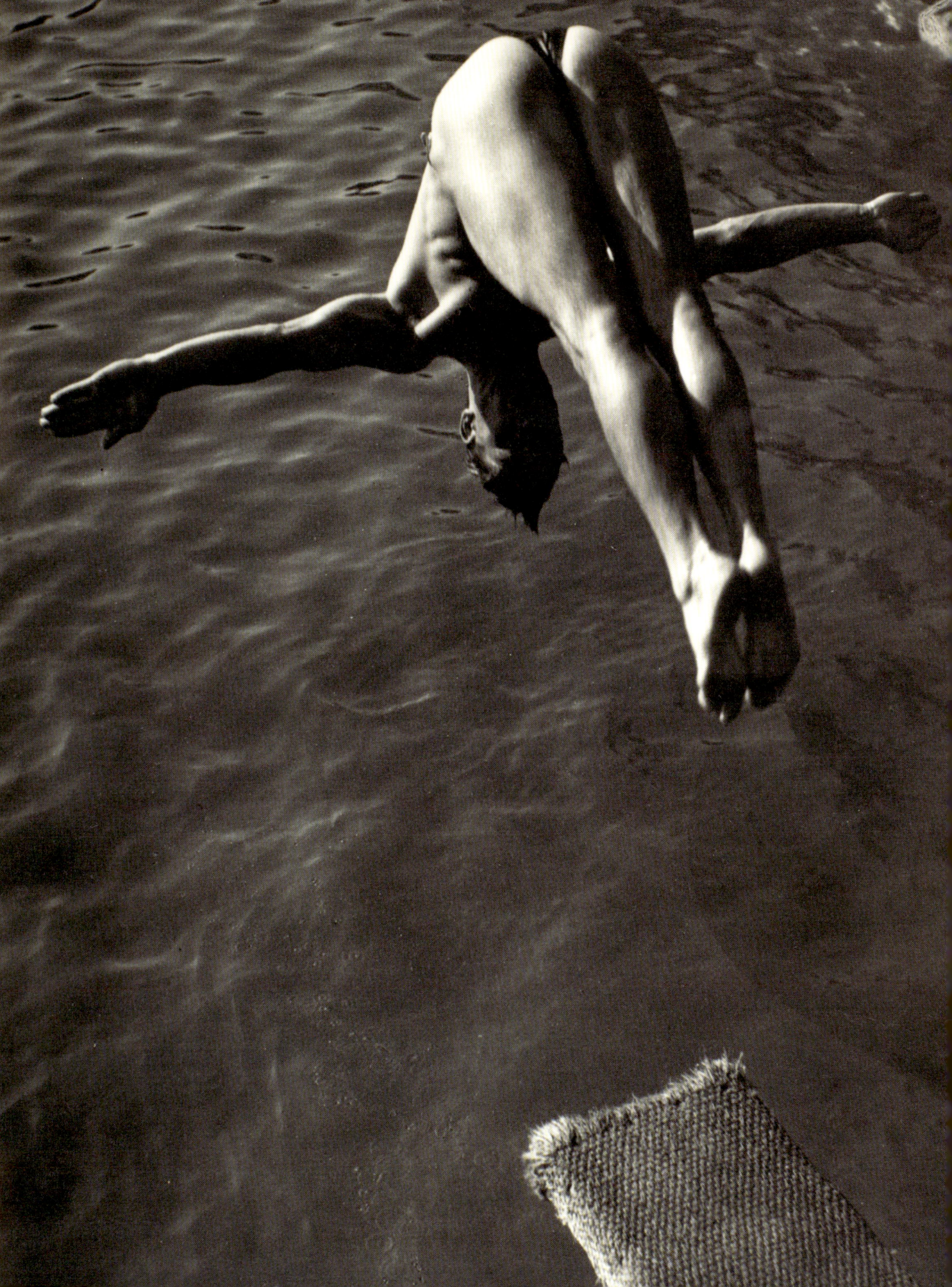

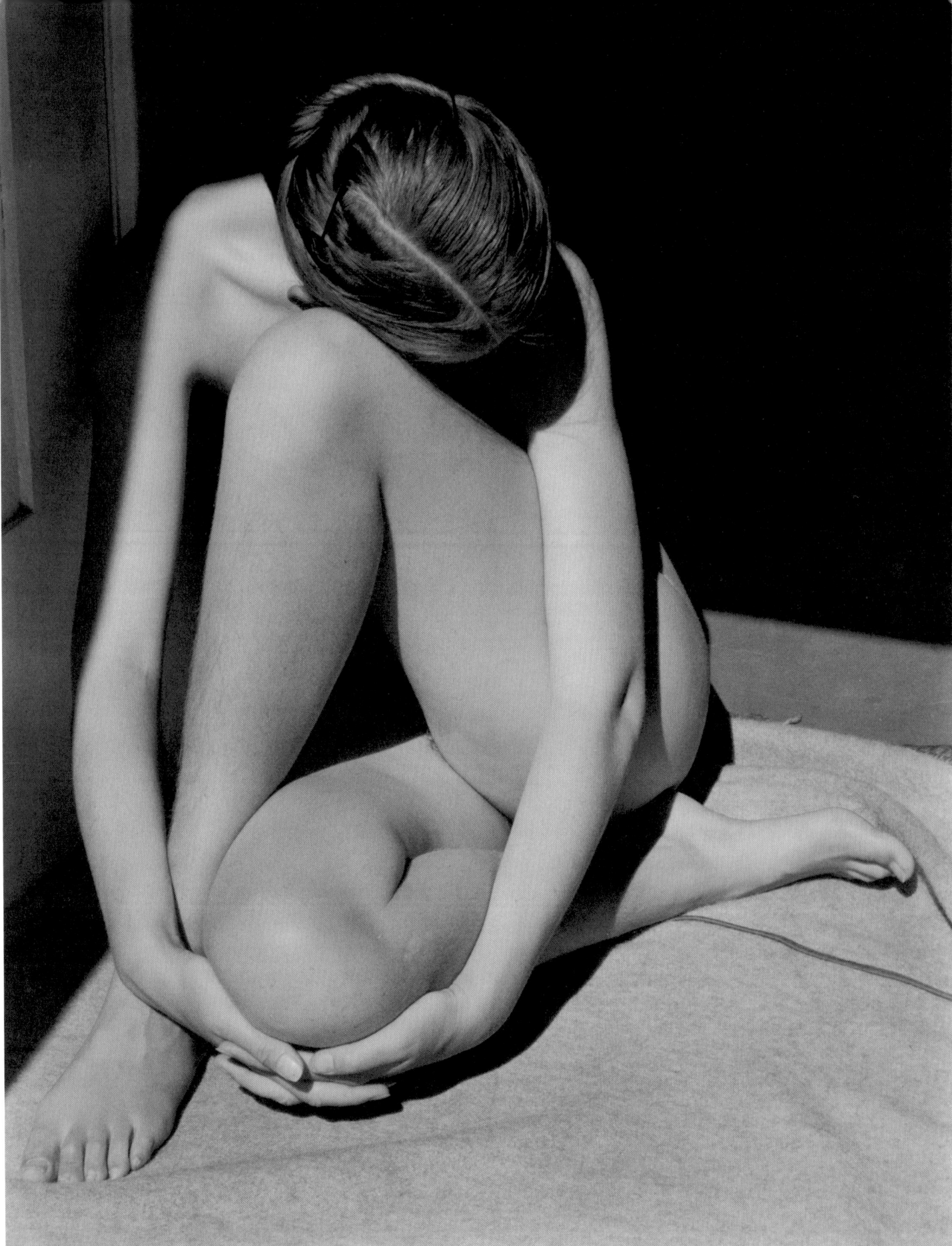

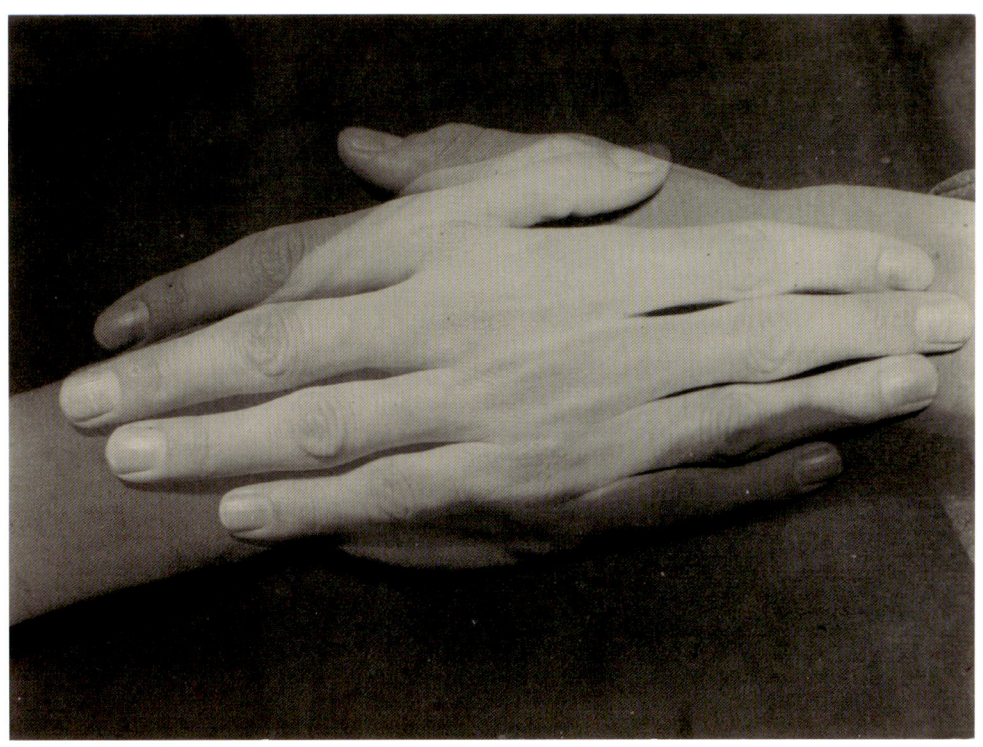

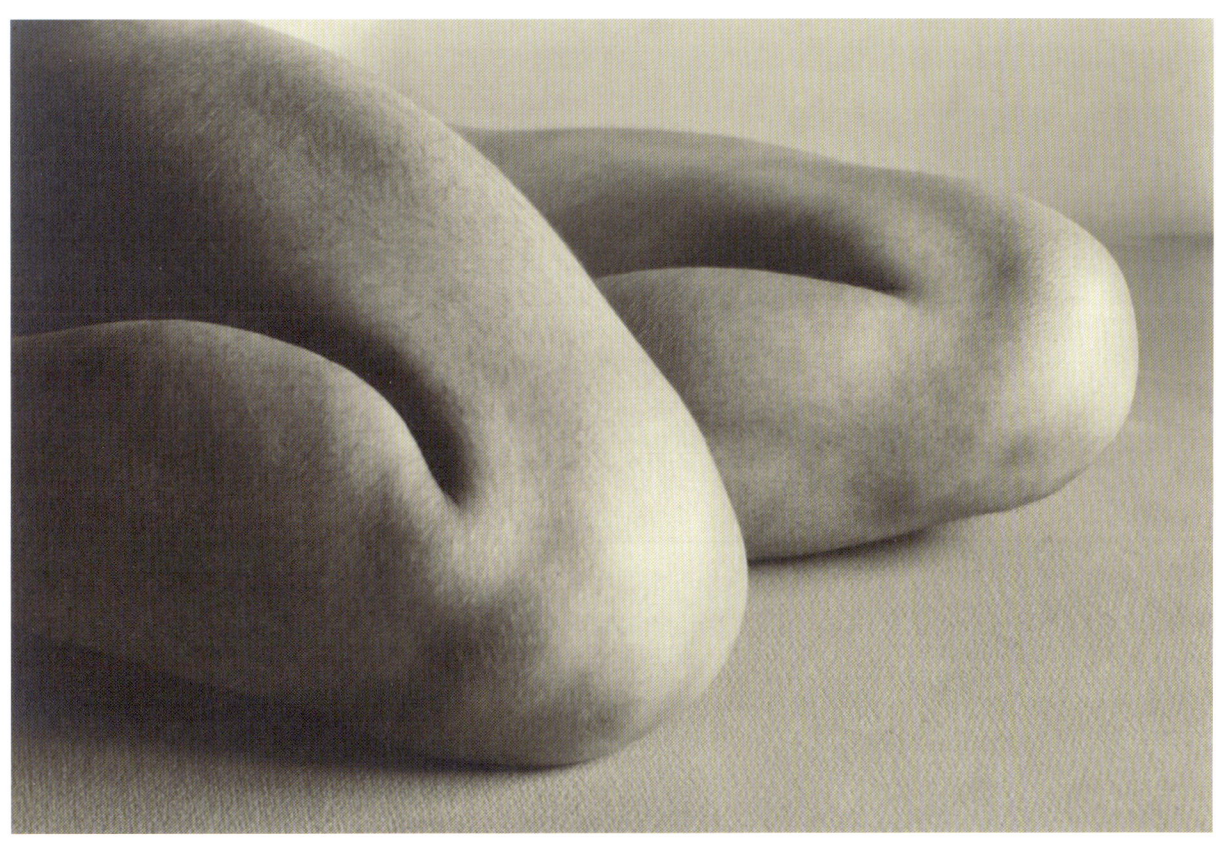

Opposite: **EDWARD WESTON** *Nude* 1936
24.1 × 19.1 cm

Top: **ELFRIEDE STEGEMEYER** *Otto's Hands* 1933, 12.7 × 17.8 cm
Above: **EDWARD WESTON** *Nude* 1927, 15.6 × 23.2 cm

153

HEINZ HAJEK-HALKE *Untitled (Nude)* c.1930, 23.5 × 17.1 cm

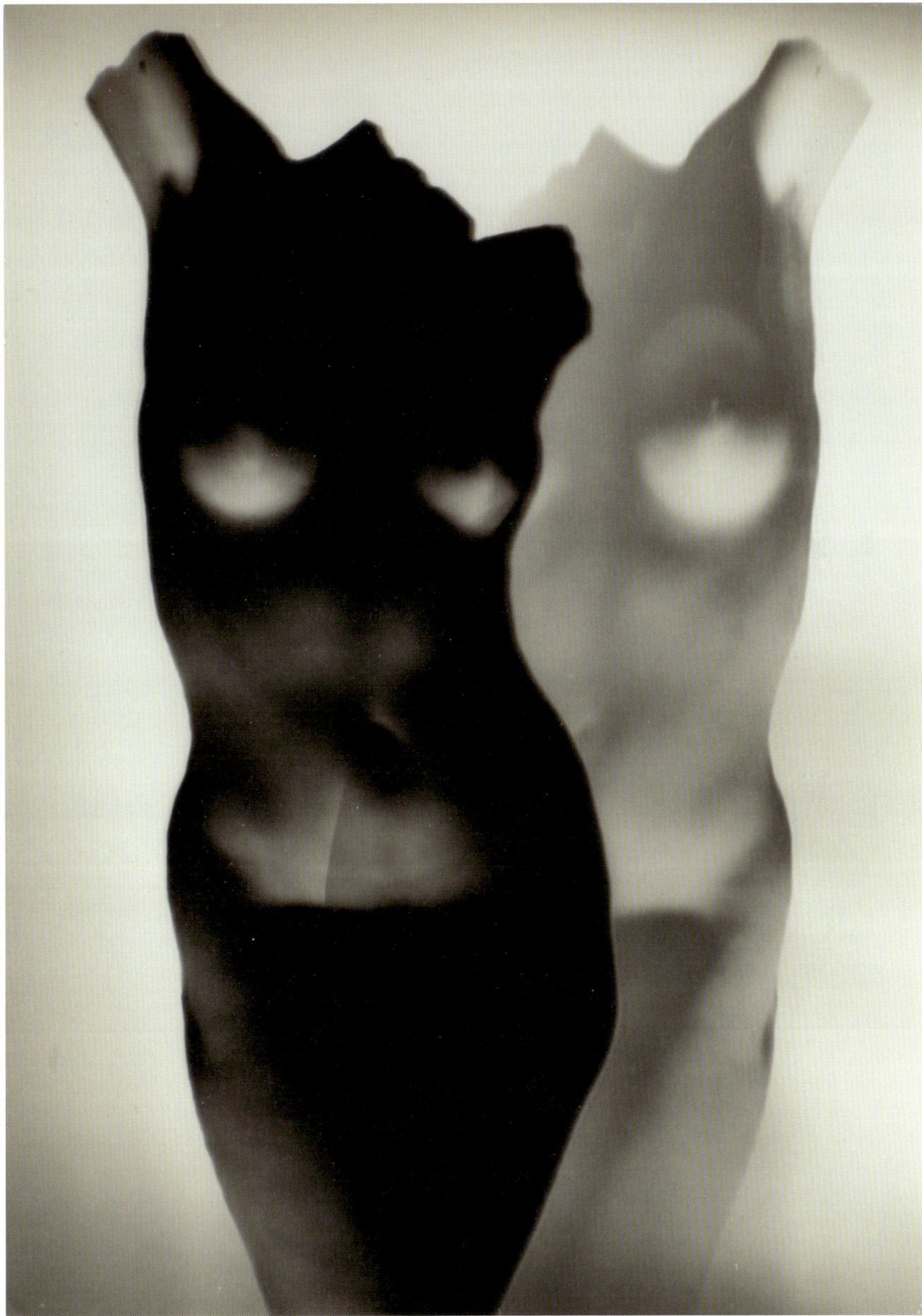

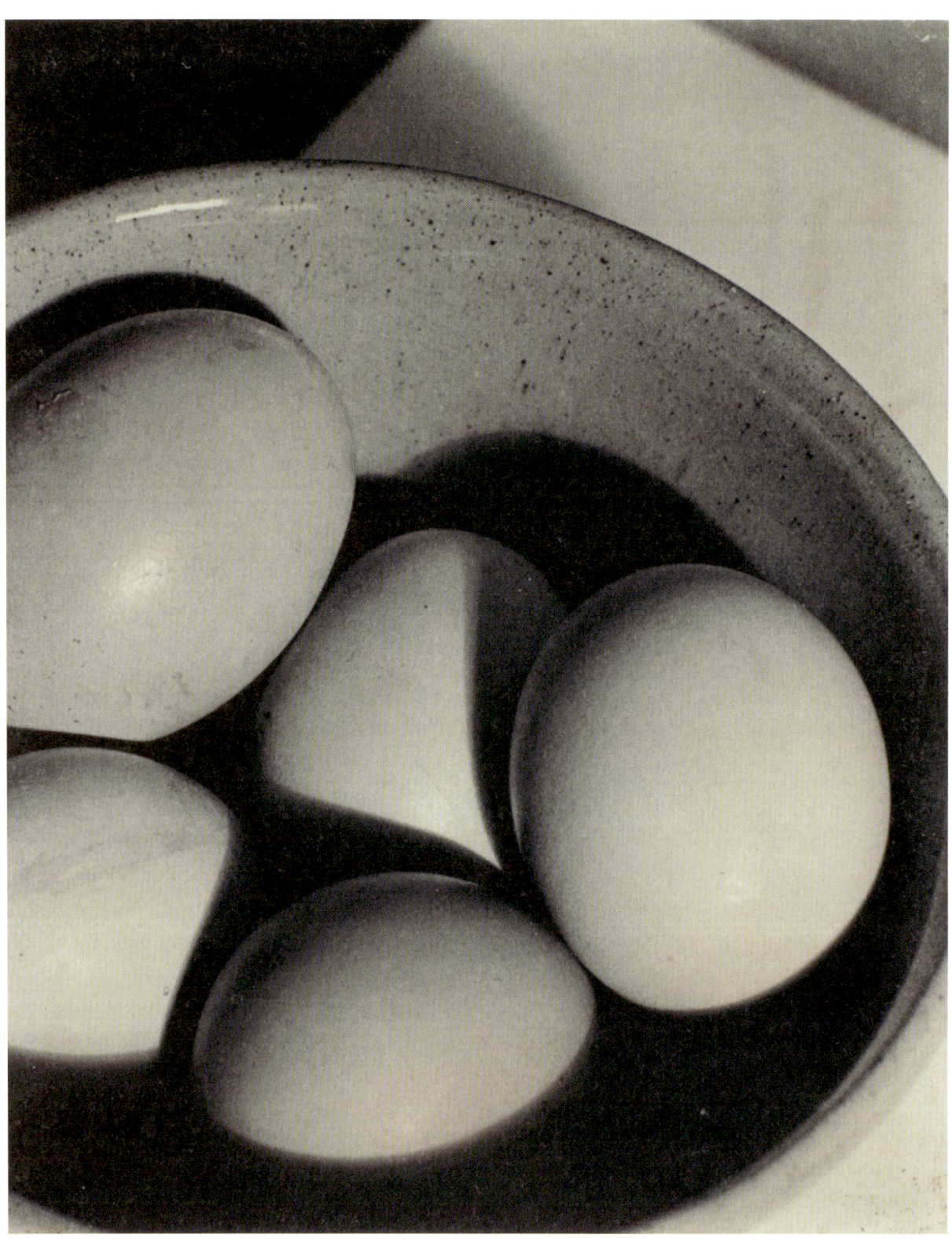

PAUL OUTERBRIDGE
Eggs in Bowl 1922
platinum print, 8.6 × 7.3 cm

OBJECTS

The still-life composition was one of photography's most important genres from its very earliest days. Not only did it suit the static subject matter necessitated by the minutes-long exposure times of early cameras, but it also provided the opportunity to illustrate photography's worth as fine art by replicating one of the most important traditions in painting.

By the first decades of the twentieth century, exploration of the camera's many possibilities had led to a shift away from the traditional still life – which featured organic subjects such as fruit and flowers, brought together for their symbolic significance – towards studies in which form took precedence. In place of objects arranged together for representational meaning were compositions featuring geometric lines and reflective surfaces, which echoed the fractured perspectives of cubist painting. Unconventional angles or extreme close-ups often replaced the customary frontal view, while the inclusion of man-made objects and synthetic materials not only celebrated industry, mechanisation and the ephemera of modern life, but also suggested that of all the media available to the artist, it was the camera that was best equipped to represent them.

One of the defining principles of modernist photography was the emphasis placed on the camera's ability to reveal the underlying truth of the subject. Not to aestheticise or interpret, but to allow the viewer to 'see' – in a way that the eye does not – through judicious use of lighting, composition, angle and proximity. This 'pure' or, as it would come to be known, 'straight' photography had been promoted by Paul Strand in the journal *Camera Work* as early as 1917 and would later be investigated and refined by photographers associated with Neue Sachlichkeit (New Objectivity) in Germany and, in the United States, with Group f.64 (on the West Coast) and precisionism (on the East).

At the Bauhaus in Germany – which was highly influential in collapsing the boundary between fine and applied art – foundation courses included 'object lessons' in which students' understanding of how texture and form translate photographically was developed. Experimentations with table-top arrangements of everyday things – from the organic (eggs), to the material (string), or the technical (mathematical equipment, for example) – helped demonstrate balance in composition, how light and shadow can transform how we read surfaces, or even the visual satisfaction to be gleaned from a straight line or a curve in their purest form.

Some of the most instructive examples of modernist object studies produced internationally were advertisements for products. In America, significant contributions to the commercial still-life genre emanated from the Clarence H. White School of Photography. Though White had led the pictorialist movement there, his school's design-led curriculum equipped the younger generation with techniques that could be successfully applied to commercial commissions, including exercises in still-life design. From the early 1920s, popular magazines were filled with the work of its alumni, among them Margaret Bourke-White, Ralph Steiner and Paul Outerbridge. EL

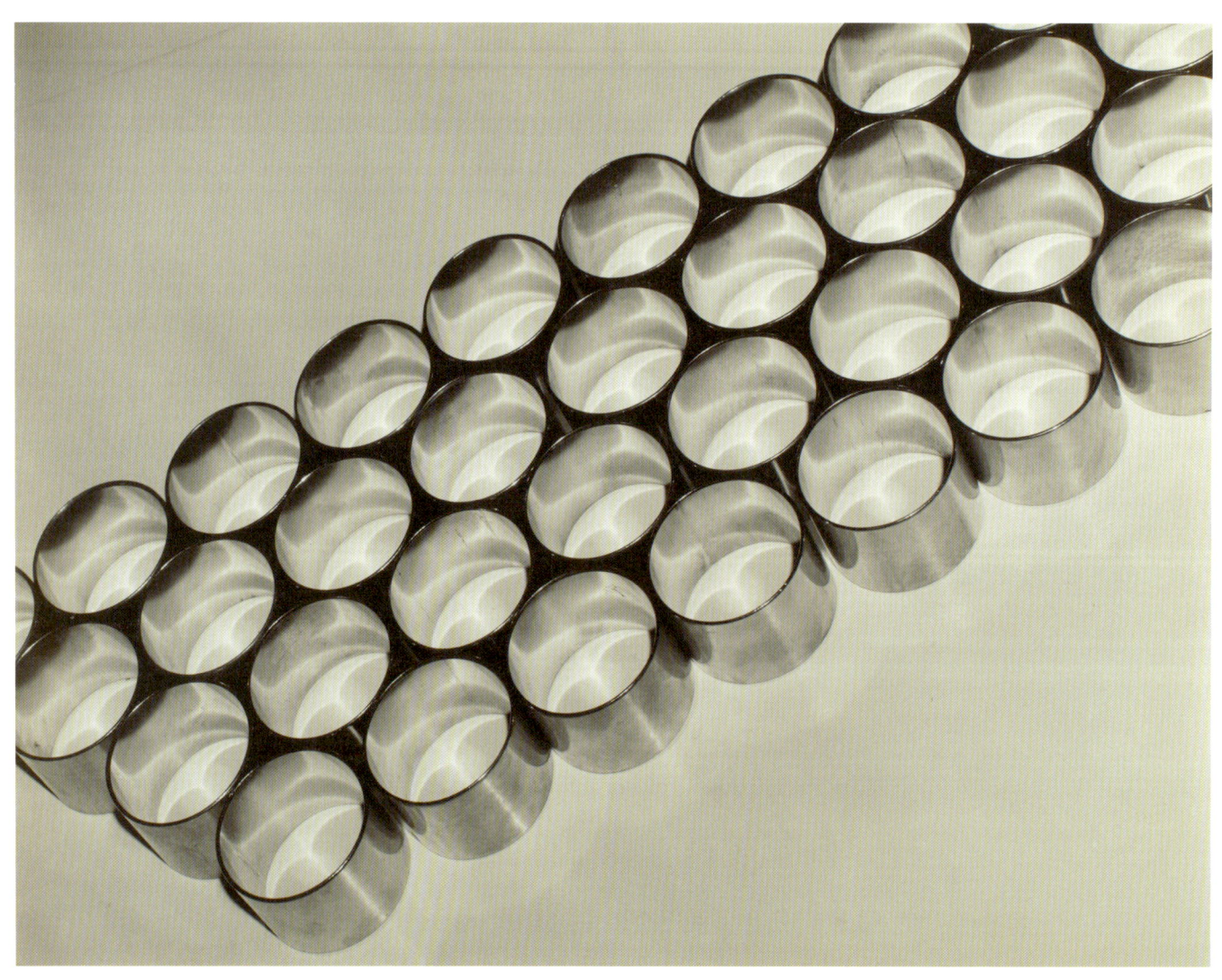

Emmanuel Sougez *Interference* c.1930s, 27.6 × 36.5 cm

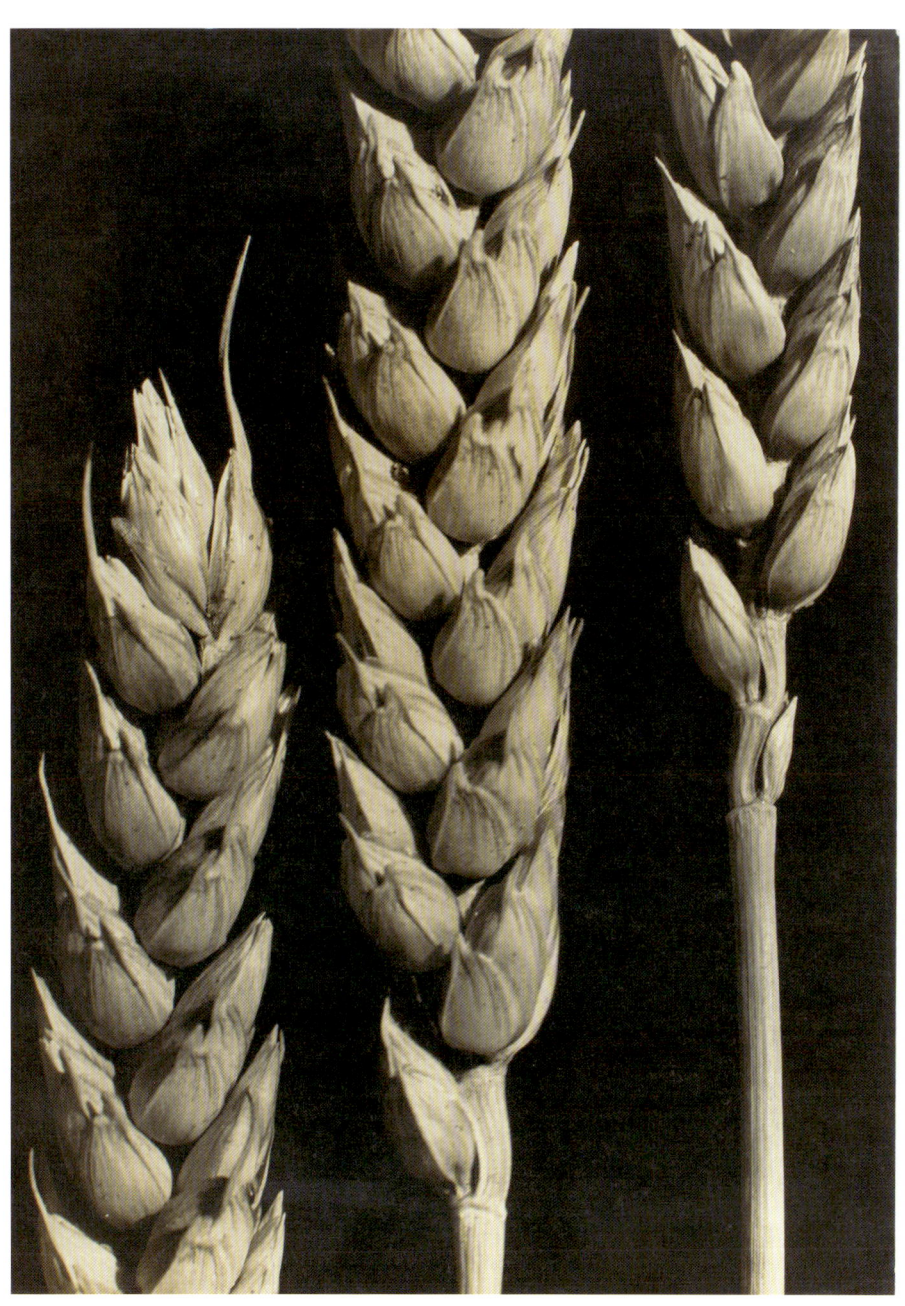

Emmanuel Sougez *Three Ears of Wheat* 1929, 37.8 × 27 cm

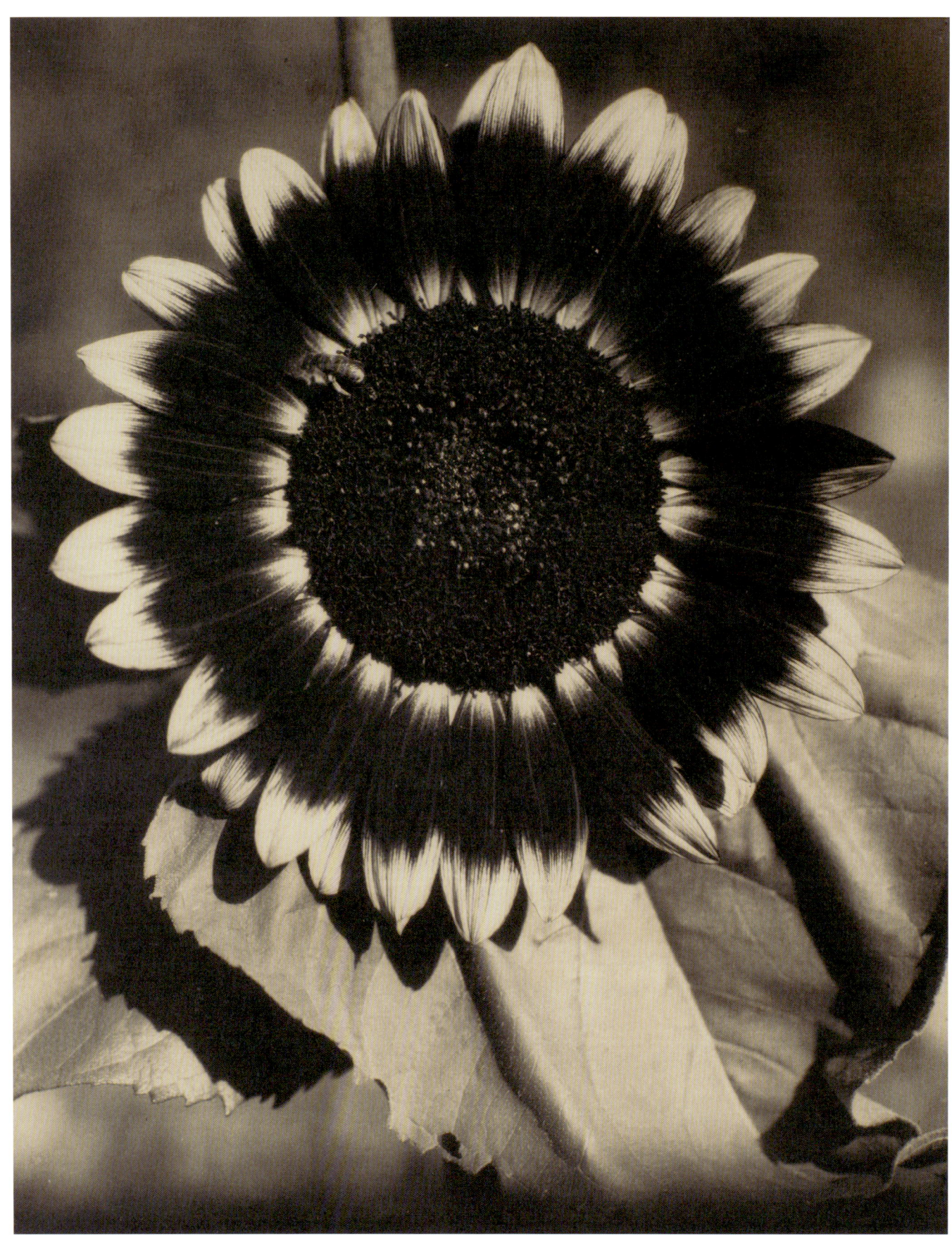

EDWARD STEICHEN *A Bee on a Sunflower* c.1920
palladium print, 24.1 × 19.7 cm

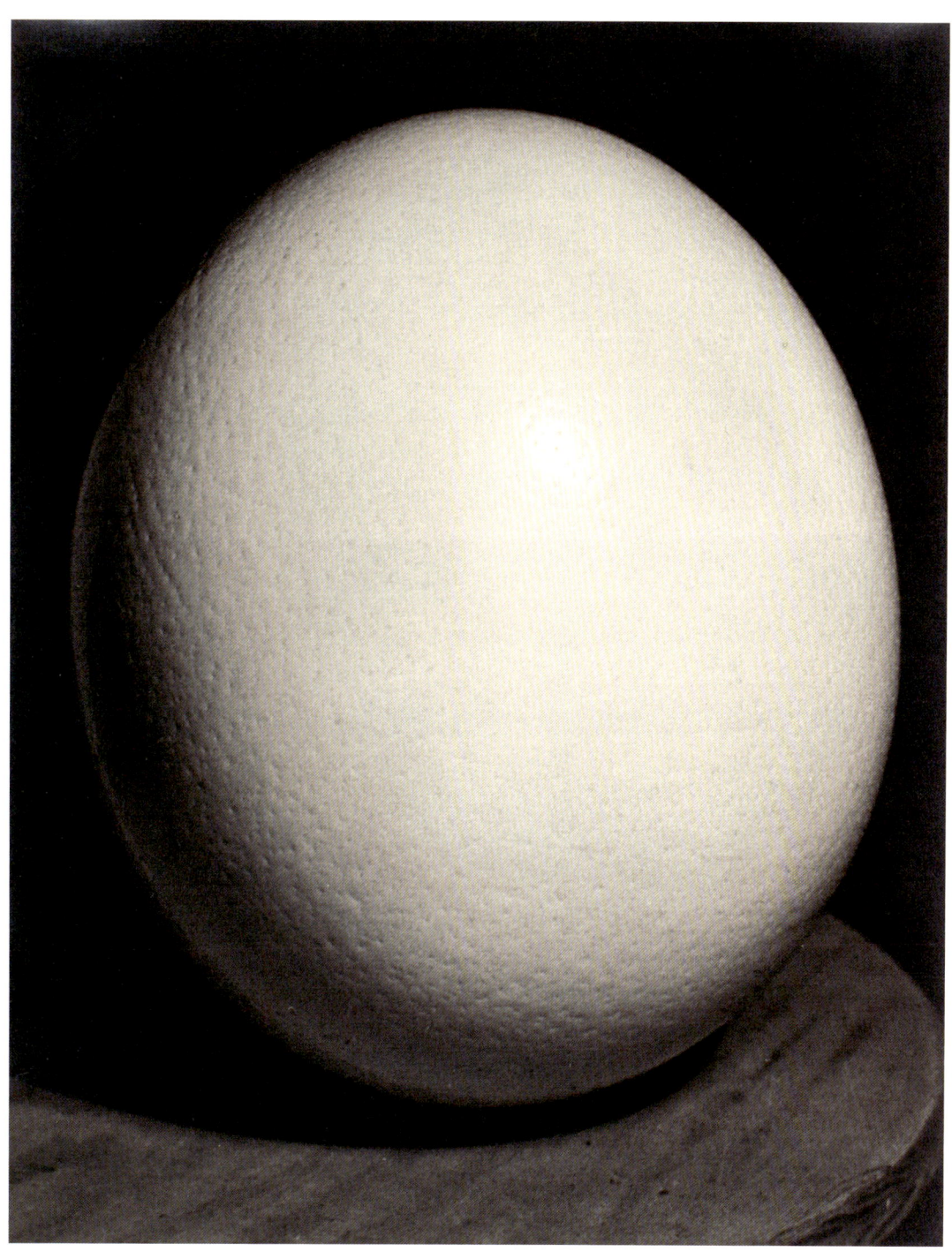

MAN RAY *Ostrich Egg* 1944, 25.1 × 22.2 cm

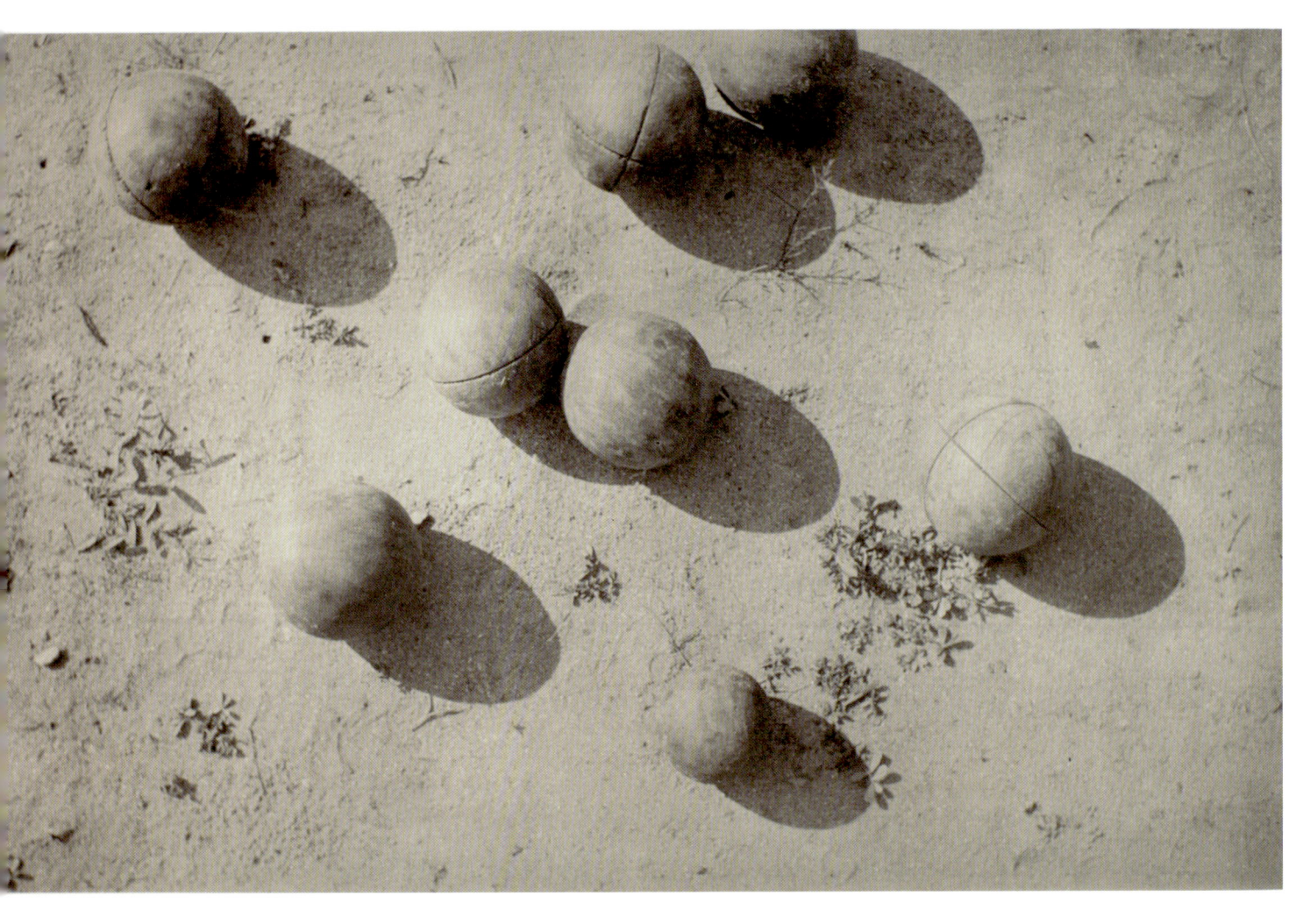

HERBERT BAYER *Boules* 1928, 14 × 21 cm

JOSEF SUDEK *Ladislav Sutnar China (Tea Cups)*
c.1930, 16.2 × 22.5 cm

162

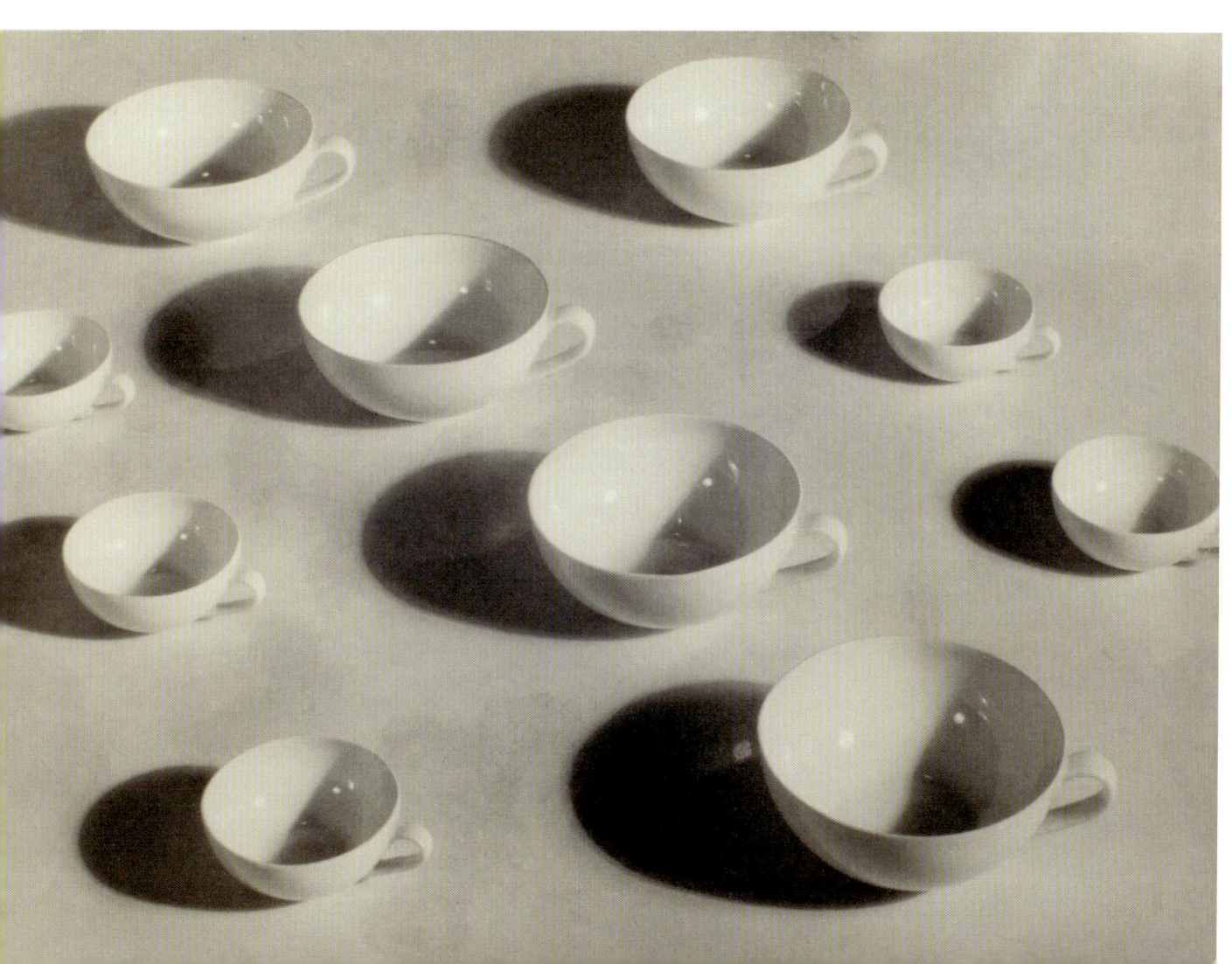

Imogen Cunningham *Magnolia Blossom* 1925, 19.1 × 23.5 cm

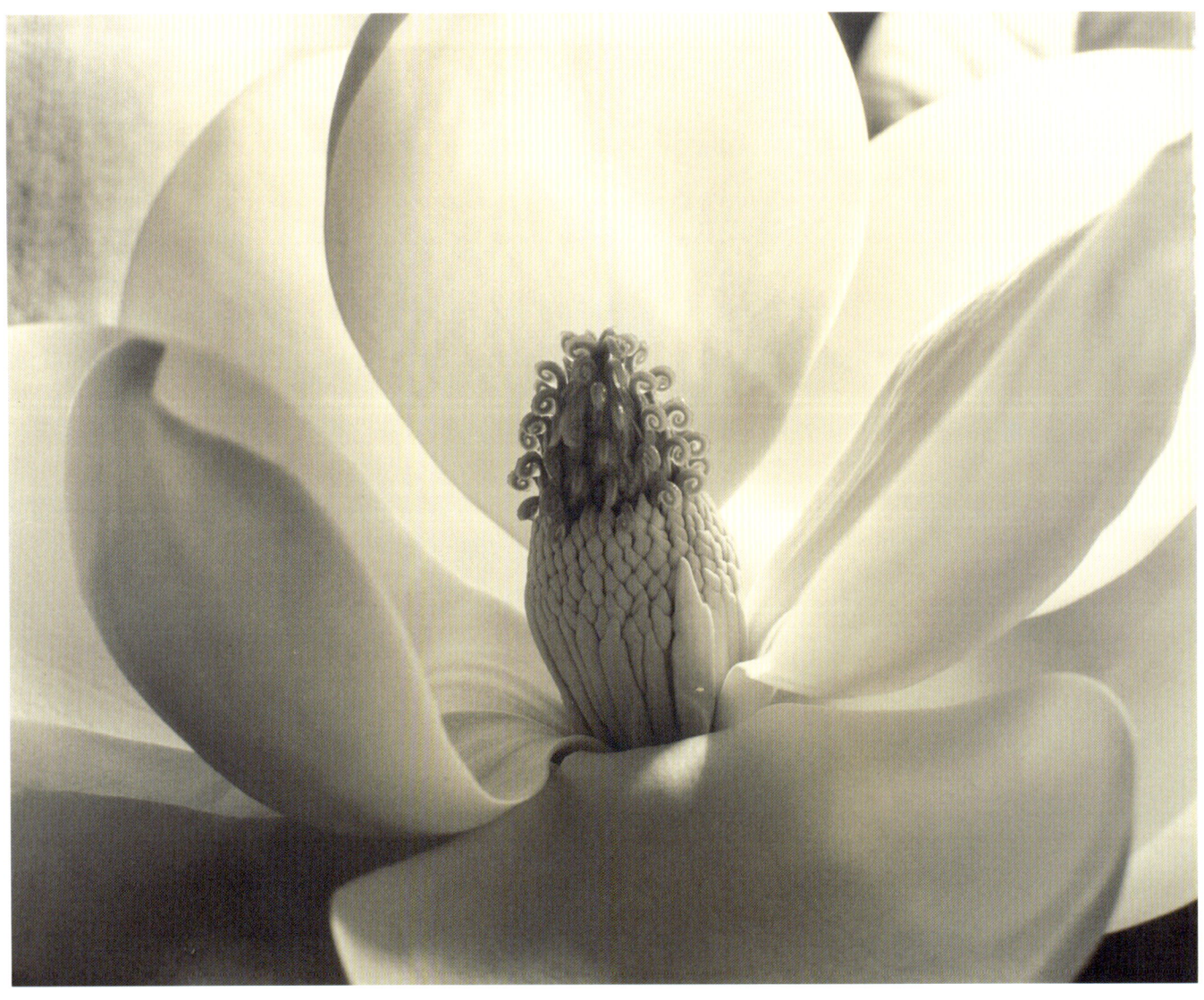

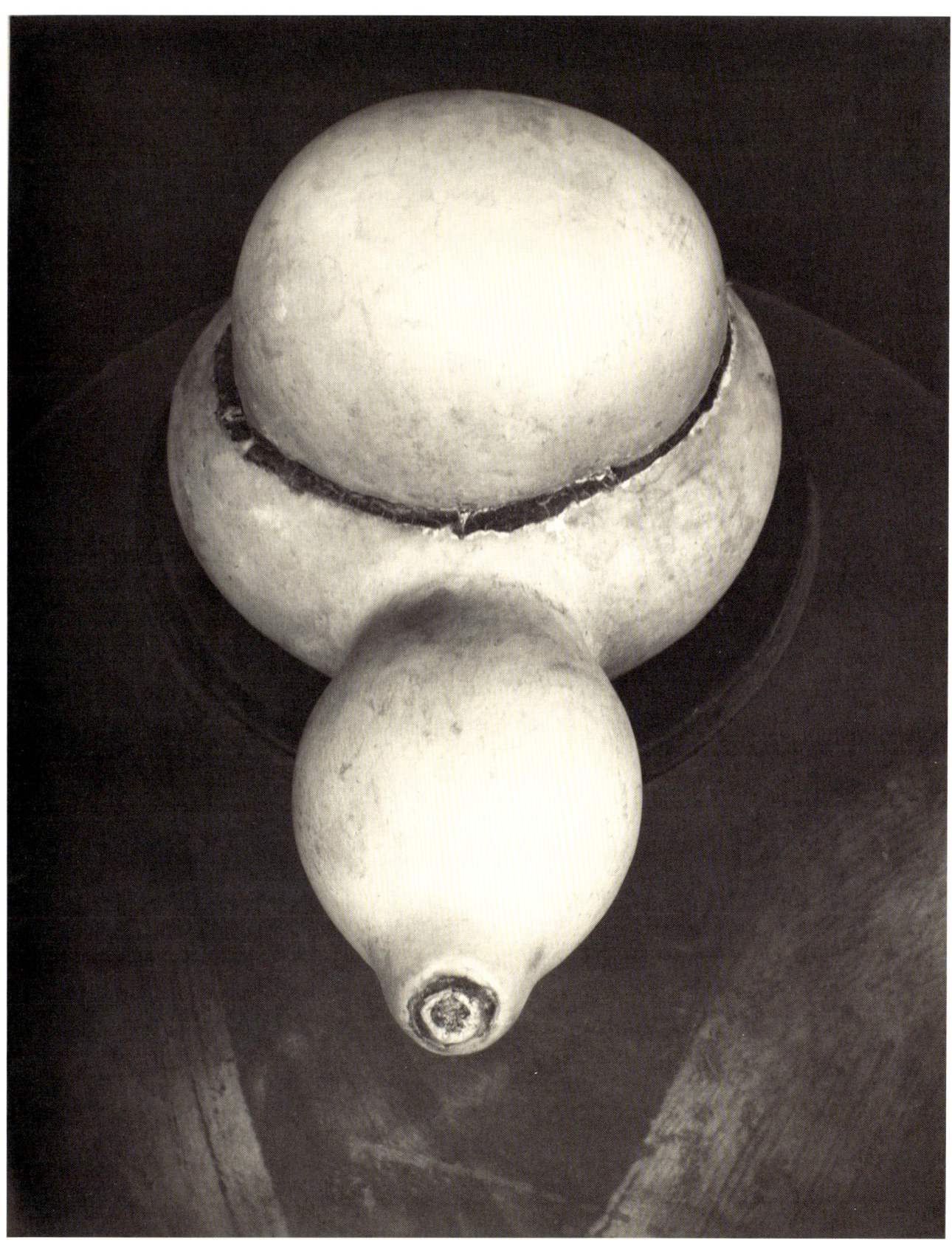

EDWARD WESTON *Gourd* 1927, 24.1 × 19.1 cm

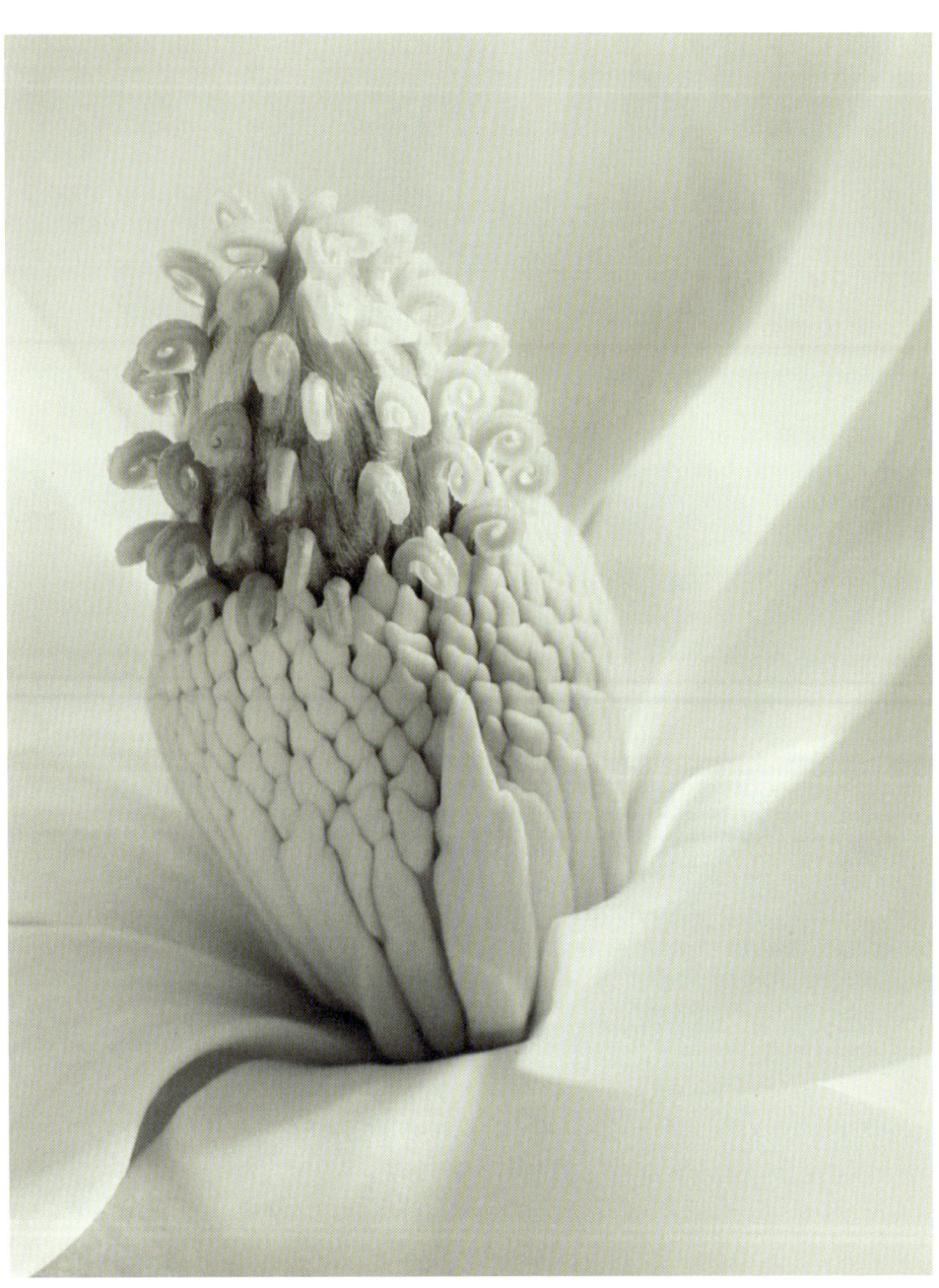

IMOGEN CUNNINGHAM *Magnolia Blossom, Tower of Jewels* 1925, 24.1 × 18.4 cm

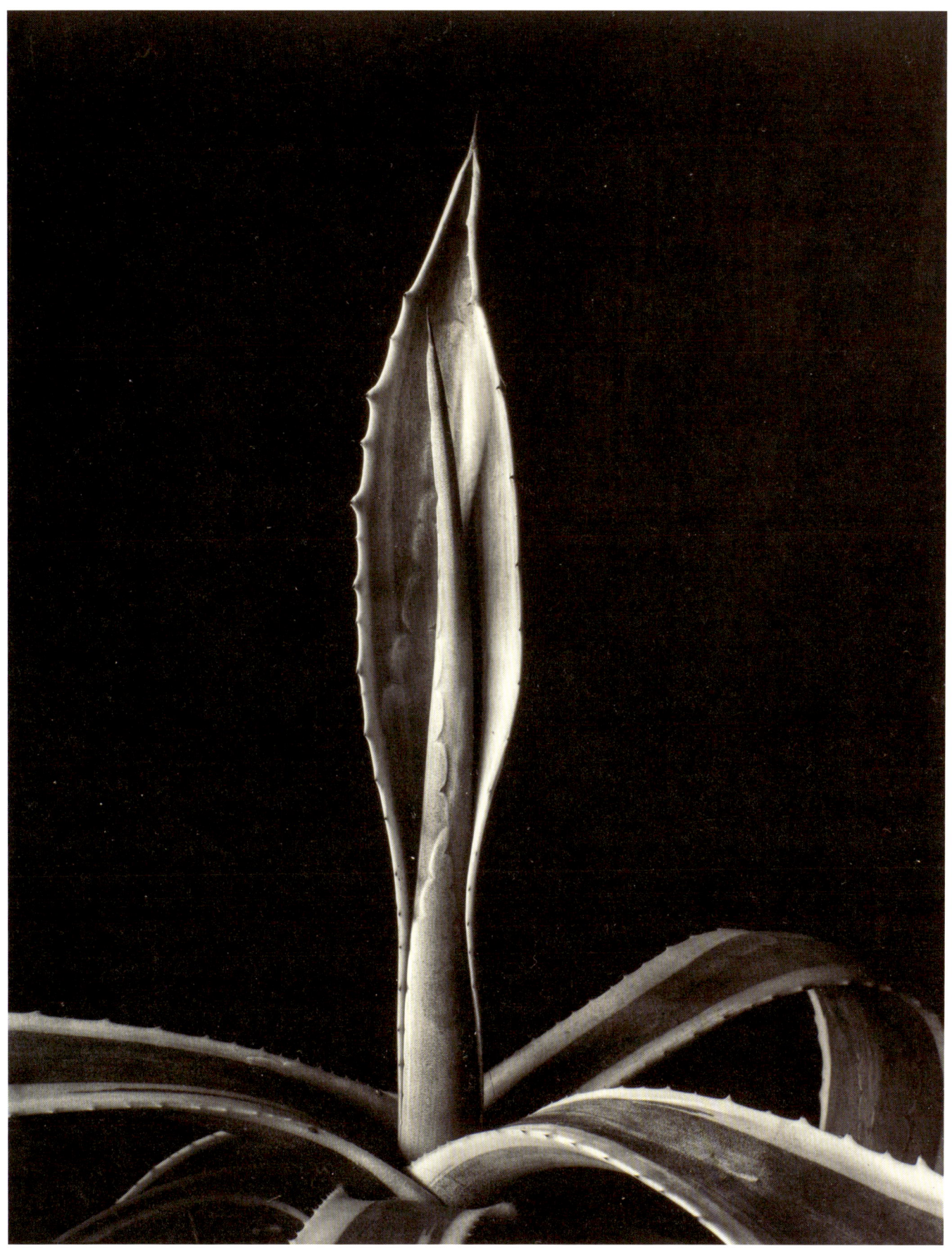

Imogen Cunningham *Agave* 1920s, 24.1 × 19.1 cm

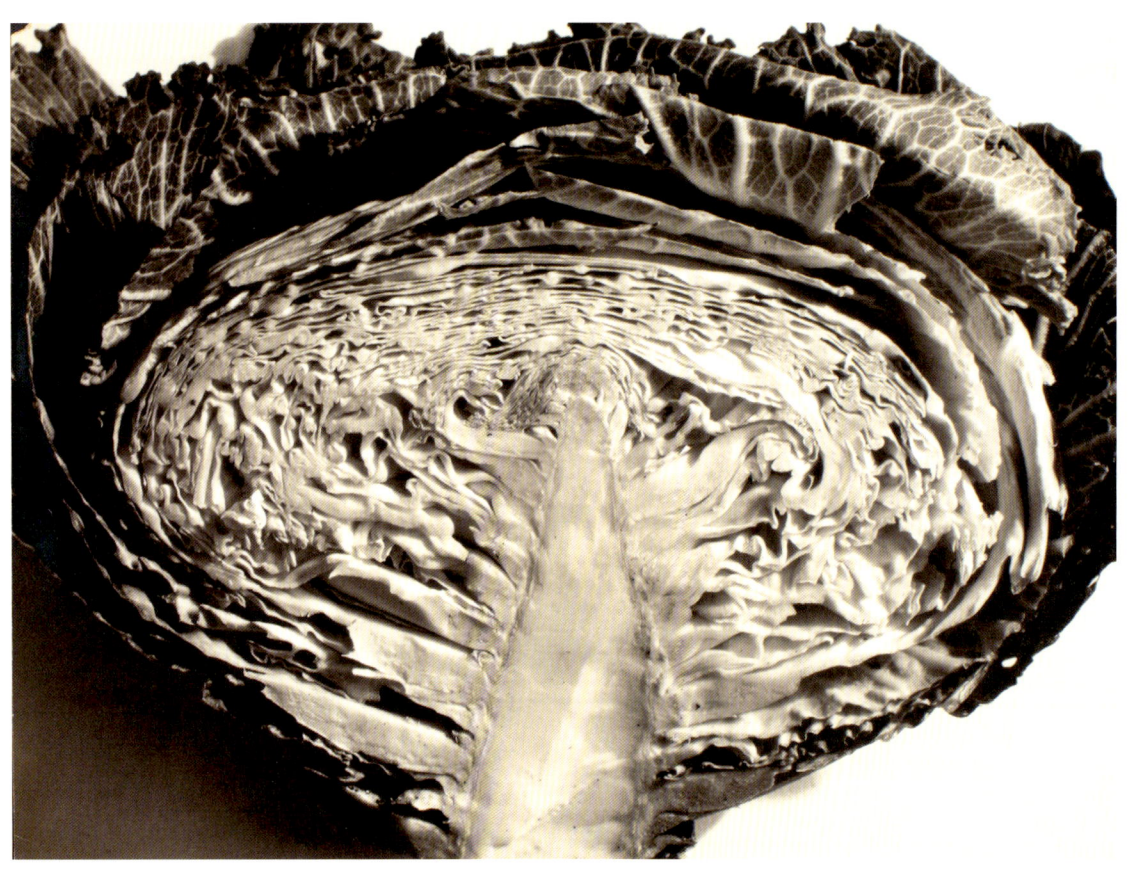

EMMANUEL SOUGEZ *Cabbage* 1929, 27.3 × 37.1 cm

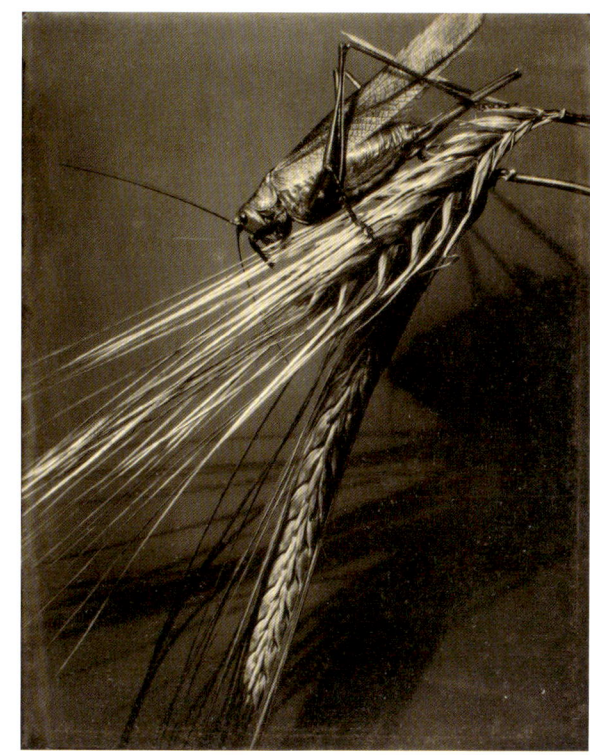

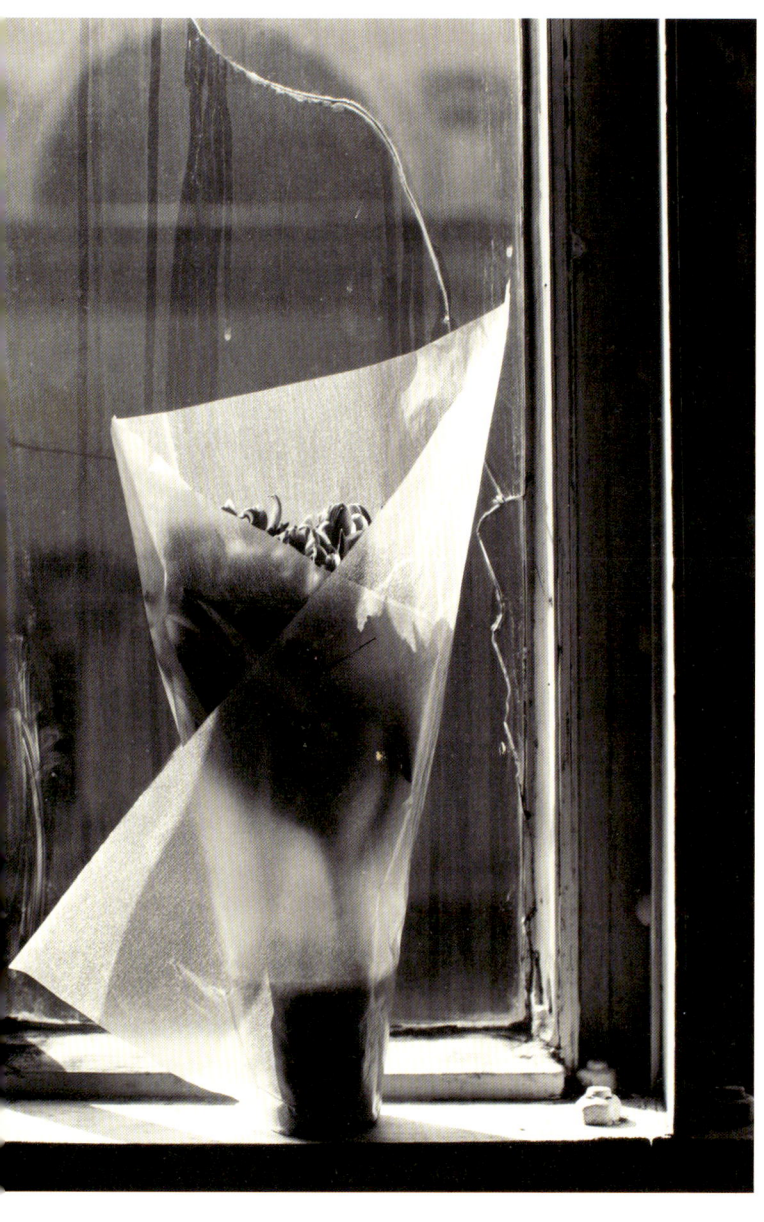

Above: **EDWARD STEICHEN** *Grasshopper on Wheatstalk*
c.1920, 25.4 × 20.3 cm

Left: **EMMANUEL SOUGEZ** *The Pot of Tulips*
1932, 35.9 × 27.3 cm

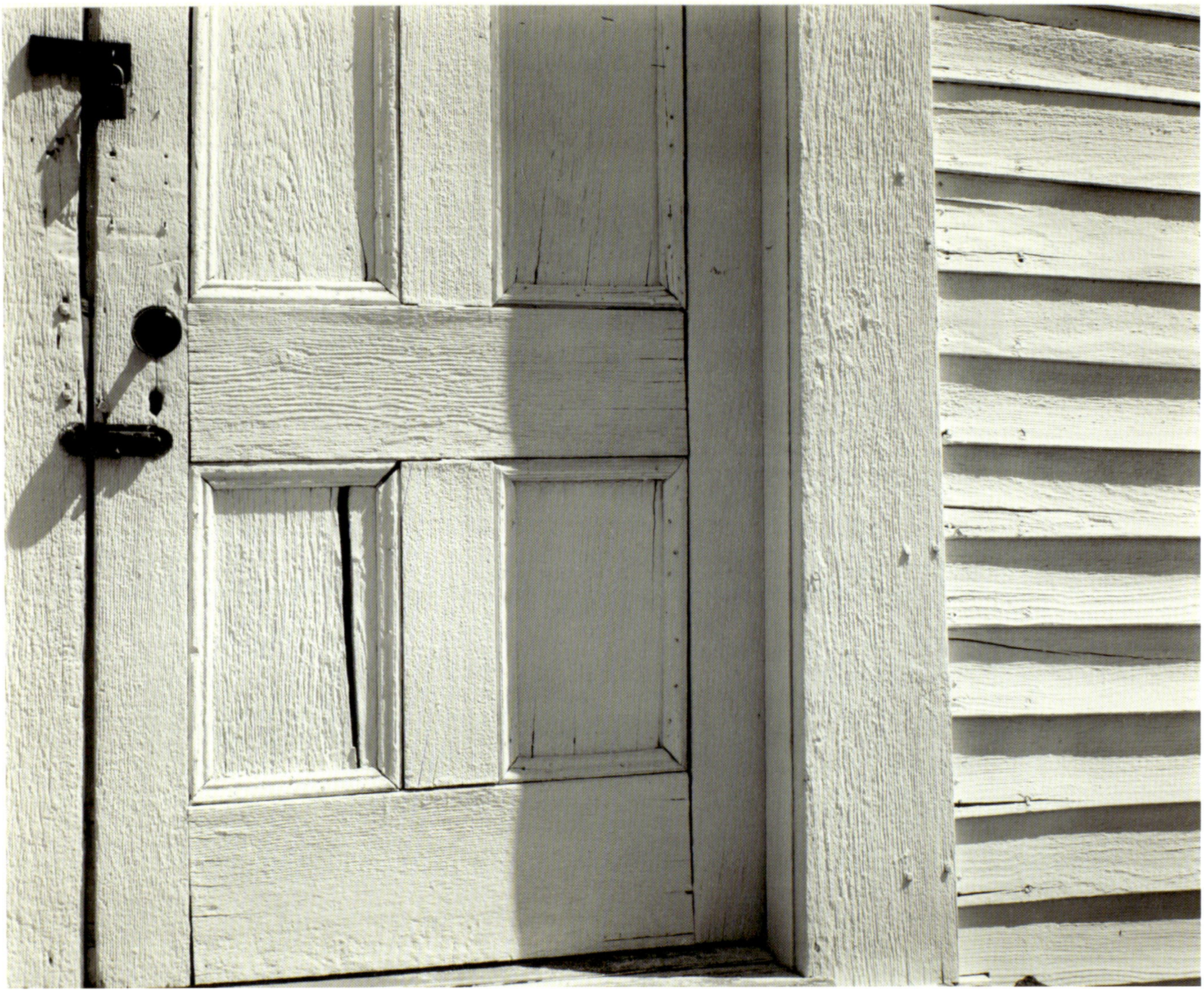

Above: **EDWARD WESTON**
Church Door, Hornitos
1940, 19.1 × 24.1 cm

Right: **ANDRÉ KERTÉSZ**
Homing Ship, Central Park,
New York 1944, 11.7 × 15.2 cm

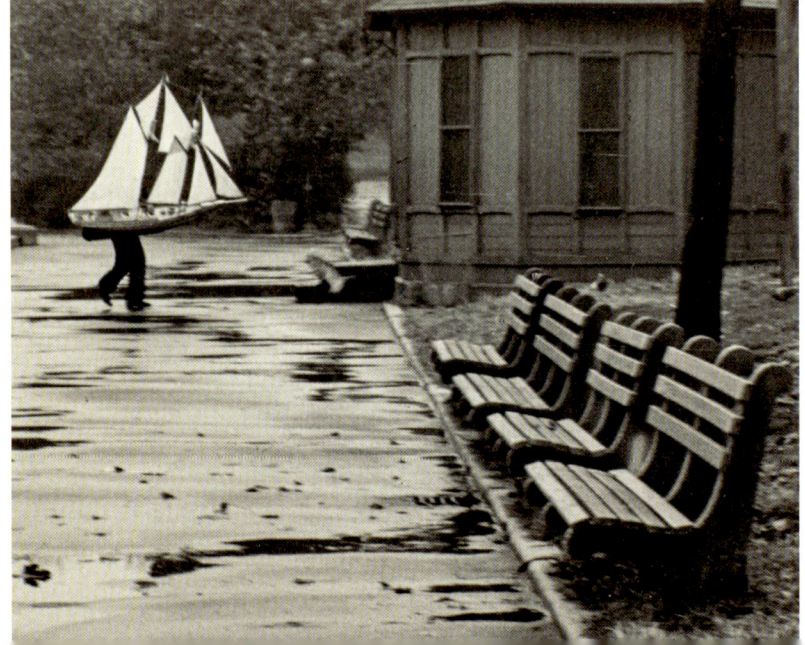

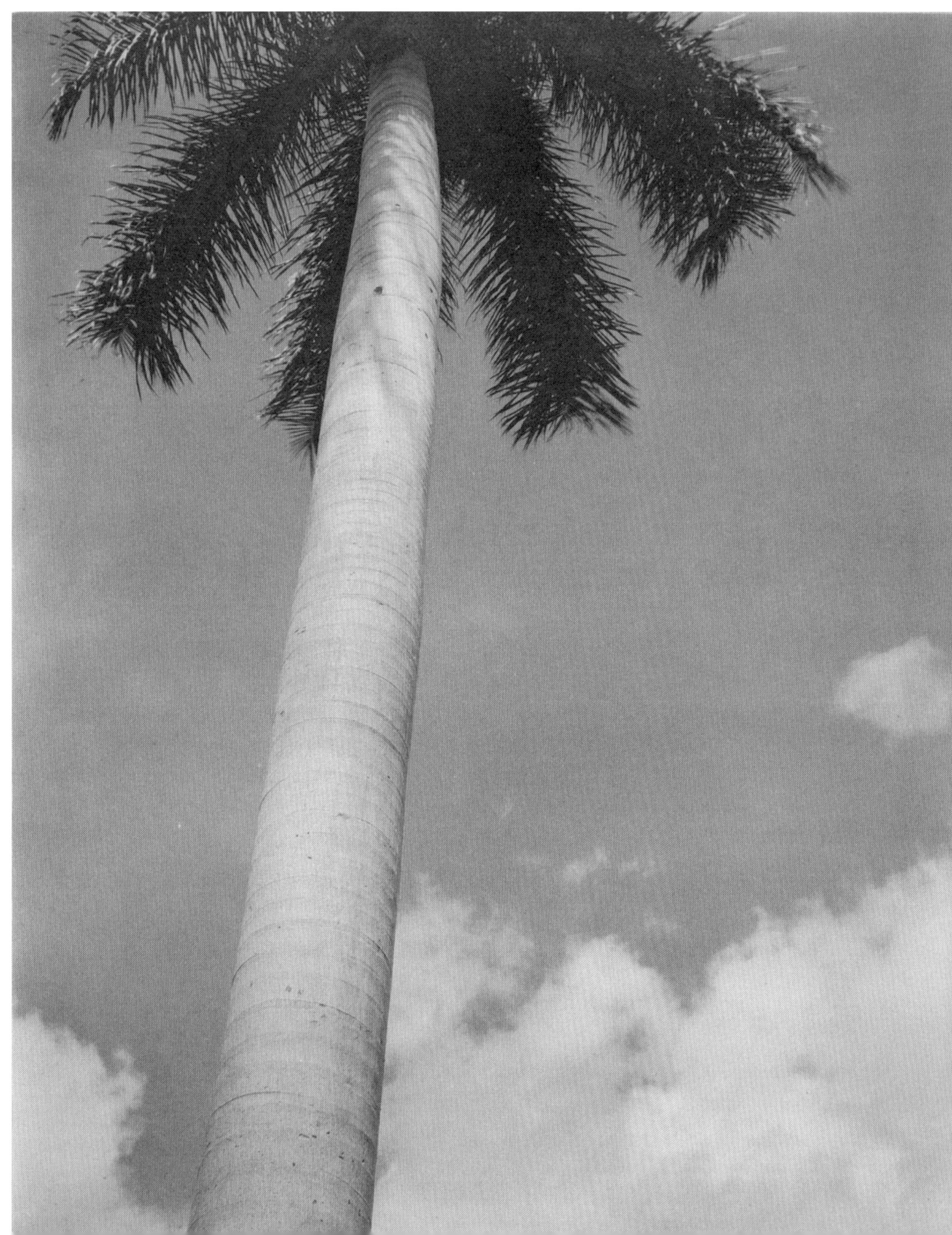

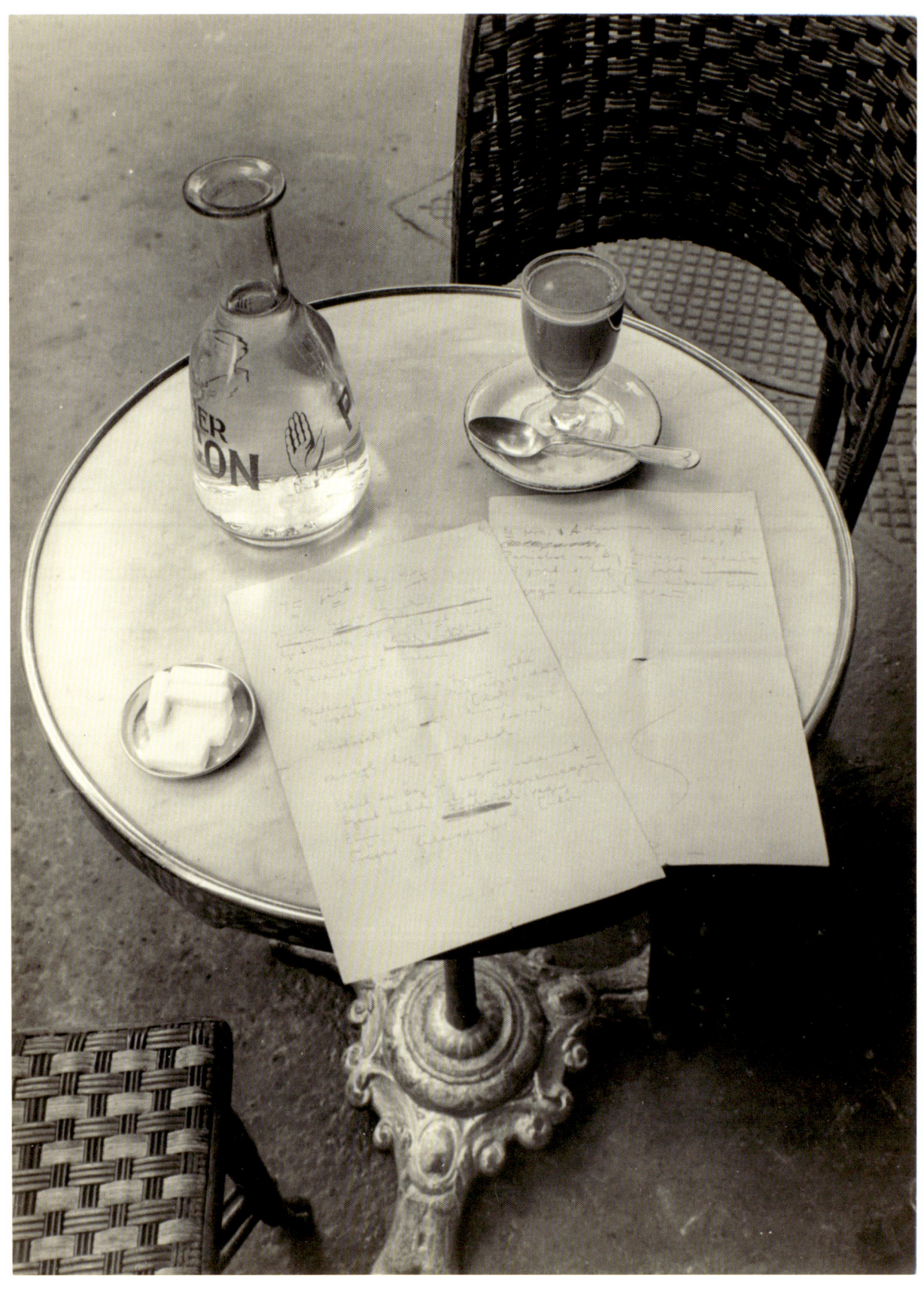

André Kertész *Ady's Poem* 1934, 22.9 × 17.1 cm

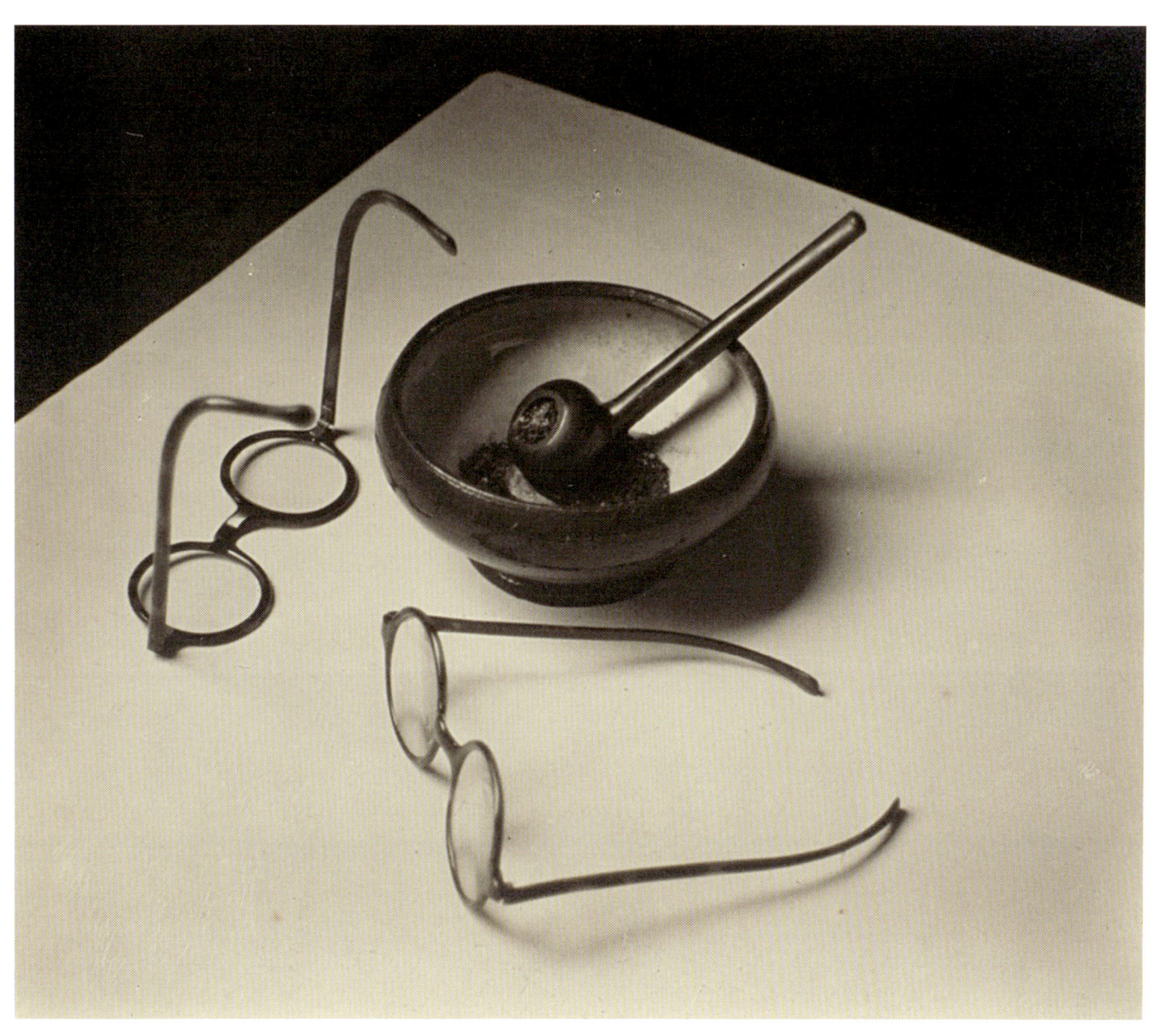

André Kertész *Mondrian's Eyeglasses and Pipe, Paris 1926, 7.6 × 8.9 cm*

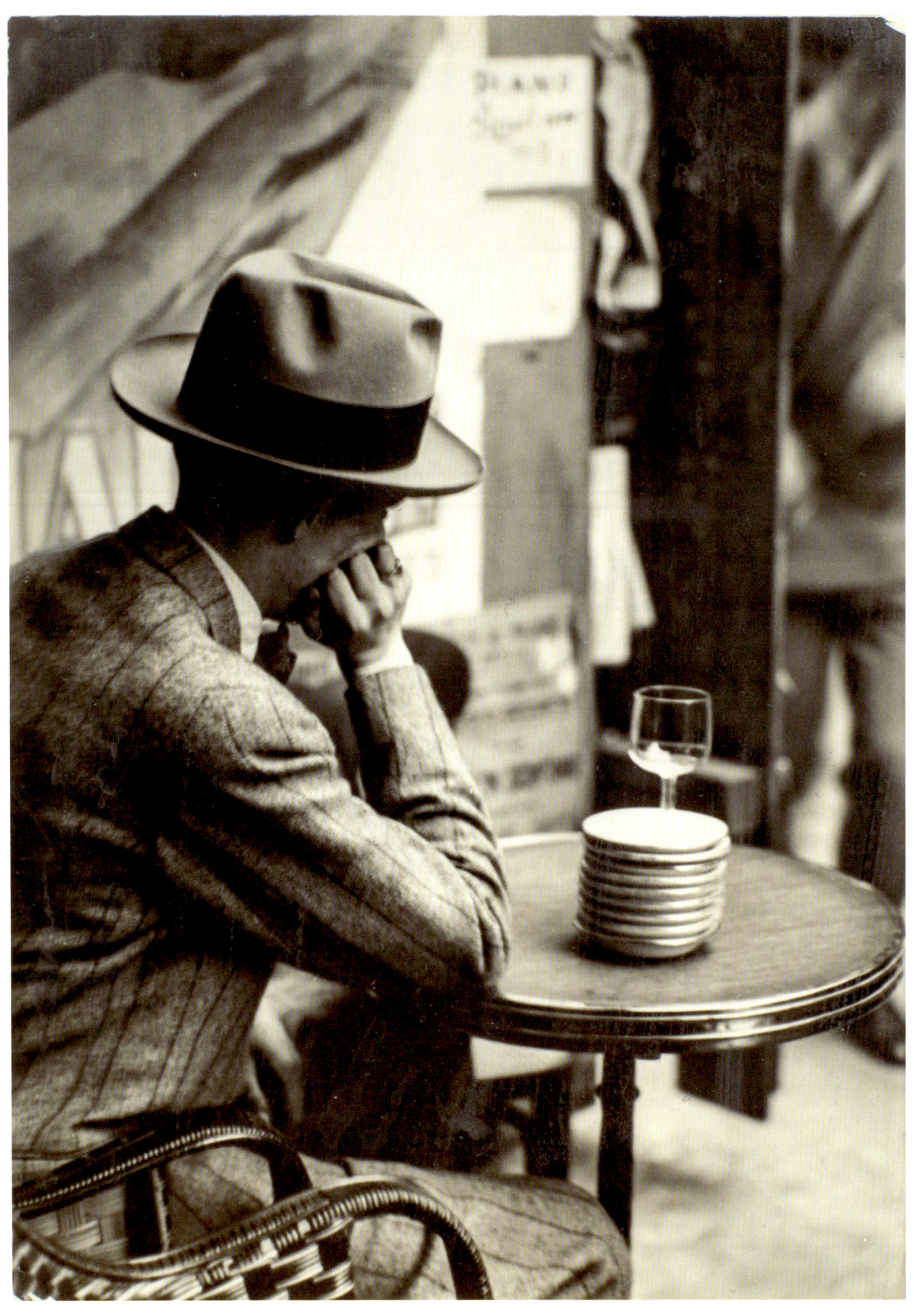

André Kertész *Outside Café*, Paris c.1928, 20 × 14.6 cm

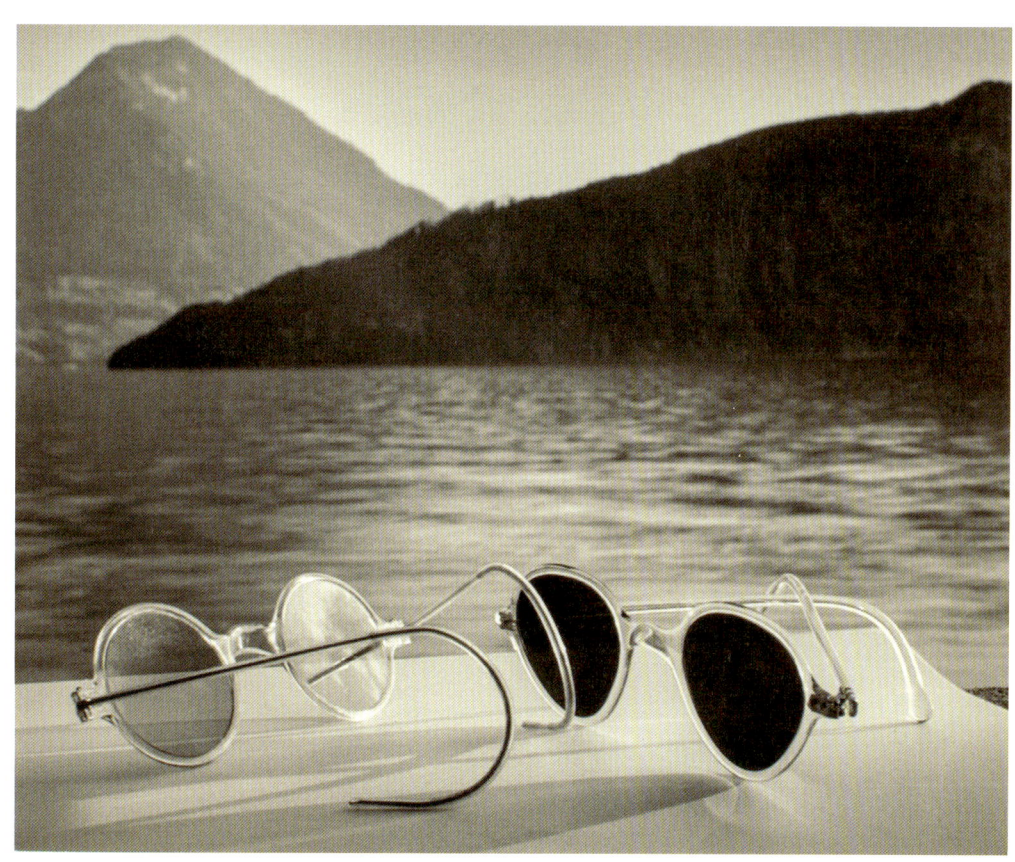

Herbert List *Lake Lucerne, Switzerland 1936, 22.2 × 27.9 cm*

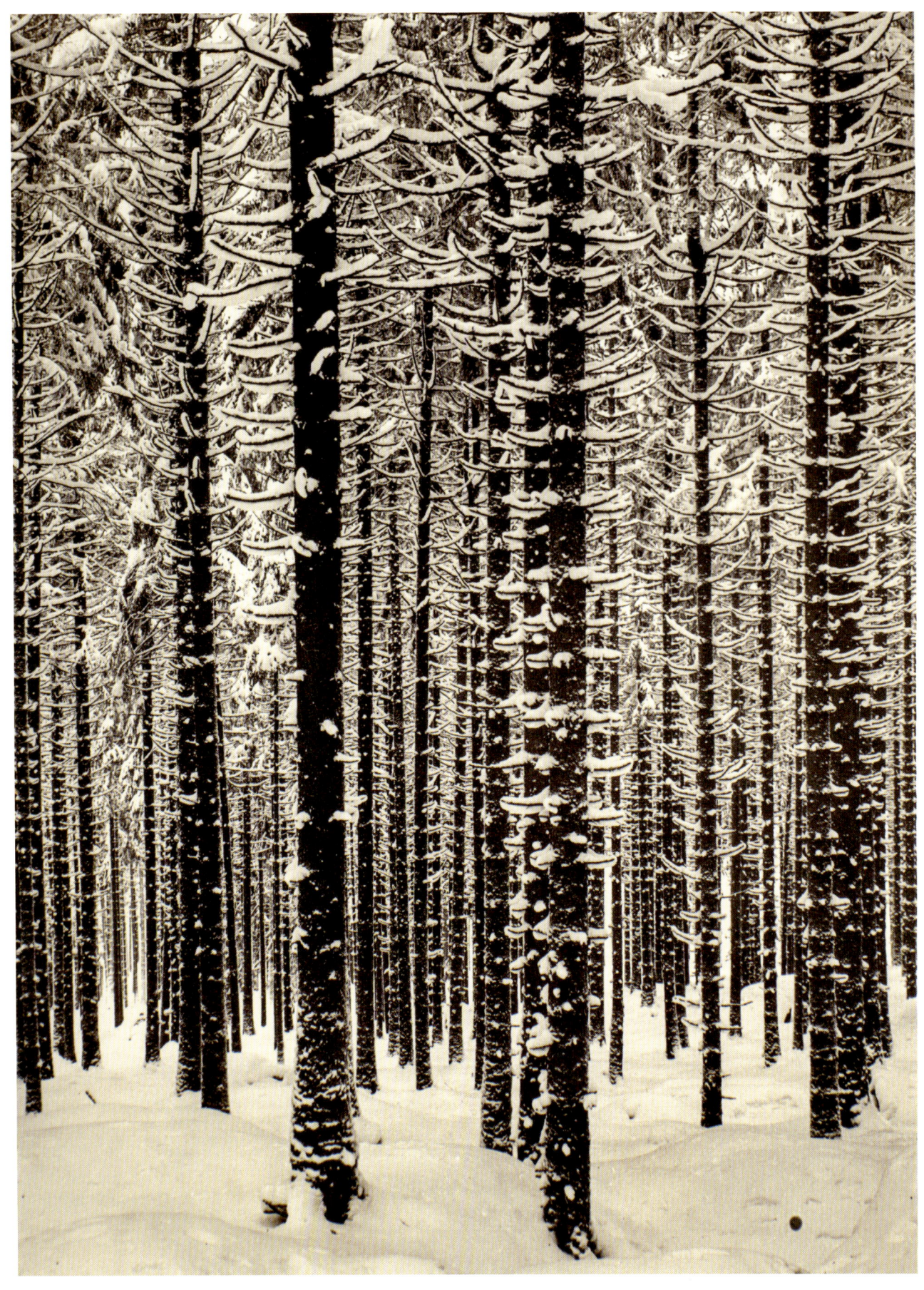

ALBERT RENGER-PATZSCH *Mountain Forest in Winter* 1926, 22.5 × 16.5 cm

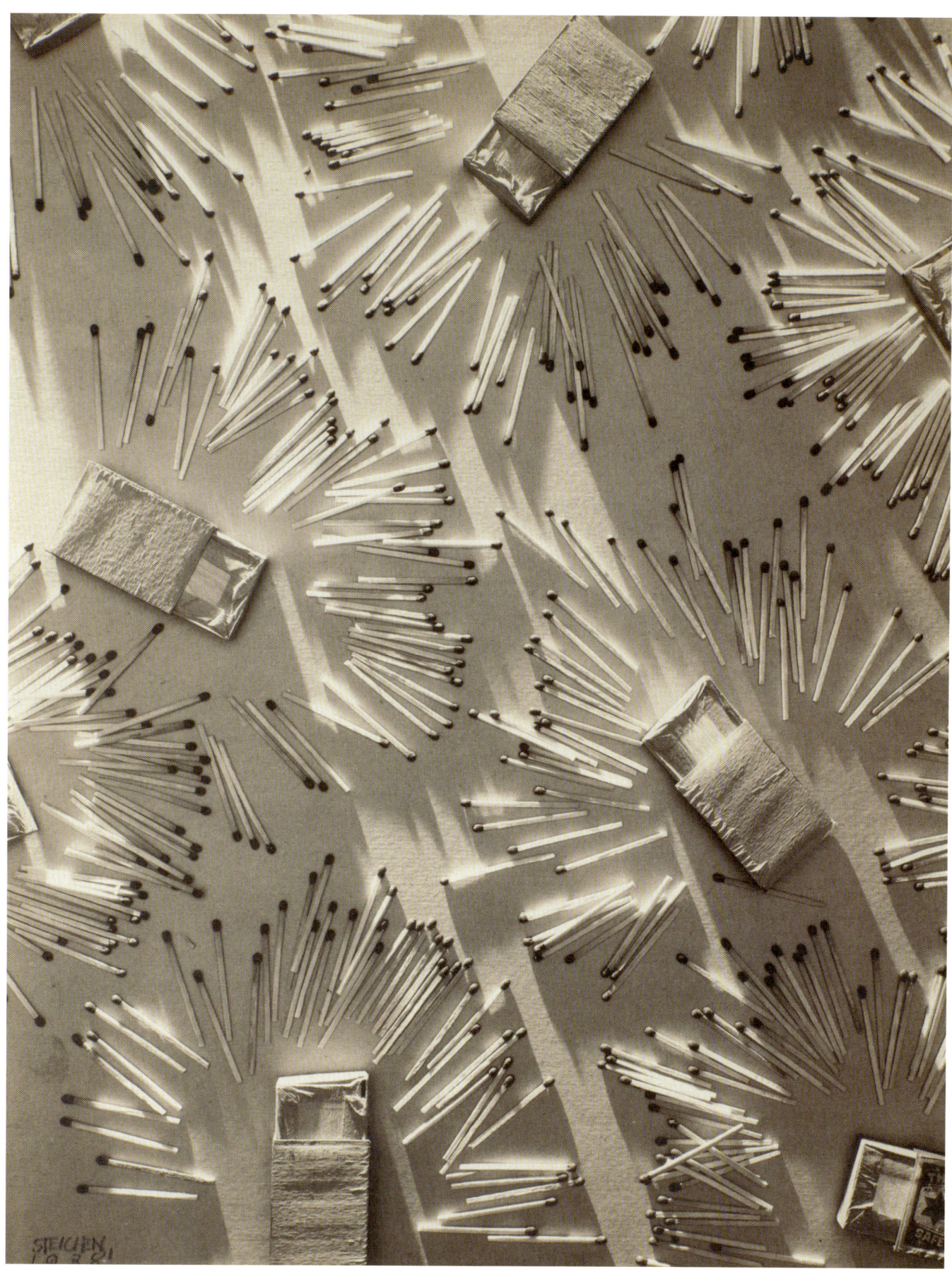

Edward Steichen *Matches and Matchboxes, Fabric Design for Stehli Silks* 1926, printed 1938, 23.5 × 19.1 cm

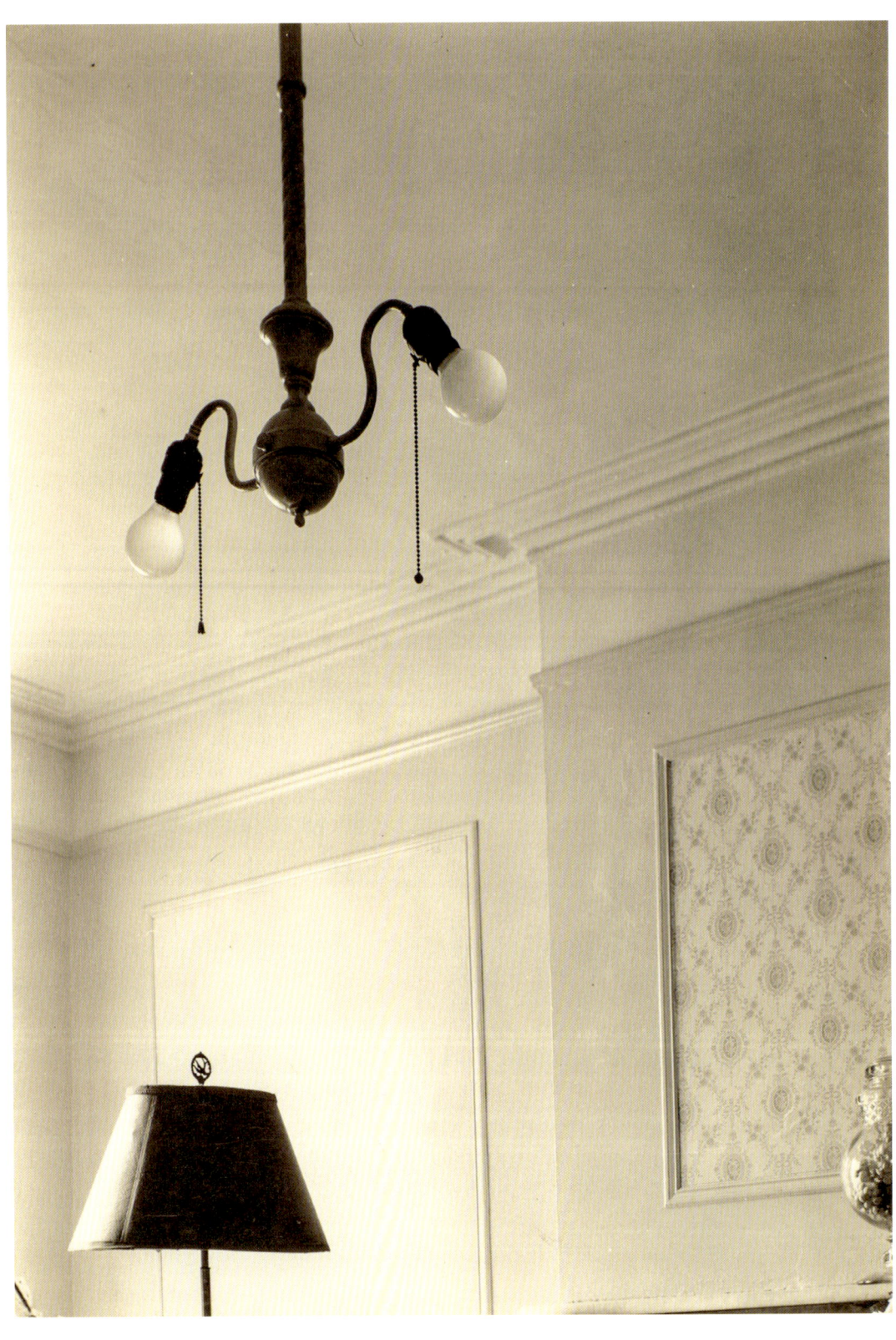

DIANE ARBUS *Room with Lamp and Light Fixture,*
New York City 1944, 16.5 × 14 cm

EMMANUEL SOUGEZ *Still Life with Cloth*
and Guitar 1911, 39.1 × 29.5 cm

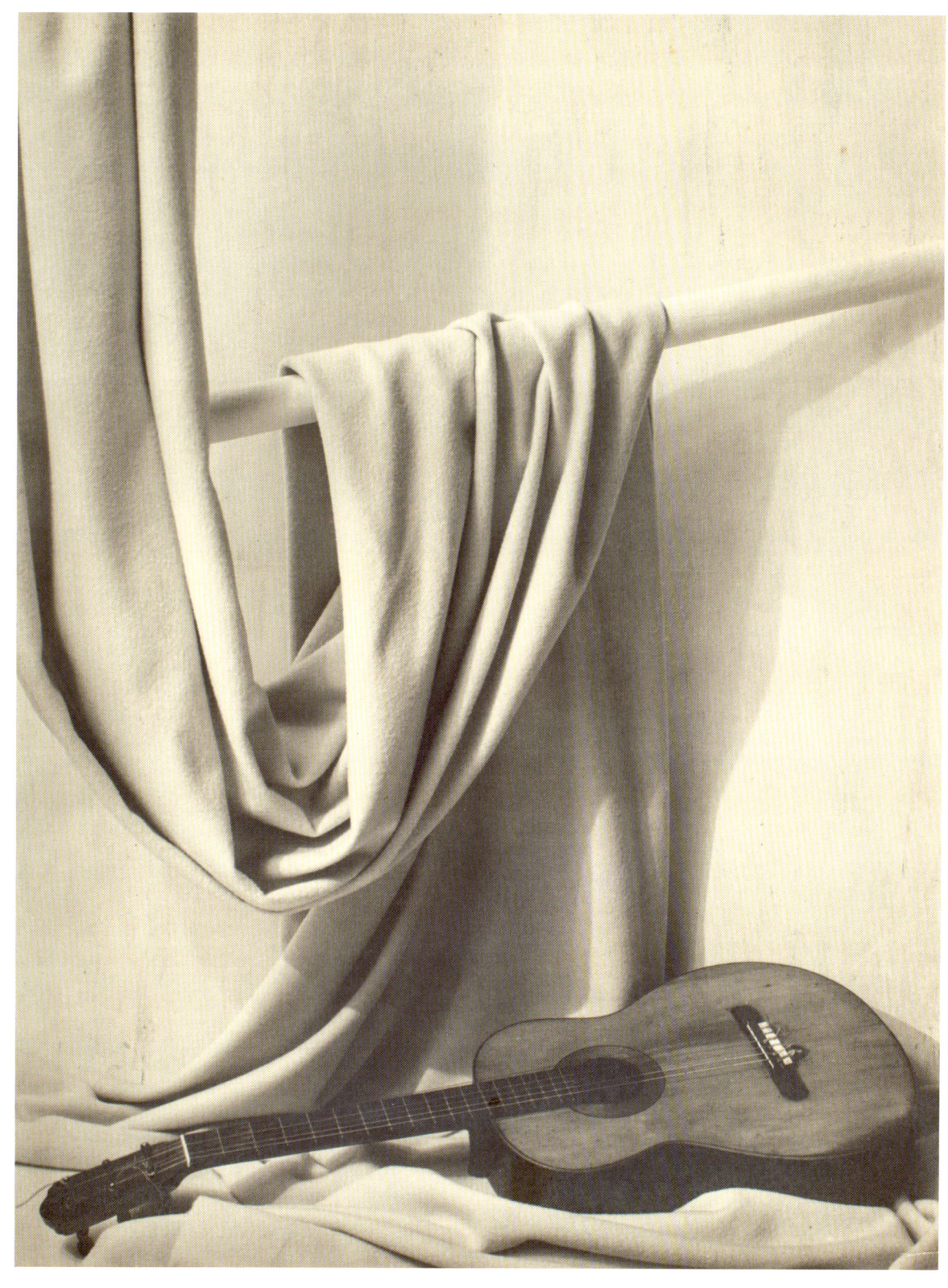

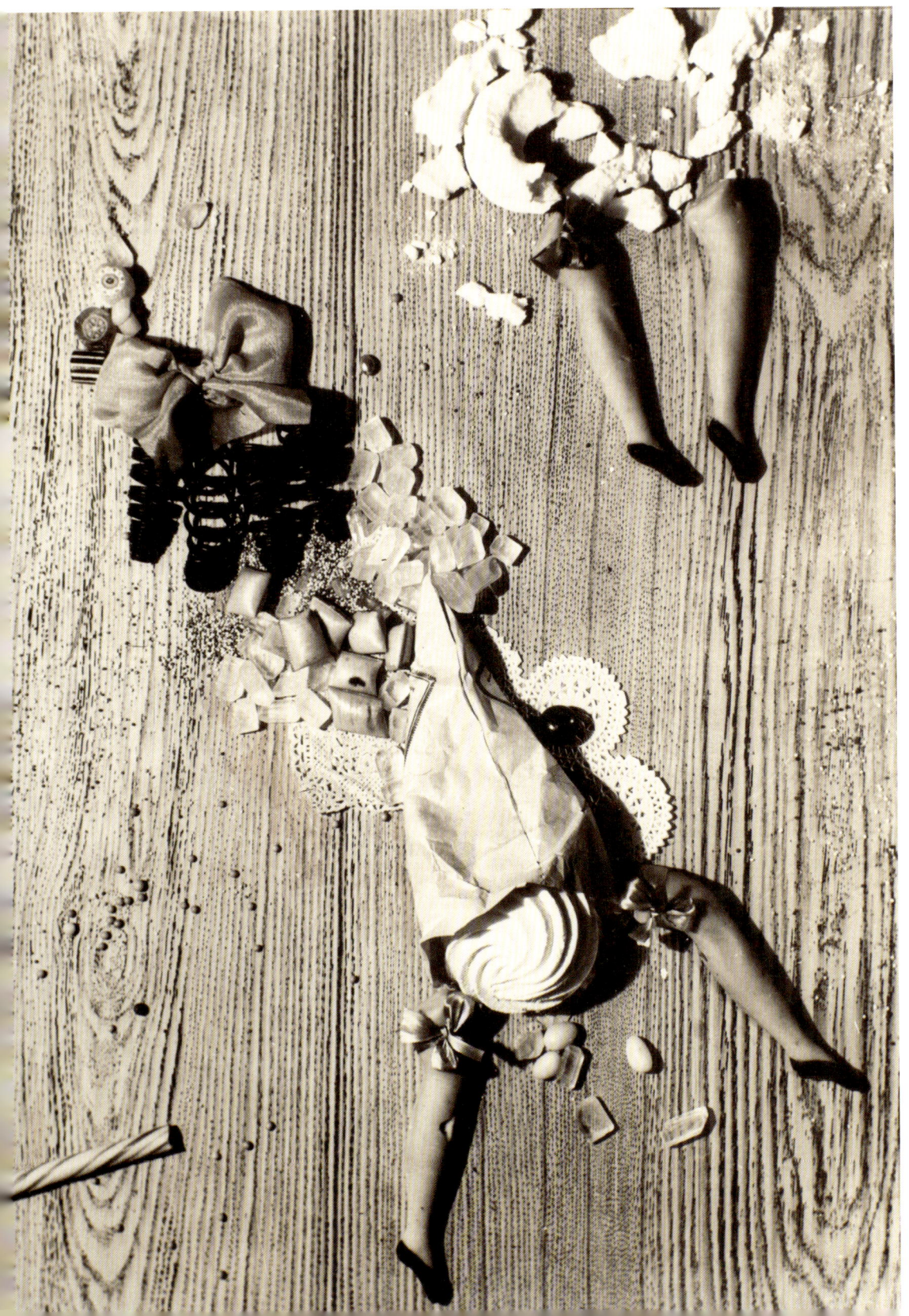

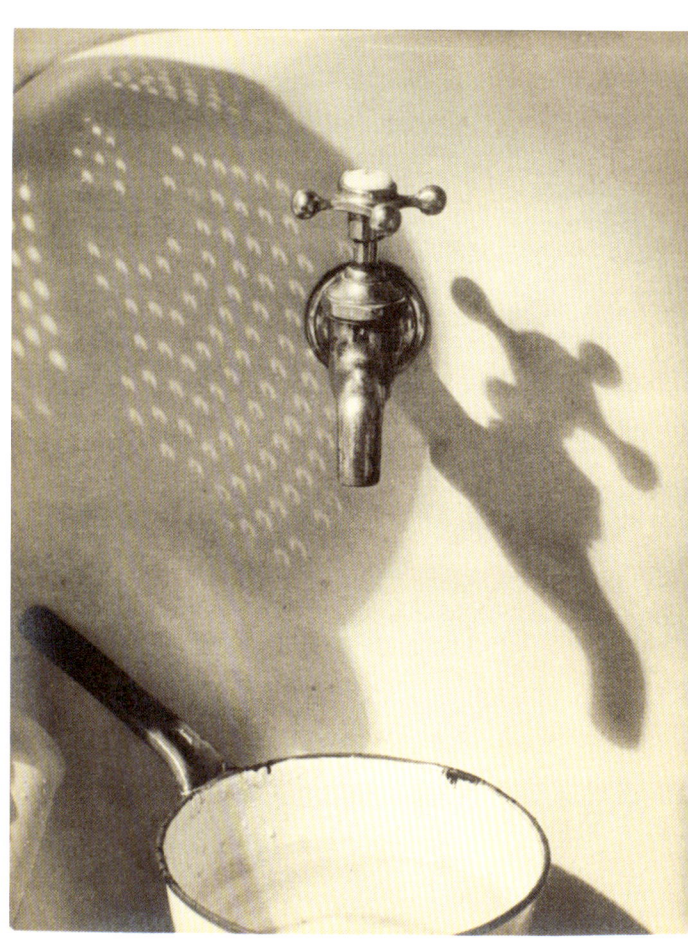

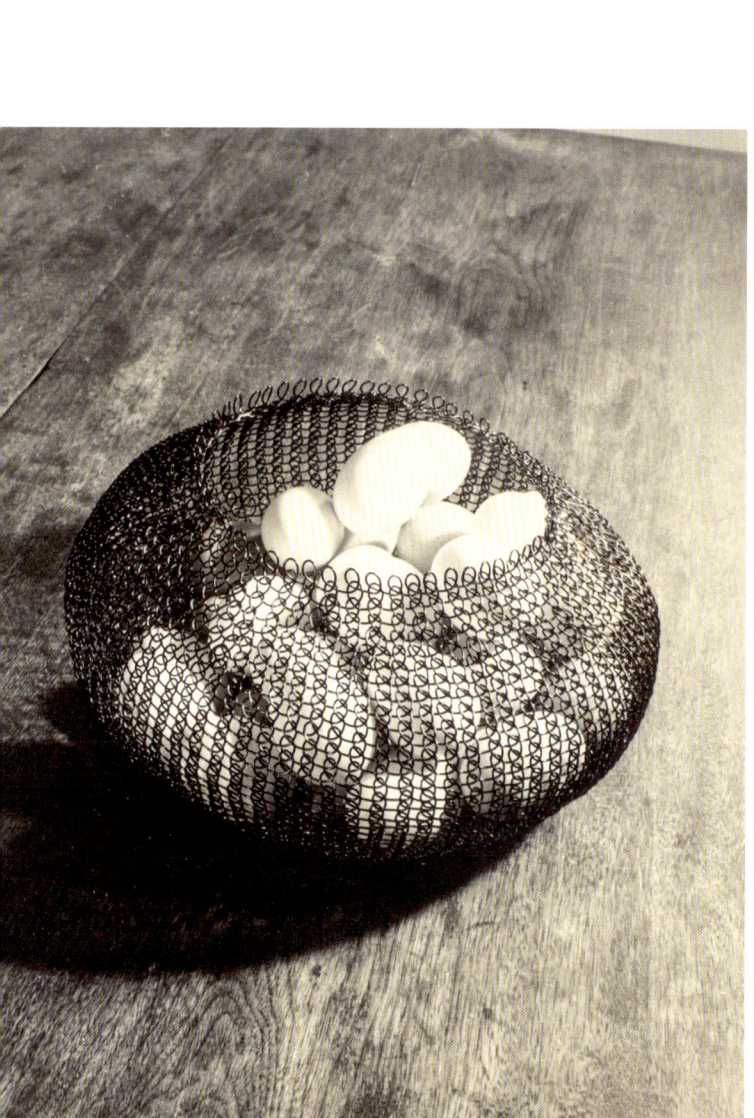

IMOGEN CUNNINGHAM *Eggs* c.1930, 12.7 × 9.8 cm

GORDON COSTER *The Spigot and the Shadows*
1927, 22.9 × 19.1 cm

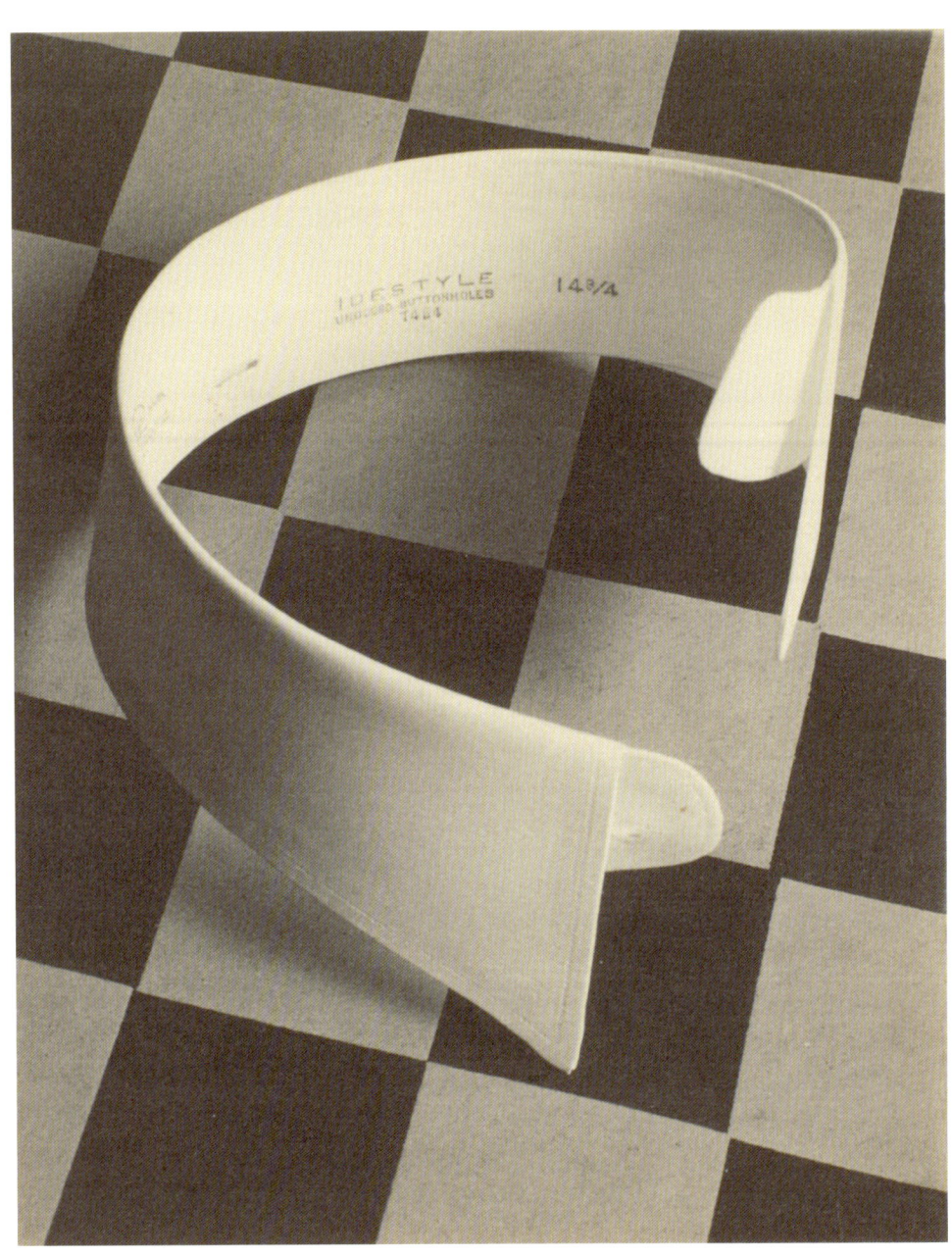

Paul Outerbridge *Ide Collar* 1922, platinum print, 11.1 × 9.2 cm

PAUL OUTERBRIDGE *Saltine Box* 1922, platinum print, 8.9 × 10.8 cm

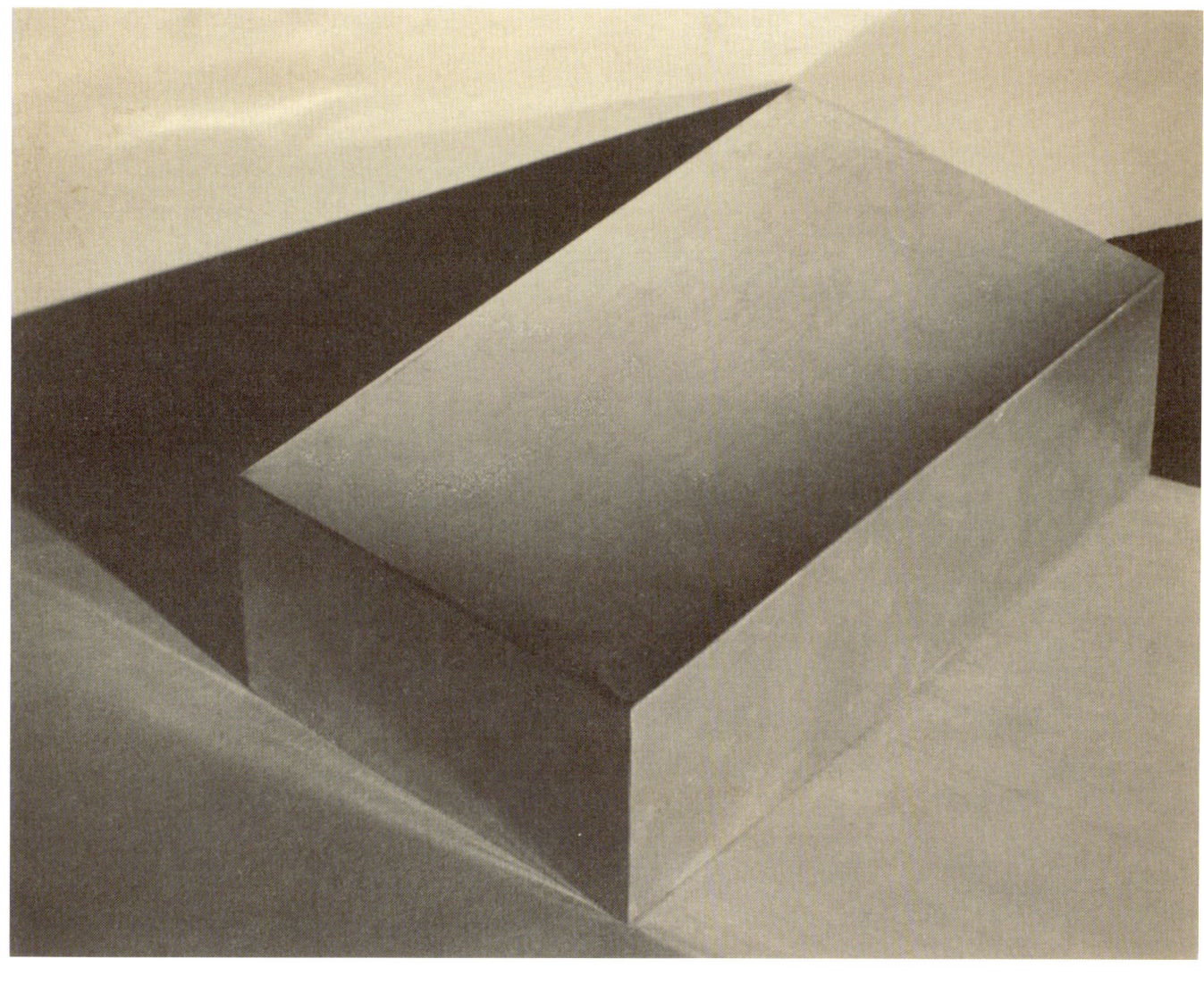

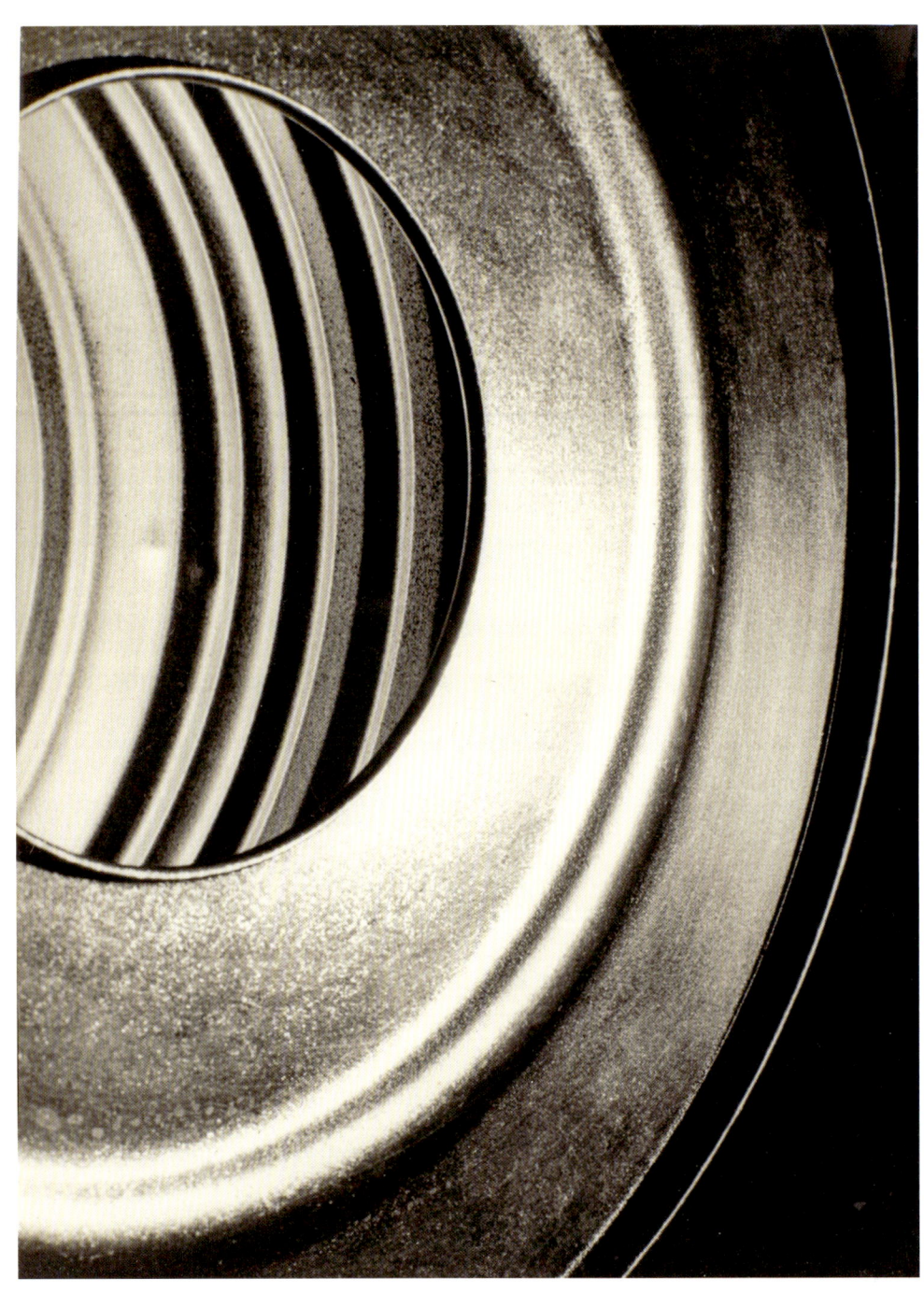

PIM VAN OS *Abstraction at Van Leer's Barrel Factory* c.1950, 23.5 × 17.1 cm

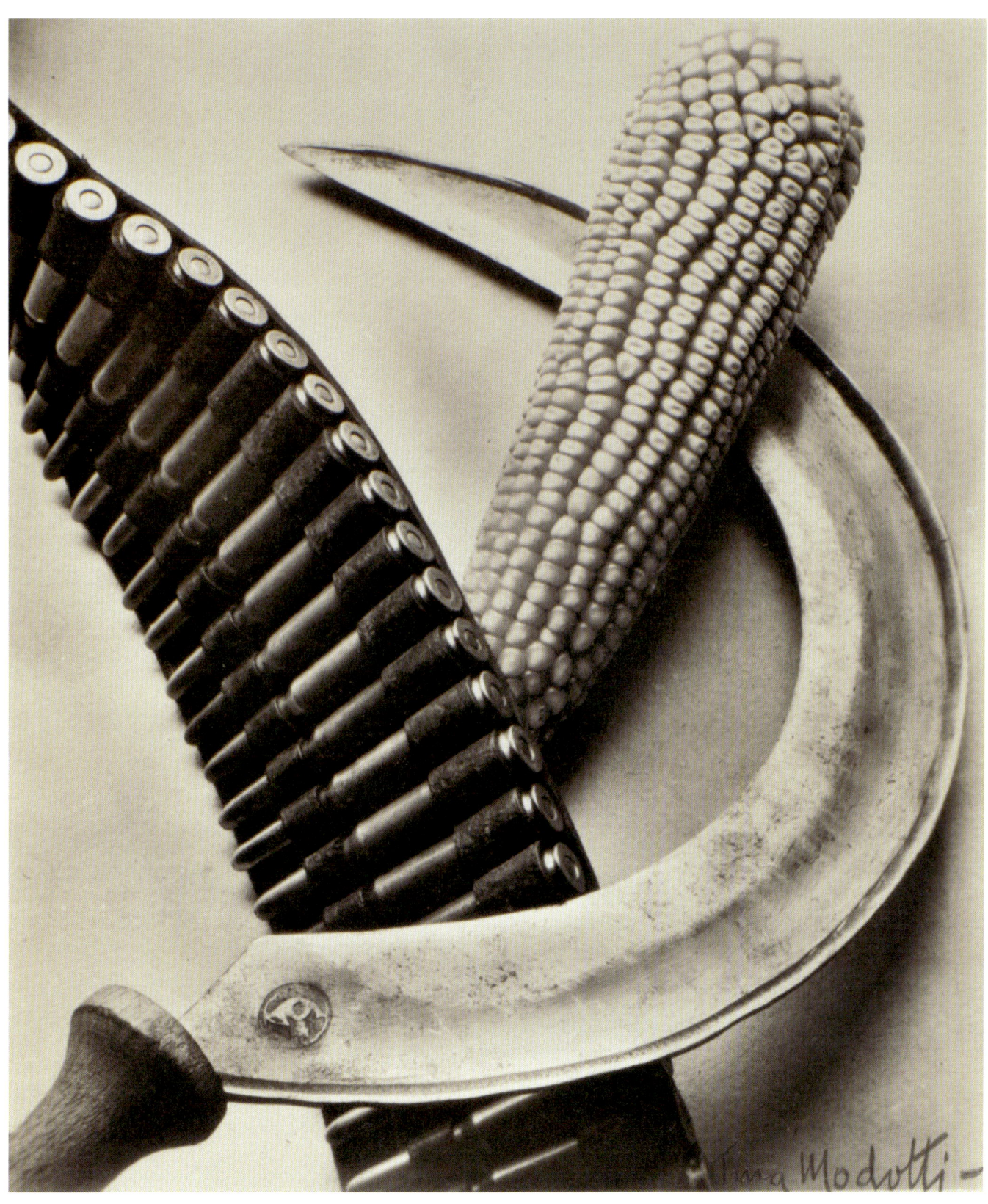

TINA MODOTTI *Bandolier, Corn and Sickle* 1927, 9.5 × 7.9 cm

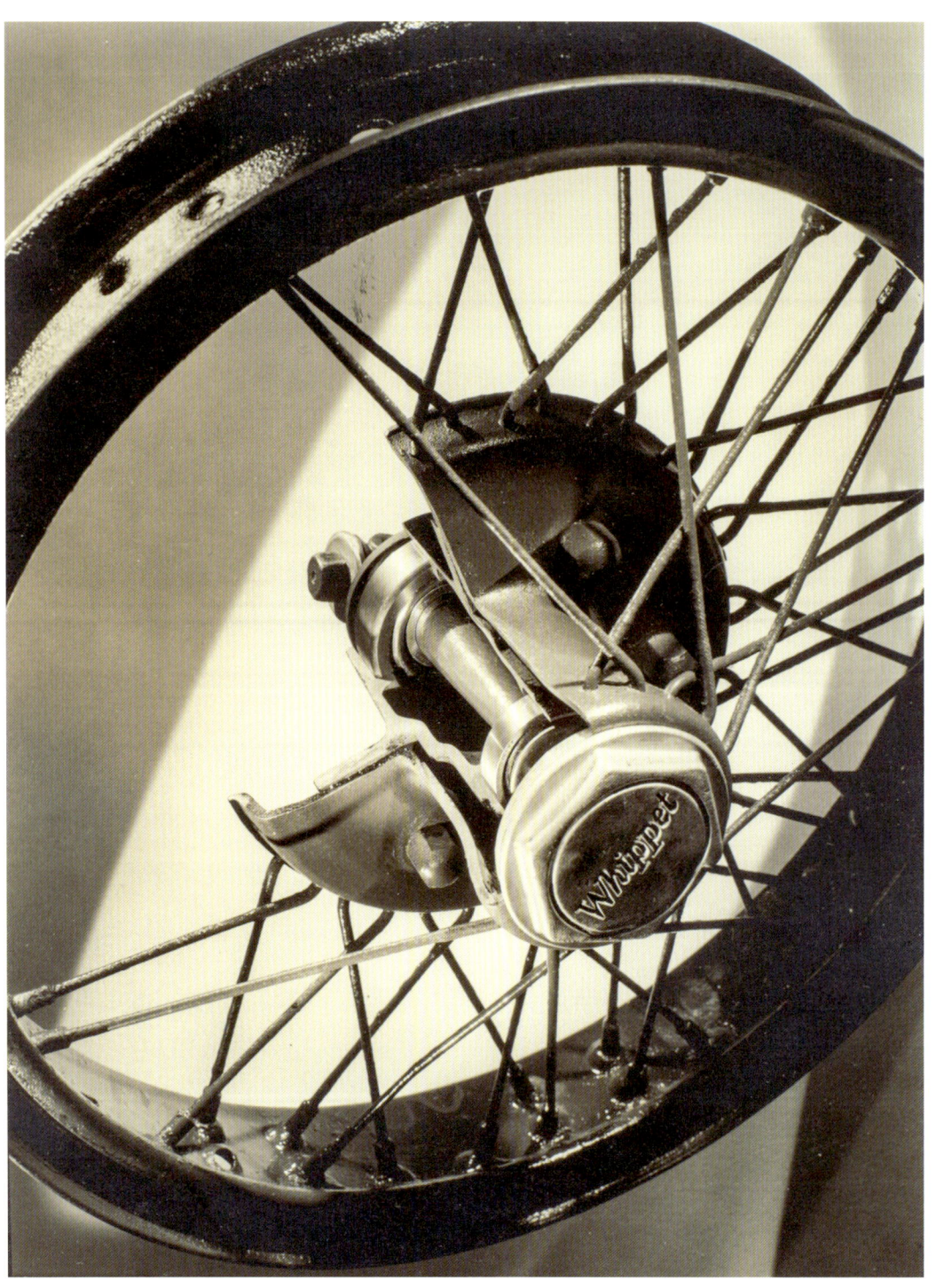

EDWARD QUIGLEY *Whippet Wheel* c.1930, 14.9 × 9.5 cm

EDWARD QUIGLEY *Gear and Ball Bearings* c.1936, 11.1 × 15.2 cm

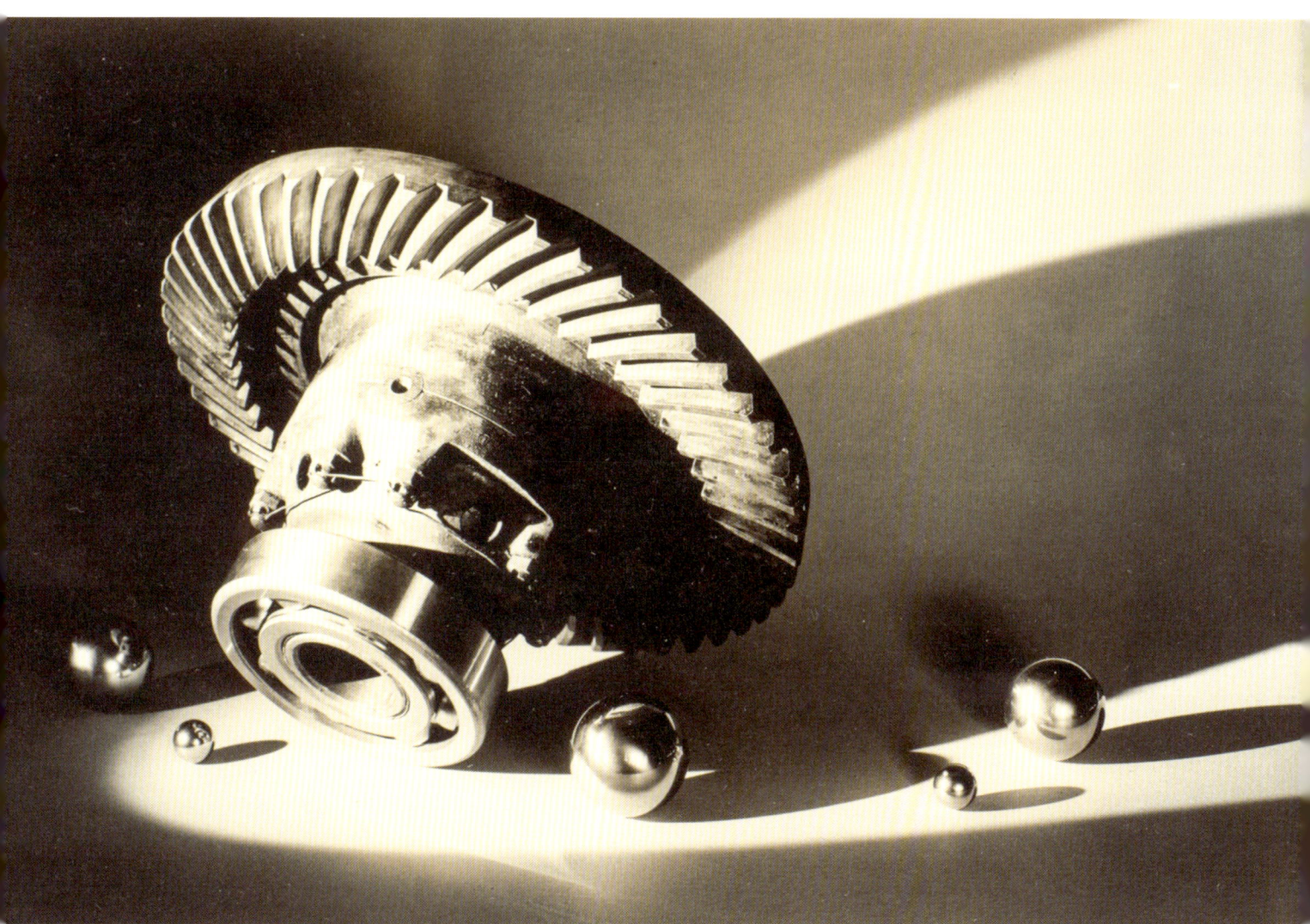

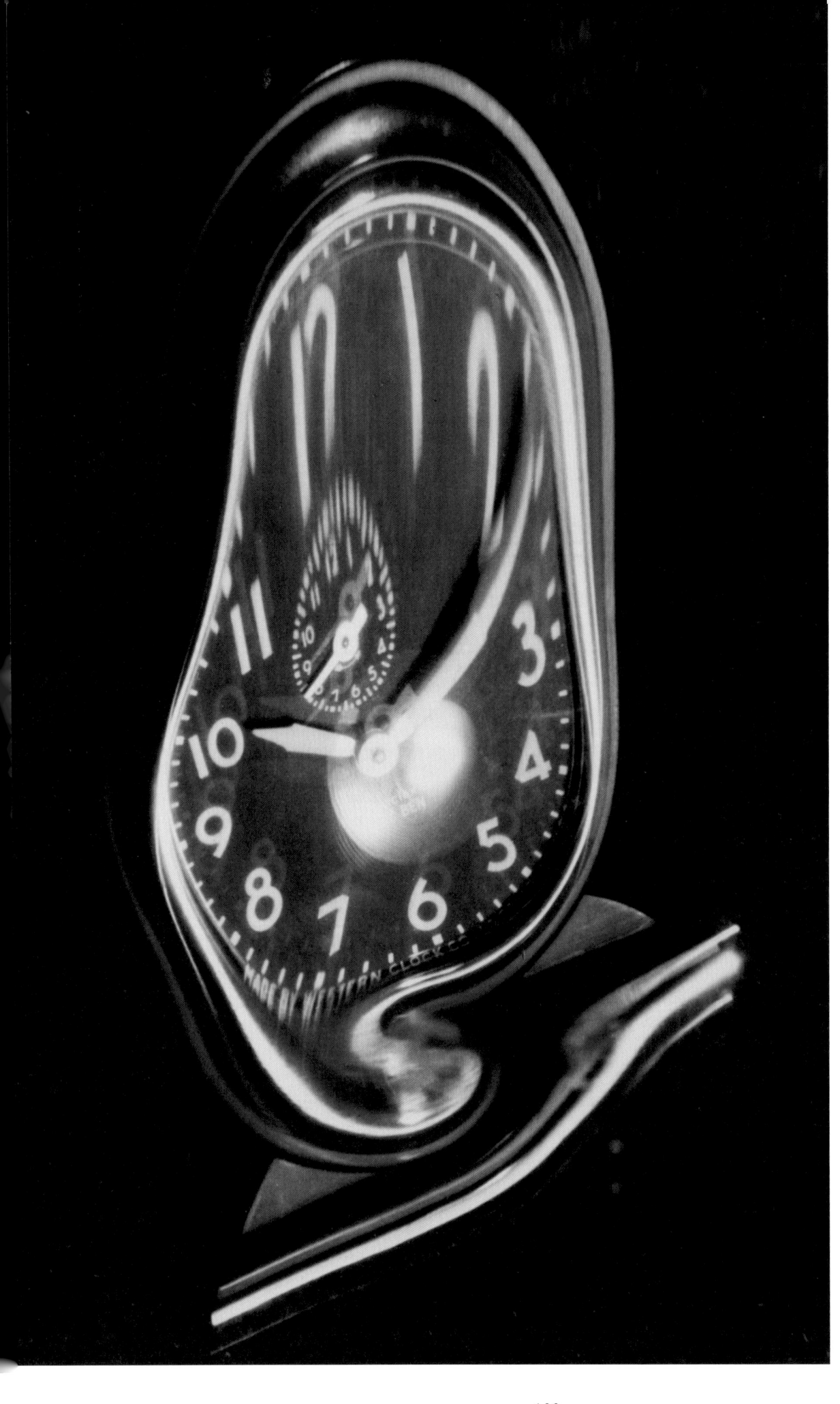

André Kertész
Clock Distortion
1938, 22.9 × 14.6 cm

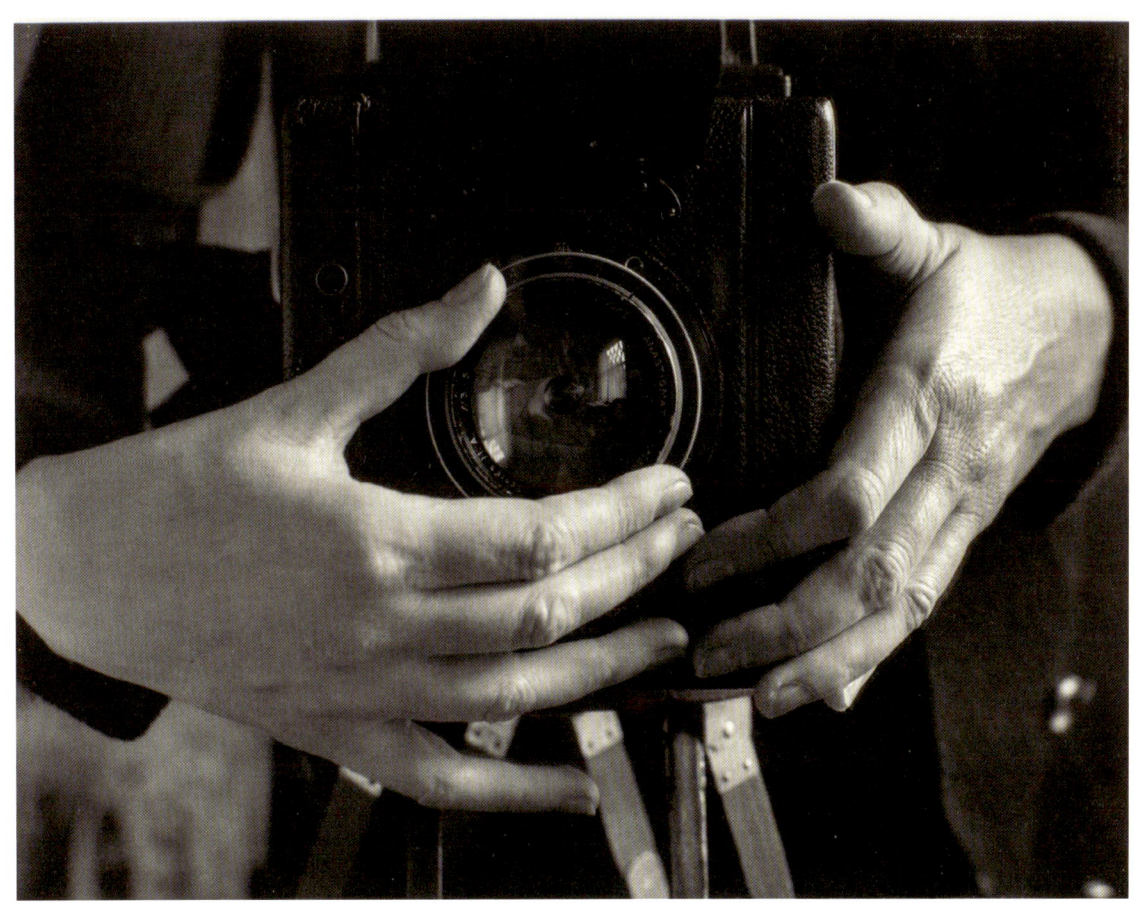

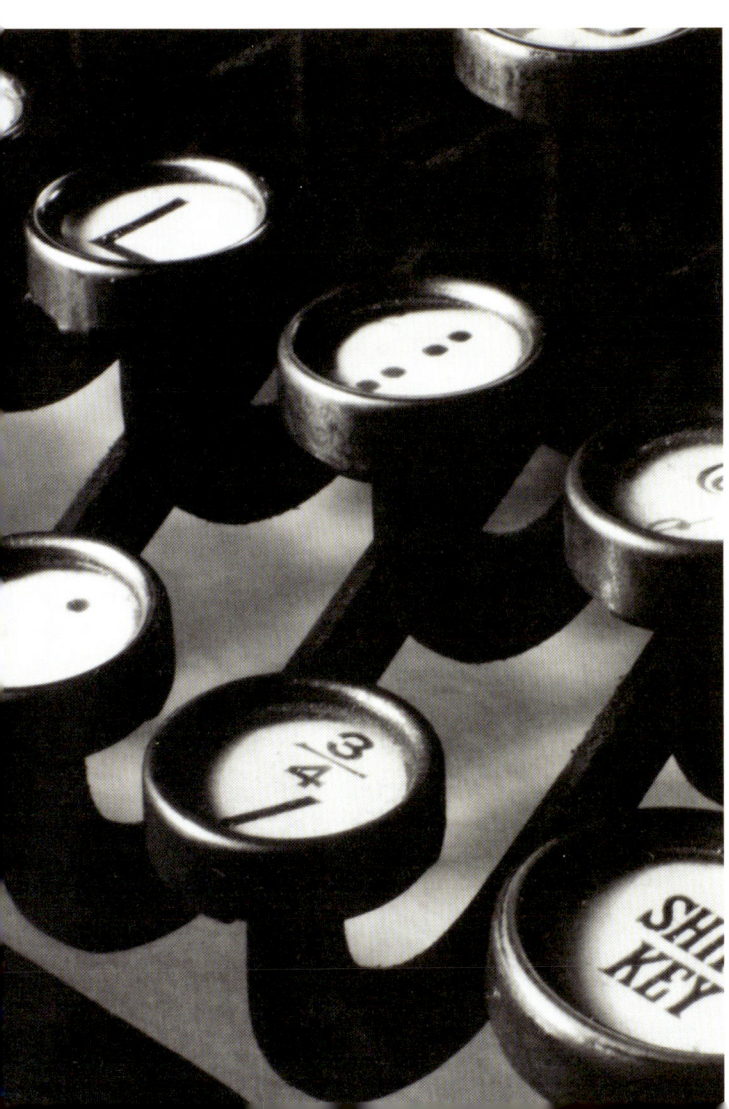

Top: **Alma Lavenson**
Self-Portrait 1932
16.8 × 22.2 cm

Left: **Ralph Steiner**
Typewriter Keys c.1921
19.7 × 14.6 m

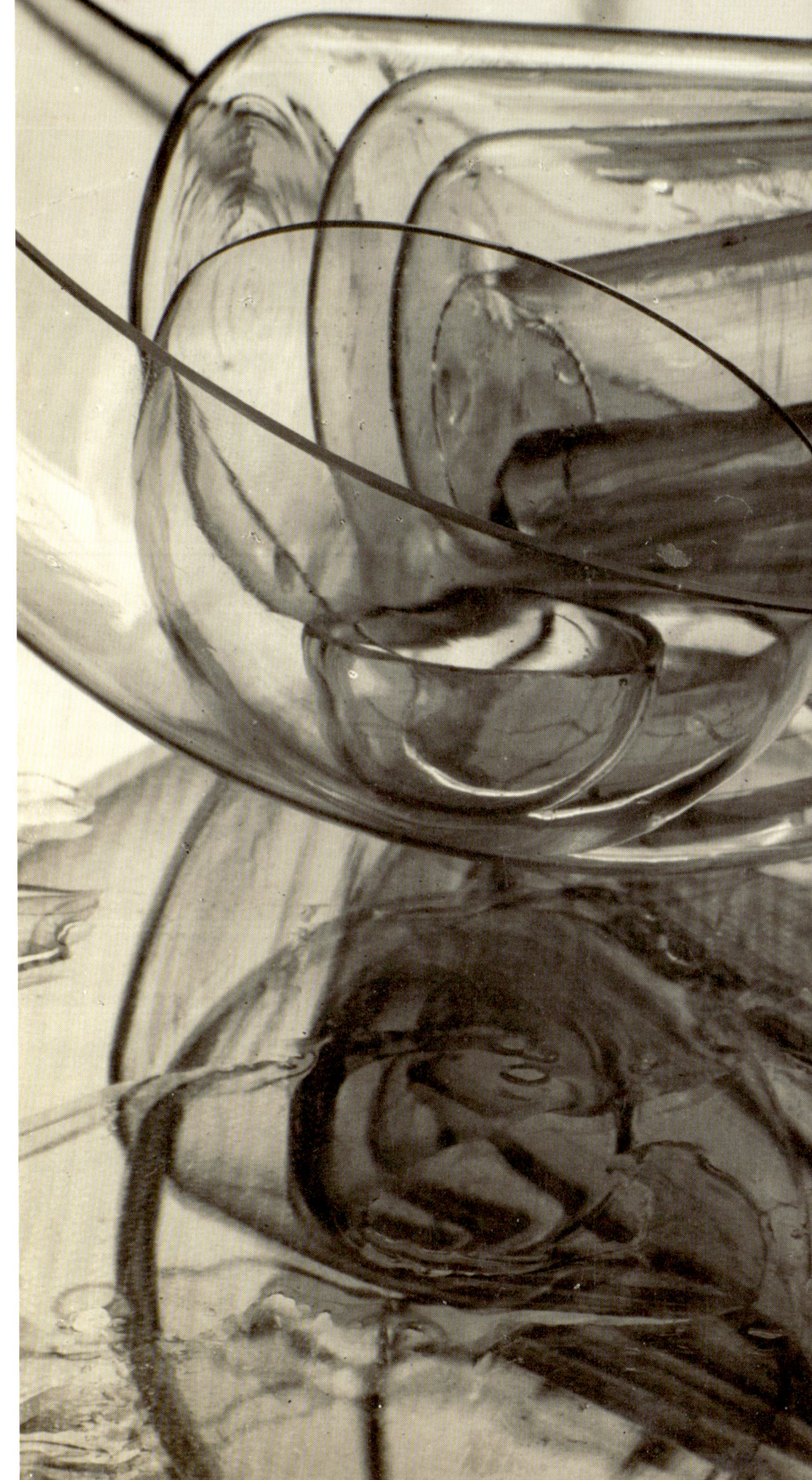

WILLY ZIELKE
Homage to
Wagenfeld
(Glass) 1929
15.9 × 21.9 cm

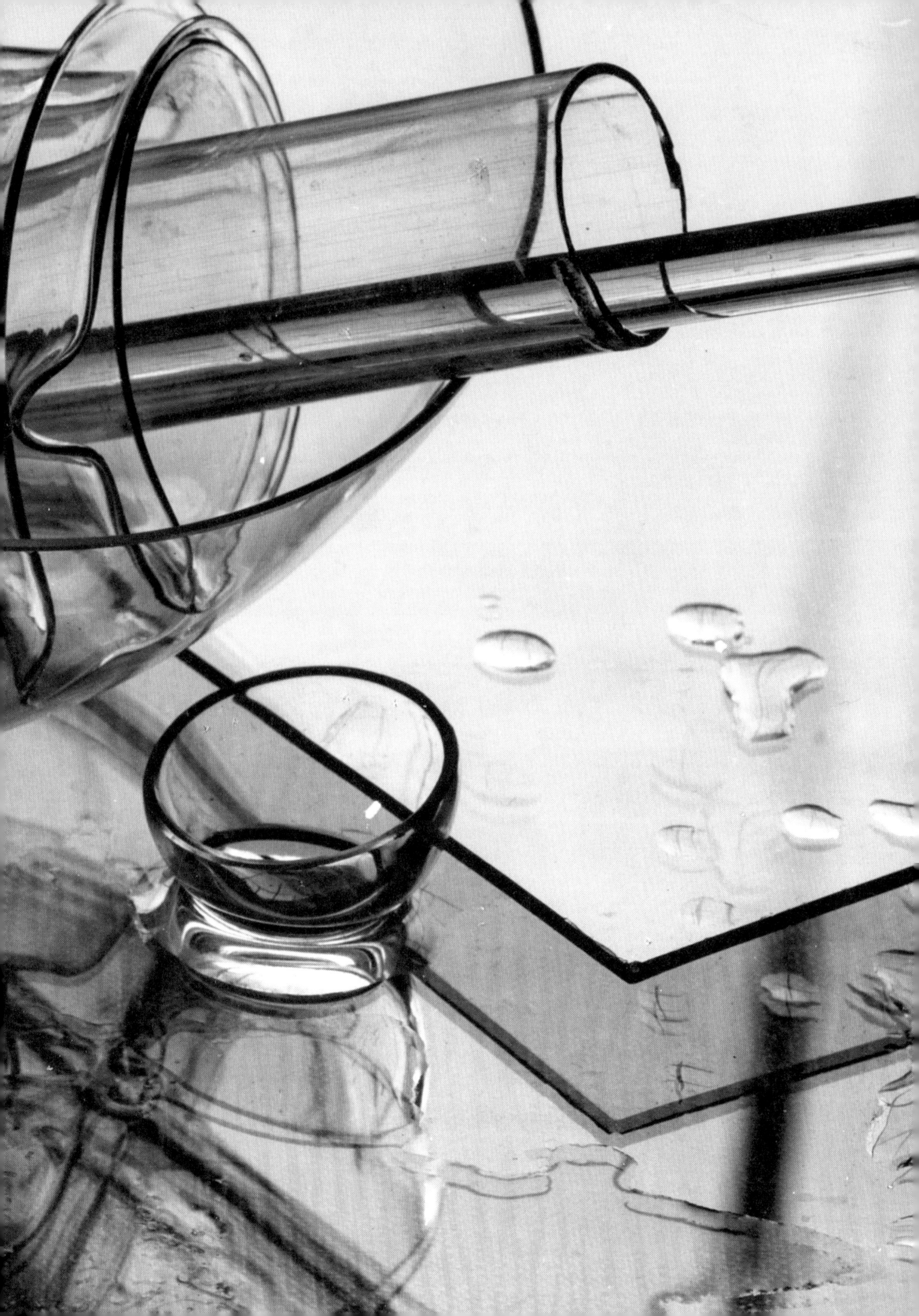

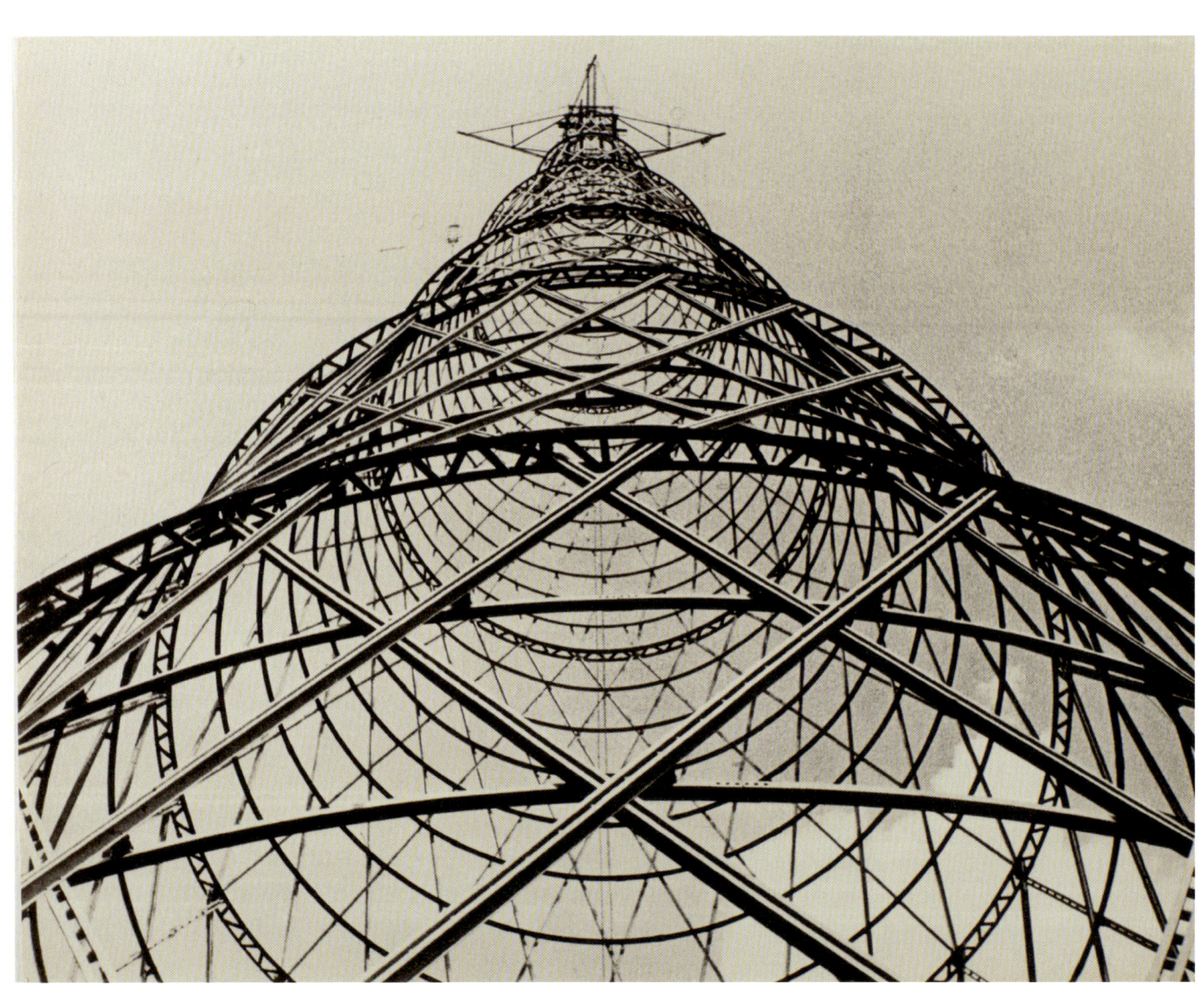

Aleksandr Rodchenko
Shukhov Tower 1927
22.9 × 27.9 cm

PERSPECTIVES

Early cameras were positioned on tripods, which meant that photographers had to capture their subjects straight-on. The popularisation of the handheld camera and roll film in the 1920s liberated photographers from working from this viewpoint, allowing them to investigate angles and perspectives in exciting new ways – just like their contemporaries in the fields of painting, drawing and sculpture. For many, like the constructivist theorist Osip Brik, the unexpected vantage point represented a new outlook that came with mechanised travel: 'There was a time when we thought it was just enough to photograph objects at eye level,' he wrote in 1926, 'but then we began to move around, to climb mountains, to soar in airplanes and drop to the bottom of the sea. And we took our camera with us everywhere, recording whatever we saw.'

Early explorations of dynamic perspectives in modernist photography were pursued by Brik's peers in post-revolutionary Russia. Throughout the 1920s and 1930s photographers and filmmakers embraced many of the same radical social theories about the visual arts and used similar techniques to break down preconceptions. Aleksandr Rodchenko interacted with pioneering filmmakers, such as Dziga Vertov, who employed cinematic montage to replicate the way the brain takes in its surroundings: rapid-fire and disjointed, as opposed to one continuous, linear narrative. Both Rodchenko and Vertov embraced the heightened perception offered by the *kino-eye* (camera-eye); a new language that scorned the laws of gravity. Vertov described himself as being in 'constant motion', employing a dizzying vocabulary of 'crawling', 'climbing', 'galloping', 'plunging', 'ascending' and 'falling' that suggested the visual roller-coaster ride experienced by the viewer.

For Rodchenko the most interesting angle was 'from below upwards' and 'from above downwards' – anything but 'photography from the belly button'. These worm's eye and bird's eye angles shifted the vanishing point to create extremely foreshortened images. The notion that this would change how we experienced the world became a defining tenet of modernist vision throughout the 1920s. Later, in his influential text *Language of Vision* (1944), the artist, designer and educator György Kepes explained these new perspectives in terms of an evolutionary tool: another step in our use of the visual image to orientate ourselves in an ever-changing environment – one that now encompassed skyscrapers, trains and subways.

In the United States, photographers developed their own visual language dedicated to growth and progress by evoking the monumentality of modern structures. Their formal simplicity and use of sharp geometric lines echoed the aesthetic employed by painters of the precisionist movement, who were, in turn, indebted to the minimalist views of the cityscape created by photographers such as Paul Strand. While their contemporaries on the West Coast were registering the expansive beauty of natural landscape, those based in the industrial centres of the East Coast were looking up to looming towers, or through structures whose outlines created cobwebs of geometric lines. These perspectives distilled and abstracted the architecture of the city, acquainting the viewer with the rhythm of shapes, patterns and forms that characterised the new metropolis. EL

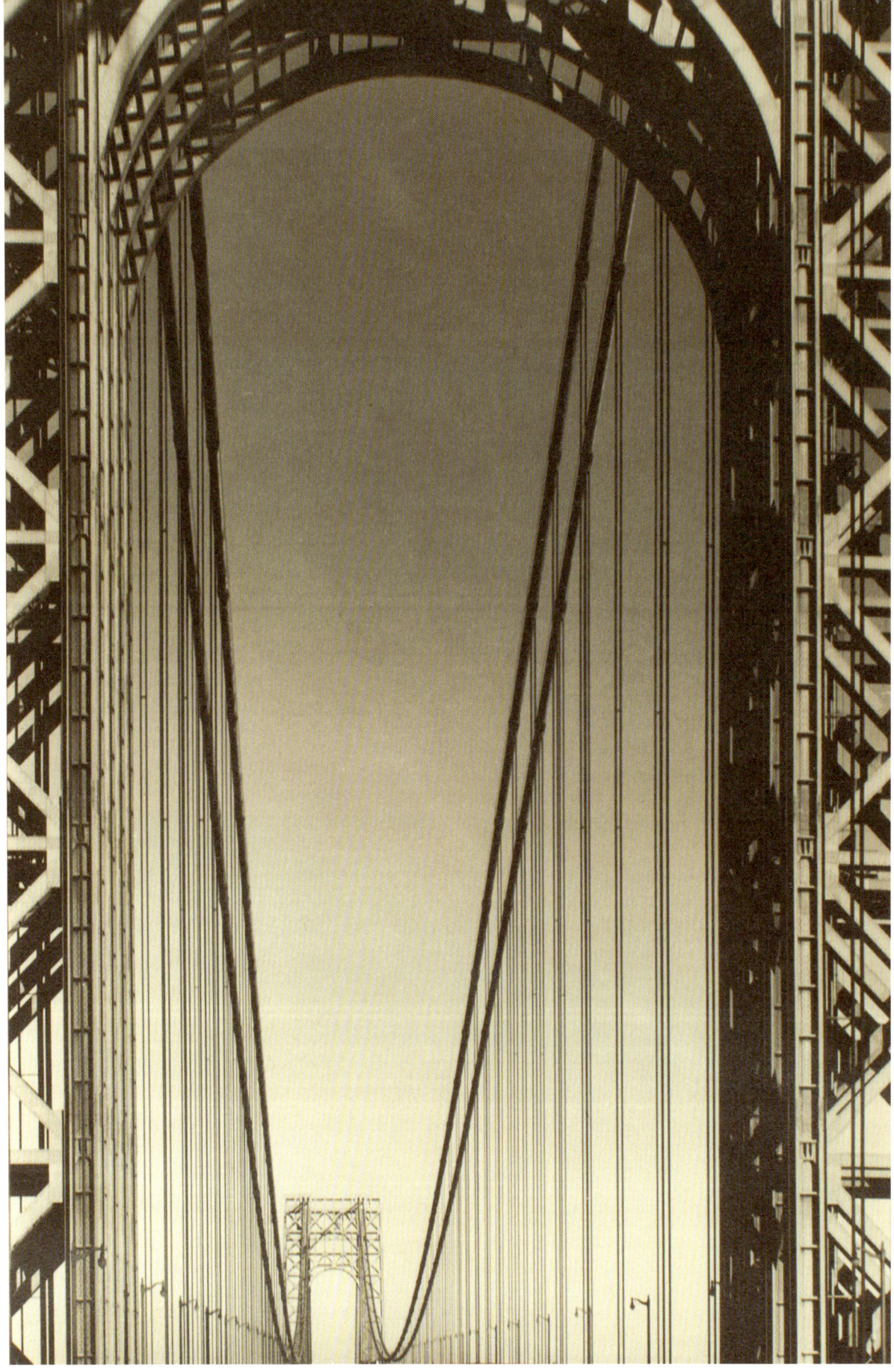

MARGARET BOURKE-WHITE
George Washington Bridge 1933, 34.3 × 22.5 cm
Photo © Estate of Margaret Bourke-White/Licensed by VAGA, New York, NY

MARGARET BOURKE-WHITE
NBC Transmission Tower c.1934, 33 × 26 cm
Photo © Estate of Margaret Bourke-White/Licensed by VAGA, New York, NY

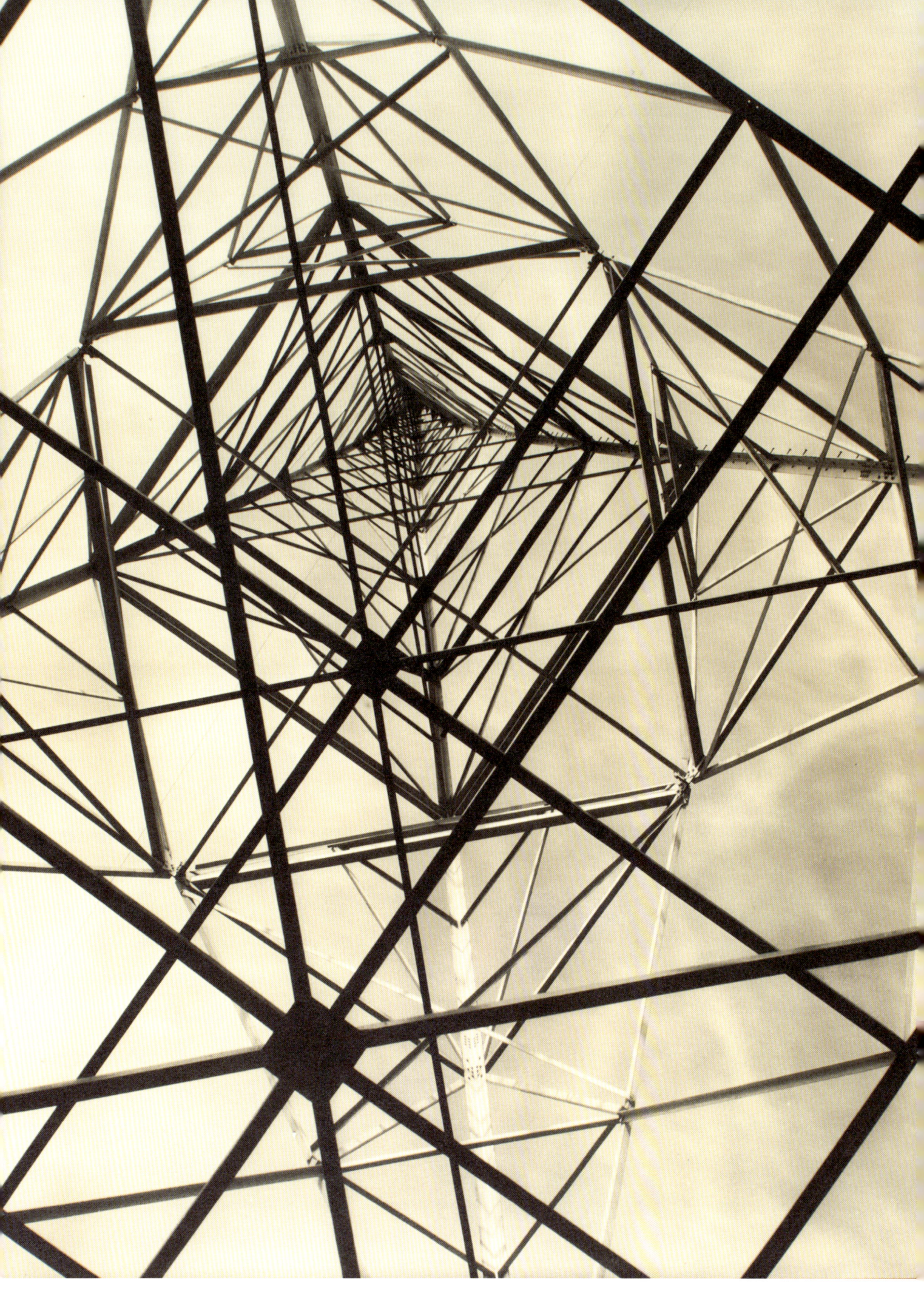

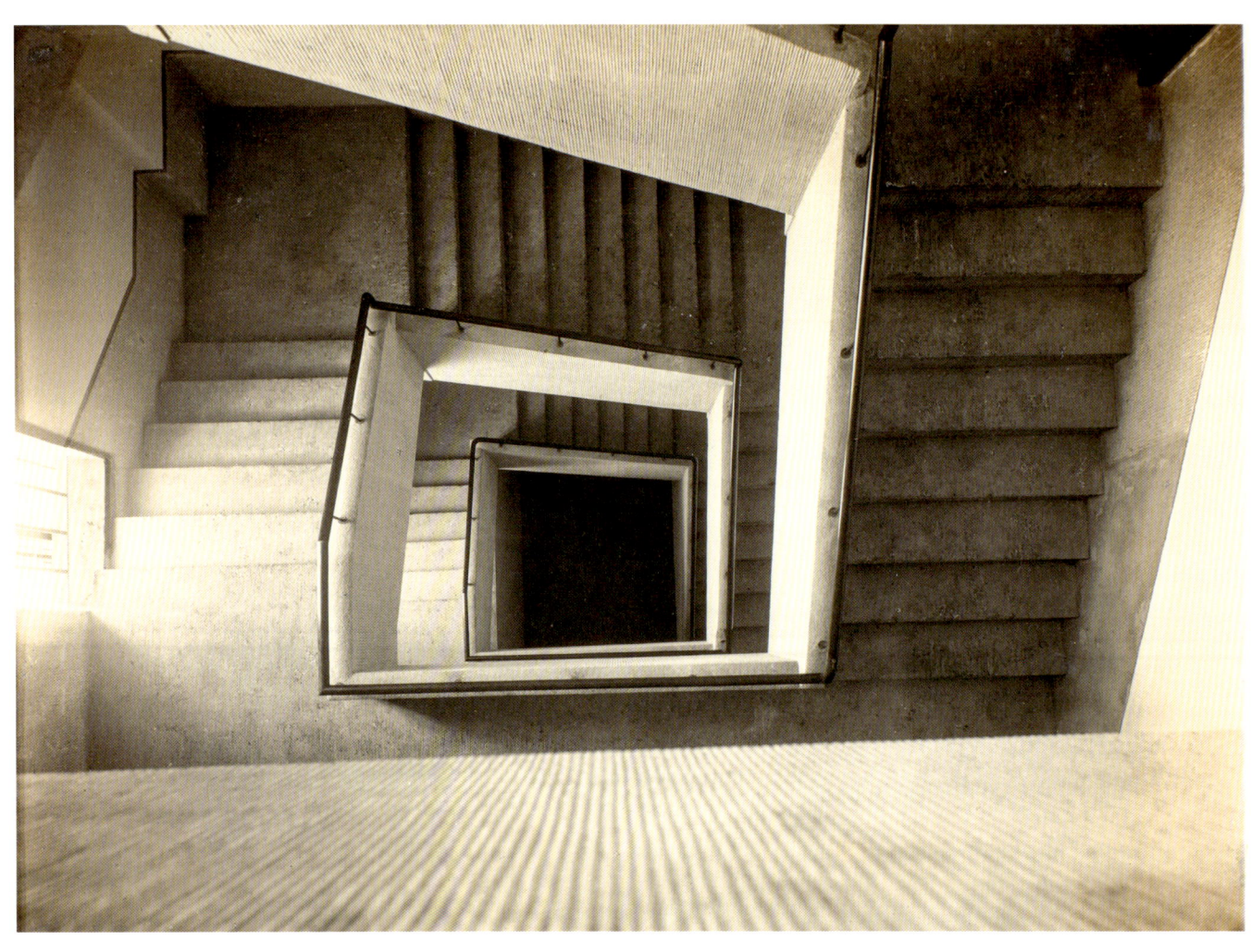

WERNER MANTZ *Staircase* c.1928, 16.5 × 22.9 cm

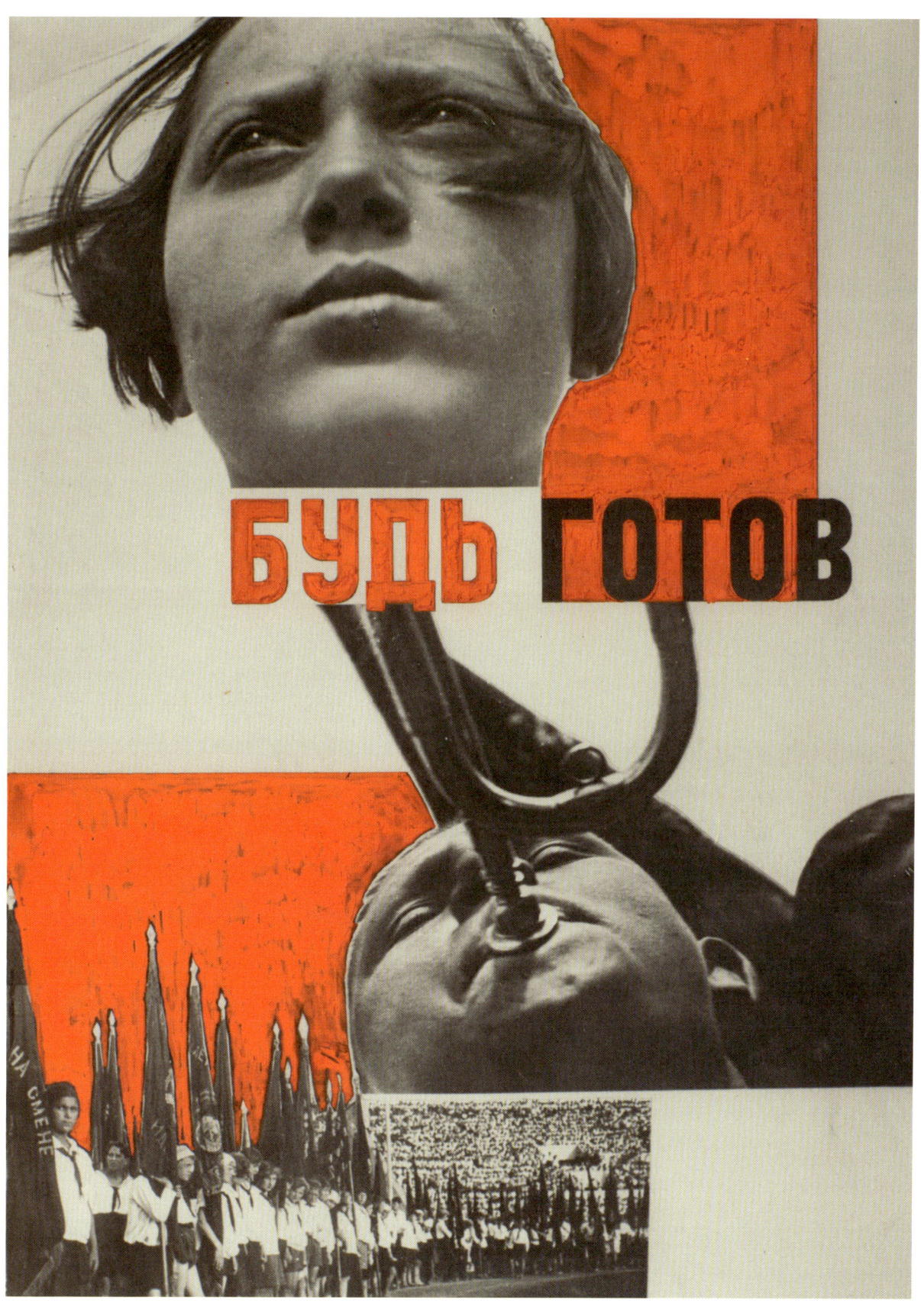

Varvara Stepanova and Aleksandr Rodchenko *Be Ready!* 1934
photomontage, gelatin silver print with gouache, 22.9 × 17.1 cm

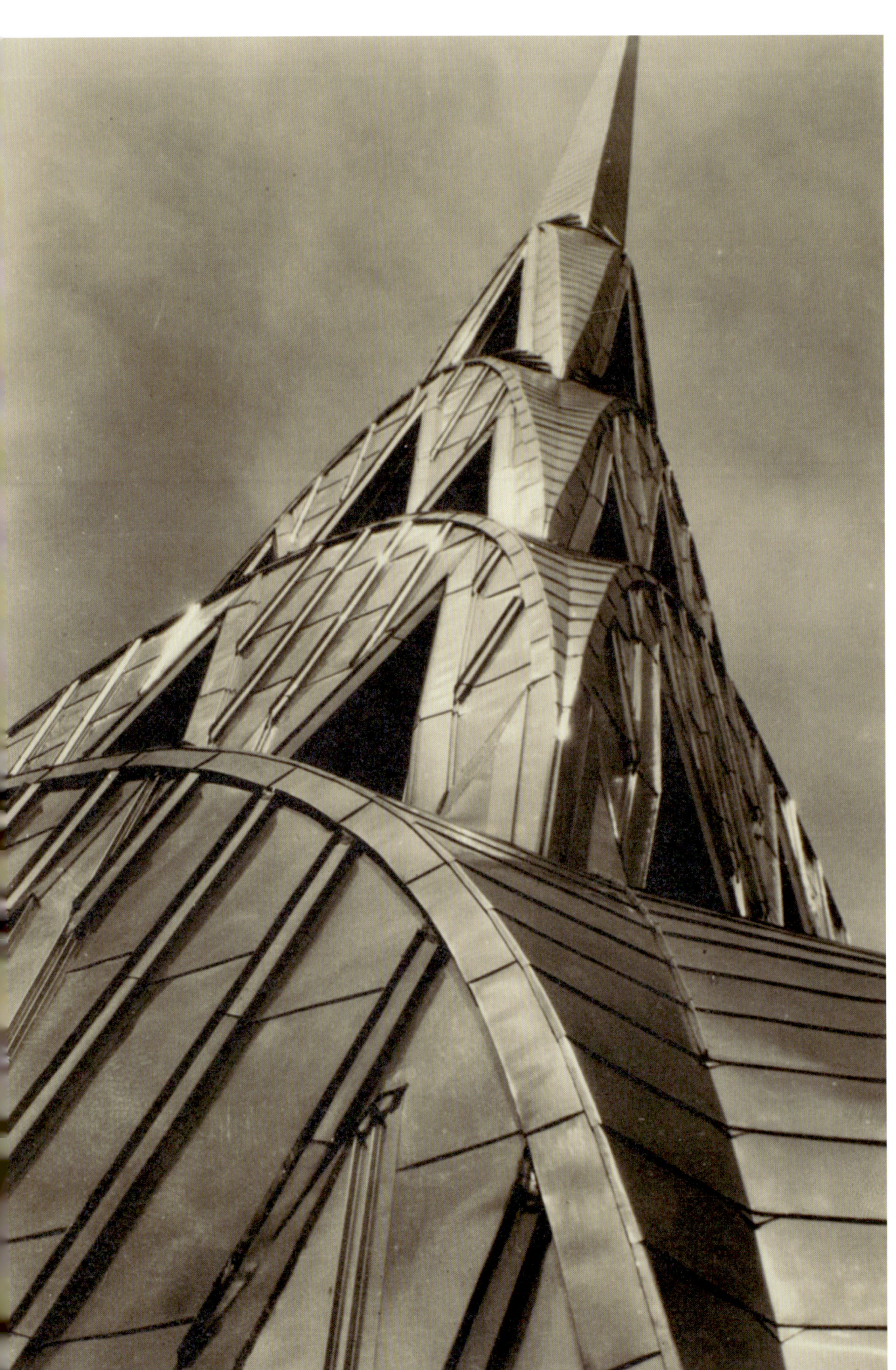

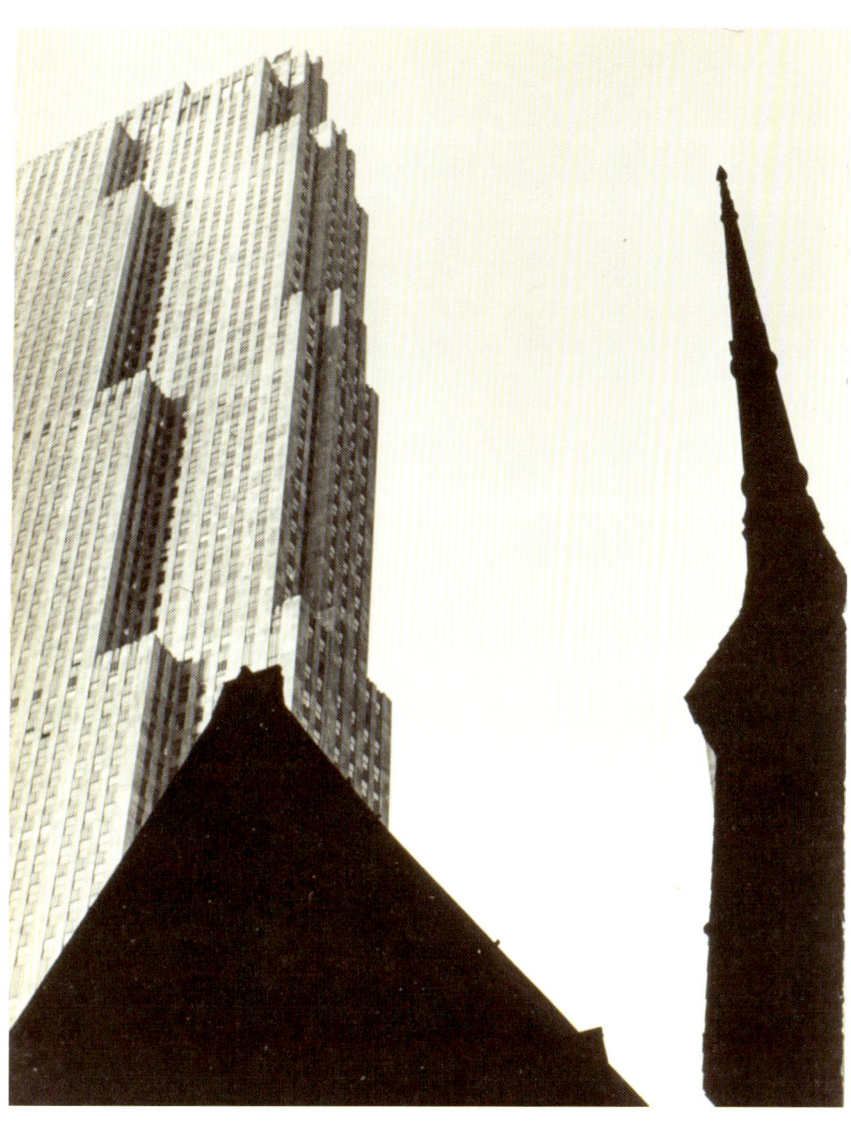

MARGARET BOURKE-WHITE
Chrysler Building, New York 1930, 12.7 × 9.8 cm
Photo © Estate of Margaret Bourke-White/Licensed by VAGA, New York, NY

DOROTHY NORMAN *Rockefeller Center Church IX*
c.1930, 22.9 × 18.1 cm

199

HERBERT LIST *Nocturnal Wall, Hamburg* 1930, 26.7 × 22.2 cm

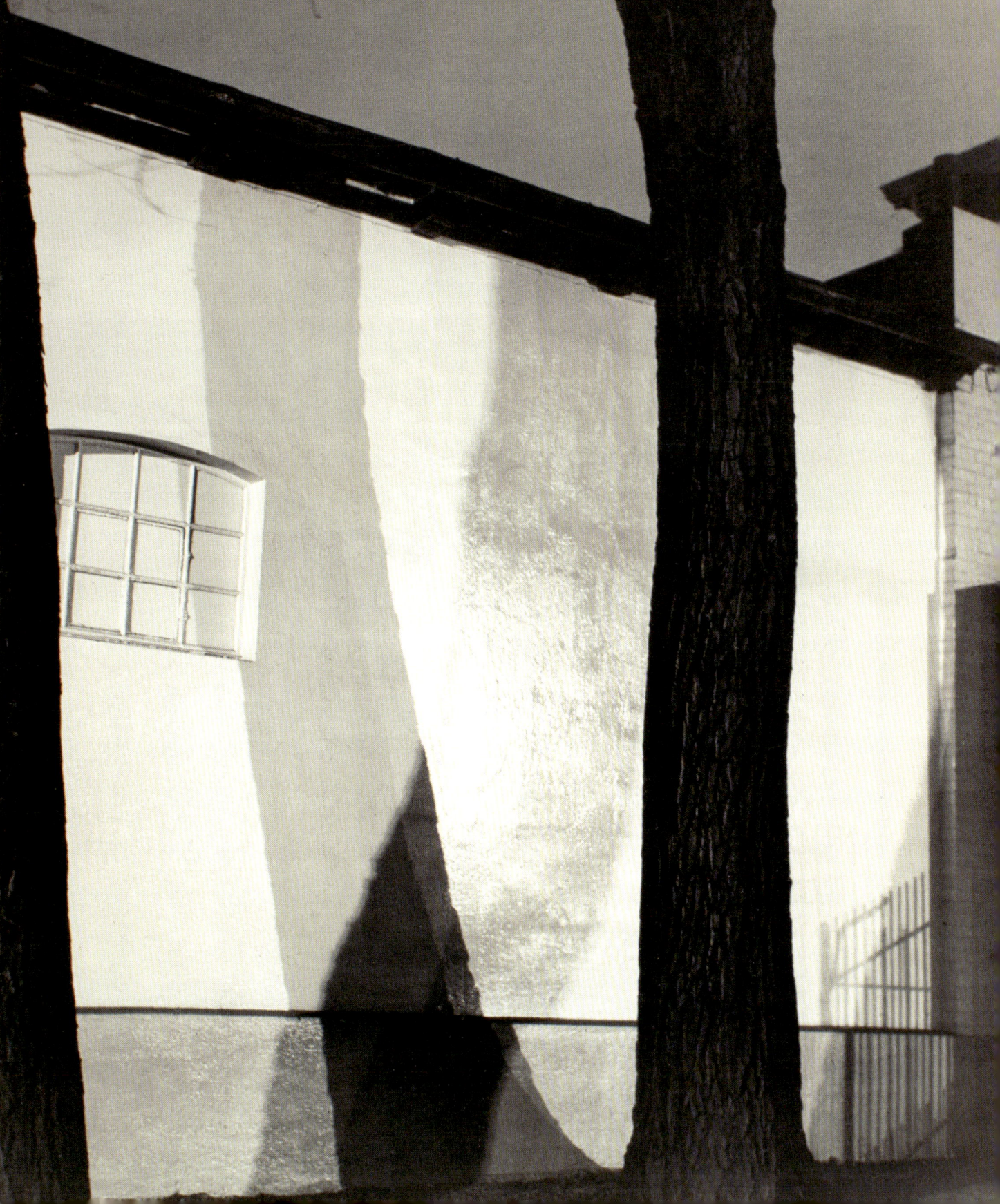

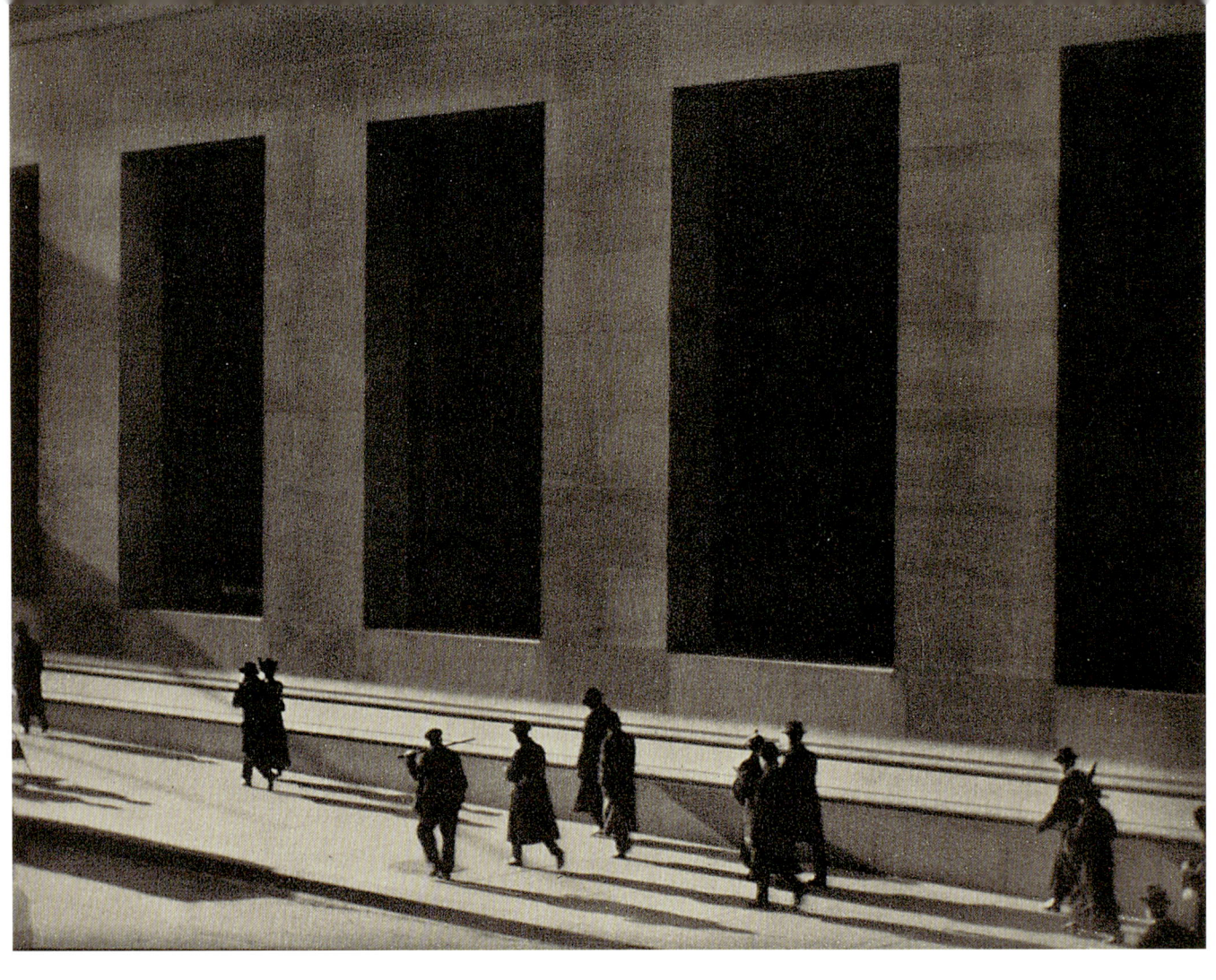

PAUL STRAND *Wall Street, New York* 1915, photogravure, 14 × 16.5 cm

Norman Parkinson *After the Shower, Trafalgar Square, London, 3 February 1947, 41 × 33.7 cm*

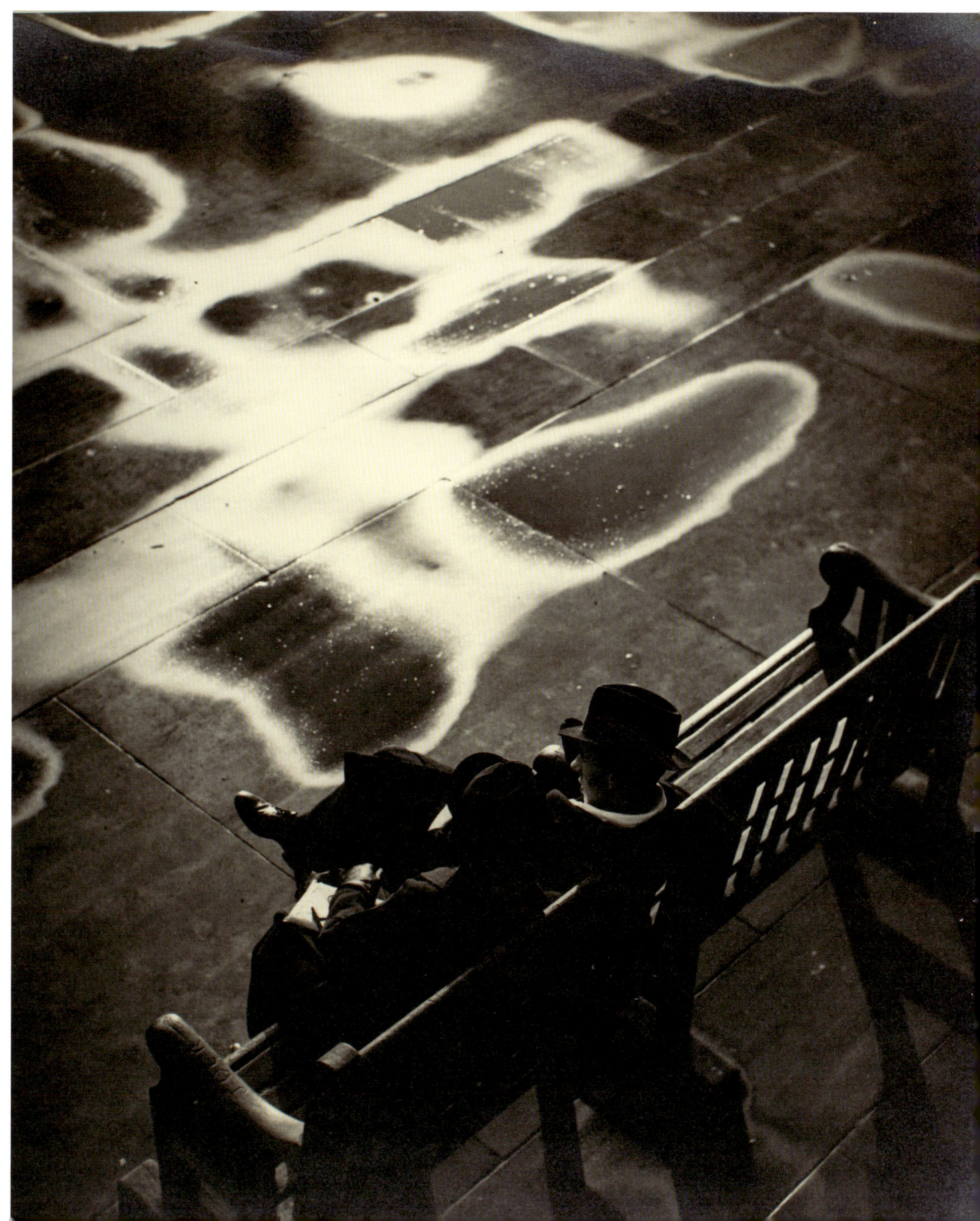

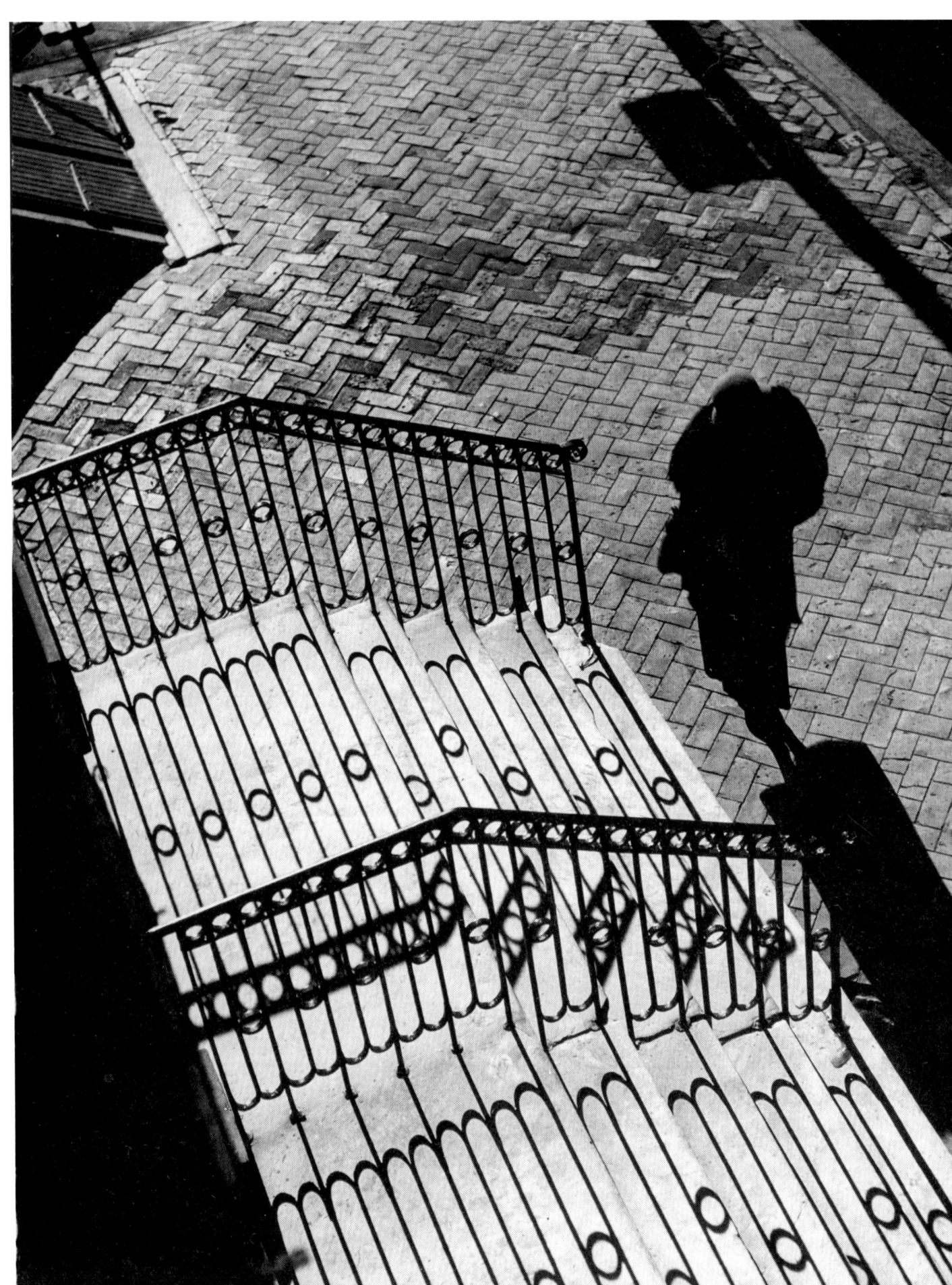

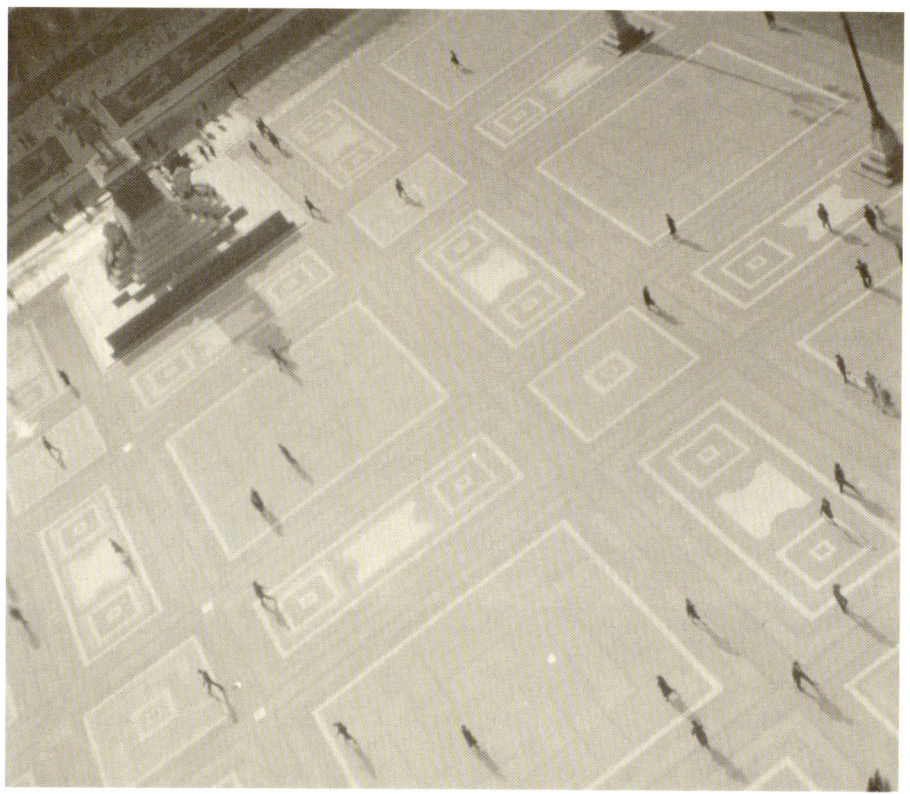

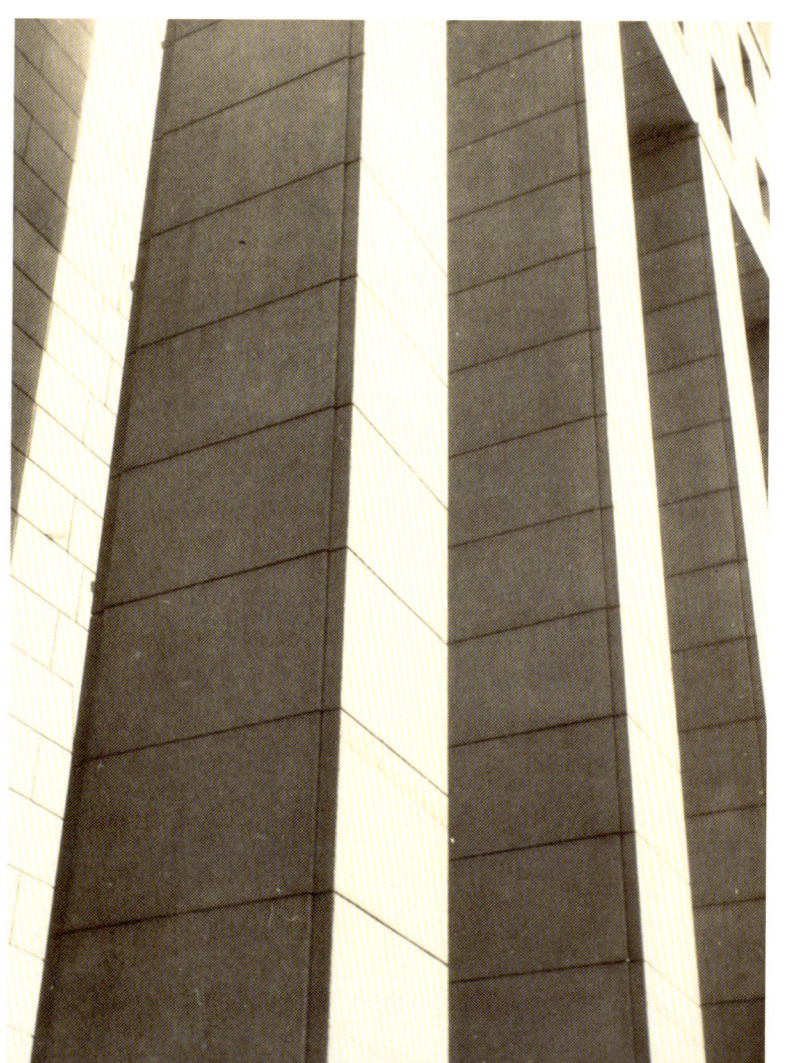

Above: **Arnošt Pikart**
Piazza del Duomo, Milan
1926, 6.5 × 7.6 cm

Left: **Iwao Yamawaki**
Building Facade c.1931
8.9 × 6.7 cm

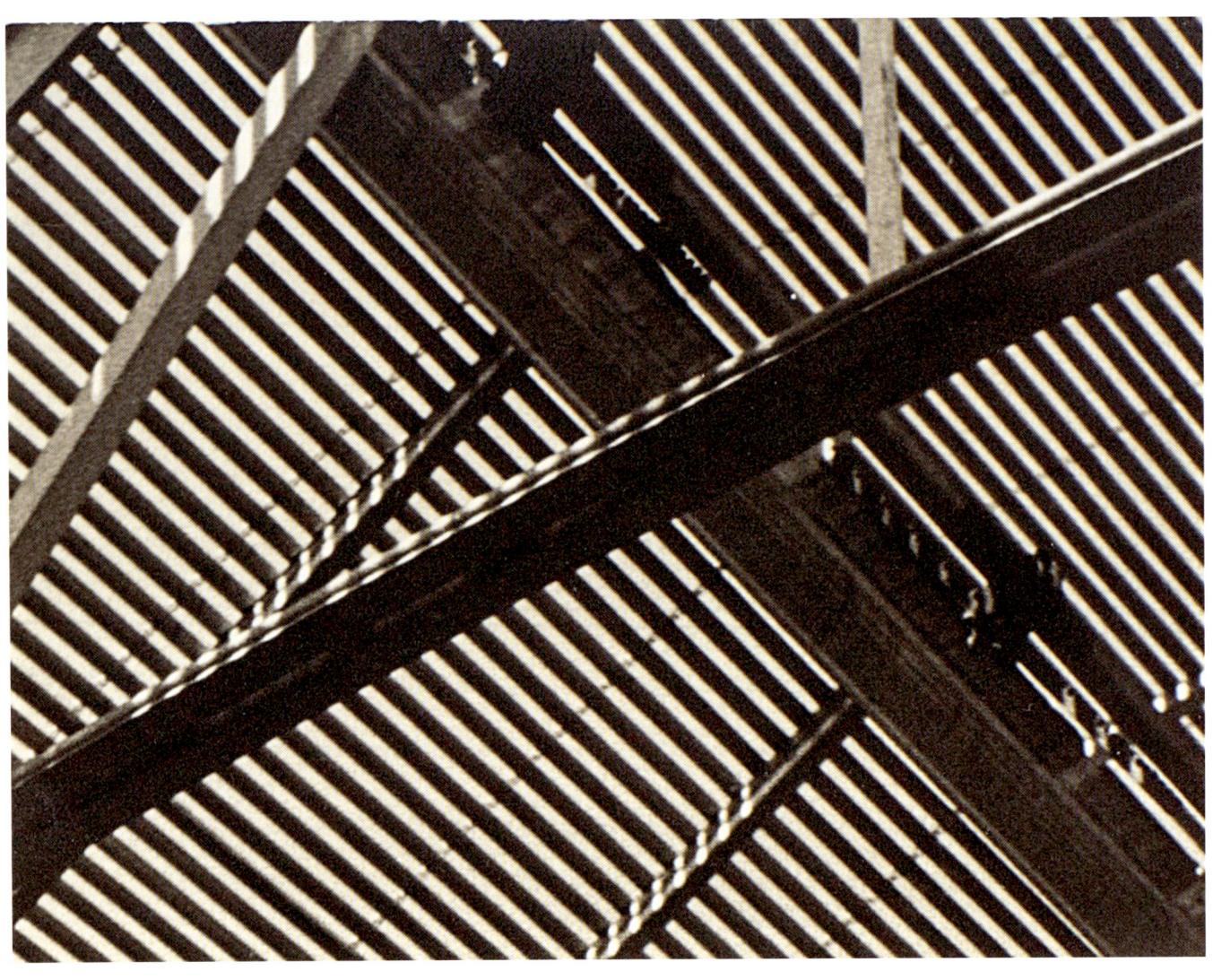

Above: **RALSTON CRAWFORD** *Untitled (Roof in Sunlight)*
1941, 6.4 × 8.3 cm

Right: **TONI SCHNEIDERS** *Rail Spider, Hamburg-Altona*
1950, 28.6 × 40.6 cm

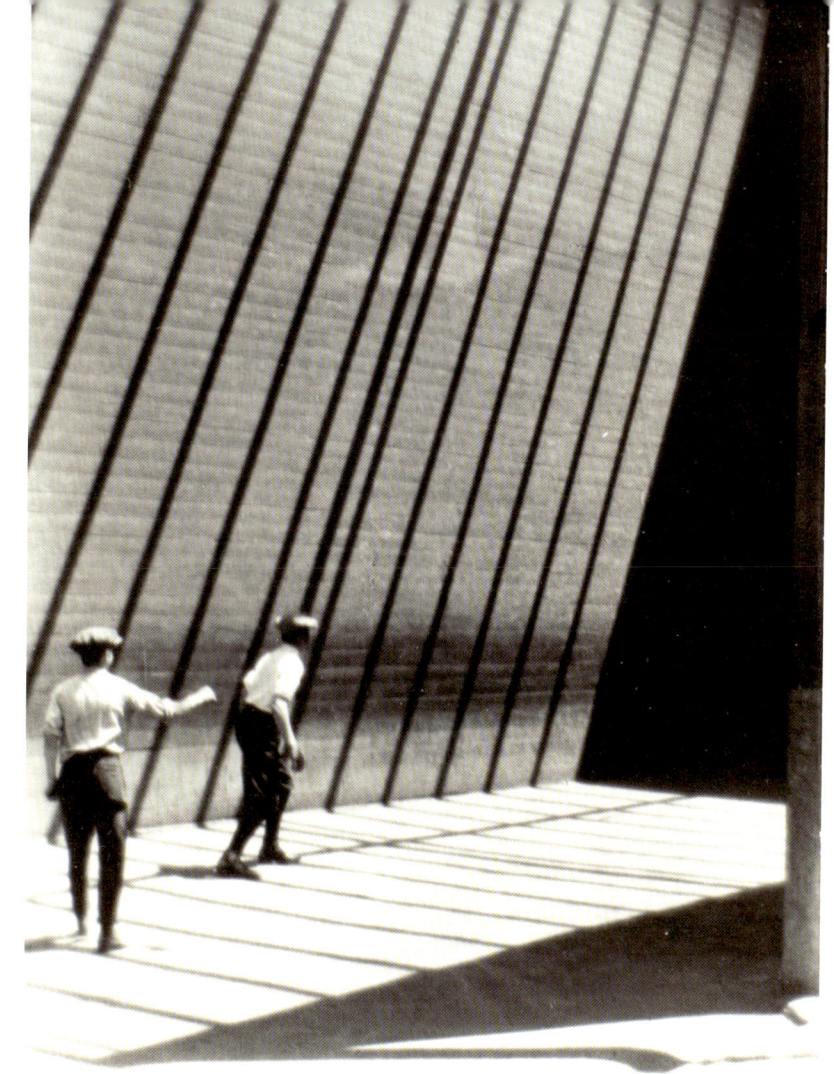

JOHAN HAGEMEYER *Untitled* 1921
printed c.1948, 12.1 × 8.9 cm

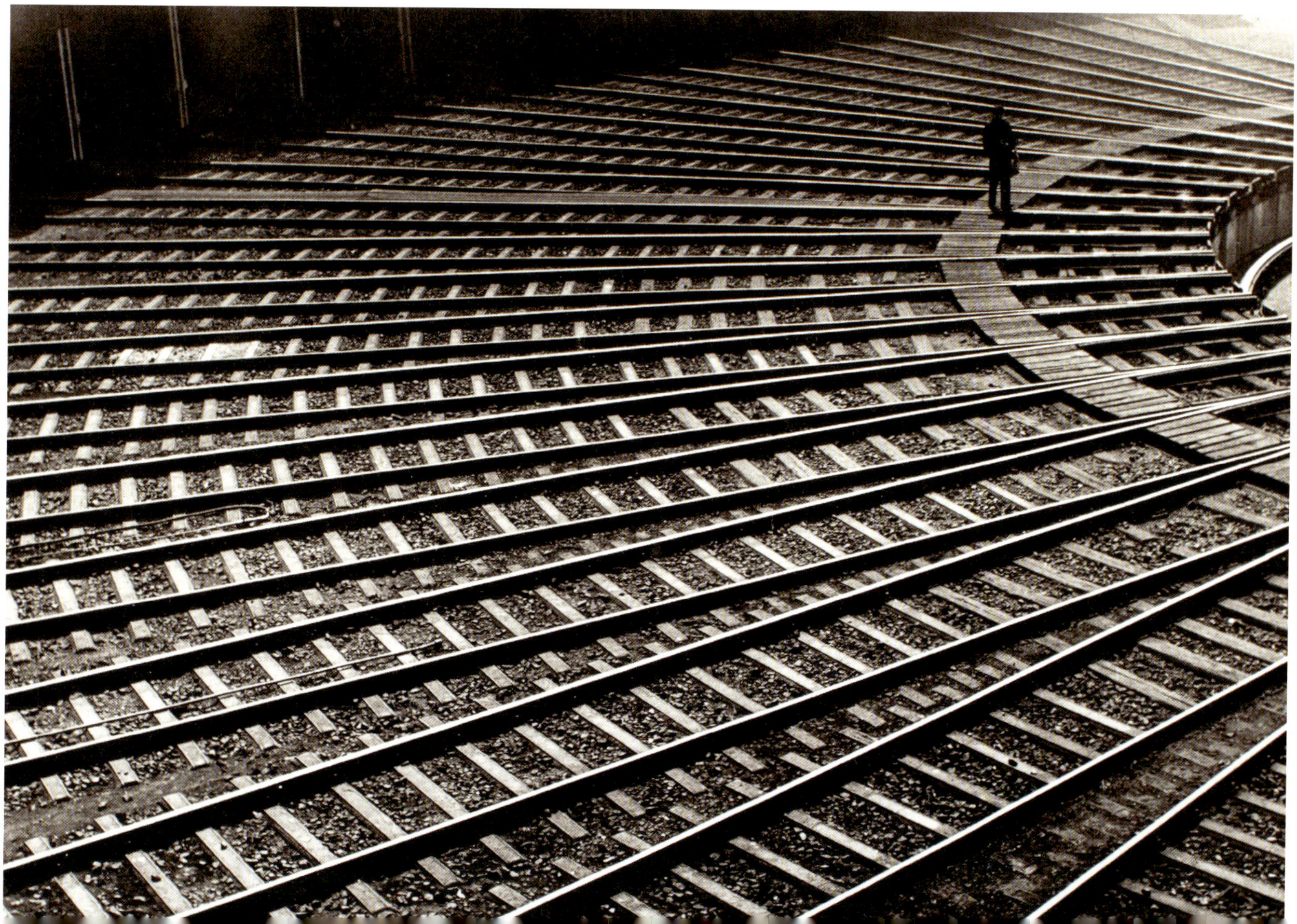

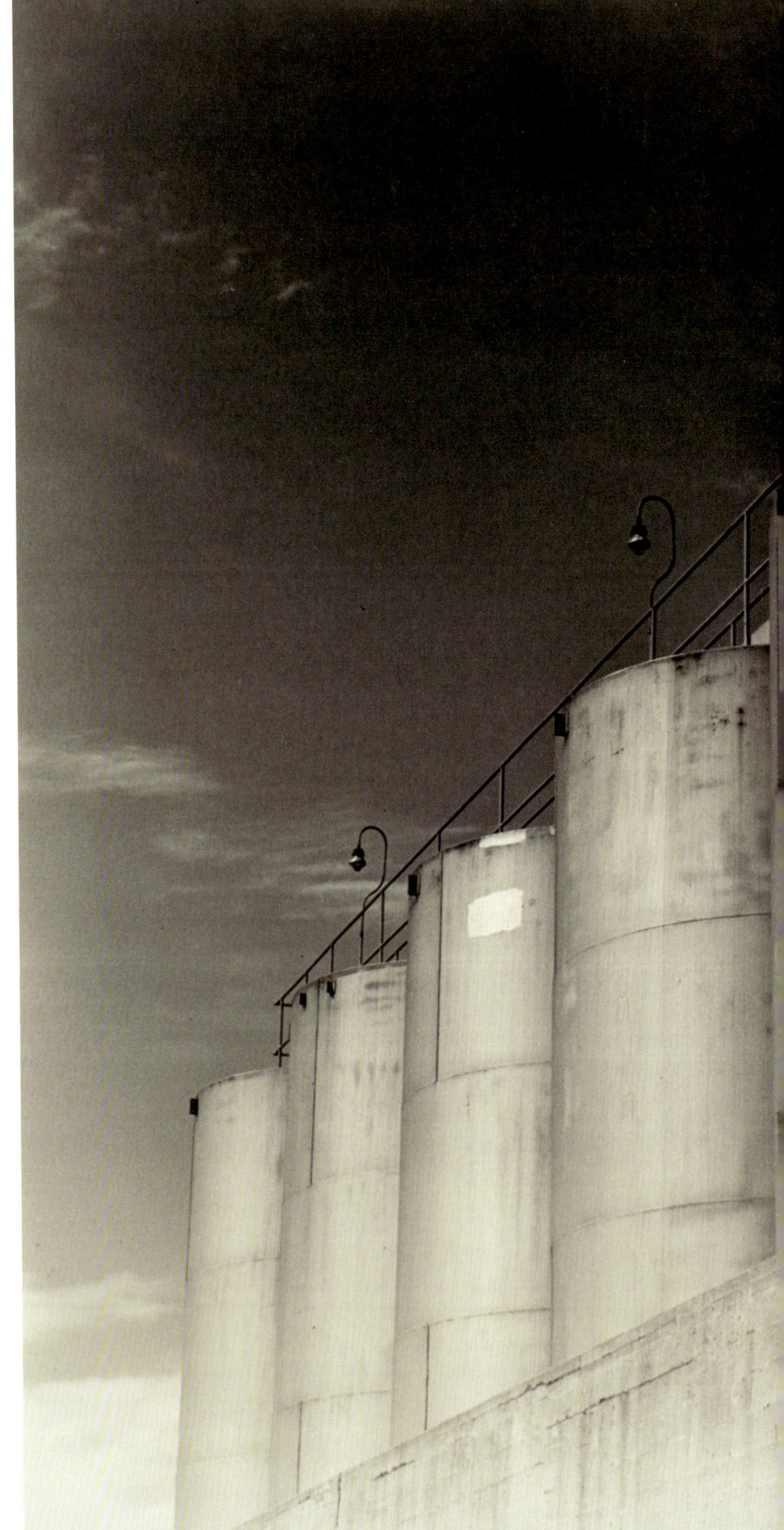

IMOGEN CUNNINGHAM
Oil Tanks 1940
18.7 × 24.4 cm

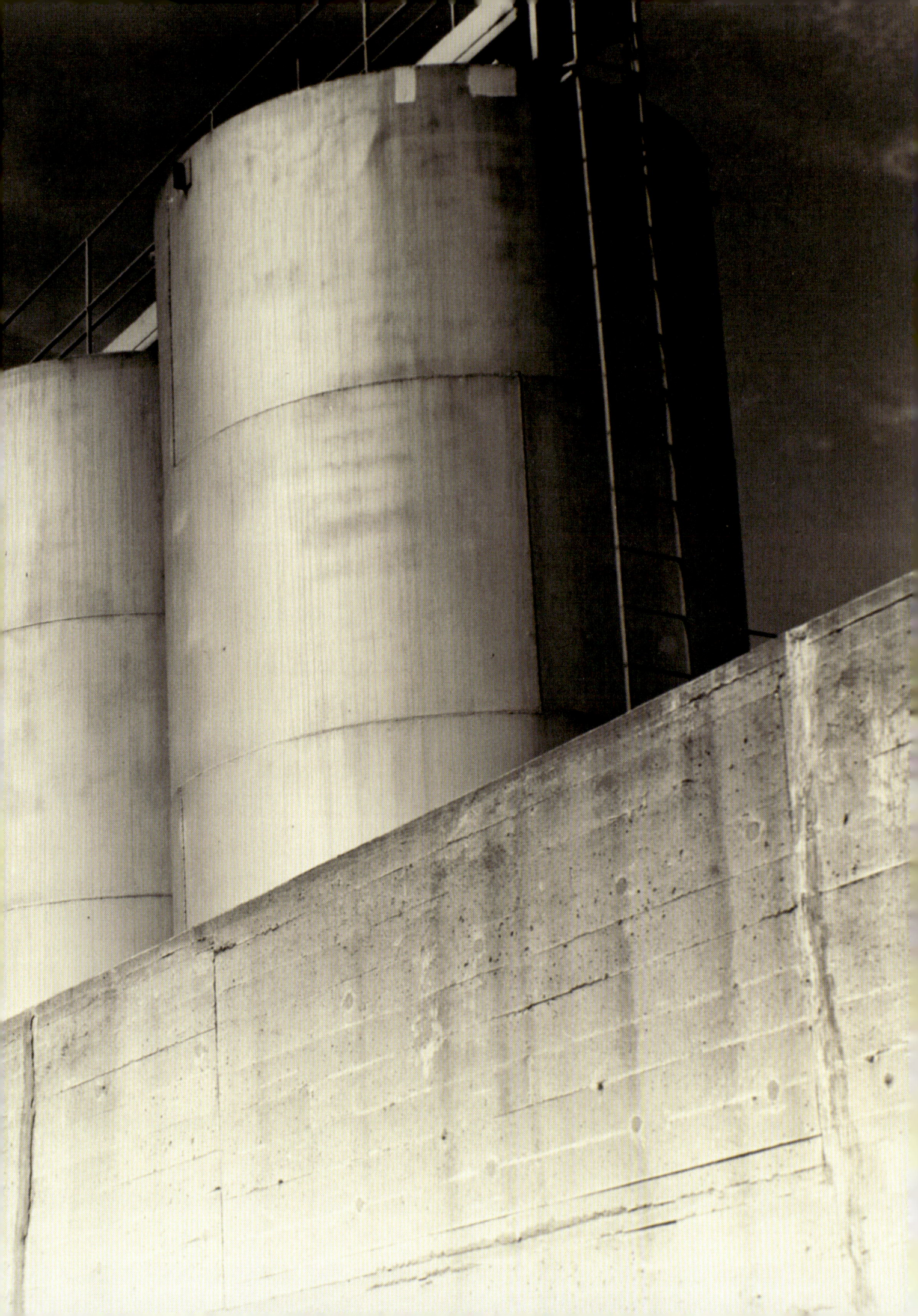

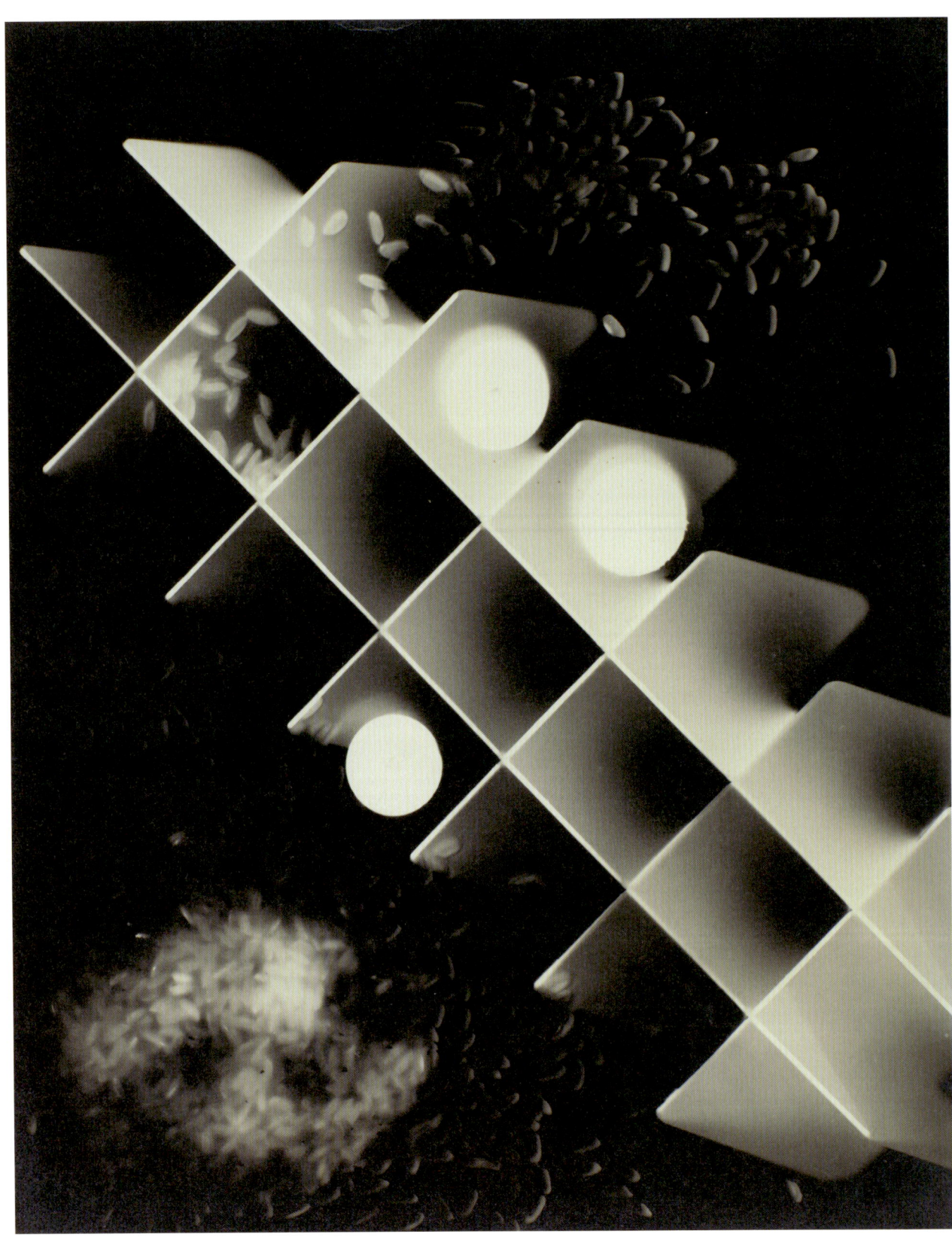

Margaret De Patta
Ice Cube Tray with Marbles and Rice
1939, 25 × 20 cm

ABSTRACTIONS

In the first decades of the twentieth century, representation by means of the camera was pushed to new limits. Photographers explored the penetrating views, intense close-ups and motion studies of the latest scientific technologies, such as the x-ray, photomicrography and chronophotography. They borrowed the visual language of modernist painters and sculptors, who were no longer concerned with showing an object in three dimensions, but proceeded to break it down into different shapes, which they then fragmented and collaged to manipulate perspective and confound perception.

Photographers found that abstraction could be achieved in-camera, through the disorientating effect of extreme angles and close-ups; in the darkroom, by distorting the negative or print with chemicals or light; and in reproduction, by isolating a detail from its context. They also found that entirely abstract images, with no grounding in reality at all, could be created by the refraction of light through mirrors and prisms. The most fertile site for photographic abstraction during this period was the photogram, an image made without a camera. Light was allowed to fall directly onto sensitised paper, tracing the patterns and shapes, or registering the shadows and outlines, of objects placed upon it.

This camera-less technique was not new: William Henry Fox Talbot had discovered the same basic process in 1835. He called it 'photogenic drawing' and it was the earliest successful attempt at recording light. From the end of the 1910s, the photogram was resuscitated by some of the most experimental photographers of the time. The dada artist Christian Schad made his 'schadographs' using scraps of discarded material; Man Ray's 'rayographs' mixed bold, graphic shapes with a lyricism that appealed to surrealist sensibilities; while the constructivists put the photogram – often together with combined negatives, reversed images and photomontage – to use in advertising and graphic design.

Experimentation with this technique continued long after the movements of the European avant-garde had declined. A major contribution was provided by László Moholy-Nagy's book *Painting Photography Film* (1925). There, he laid out images of photograms alongside examples of new scientific photography and constructivist painting to explore ideas of heightened perception. Later in the modern period, abstraction was considered in increasingly poetic and emotive terms: a 1932 exhibition review described Edward Quigley's photograms as 'light paintings' that represented 'magic realms near the metaphysical and the abstract'. In 1940 Czech photographer Jaromír Funke would provide one of the period's most complete statements on the abstract photograph in *From the Photogram to Emotion*. There, his emphasis on the poetry and magic of the camera-less photograph articulated a more brooding and emotional direction in abstraction, which would be explored further in the subjectivist movement of the following decade. EL

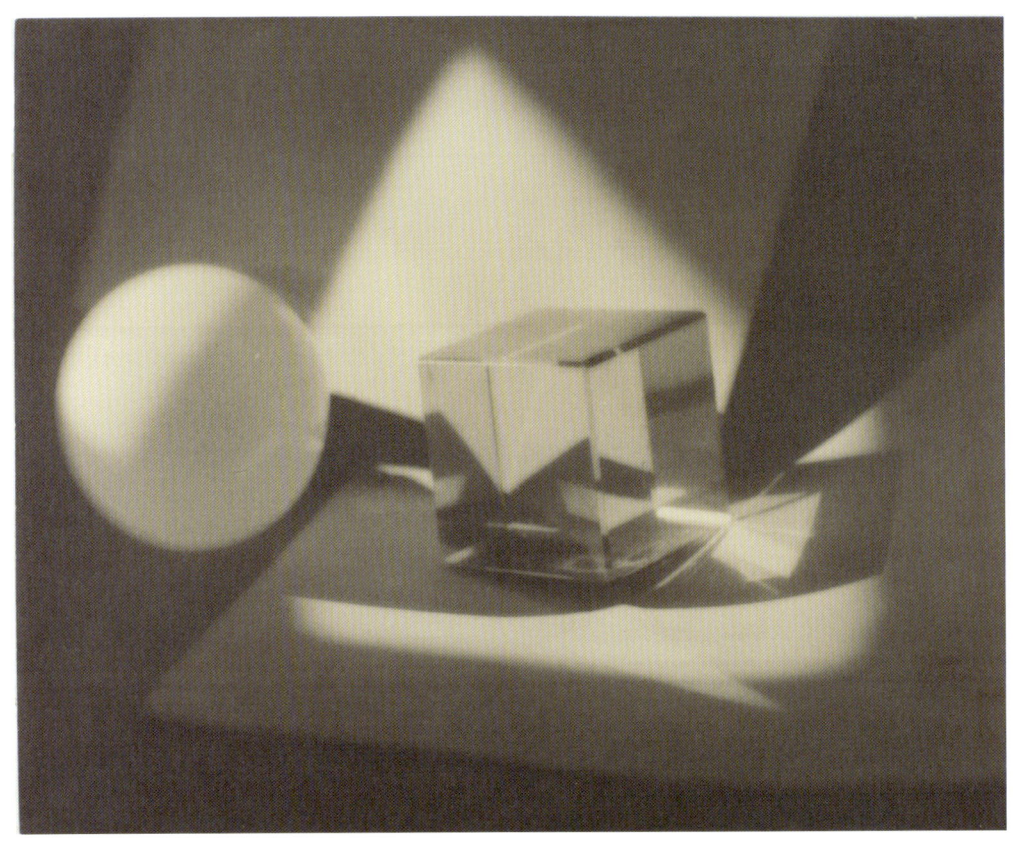

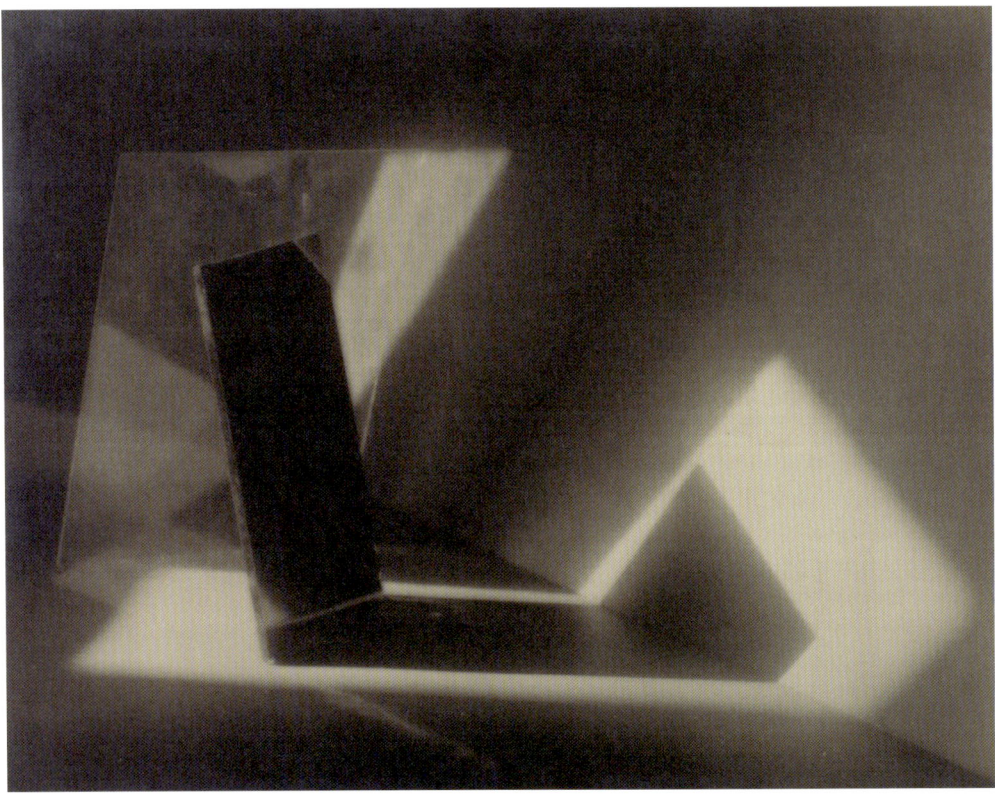

Top: **JAROMÍR FUNKE** *Photographic Construction*
c.1923, 22.9 × 28.9 cm

Above: **JAROMÍR FUNKE** *Composition* c.1924
22.9 × 29.2 cm

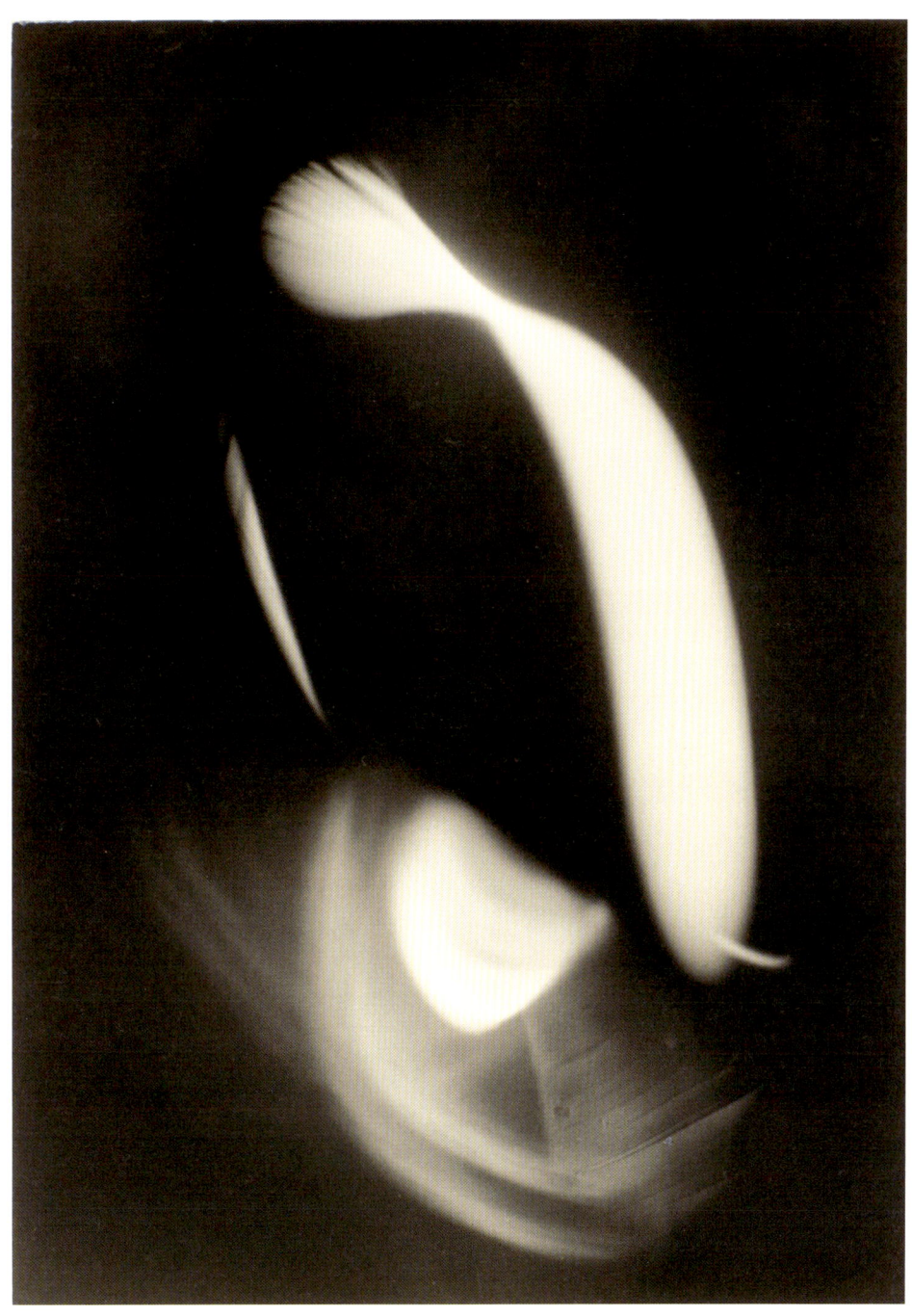

Edward Quigley *Light Abstraction* c.1931, 15.2 × 11.1 cm

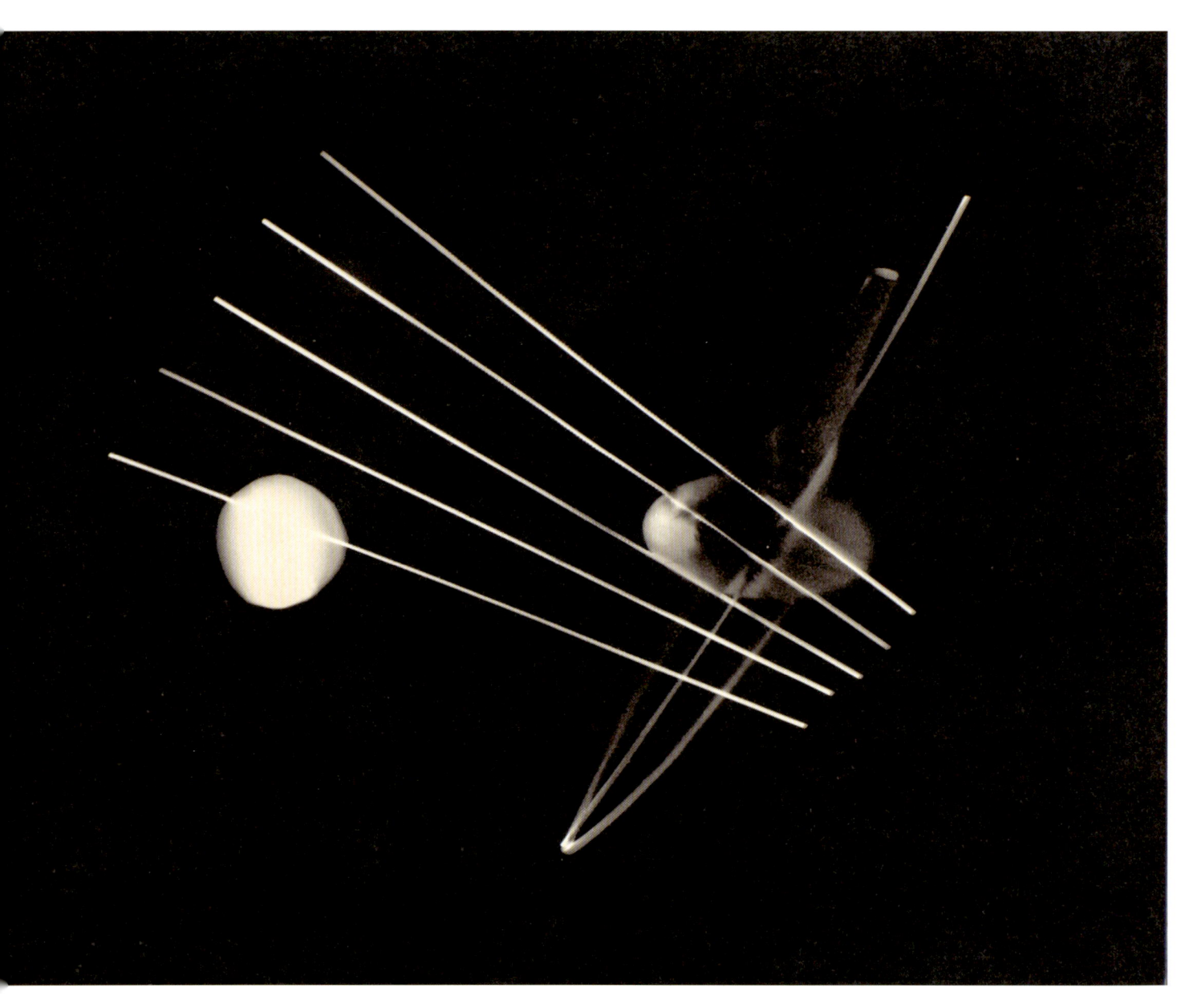

Margaret De Patta *Jewellery Design* 1939, 16.5 × 21 cm

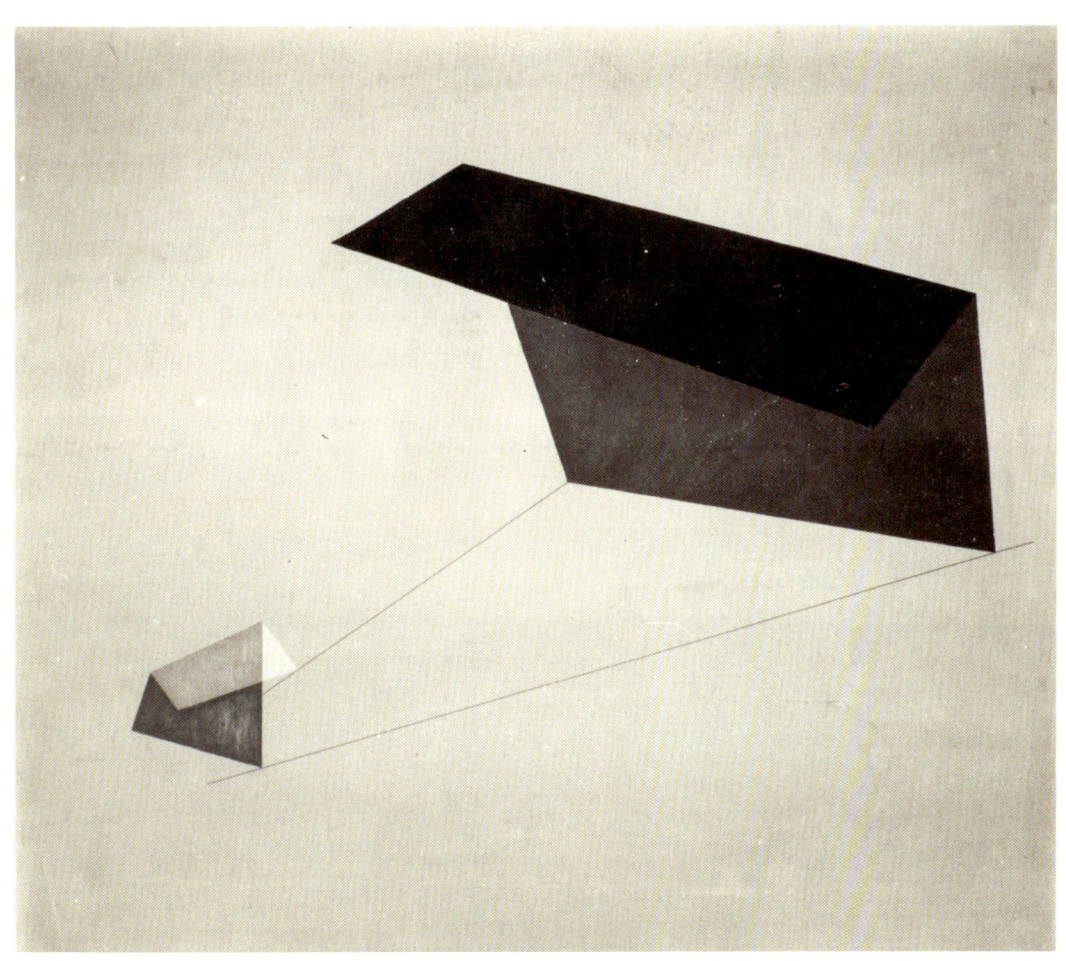

László Moholy-Nagy *LK II* 1936, 12.1 × 14 cm

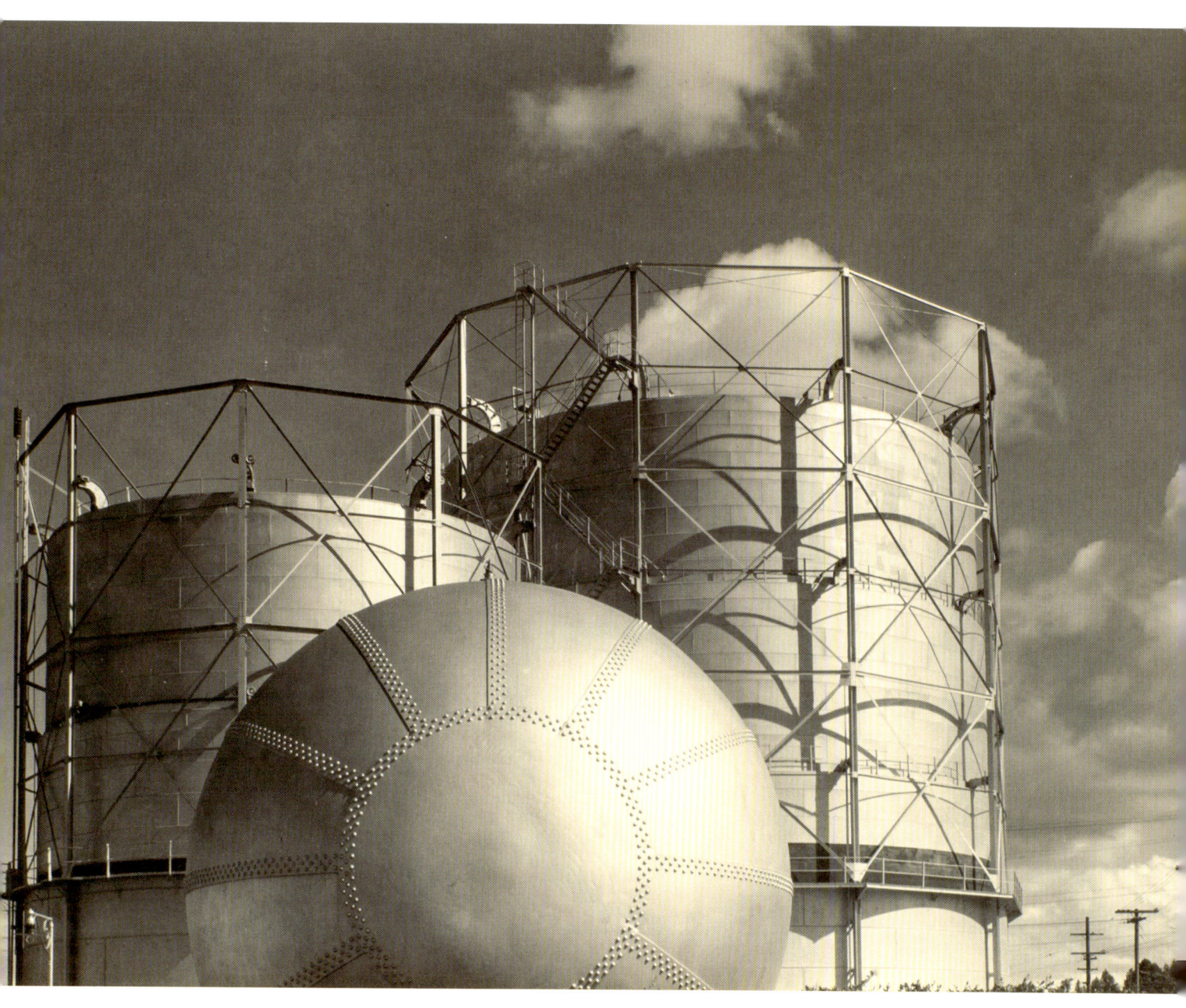

IMOGEN CUNNINGHAM *Gas Tanks* 1927, 15.2 × 20.3 cm

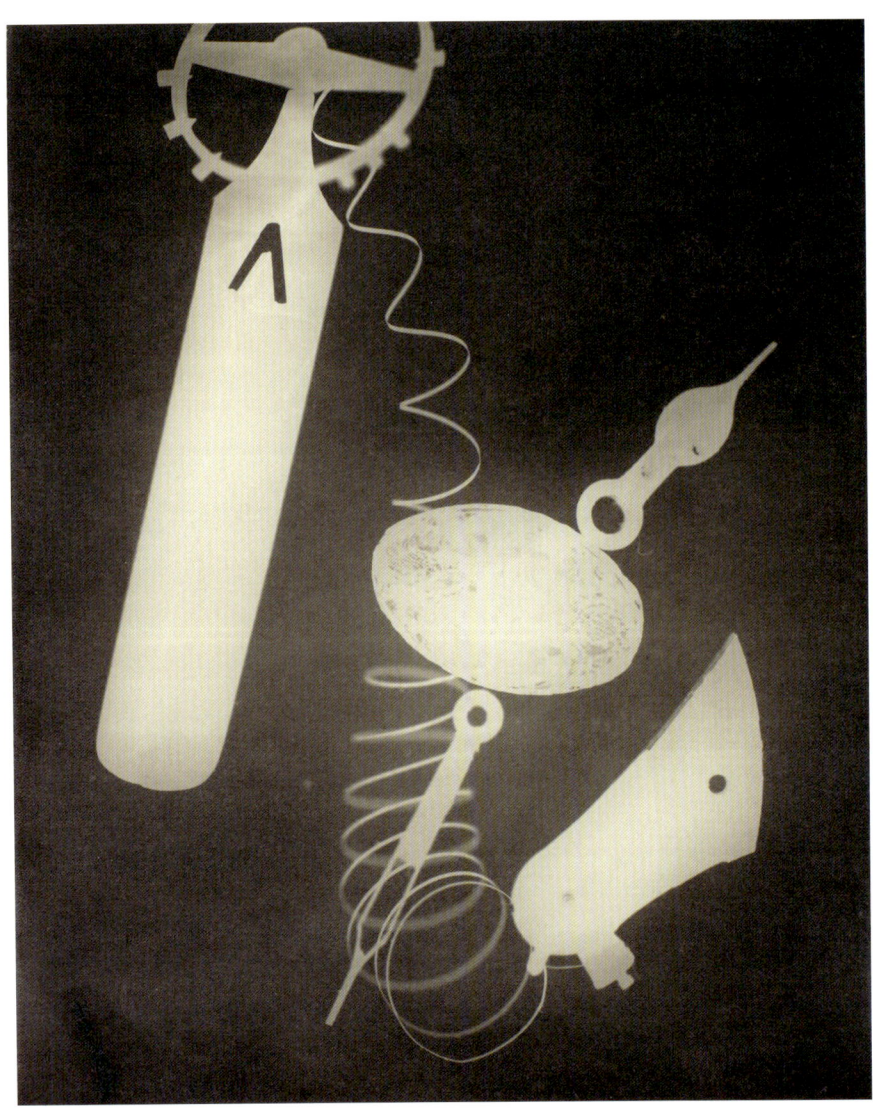

Man Ray *Rayograph* 1923, 28.3 × 22.5 cm

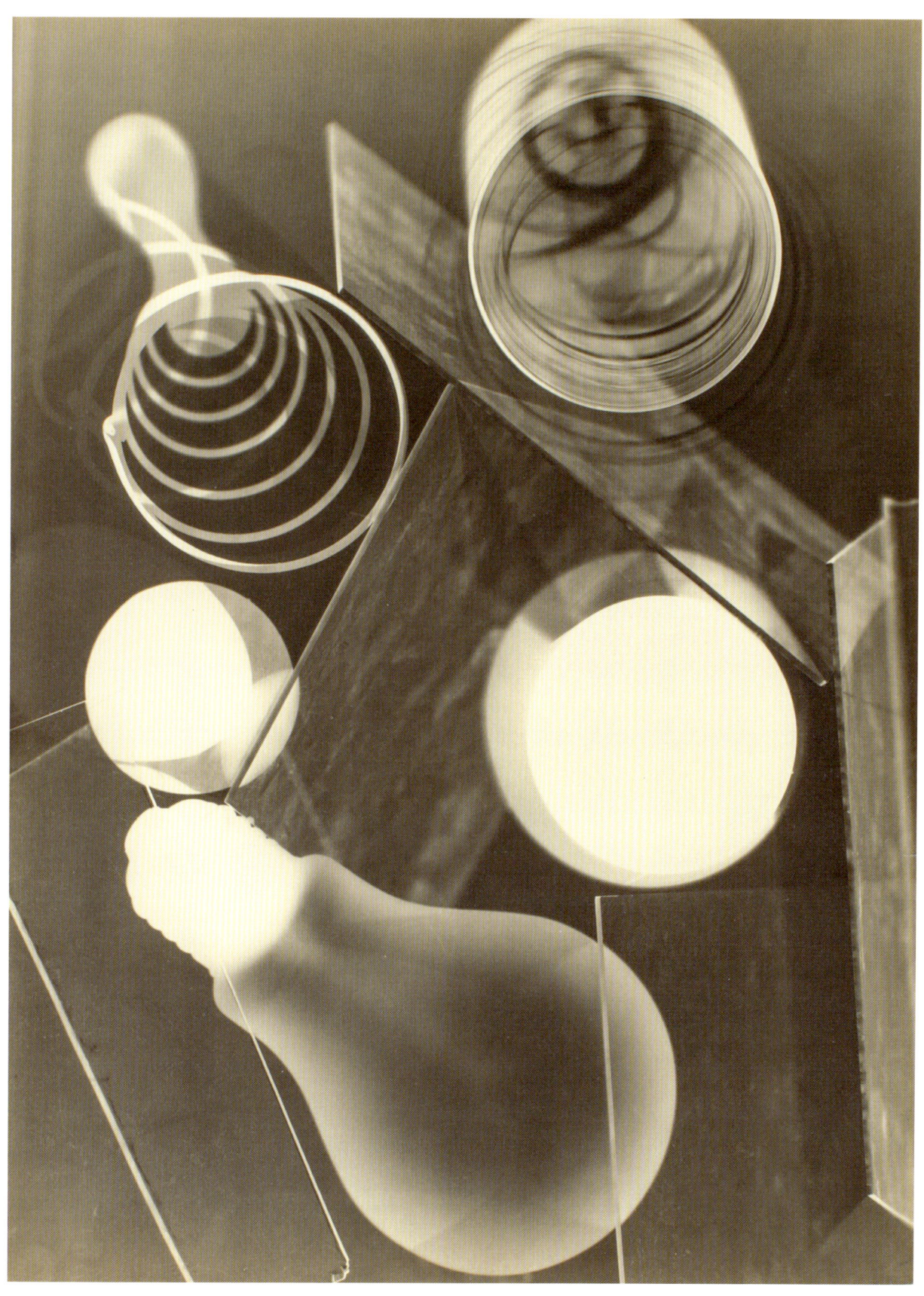

ELFRIEDE STEGEMEYER *Light Bulb, Springs, Squares and Circles* 1934, 23.5 × 17.1 cm

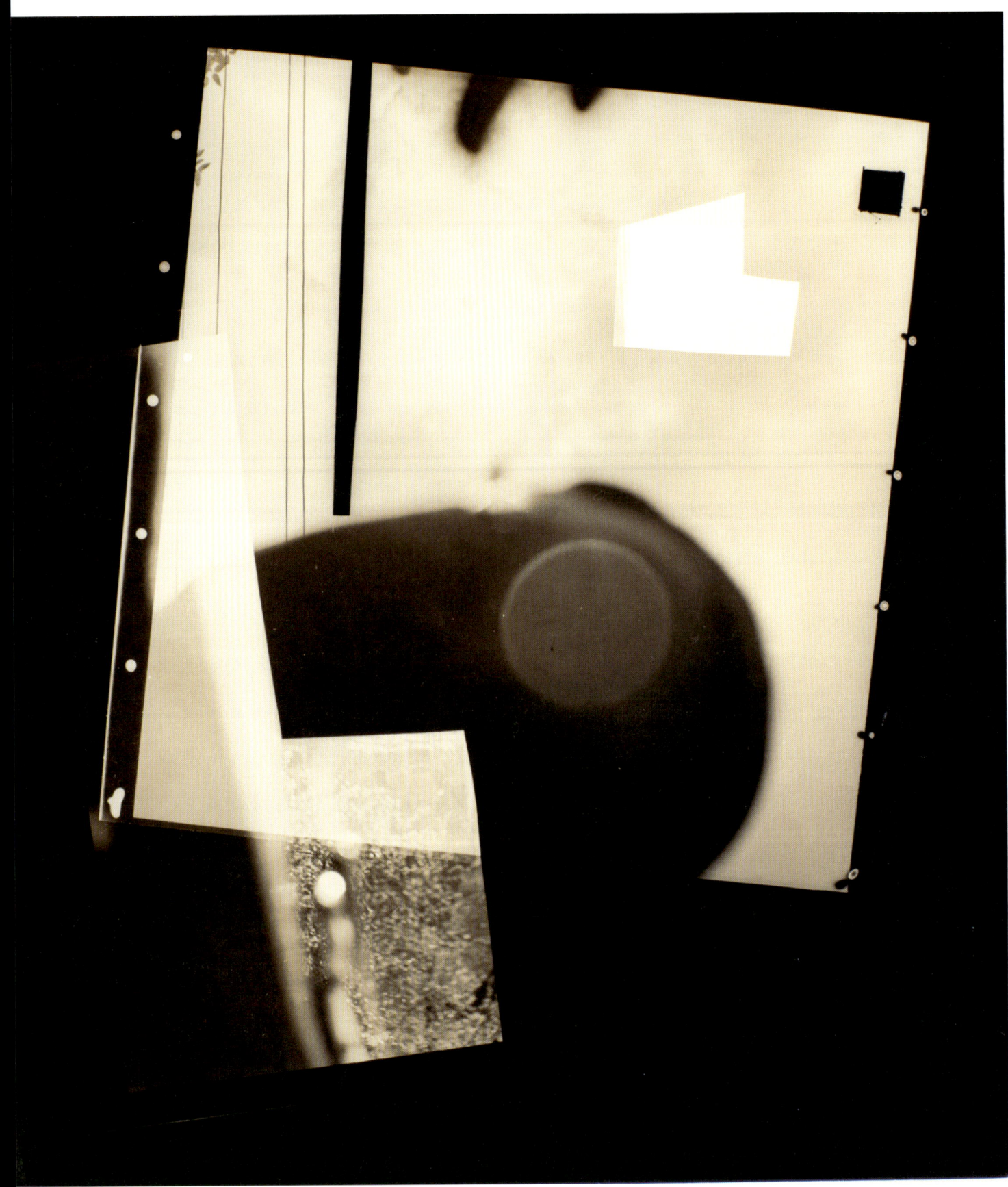

PIM VAN OS *Photogram* c.1950, 20.3 × 18.7 cm

Pim Van Os *Untitled, Geometric Abstraction* c.1950, 22.9 × 16.2 cm

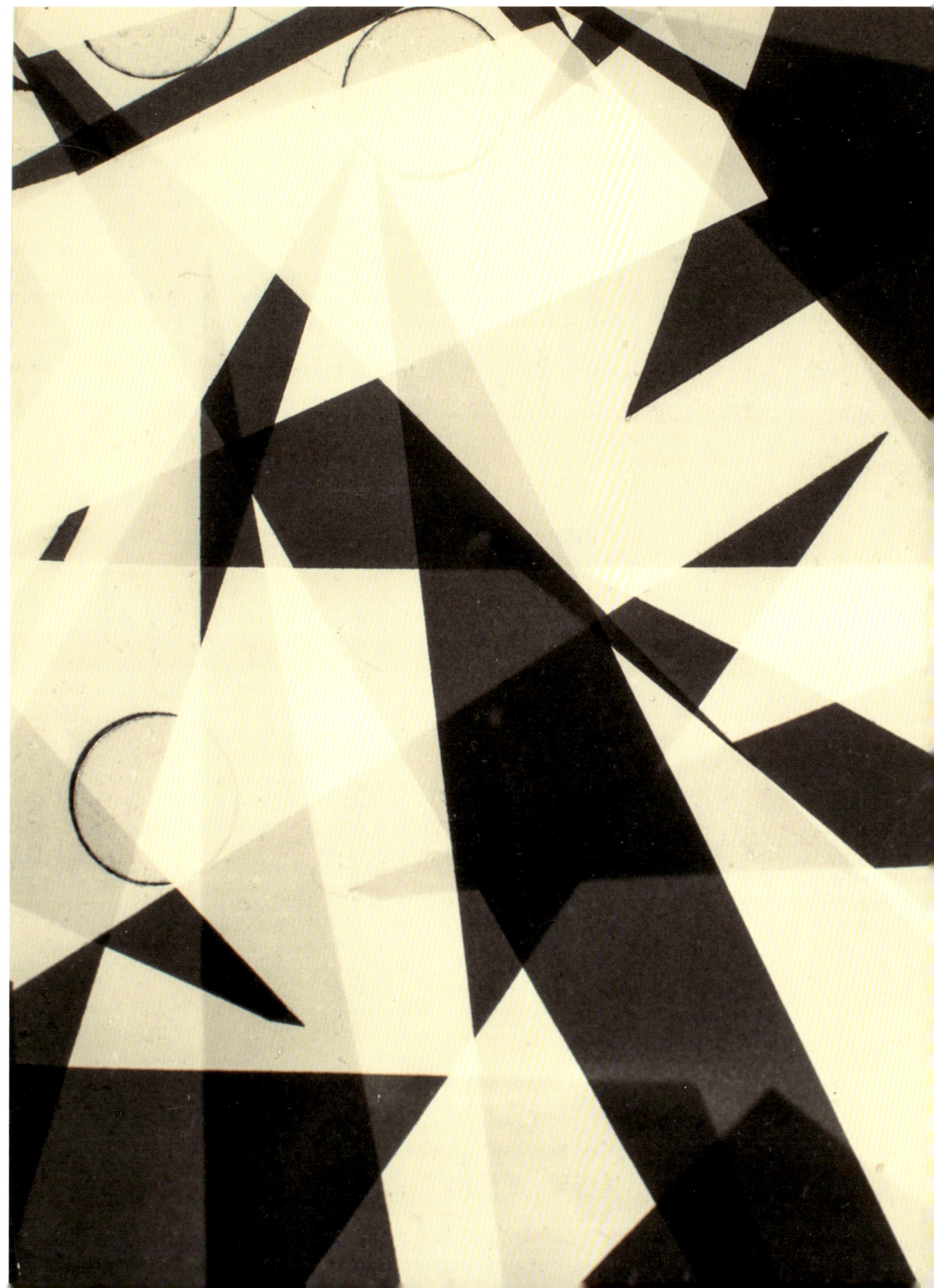

Klara Langer *Ribbon* c.1930, 7.6 × 9.2 cm

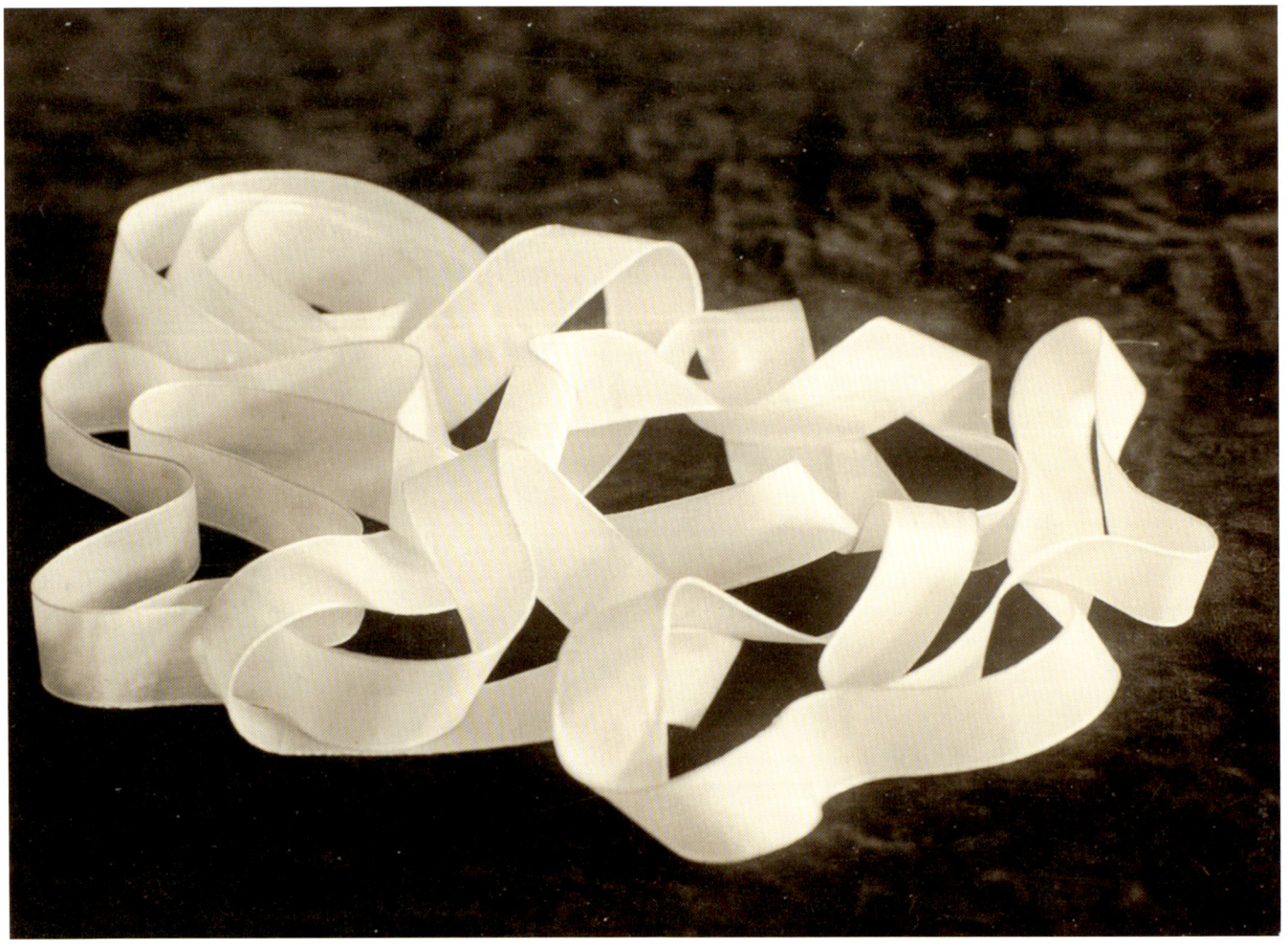

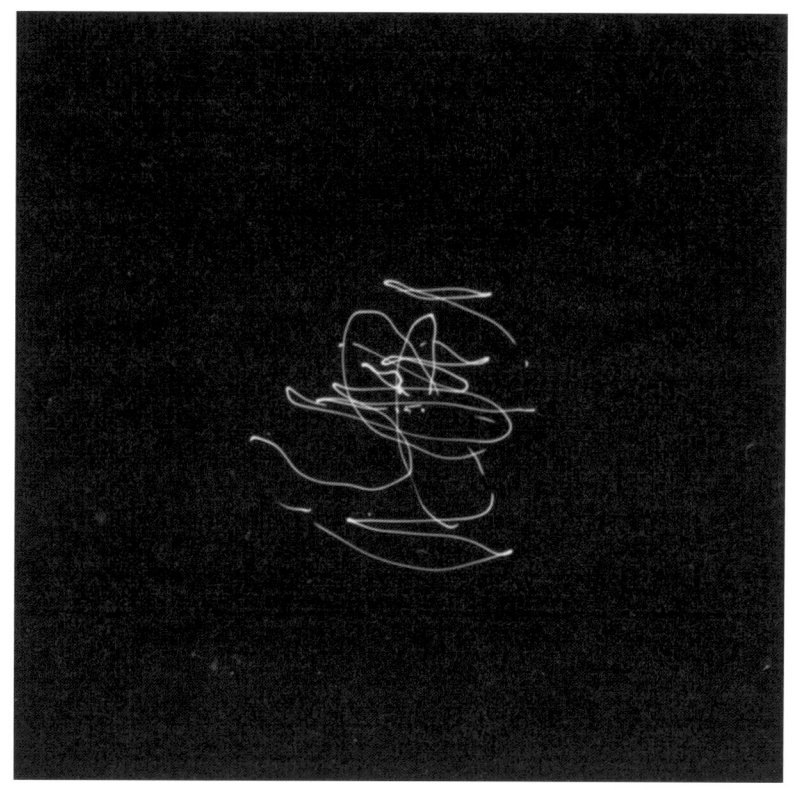

HARRY CALLAHAN *Camera Movement on Flashlight* c.1946, 5.1 × 5.1 cm

223

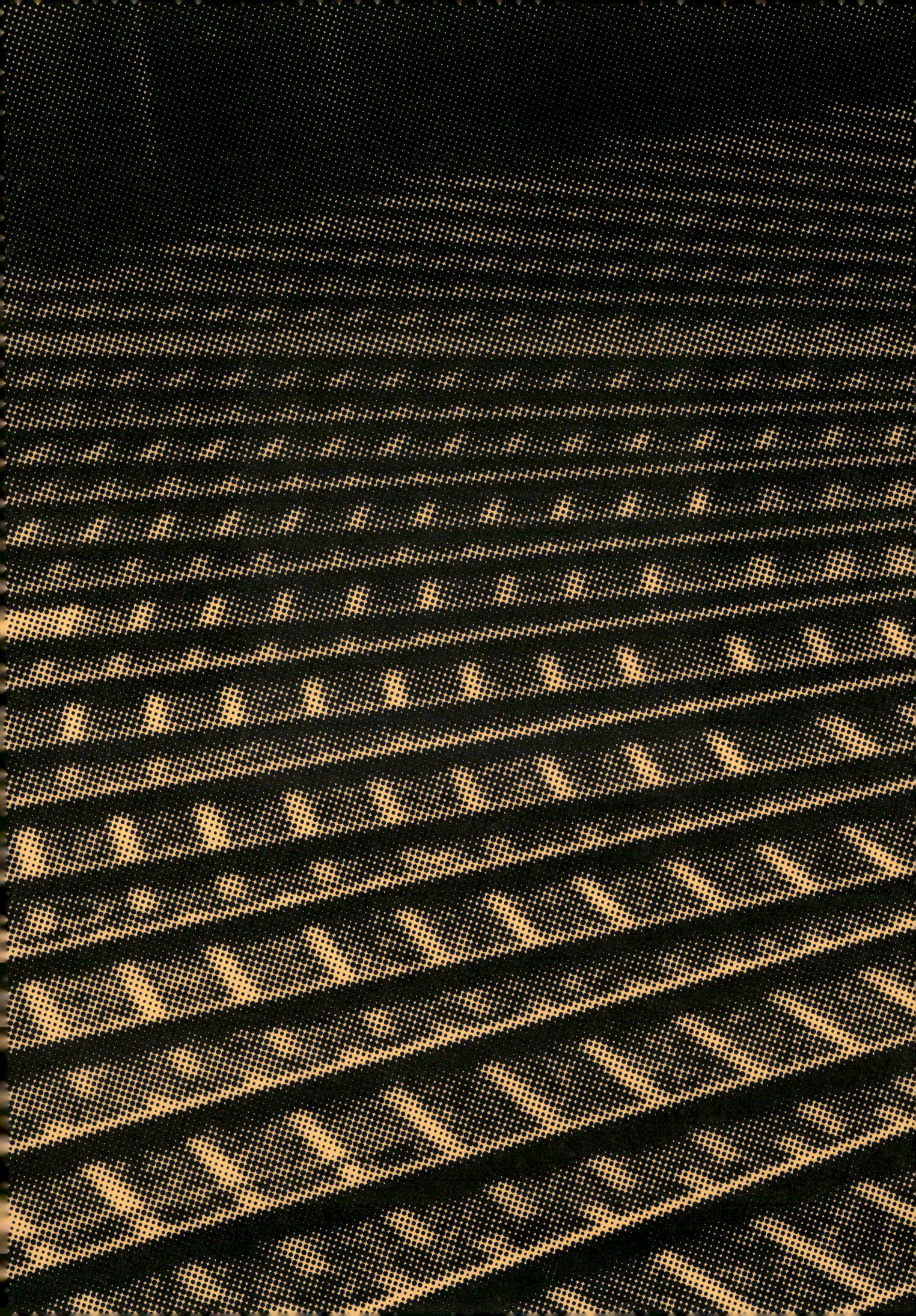

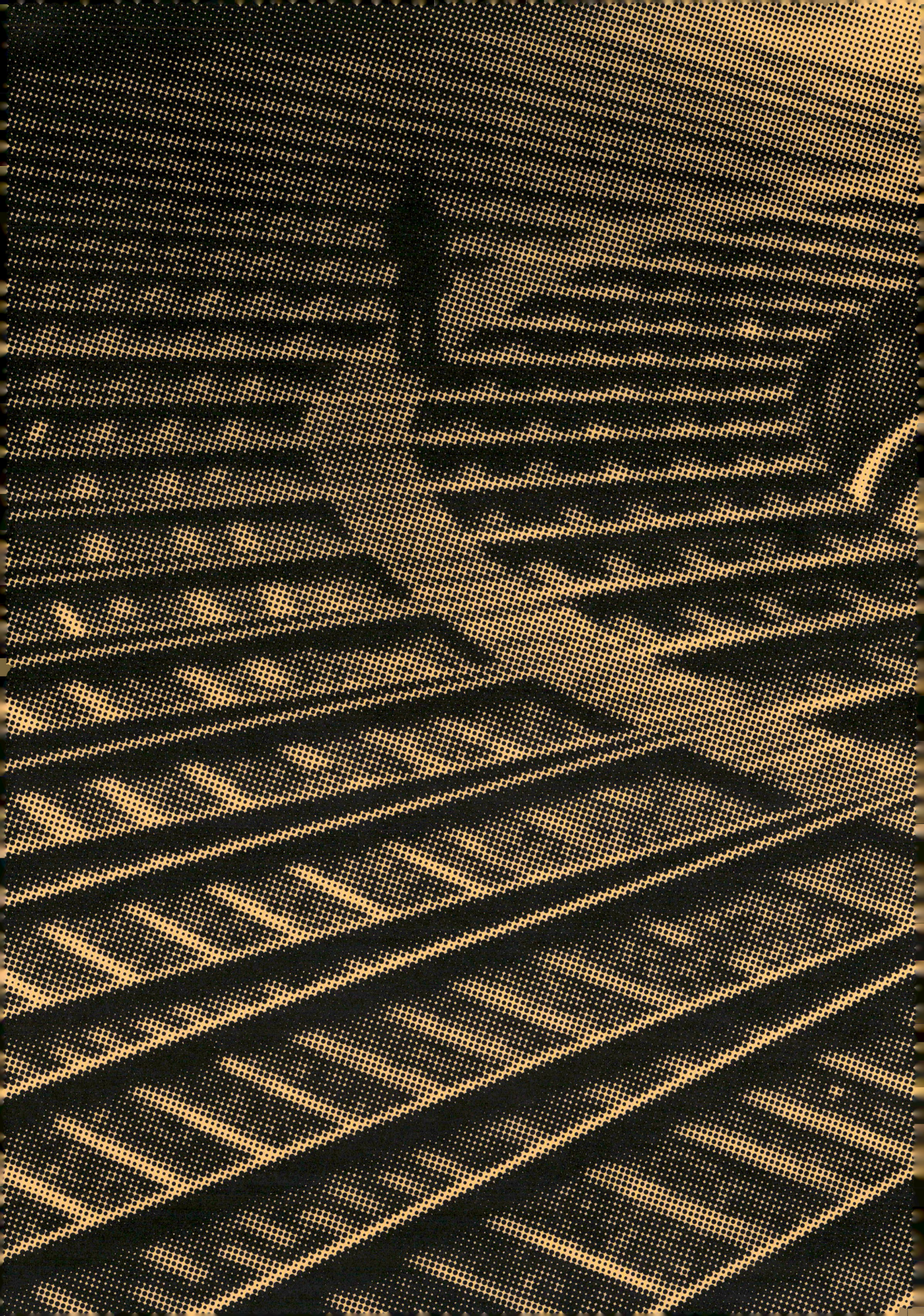

The birth of modernist photography was both a product of, and response to, rapid technical innovations in the mechanical age; a period when increased change was occurring throughout society with the industrialisation and urbanisation of the modern world. Photography, along with film, both mediums that symbolised progress, had by the 1920s become central to daily life, the importance of which was underlined by László Moholy-Nagy's comment that 'a knowledge of photography is just as important as that of the alphabet. The illiterates of the future will be ignorant of the use of camera and pen alike.'[1] Three major factors contributed to photography's ability to shape and transform visual language in the modernist period. First, rapid technical innovations allowed images to be reproduced and distributed easily and affordably throughout mainstream society, thus enabling photography to become an instrument of mass communication. Second, unlike other traditional mediums, photography could objectively record the everyday world in precise detail, expanding the field of human vision. Third, changing attitudes meant that artists approached photography with a more experimental attitude, playing with ideas of abstraction, defying all its inherent rules and characteristics. The capacity of photography to harness technical innovation, even to the extent of the manipulation of its own process, developed into a unique regeneration of its own visual language offering radical new perspectives on modernity.

What was originally seen as the medium's downfall – its ability to be reproduced, and later, mass-produced – had, by the turn of the century, become its biggest strength. The ability to mass-produce photographic images was largely due to advancements in the development of half-tone photomechanical printing techniques in the late 1880s; the half-tone process allowed images to be printed directly onto paper by translating the black, white and grey tones of a photograph into dots of various sizes with the use of a screen.[2] More traditional printing techniques, such as photogravure and collotype, delivered excellent quality but were costly and time consuming, whereas the new half-tone print was fast and cost-effective, allowing for true mass production of the photographic image. As a result, the popularity of illustrated magazines surged in the first decades of the twentieth century, one of the most popular in Europe being the German-based magazine *Berliner Illustrirte Zeitung* (*BIZ*) with a circulation of more than one million by 1920 and more than two million in the 1930s. *BIZ*'s innovative format, placing the photographic image at its heart, became the template for other mass-market publications such as Henry Luce's *Life* magazine.[3] Originally illustrated with a mixture of hand-drawn images in the late nineteenth century,

these magazines began to move over to the photographic image and, by the 1930s, they were almost exclusively photographic. Kurt Korff, the editor of *BIZ*, encapsulated these changes:

> To the extent that life became more hectic, and the individual was less prepared to leaf through a magazine in a quiet moment, to that extent it became necessary to find a sharper, more efficient form of visual representation, one which did not lose its impact on the reader even if he only glanced fleetingly at the magazine page by page.[4]

Photography brought with it a shift in pace and perception. The act of viewing changed and rather than contemplating a painting, the viewer now absorbed several photographic images in quick secession. This transformation in visual communication was reinforced by thinkers across Europe and North America. As writer Lincoln Kirstein observed when discussing Walker Evans's photographs: 'It is a good deal easier to look at a picture than to read a pararaph. The American reading public is fast becoming not even a looking public, but a glancing or glimpsing public',[5] suggesting that even in the 1940s social commentators were acknowledging the shortened attention spans and rapid absorption of information that we attribute to the digital generation today.

Now a familiar part of everyday life, as artist Johannes Molzahn stated in an article aptly titled 'Stop Reading! Look!', 'it is the photo that continually informs us ... through the penetrating language of the image'.[6] Modern society now knew how to read an image, with all its complexity and layers of meaning, a development crucial to the acceptance of avant-garde techniques into mainstream media, such as magazines, advertisements and publications. Harnessing and exploiting the visual power of the photographic image also played a central role in cultural and political movements of the time. As the appetite for image-based material increased, traditional, non-mechanical art forms seemed less relevant and, indeed, less popular among the avant-garde. As the Russian artist El Lissitzky pointed out in relation to post-revolutionary Russia, 'The (painted) picture fell apart together with the old world which had created it for itself', referring to how traditional mediums represented the past, not just artistically but culturally and politically, adding 'the new world will not need little pictures. If it needs a mirror, it has the photograph and the cinema.'[7] In Germany, following its defeat in the First World War, and in Russia, following the 1917 revolution, the past had lost its attraction and photography was championed as the medium of the future. In Germany, at least, photography

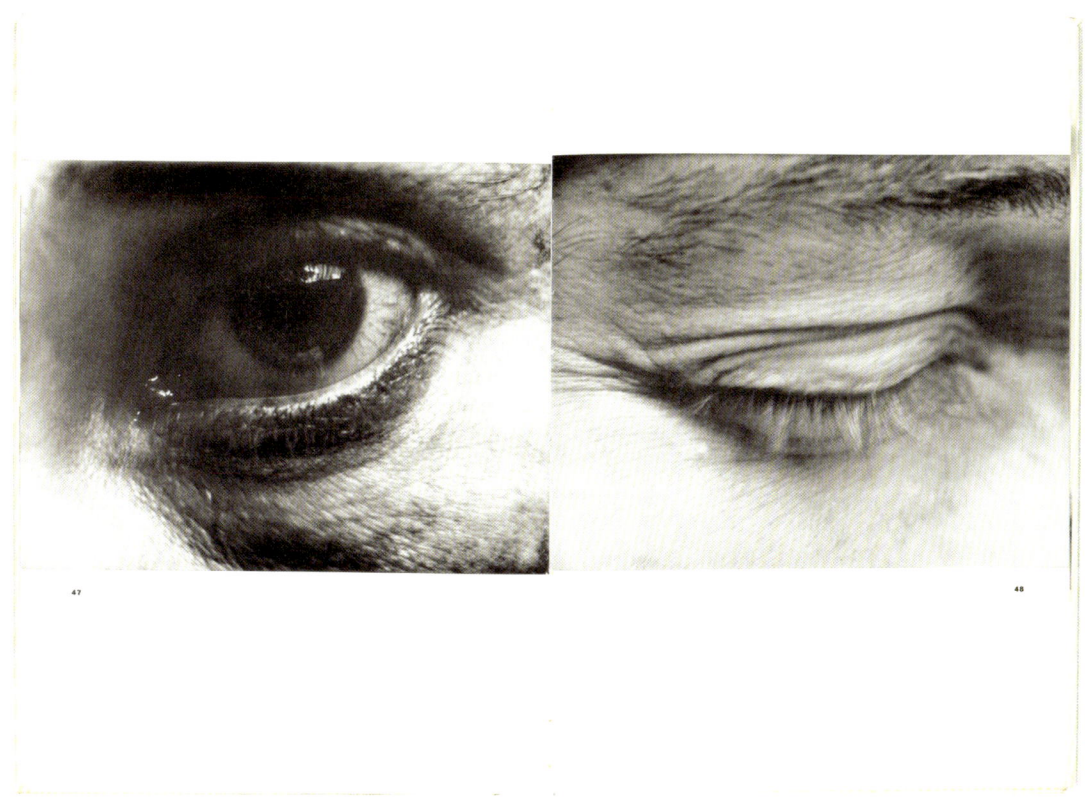

was seen as an important tool that could unite art and technology philosophically; a way of bringing together ingenuity, manufacturing and design in a modern world. Similarly, in Russia photography was seen as a means of documenting and delivering the aims of the newly established Soviet regime, its goal to communicate and cement the message of the revolution.

The camera, with its capacity to 'complete or supplement our optical instrument, the eye',[8] and the reproducible photographs, were widely embraced as the instruments through which a new visual language could be constructed. From this universal acceptance, different and often opposing ideas emerged as to which direction it should take. In the first issue of the photographic annual *Das Deutsche Lichtblid* (1927), two opposing statements appeared outlining the possibilities of the photographic medium, statements that would dominate aesthetic and theoretical debates for decades to come; one by Albert Renger-Patzsch, championing precision, and the other by Moholy-Nagy, advocating a move towards abstraction. Renger-Patzsch believed that 'the secret of a good photograph resides in its realism'.[9] In his view, the mechanical age with its new technically advanced tools gave artists the opportunity to strive towards precision, to embrace the inherent mechanical qualities of the medium

and present the world in all its detail. This reflected the ideas of Neue Sachlichkeit, known internationally as New Objectivity, a movement that emerged in Germany in the interwar years, first in painting and then embraced by photographers with the intention of capturing the everyday world in a clear and objective way. At the opposing end of this spectrum was Moholy-Nagy, who believed that photography could be used to deconstruct reality through abstraction, a concept that lay at the heart of what he referred to as 'the new vision' and was showcased in his seminal publication *Painting Photography Film* (1925).

PRECISION

In the movement towards precision, the camera, with its perceived ability to record objectively and in detail, was of the utmost importance. In an approach related to scientific or medical photography, artists used the camera to view close-up details, invisible to the naked eye. Renger-Patzsch, for example, saw the camera as an instrument to 'extend human vision so that forms too small to see with the unaided eye could be examined and appreciated'.[10] This study of beauty in the everyday, both natural and man-made, presented ordinary objects in a fresh and exciting way, as published in his photobook *Die Welt ist Schön* (The World

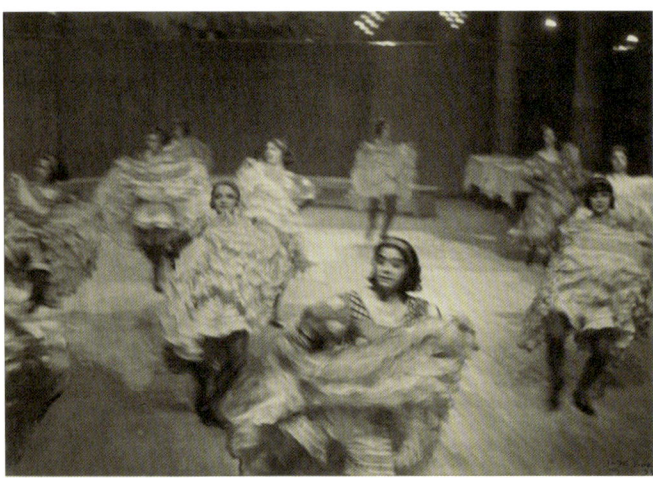

is Beautiful) of 1928. This same direct approach, exposing what is usually overlooked, was also applied to the human body in works such as Aenne Biermann's *Open and Closed Eye* (fig.14). These close-up, detailed images allow the viewer to examine part of the human body in detail, in this case through the intimate form of the photobook, which opens up a new perspective, a means of study unconstrained by time that would not be available without the aid of the camera. Although such images exhibited extreme precision and detail which suggests a certain degree of truth, they were also manipulated by cropping, which changed the context, or meaning, of the image by both revealing and concealing information simultaneously. For example, the viewer can examine the eye in extreme detail; however, the viewer does not know who the eye belongs to. This precise, detailed and measured approach to the photographic medium was echoed in many contexts. American photographer Imogen Cunningham worked in a similar style, as demonstrated by *Magnolia Blossom, Tower of Jewels* (p.166), which reflected her involvement in Group f.64. Founded on the West Coast of the United States in 1932, Group f.64 took its name from the smallest aperture on a large format camera, underlining its dedication to the mechanical nature of photography. By faithfully using this setting, the photographers were able to record the greatest depth of field which, in turn, allowed for the majority of the pictures to be in sharp focus.

Seemingly insignificant details in the everyday environment now attracted attention and assumed a new importance. Gustav Stotz, director of the *Film and Photo* exhibition wrote in 1929:

A new optic has developed. We see things differently now, without painterly intent in the impressionistic sense. Today things are important that earlier were hardly noticed:

for example shoe laces, gutters, spools of thread, fabrics, machines etc. They interest us for their material substance, for the simple quality of the thing-in-itself; they interest us as means of creating space-form on surfaces, as the bearers of the darkness and the light.[11]

It was this willingness to embrace the mechanical nature of photography, and utilise the exact features that separated it from other traditional art forms, which defined the modernist period. The human eye, in all its complexity, 'auto-corrects' the world so that it is seen in a 'normal' perspective. The camera, however, can be manipulated and pushed to extremes to reveal something new. The joy derived from embracing the potential of the machine, in a cinematic context, was described by Russian filmmaker Dziga Vertov as early as 1923: 'I, the machine, show you the world as only I can see it. I emancipate myself ... from human immobility. I am in constant motion ... My path leads towards the creation of a fresh perception of the world.'[12]

Ground-breaking technical and mechanical innovations expanded the development of photography during this period. At the forefront of German engineering, the Leica, released in 1925, was the first camera to use roll film; this development employed 35mm cinema film stock adapted for a still camera, which allowed for twenty-four or thirty-six frames, or exposures, to be captured in sequence. The small negatives were then enlarged in the darkroom to make a print. Although not as crisp as a plate negative, what it lacked in detail it made up for in versatility. With a range of film speeds, the Leica could capture movement and adapt to different lighting conditions, making it the ultimate hand-held camera. Its design and the use of roll film were replicated worldwide and became the standard in mainstream photographic technology until the advent of the digital camera.

Now, with several options available, photographers could choose the tool to fit their purpose, often switching between cameras depending on the task, as described by Moholy-Nagy in his photobook *Street Markets of London* (1936): 'As a rule I prefer to work with a large camera in order to obtain the minutely graded white-grey photovalues of the contact print, impossible to achieve in enlargement. But ... for taking rapid shots without being observed ... I always return to the Leica.'[13] With the invention of the hand-held camera, what was once a cumbersome device began to blend into everyday life, fostering the development of street and documentary photography. The candid quality inherent in this now small and versatile machine went on to transform photography, particularly photojournalism, and was crucial in the development of theories such as Henri Cartier-Bresson's 'decisive moment'. With innovation came choice and with choice came tighter scrutiny of the medium; photographers could now adapt the machine to the practice; photography was no longer limited by one set of technological parameters but rather encompassed many variants with multiple possibilities and results.

An affiliation with a certain technology or technique often became synonymous with a specific photographer's work. This can be said of Ilse Bing, who Emmanuel Sougez described in his review of the 29th Salon International d'art photographique in 1934 as the 'Queen of the Leica'.[14] Bing built a career around this new camera, adopting it early on and pushing the technology to its limits by photographing moving subjects in lowlight. The results, such as *Can-Can Dancer, Moulin Rouge, Paris* (fig.15), which were sometimes blurred with a visible grainy quality, injected dynamism into a medium that is often fixated on freezing movement. Bing also captured movement in crisp perfection, seen in *Dancer, Willem van Loon, Paris* (p.148), signalling that artists with a willingness to experiment could operate between precision and abstraction, producing sharp detail alongside suggestive blur, resulting in an interesting and diverse body of work.

The assumed ability of the camera to provide a mirror onto the world was enhanced by the fact that not only could it record what the human eye saw, it could also document beyond the eye's capabilities. As Moholy-Nagy put it, the 'camera has offered us amazing possibilities which we are only just beginning to exploit. The visual image has been expanded and even the modern lens is no longer tied to the narrow limits of our eye'.[15] As photographers abandoned heavy equipment for lighter alternatives, they could now remove the camera from its tripod and place it on the floor, or at a high vantage point, to reveal a totally new perspective – what Moholy-Nagy referred to as the 'bird's eye' and 'worm's eye' views. These new perspectives were not solely due to more versatile photographic equipment; they were also the result of feats of modern engineering. The perceived limits of human endeavour were constantly shifting as high-rise buildings, radio towers and steel bridges (pp.8, 192, 195, 198, 199) reached dizzying heights. Aerial photography, first commandeered for reconnaissance work during the First World War, was now used for civilian purposes, capturing the landscape from the altitude of an airplane (fig.16), itself a relatively new invention.

Although this was an intense period of experimentation, it was not so much a period of discovery as one of re-discovery. Experiments that had taken place in the nineteenth century, then deemed improper, were re-visited and embraced by artists with a new, broad-minded outlook. Art history considers that photography (discounting the medical and scientific practices) had until this point developed along a linear trajectory, a purist approach closely mimicking painting, and anything that did not fit within this conservative framework was regarded as unacceptable. For modernist photography, however, the idea of what was achievable through the photographic process expanded; influenced by manifestos, such as Moholy-Nagy's *Painting Photography Film*, this linear line of development was shattered, making way for more open and varied possibilities. Art historian Franz Roh defined the different forms that the photograph could now take: photography could be not just the 'reality-photo' but also 'a photogram, photomontage, photos with etching and painting and photos in connection with typography.'[16] Transforming pre-conceptions of the medium, photography was no longer limited to a quest for perfection; it could also embrace the imperfect and explore abstraction.

A combination of circumstances led to this reinvigoration of the medium, including ground-breaking, cross-disciplinary approaches to teaching. Highlighted as an important underlying principle of the Preliminary Course, taught in the first year of the Bauhaus in Germany, was a practice now referred to as 'creative cognition'. Prioritising the importance of formal game play, the year-long course taught the 'categorical reduction of visual media itself',[17] or understanding an image purely in its own terms, described by theorists as 'a shift from categorising an object at the basic level to categorising it more abstractly in terms of its underlying or constituent properties'.[18] The simple act of 'improvisation with constraints', as the Bauhaus theorists described it, encouraged random and unrestricted creativity, which, in turn, could be applied to more practical purposes. These ideas of improvisation without intent are interesting when applied to photography and technology. The notion of play is often an inherent human response when confronted with new technology; we want to 'play with our new toy'. By exploiting the inbuilt relationship between play and technology, artists could investigate in a more curious, inquisitive way, seeking to master the process by playing with it, manipulating it and, at the same time, testing its limitations and boundaries. Testing limits was crucial in moving to the next stage, as once the technique was learned, the rulebook could be abandoned and the artist could truly explore. In tandem with the Bauhaus approach was the fact that many artists using photography were untrained, and mastered the techniques through a degree of trial and error, which gave them a willingness to improvise and make mistakes. This marked difference in attitude between trained photographers and untrained artists led many leading thinkers to include 'un-authored' works alongside those of established

16 Franz Roh and Jan Tschichold
Photo-eye: 76 Photos of the Time, 1929
Left: Günther Petschow, *Corn Field*
Right: Günther Petschow, *Tug-Boat on the Elbe*

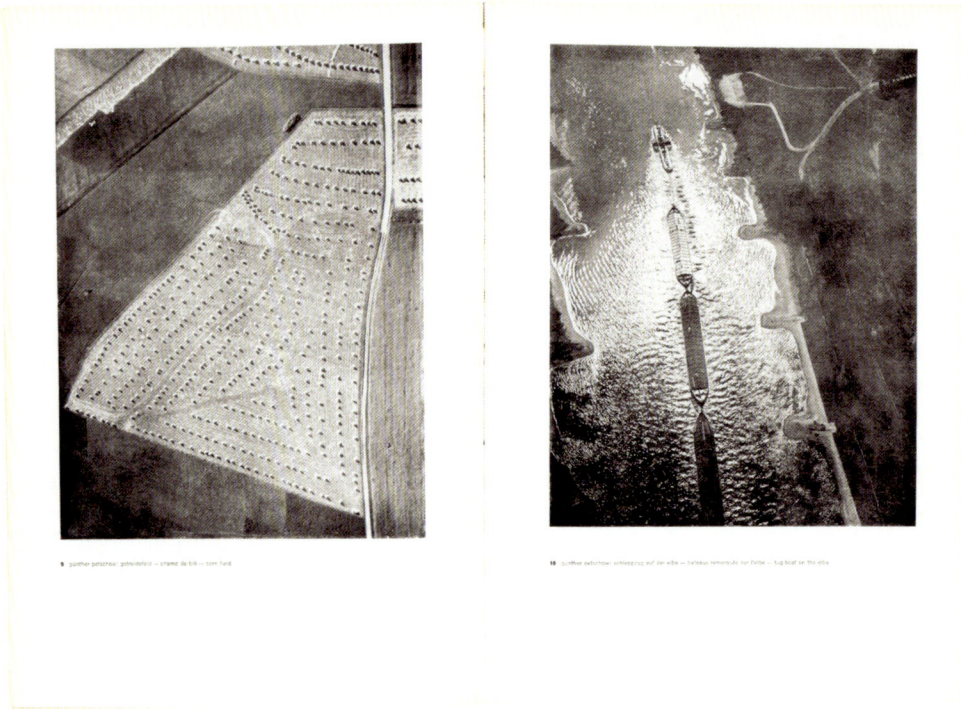

photographers, as seen in Franz Roh and Jan Tschichold's *Photo-eye: 76 Photos of the Time* (figs.16, 17). Amateur, or vernacular, works were also present in the landmark exhibition *Film and Photo* in Stuttgart in 1929, which helped to broaden the aesthetic language of the medium.

ABSTRACTION

From around 1917 onwards, going against the medium's inherent ability to record objectively and represent the world in realistic detail, artists began intentionally to experiment with abstraction using photography. Abstraction, which was already central to avant-garde painting and sculpture, disregarded reality, instead embracing shape, form and gesture. The shift towards abstraction relied on artistic curiosity to identify gaps or flaws in the medium, exploiting them to creative advantage. Photography, we must not forget, is also a technical process and in order to produce a precise image every single one of the many steps - from setting the camera, to focusing the image, to making the print - needs to be followed and the correct methods and instructions adhered to. If even one of these rules is ignored, then the result will be unexpected and, in most people's opinion, undesirable. However, it is in these flaws that the opportunity for unique creative experimentation lies; by disregarding or subverting the photographic process, the meaning of the image can be transfigured. The most straightforward example of this is in the negative printing process. Traditionally, a negative is used to produce a positive print in the darkroom. However, the process

in the darkroom can be defied to produce a negative print, such as Man Ray's *Noire et Blanche* (p.83). This simple intervention transformed the image, adding layers of complexity in both technique and meaning. The approach was not a mistake but a deliberate action, intended to break the rules in order to produce something new. This openness to the misuse of the medium took on many different forms, both with regard to the camera and in the darkroom.

The camera, a machine engineered to record that which is actually experienced or seen, was used by artists to create a deliberately distorted version of reality, as in André Kertész's *Clock Distortion* (p.188) and *Self-Portrait with Carlo Rim, Luna Park* (p.90), and Berenice Abbott's *Portrait of the Artist as a Young Woman* (p.91). Captured using props, or tricks such as concave and convex glass or mirrors, or made by curving the paper under the enlarger in the darkroom, these distorted images signalled the shift away from a desire to replicate reality towards a more playful experimentation, redefining the parameters of photography's relationship to truth and objectivity.

Emphasising the undesirable and embracing mistakes in the modernist period brought about an enlightening and often unexpected visual experience, as artists investigated different ways to deconstruct the medium. The identification of gaps, flaws or loopholes could occur at any point in the photographic process, from taking the image, to the final print, and all the stages in between. Opportunities to misuse, or hack, the medium existed in-camera, in the darkroom and in post-production. Utilising the

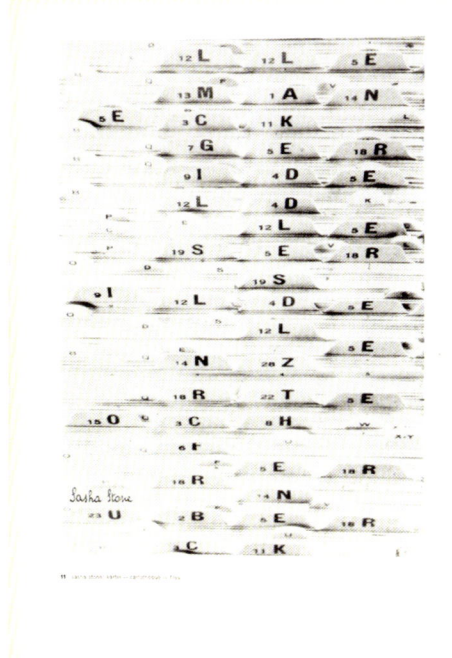

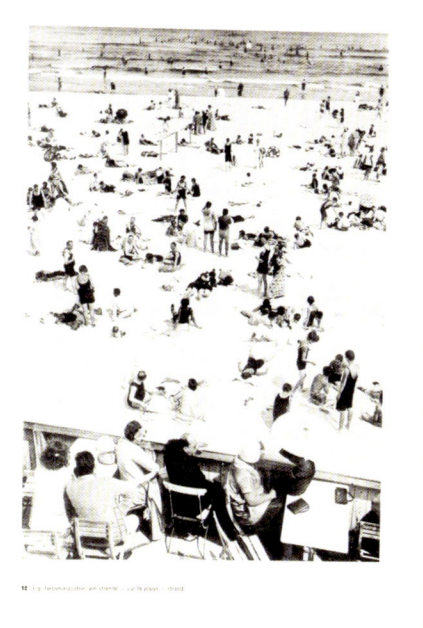

qualities inherent in photography, making a feature of attributes usually regarded as undesirable – distortion, blur, grain, and light leaks – was invigorating, creating texture and diversity, highlighting the unique materiality of the photographic medium. This approach, focusing on and harnessing specific attributes of the medium, would later be characterised and theorised as 'medium specificity'.[19]

Double exposures – referred to in the nineteenth century as 'spirit photographs', pictures in which an old image would dimly appear over a new one if the collodion plate was reused and not cleaned properly,[20] – were revived and embraced in both film and still photography as a way of creating interesting imagery and assisting narratives. These 'failed photographs', wrote Moholy-Nagy in 1926, where 'two events were recorded on the same plate, provided the inspiration for superimposition in cinema.'[21] They gave photography a means of layering imagery, both physically and metaphorically. Made either in-camera, by not winding the film forward and re-exposing the same negative twice, or in the darkroom by 'sandwiching' two negatives on top of each other in the enlarger or printing two negatives onto the same sheet of photographic paper, double exposures (or even multiple exposures) allowed for several stories to be told in the same frame, compressing time and space into one image. The relationship between the two images often varied, either complementing each other, as in the human figure and nature, or juxtaposing one against the other, as in the human figure and the machine. These combinations, often intentional, could perhaps have been loosely

linked to surrealism and Freudian ideas of personality. The effect was used in advertising and semiotics in order to provoke certain connections between unrelated things, while other experiments were made purely for aesthetics. Harry Callahan was a master of the double exposure, sometimes exposing the same negative in-camera dozens of times, resulting in a chaotic and fragmented image. He also used the technique to create the illusion of texture on the surface of an otherwise sleek composition by layering a close-up abstract image of foliage over a traditional portrait of his wife Eleanor (p.95).

Perhaps, rather romantically, it is useful to think of the darkroom as the place where moments of creativity materialise. The darkroom holds all the elements central to the exploration of the medium: light-sensitive paper, chemicals, the enlarger. Light is the lifeblood, but also the knife-edge in the relationship; it is essential in the photographic process and can both create, by exposing the negative and paper, or destroy, by being unintentionally leaked. It is the photographer's task to use and control light to produce an image; light is banished from the darkroom and added only at controlled intervals. Embracing mistakes, however, was important in fostering the development of the modernist aesthetic, as was the acceptance of alternative darkroom processes including solarisation, where the print or negative is exposed to light during the developing process to create a partial reversal of light and dark tones.[22] The technique was popularised in the late 1920s when Man Ray adopted the approach. It may be a myth, but it is widely recounted that Man

Ray and Lee Miller discovered solarisation accidentally when Miller, Man Ray's darkroom assistant at the time, switched on the light in error during the developing process.[23] The technique had astonishing effects, bringing out silvery reflections, partially reversing shadows and highlights from positive to negative, skewing reality. Particularly successful when applied to the contours of the human body, as seen in Man Ray's *Male Nude* (p.139), solarisation offered an abrupt shift in perception, not by means of staging or any formal arrangement by the artist but caused purely by the chemical methods inherent in the photographic process. In essence, solarisation is a way of influencing the medium to bring upon itself its own destruction, and then abruptly halting the process before it is too late. Acknowledging an ever-present frisson between creation and destruction, between experimentation and control, and embracing the unknown were key factors in many of these techniques.

Another darkroom process practised by modernist photographers was that of the photogram. Almost as old as photography itself, it dates back to the development of 'photogenic drawing' by William Henry Fox Talbot in 1834, in which objects were used to outline silhouette exposures instead of images being captured through the lens. Talbot first used the technique to record botanical specimens, as did Anna Atkins who embraced the process to illustrate *British Algae: Cyanotype Impressions* (3 vols, 1843–53), the first publication to use a photographic process for its illustrations. However, as attention shifted to perfect lens-based image techniques, the photogenic drawing fell out of favour, lying relatively dormant until it was revived with enthusiasm at the beginning of the twentieth century by practitioners such as Christian Schad, Man Ray and Moholy-Nagy. During its rebirth the photogram assumed many different titles, artist Tristan Tzara naming Schad's works 'schadographs', Man Ray coining the word 'rayographs' and Moholy-Nagy adopting 'photogram', which became the colloquial term. Although each iteration took a different conceptual approach, the purpose remained largely the same; to record an image without the use of a camera or optics by placing objects directly onto the surface of a light-sensitive material and exposing it to light, revealing a negative representation of the shadow, outline or form of the object.[24]

Although relatively simple to produce, the photogram had radical results and was quickly taken up, becoming an important element of the new vision. Schad, a member of the Swiss and later Berlin dada group, produced around 1917 what could be considered the earliest intentionally abstract photographs, the first of which were made with printing-out paper and exposed by means of daylight.[25] Using found, worthless objects or scraps of cut paper, Schad constructed layered compositions while, at the same time, acknowledging that the process relied largely on chance. Embracing this element, Schad considered his schadographs 'his most important contribution to Dada' in that he refuted the camera's claim on truth and, by doing so, gave additional room to the unexpected.[26]

Similarly, a contrasting rationale and variant techniques informed the photograms of Man Ray and Moholy-Nagy. For Man Ray, as for artists like Margaret De Patta, Pim Van Os and Elfriede Stegemeyer (pp.210, 214, 218, 219, 220), the excitement lay in the transformation of everyday objects into shape and form, which resulted in images that sat 'between abstract geometrical tracery and the echo of objects'.[27] Once frozen as a 1:1 scale representation of themselves, the objects lost their status as useful items with a specific purpose and simply existed as forms (fig.18). Sometimes combining objects in absurd juxtapositions, the photogram was embraced by both dadaists and the surrealists as part of their new approach to constructing realities. Man Ray's images, often made by exposing the same piece of paper several times with a different combination of objects, were true fabrications that had never existed as physical forms: 'the picture is a visual invention: an image without a real-life model to which we can compare it'.[28]

Perhaps the most abstract or minimalist approach to camera-less photography was illustrated by Moholy-Nagy's 'light compositions'. Abandoning the object almost completely and utilising only the medium's ability to record light on photographic paper, Moholy-Nagy used the photogram process to create images in their purist form; the objects themselves are unrecognisable and any desire to represent the real world was unimportant. Harnessing the way in which the photogram allows light to represent itself, he attempted to record light and space, or light *in* space, resulting in abstract images of light, space and movement. Similar in approach to Moholy-Nagy's light compositions, Edward Quigley, György Kepes and Callahan all experimented with light abstractions and the photogram (pp.213, 223).

In strictly technical terms the photogram is not a photograph but perhaps has more in common with an x-ray, or with print-based mediums such as a photocopy or a digital scan. However, due to its reliance on photographic materials, it has always sat within the umbrella of photography. Unlike other photographic processes, the photogram, as we have seen, has more to do with chance than technical precision and, although it can be learned, it is still to a large degree unpredictable. It can be considered the most pared back approach to photography and, in turn, the most radical. By abandoning the camera and utilising only

18 László Moholy-Nagy
Painting Photography Film, 1925
Left: László Moholy-Nagy, *Photogram*
Right: Man Ray, *Photogram*

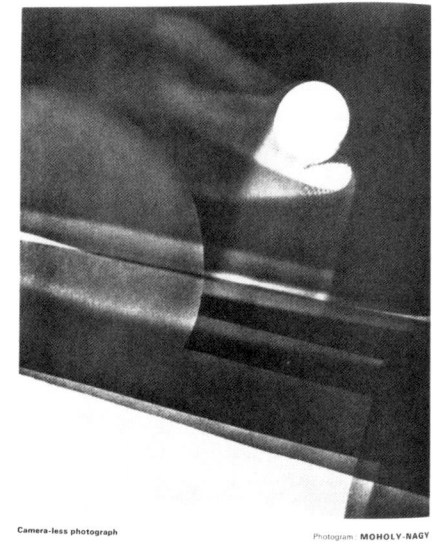

Camera-less photograph   Photogram: **MOHOLY-NAGY**

76

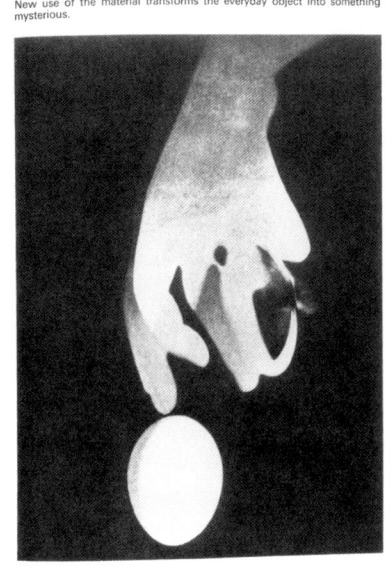

Camera-less photograph   Photogram: **MAN RAY/PARIS**
New use of the material transforms the everyday object into something mysterious.

77

light-sensitive paper and chemicals, by disregarding the rules of photography that assume the camera is the central part of the process, the photogram now hinted at the abstraction that would dominate the art of the decades to come. In an era preoccupied with the reproducibility of the photographic medium, the photogram offered a mode of production, rather than reproduction.[29] It allowed artists to literally 'paint with light', producing unique, one-off compositions.[30]

Moving out of the darkroom and into post-production, the manipulation of photographic images, which we associate so closely with the post-Photoshop digital age, has in fact been an important and much debated part of photographic history since the nineteenth century. Adopted by amateurs and professionals alike, composite images made from multiple negatives were common, albeit controversial; they were prohibited by the more conservative photographic societies, being deemed not true representations of reality.[31] Compositions made from multiple negatives were, however, used in popular culture as 'trick' and 'novelty' photography designed to amuse the masses. These novelty images, with their obvious disregard for reality, are perhaps closer relatives to the collage and photomontage of the modernist period. The acceptance of the manipulated image into the new visual language, be it the 'cut and paste' photocollage, the purely constructed photomontage, or the mixed-media collage using photographic imagery alongside other mediums such as paint, inks and drawing, produced an array of experimentation.

Deriving from the form of collage popular with cubists and futurists, the term photomontage, meaning to assemble, was first used by the Berlin dadaists to describe their works, which included photographs. Recounting the origin of the term, Raoul Hausmann reasoned that he and the rest of the group, including Johannes Baader, George Grosz, John Heartfield and Hannah Höch, chose the name photomontage as 'this term translates our aversion at playing the artist and, thinking of ourselves as engineers (hence our preference for workmen's overalls), we mean to construct, to assemble our works'.[32] Embracing the mechanical, reproduced nature of photography, the group were keen to engage with the medium, using it to establish themselves within the context of the mechanical world, their purpose being to 'integrate objects from the world of machines and industry into the world of art,' explained Höch.[33]

Photomontage was adopted for political as well as commercial use, and in the turbulent times of the 1930s was used to articulate official propaganda. Conversely, the same imagery was often commandeered to make a case for the opposition, using the same language as that employed by those in positions of power, and adopting the same forms of mass distribution via the regular press such as *Arbeiter-Illustrierte-Zeitung* (*AIZ*). The act of cutting up a photographic image (essentially destroying it), hacking it and changing its meaning, could also be interpreted as an act of violence, respect for the original art object having given way to the desire to construct a different narrative.

233

In photomontage several unrelated images could be placed side by side to fashion a new reality; or a new image could be produced from several fragments, brought together from various sources. This act of cutting, splicing and pasting removes and frees an image from its original context and allows new connections to be made between unrelated images. As well as being used for political propaganda, photomontage was utilised by advertising agencies as a means of drawing rapid visual links between usually unrelated products. Herbert Bayer's work, which drew on surrealist ideas, illustrates his mastery of the technical skills of photomontage, with images that defied reality such as *Humanly Impossible (Self-Portrait)* (p.18). Working across the fields of advertising, design and photography, often incorporating graphic elements alongside text and image, Bayer's approach could be seen as a precursor to the dominance of graphic design seen in the later part of the twentieth century.

As with many techniques in the modernist period, photomontage went through several phases as processes were refined, and directions and opinions shifted. An advocate of such experimentation, Moholy-Nagy referred to his works, in which photographs were seamlessly fused rather than cut and pasted together, as 'photoplastics':

> They [photoplastics] are pieced together from various photographs and are an experimental method of simultaneous representation; compressed interpenetration of visual and verbal wit; weird combinations of the most realistic, imitative means which pass into imaginary spheres. They can, however, also be forthright, tell a story; more veristic 'than life itself'. It will soon be possible to do this work, at present still in its infancy and done by hand, mechanically with the aid of projections and new printing processes.[34]

Foreseeing the widespread use of the image and text combination, Moholy-Nagy praised the photomontage for its ability to construct a narrative and communicate with the masses. Here, he also predicts that the physical cutting and pasting of the image will soon give way to a more streamlined means of production, which we now see in digital photographic practice.

In the many stages of possible intervention with the photograph, the act of altering the surface of the printed image is perhaps the final opportunity for the artist to mediate. Toning, bleaching and hand-colouring were all popular techniques in the nineteenth century, used either as an aesthetic feature, in the case of techniques such as sepia toning, or in order to more closely resemble the real world by adding colour to a black-and-white image. Unlike a technically trained commercial photographer, who would apply colour in a precise and realistic way to faithfully fill in details missing in a black-and-white print, artists experimented with colour not to mimic reality but to create a different version of it. Josef Breitenbach shifted between these two approaches to post-production, adding colour to the surface of the print in both a traditional and an experimental way. Breitenbach was a seasoned photographer with his own studio, creating portraits of Munich's bohemian circles. In *Hans Wolf Breitenbach, Munich* (p.106) he added delicate and precise colour, creating a soft, yet slightly surreal image not too far removed from a commercial studio portrait. Alongside this work, however, he used the photograph to experiment with paint and pigment, as in *Patricia, New York* (p.88). In this case, the photograph acts almost as a base, or foundation, for layers of colour that are applied as abstract forms to the surface of the print. Breitenbach achieved this by using the same colour-printing techniques that pictorialists used to mimic soft colour, but instead used this process to apply heavy blocks of abstract colour.[35]

These two parallel trajectories – towards precision on the one hand and abstraction on the other – informed the complex and varied visual language that photography became. The camera's technical prowess in capturing detailed reality objectively developed alongside, rather than in opposition to, abstraction, investigating the possibilities beyond photography's prescribed use harnessing the medium's ability to produce rather than document and reproduce. The experiments and innovation in the modernist period comfortably drew from the past and daringly predicted, or at least alluded to, a future in which images would play a central role in communication throughout society, not unlike what we experience today. New photographic techniques changed optics in a way that, as Moholy-Nagy put it at the time, 'almost amounts to a psychological transformation of our eyesight'. Photography then 'imparts a heightened or, (in so far as our eyes are concerned), increased power of sight in terms of time and space'.[36] So photography changed the way we produced, viewed and interpreted images. The effect that photography, technology and experimentation had in the 1920s and throughout the twentieth century, a revolution into an image-based medium that was as accessible as it was creative, foreshadowed the digital revolution of today. The ability of the medium to produce and reproduce, reveal exquisite detail, to construct, deconstruct and question its own form, has transformed, and continues to transform, not only art but also the social constructs that determine the way we envision and interpret the world.

NOTES

1 László Moholy-Nagy, 'A New Instrument of Vision', in Moholy-Nagy [1932] 2011, pp.34-6.

2 Half-tone refers to a mechanical printing method in which different tones are produced by arranging a large number of different-sized small dots. The result mimics the continuous tonality of a photograph. See Peres 2007, p.192.

3 Abbaspour, Daffner and Hambourg 2014; www.moma.org/objectphoto.

4 Kurt Korff, *Die illustrierte Zeitschrift* (The Illustrated Magazine), 1927; trans. in Kaes, Jay and Dimendberg 1994, pp.646-7.

5 Lincoln Kirstein, 'Photographs of America: Walker Evans', in Evans 1938; repr. 2012, p.193.

6 Johannes Molzahn, *Nicht mehr lessen! Sehen!* (Stop Reading! Look!), *Das Kunstblatt* 12, no.3, March 1928; trans. in Kaes, Jay and Dimendberg 1994, pp.648-9.

7 El Lissitzky, 'The Conquest of Art', *Ringen*, 109, 1922, pp.32-4; trans. Michael Steinlauf, in Nisbet et al. 1987, p.61.

8 Moholy-Nagy [1925] 1973, p.28.

9 Albert Renger-Patzsch, 'Aims', 1927; trans. Joel Agee, in Phillips 1989, p.104.

10 Van Deren Coke 1980-1, p.18.

11 Gustav Stotz, 'Werkbund-Austellung "Film und Foto" Stuttgart 1929', *Das Kunstblatt*, 13, no.5, May 1929.

12 Dziga Vertov, 'Kinoki. Perevorot' (Kinoks. A Revolution), *Lef*, no.3, 1923, p.141; trans. in Richard Taylor and Ian Christie (eds), *The Film Factory: Russian and Soviet Cinema in Documents 1896-1939*, London 1988, p.93.

13 Mary Benedetta and László Moholy-Nagy, *Street Markets of London*, London 1936, pp.vii-viii.

14 Emmanuel Sougez, 'Le XXIX Salon international d'art photographique 1934', *Bulletin de la Société française de Photographie*, no.9, September 1934, p.182.

15 Moholy-Nagy [1925] 1973, p.7.

16 'Mechanismus und Ansdruck' (Mechanism and Expression), in Roh 1929, p.16.

17 Phillip Prager, 'Making Sense of the Modernist Muse, Creative Cognition and Play at the Bauhaus', *American Journal of Play*, vol.7, no.1, Fall 2014.

18 Ronald A. Finke, Thomas B. Ward and Steven M. Smith, *Creative Cognition: Theory, Research, and Applications*, Cambridge MA 1992, p.140.

19 Medium specificity was first discussed in relation to photography in Newhall 1938.

20 Ades [1976] 1986, introduction, p.7.

21 László Moholy-Nagy, 'Fotoplastisch Reklame', in *Offset Buch und Werbekunst*, 1926; repr. in Peter Hahn, *Bauhaus-Heft der Zeitschrift*, Munich 1980, p.391.

22 Solarisation can be done either when developing the negative, producing a solarised negative, or at the printing stage, producing a solarised print from a standard negative. For more information, see Peres 2007, p.182.

23 Terence Pepper and Marina Warner, *Man Ray Portraits*, exh. cat., National Portrait Gallery, London 2013, p.193.

24 Photograms were made using a variety of light-sensitive materials such as daguerreotype plates, cyanotype paper, printing-out paper, or gelatin silver paper. See Peres 2007, p.101.

25 Other artists, such as Alvin Langdon Coburn, were using photography to produce intentionally abstract images at the same time. See Pamela Roberts, *Alvin Langdon Coburn*, exh. cat., Fundación Mapfre, Madrid 2014.

26 Gabriele Sterner, *Christian Schad: Etchings, Woodcuts, Schadographs*, exh. cat., Leinster Fine Art, London 1981.

27 'Mechanismus und Ansdruck' (Mechanism and Expression), in Roh 1929, p.16.

28 John Szarkowski, *MoMA Highlights*, The Museum of Modern Art, New York 1999; revised edn 2004, p.126.

29 Moholy-Nagy [1925] 1973, pp.30-2.

30 Although photograms are generally thought of as a one-off, this can never be truly proven as photograms can be re-photographed and several prints produced from the resulting negative.

31 Scharf 1974, p.109.

32 Raoul Hausmann, *Courrier Dada*, Paris 1958, p.42; trans. in Ades [1976] 1986, p.12.

33 Scharf 1974, p.211.

34 Moholy-Nagy [1925] 1973, p.36.

35 For information on popular pigment printing process, see Peres 2007, p.98.

36 László Moholy-Nagy, 'A New Instrument of Vision', in Moholy-Nagy [1932] 2011, pp.34-6.

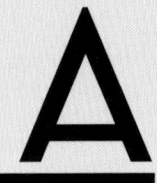

Berenice Abbott (b. 1898 Springfield, Ohio, USA; d. 1991 Monson, Maine, USA). Following an early career in journalism in New York City, Abbott moved to Europe to study fine arts in Berlin and Paris. She was hired in 1923 as a darkroom assistant to fellow American Man Ray, whose introduction to photography encouraged her to pursue her own practice. Primarily working in the genre of portraiture, with artistic and literary avant-garde figures as her subjects, she exhibited frequently in Paris alongside Man Ray and artists such as André Kertész. In 1925 Man Ray introduced Abbott to the work of Eugène Atget, whose archive she purchased upon his death, and whose work she continued to publish and promote throughout her life. Atget's photographic documentation of Paris inspired her to return to New York in 1929 to commence her own series entitled *Changing New York,* dedicated to the city's urban transformation. ZZ

Ansel Adams (b. 1902 San Francisco, California, USA; d. 1984 Monterey, California, USA). A photographer and avid environmentalist, Adams is best known for his iconic depiction of the American West. He took up photography at the age of fourteen following a trip to Yosemite National Park, which, in addition to joining the Sierra Club in 1919, initiated a lifelong commitment to both the preservation and documentation of the country's natural landscape. Adams's prodigious technical mastery of the medium garnered the praise of friends and collaborators such as Edward Weston, Alfred Stieglitz and curator Beaumont Newhall, with whom Adams helped to establish the first department of photography at New York's Museum of Modern Art in 1940. ZZ

Manuel Álvarez Bravo (b. 1902; d. 2002 Mexico City, Mexico). Álvarez Bravo began taking pictures in a post-revolutionary Mexico, when Mexico City was subject to both intense modernisation and a great influx of the rural poor. Initially working in the pictorialist style, he then moved towards modernism and from the late 1920s associated with an international avant-garde drawn to the invigorated city, including Henri Cartier-Bresson and André Breton. Dedicated to conveying Mexico's unique history, culture and identity, he documented everyday life, paying special attention to traditional themes and motifs, and occasionally capturing political action. His work also circulated further afield, through his joint exhibition with Cartier-Bresson in Mexico and New York in 1934-5, Breton's 1940 surrealism exhibition in Paris and Edward Steichen's seminal exhibition *The Family of Man* in 1955. SG

Diane Arbus (b. 1923; d. 1971 New York City, New York, USA). Born into the wealthy Nemerov family in New York City, Arbus married her husband Allan at the age of eighteen. After the Second World War they worked together in a fashion photography business in New York, with Diane acting as a stylist. This professional working relationship ended in 1956. Arbus took photography classes with Lisette Model, who was renowned for her own candid portraits, and developed her inimitable style, focusing on average middle-class subjects as well as on those whose way of life or appearance positioned them outside the mainstream, an approach that was a major contributor to the revitalisation of documentary photography in the United States during the 1950s. SG

Herbert Bayer (b. 1900 Haag am Hausruck, Austria; d. 1985 Montecito, California, USA). A leading figure at the Bauhaus in Weimar and Dessau – where he had studied between 1921 and 1923 before returning to teach at Dessau in 1925 – Bayer made an important contribution across the fields of applied art and design. Moving to Berlin in 1928 as art director of German *Vogue*, he was exposed to dada, surrealism and the avant-garde. His two main bodies of photographic work, *photomontagen* (1931-2, resumed in 1956) and *fotoplastiken* (1936), combined an advanced understanding of spatial properties and photographic technique with surrealist ideas. In 1938 Bayer immigrated to America. From his exhibition design for *Bauhaus 1919-1928* at the Museum of Modern Art, New York, in 1938 to his cultural rejuvenation of Aspen, Colorado, from 1946, he was instrumental in extending Bauhaus principles across the Atlantic. EL

Hans Bellmer (b. 1902 Katowice, Silesia [now Poland]; d. 1975 Paris, France). Bellmer's artistic career focused upon the eroticism of the female figure, expressed through drawings, sculpture and photographs. His constructions of fetishistic dolls were the basis of his most influential works. Abandoning his engineering studies in Berlin in 1924, Bellmer turned to illustration and design, studying with artist George Grosz before opening his own studio in 1926. In opposition to the rise of Nazism, in 1933 Bellmer halted his commercial work to prevent it being used by the state. That year he built and photographed his first doll; in 1934 a series of photographs was published as *Die Puppe* (The Doll); a further series would be published in the surrealist journal *Minotaure*. Fleeing Germany in 1938, Bellmer continued his association with the surrealists in Paris. SG

Ilse Bing (b. 1899 Frankfurt, Germany; d. 1998 New York City, New York, USA). Having acquired a 35mm Leica camera in 1929, Bing began taking on commissions for the Frankfurt-based supplement *Das Illustrierte Blatt*, while collaborations with Bauhaus teacher and architect Mart Stam formed a crucial introduction to avant-garde principles. In 1930 she moved to Paris and worked across advertising, portraiture and photojournalism throughout the decade, applying her modern style to commissions for German, French and American publications, including *L'Illustration*, *Vogue* and *Harper's Bazaar*. She continued her artistic work, however, and was noted for her inquisitive eye and use of dynamic perspectives. Dubbed 'Queen of the Leica' by photographer Emmanuel Sougez, her work featured in curator Beaumont Newhall's important 1938 exhibition *Photography 1839-1937* at the Museum of Modern Art, New York. EL

Margaret Bourke-White (b. 1904 New York City, New York, USA; d. 1971 Stamford, Connecticut, USA). Bourke-White founded her own commercial studio in Cleveland, Ohio, in 1927, but soon established herself as one of the leading figures in the burgeoning field of photojournalism. Between 1929 and 1935 she was associate editor and staff photographer for *Fortune* magazine, for which, in 1930, she photographed Soviet industrialisation – the first woman to do so. In 1936 she became a founding member of *Life* magazine and in 1946 she was dispatched to document the India-Pakistan partition, one of her most important assignments. In addition to her skills as a reportage photographer, Bourke-White's visual record of conditions wrought by the Dust Bowl and her portrayal of the Great Depression, published in *You Have Seen Their Faces* (1937), represent a significant contribution to the documentary genre. EL

Brassaï (b. 1899 Brassó, Transylvania, Austria-Hungary [now Romania]; d. 1984 Eze, France). Born Gyula Halász, Brassaï studied fine arts in Budapest and Berlin before moving to Paris to work as a journalist in 1924. Under the tutelage of fellow Hungarian André Kertész, he turned to photography to capture the life and streets of his adopted city, as well as members of its artistic and literary circles such as Salvador Dalí, Pablo Picasso and Henry Miller. Brassaï's first photographic publications, *Paris by Night* (1933) and *Paris after Dark* (1935), afforded him international acclaim. He continued as a street photographer upon immigrating to New York City in 1936, and also worked commercially for magazines such as *Harper's Bazaar*. In 1948 the Museum of Modern Art, New York, staged his first solo exhibition. ZZ

Josef Breitenbach (b. 1896 Munich, Germany; d. 1984 New York City, New York, USA). Born in Munich, into a wealthy Jewish family, Breitenbach studied art history and philosophy at university after which, in 1930, he set up a photographic portrait studio catering to the city's theatre circles. In 1933, when Hitler became chancellor, he fled his homeland for Paris. Although he never became an official member of the group, he adopted many of the photographic techniques of the surrealists, such as solarisation, collage, photograms and hand-tinting, all of which challenged traditional forms of the medium. In 1941 he became a refugee once again, escaping France for New York. Breitenbach continued his commercial work, also teaching at the progressive Black Mountain College and Cooper Union. After his death in 1984 his photographs were rediscovered, securing his reputation as a leading modernist photographer. NH

Alexey Brodovitch (b. 1898 Ogolichi, Russian Empire [now Belarus]; d. 1971 Avignon, France). Brodovitch began his career in Paris, among a cultural milieu of fellow Russian émigrés, painting backdrops for the Ballets Russes and creating layouts for leading art and design journals. In 1930 he was appointed head of advertising design at Pennsylvania Museum School of Industrial Art, Philadelphia, where he established the renowned Design Laboratory for students of illustration, graphic design and photography. In 1934 Brodovitch became art director at *Harper's Bazaar*. His progressive, directional approach to fashion photography – favouring location shoots, narratives and use of cropping and perspective to create unexpected views – as with his approach to typography and design, transformed the magazine industry. Brodovitch's personal photographic work, focusing on ballet companies that visited New York, is considered a masterpiece of motion study and layout. EL

Harry Callahan (b. 1912 Detroit, Michigan, USA; d. 1999 Atlanta, Georgia, USA). Callahan pursued a degree in chemical engineering at Michigan State University before joining Chrysler Motor Parts Corporation in 1936. He became a member of the company's Camera Club and Detroit's Photo Guild, but it was upon meeting photographers Ansel Adams and Alfred Stieglitz in the early 1940s that he decided to pursue photography, through his own practice and through education. In 1946 László Moholy-Nagy invited him to teach at the Institute of Design in Chicago. The curriculum, based on Bauhaus ideology, emphasised experimentation; this led Callahan to explore formal abstraction in his own work. Callahan taught at the Institute until 1961 and subsequently became chair of the photography department at the Rhode Island School of Design, where he remained until 1973. ZZ

Henri Cartier-Bresson (b. 1908 Chanteloup, Seine-et-Marne, France; d. 2004 Montjustin, France). Driven by a surrealist interest in spontaneity, Cartier-Bresson engaged with photography while studying literature and painting. His purchase of a hand-held Leica in 1932 led him to pursue the medium professionally. During the Second World War, he was taken prisoner by German forces but escaped in 1943. Two years later, he photographed the liberation of Paris. In 1947 Cartier-Bresson co-founded the cooperative agency Magnum Photos and the Museum of Modern Art, New York, staged *Photographs by Henri Cartier-Bresson*. He travelled and photographed extensively, documenting Mahatma Gandhi's funeral and the Chinese Civil War. Upon his return to Europe in 1952, he published the seminal *Images à la Sauvette* (The Decisive Moment), for which Henri Matisse illustrated the cover. He continued his career as a photojournalist until the 1960s. ZZ

Paul Citroën (b. 1896 Berlin, Germany; d. 1983 Wassenaar, Netherlands). After developing an interest in photography at the Academy of Arts in Berlin, Citroën immersed himself in the city's dadaist circles and frequented the influential Der Sturm gallery, the focus of Berlin's modern art scene. In 1919 he enrolled at the Bauhaus in Weimar, where he concentrated his photographic practice on photomontage and portraiture. His work was featured in the first Bauhaus exhibition in 1923, and published in László Moholy-Nagy's seminal *Painting Photography Film* of 1925. Influenced by the principles of Bauhaus education, Citroën founded the New Art School in Berlin in 1937, and later assumed a post at the Art Academy of The Hague. ZZ

Gordon Coster (b. 1907 Baltimore, Maryland, USA; d. 1988 USA). As an amateur photographer in Baltimore in his late teens and early twenties, Coster experimented with modernist techniques and his work was exhibited by international photographic salons. He forged a career in New York as an advertising and industrial photographer and photojournalist. From the late 1930s, now based in Chicago, he worked for magazines including *Life*, *Fortune* and *Time*, producing photo-essays that epitomised the new documentary mode and often reflected social welfare issues. In 1946 Coster was invited to lecture on documentary photography to students at Chicago's Institute of Design as part of László Moholy-Nagy's symposium 'New Vision in Photography', later credited with crystallising an American Bauhaus. He returned to teach at the Institute again in 1950-1 and 1960, before retiring in 1964. EL

Ralston Crawford (b. 1906 St Catherines, Canada; d. 1978 Houston, Texas, USA). The son of a ship's captain, Crawford spent his life travelling. After studying art in Los Angeles and working briefly as an illustrator for Walt Disney Studios, he spent the next decade working, studying and exhibiting his artwork internationally. Primarily a painter, he was among the pioneers of the precisionist style, characterised by geometric line and abstracted forms, and typically focused on slick, industrial architecture. Crawford took up photography in 1937, initially to provide source material for his paintings and lithographic prints. He found inspiration in the flatness and lucidity of the photographic plane, and the dynamic views created by cropping negatives. In the early 1950s he moved away from formally rigorous abstraction towards a more spontaneous documentary style, as he chronicled the lives of black jazz musicians in New Orleans. EL

Ferenc Csík (b. 1894; d. 1984 Sopron, Hungary). After studying textiles in Vienna Csík worked in the textile industry. He first picked up a camera in 1930 at the age of thirty-six, joining the Sopron Photo Club the following year. A self-taught photographer, Csík initially worked in the style of pictorialism before shifting his aesthetic in line with the Neue Sachlichkeit (New Objectivity) movement in Germany, photographing still lifes and close-ups. After 1945 Csík turned his attention to documenting the urban environment of his hometown Sopron and in 1956 he became a founding member of the Association of Hungarian Art Photographers. SM

Imogen Cunningham (b. 1883 Portland, Oregon, USA; d. 1976 San Francisco, California, USA). Cunningham began her photographic career in 1907, working in the studio of portrait photographer Edward S. Curtis. After studying photochemistry, she opened her own photography studio in Seattle in 1909, relocating to San Francisco in 1917. Cunningham became a member of the Pictorial Photographers of America in 1922 but would later become known for a sharp-focus style characteristic of the aesthetic of Group f.64, the San Francisco-based collective that she co-founded with Edward Weston and Ansel Adams, among others, in 1932. Though she eventually turned to photographing everyday scenes, Cunningham is today best known for her nude studies and a series of flower forms, *Blumenformen*, made between 1922 and 1929. EL

František Drtikol (b. 1883 Příbram, Bohemia [now Czech Republic]; d. 1961 Prague, Czechoslovakia [now Czech Republic]). Drtikol studied art in Munich (1901–3), focusing on drawing and photography. In 1910 he opened a successful photographic studio in Prague, alongside which he maintained his own artistic practice. Drtikol's style was distinguished by the disparate influences of art nouveau, symbolism and art deco, to which he had been exposed in Munich. Nude studies formed the core of his practice. Often working with dancers, he choreographed dynamic poses and used set pieces to cast geometric shadows, resulting in energetic scenes that exemplified the concept of the modern body. From 1930 he replaced the human figure with paper cut-outs, his work now used to convey key tenets of Buddhism, to which he was committed. Five years later, he ceased his photographic practice and turned his attention to painting. EL

Walker Evans (b. 1903 St Louis, Missouri, USA; d. 1975 New Haven, Connecticut, USA). Evans was instrumental in establishing the American documentary photographic tradition. Educated on the East Coast, he turned to photography on moving to New York City in 1927, in spite of earlier literary ambitions. The influence of European modernism in his early work gave way to a 'straight' approach when, in 1935, he was hired by the US Department of the Interior to document government-sponsored resettlement projects. Working alongside photographers Dorothea Lange and Arthur Rothstein, among others, his depiction of rural and small-town life not only chronicled the realities of the Great Depression, but also positioned him as a seminal documentarian of the period. His photographs appeared in myriad publications, and in 1938 the Museum of Modern Art, New York, held a retrospective of his work: *American Photographs*. ZZ

Jaroslav Fabinger (b. 1899 Prague, Bohemia [now Czech Republic]; d. 1942 Luby u Klatov, Czechoslovakia [now Czech Republic]). Fabinger took up photography during his training as a chemical engineer, and soon became an active exponent of new trends in photographic experimentation in Prague following the First World War. Alongside photographer Josef Sudek, he founded the innovative Fotoklub Praha in 1922. Fabinger primarily engaged with figurative compositions, but his practice also comprised sports and architectural photography, as well as photojournalism. In 1935 he published a widely disseminated manual on portraiture, and the following year promoted the 'Sabatier effect', a technique related to solarisation and inspired by Man Ray's photography. He later rejected manipulated processes in favour of gelatin silver and carbon printing. ZZ

Robert Frank (b. 1924 Zurich, Switzerland). Best known for his seminal photobook *Les Américains* (1958), a portrayal of the myth of the American dream, Frank's image-making is defined by his lyrical, personal approach. Born to Jewish parents, he was deeply affected by his early experience of the Second World War. Initially studying with commercial photographers such as Michael Wolgensinger, who was affiliated with the Bauhaus, Frank was influenced by Swiss graphic design and quickly realised the potential of the photobook. In 1947 he left Switzerland for New York, where he worked for fashion magazines, and moved in the circle of other European émigrés such as André Kértesz and Alexey Brodovitch. Two years later, he went freelance. Travel throughout Europe and South America enabled him to explore his status as both outsider and photographer. SG

Jaromír Funke (b. 1896 Skuteč, Bohemia [now Czech Republic]; d. 1945 Kolín, Czechoslovakia [now Czech Republic]). After studying medicine, law and philosophy at the Charles University in Prague, Funke opted to pursue a career as a freelance photographer. In 1922 he co-founded the Prague Photo Club, and, two years later, he established the Czech Photographic Society. Through his photographic practice, which featured still lifes, abstraction and photograms, he attempted to fuse the pervading trends in European photographic modernism. While a teacher at the School of Arts and Crafts in Bratislava in the early 1930s, he joined the Bauhaus-inspired photographic movement Szociofotó, whose social concerns caused him to focus permanently on documentary photography. ZZ

Johan Hagemeyer (b. 1884 Amsterdam, Netherlands; d. 1962 Berkeley, California, USA). Hagemeyer's interest in photography was accelerated in 1916 on meeting Alfred Stieglitz and other important figures in California's photography scene, including Edward Weston, to whom he became a friend and mentor. The same year he opened a portrait studio in Berkeley and in 1923 opened another in Carmel. The latter became a meeting place for local artists and intellectuals, his portraits of whom formed a central part of Hagemeyer's *oeuvre*. Hagemayer was associated with Group f.64, but while he shared some aspects of its approach – namely shooting in natural light, in medium or large format – his preference for manipulating images and his individualist mind set (he declined to participate in the 1929 exhibition *Film and Photo*, the American section of which Weston curated) meant that he remained in relative obscurity. EL

Heinz Hajek-Halke (b. 1898; d. 1983 Berlin, Germany). Hajek-Halke received formal training in fine and applied arts in Berlin, and worked in film poster design and publishing before turning to photography in 1924. He undertook commissions in advertising and reportage, later researching macrophotography and working as an aerial photographer. After the Second World War, Hajek-Halke explored photography's creative potential, experimenting with negative prints, montage, the application of atypical materials such as varnish and fish bones, and 'light graphics' (a type of photogram). His expressive, dreamlike style, reminiscent of surrealism, aligned him with the subjective photography movement and in 1950 he joined its founding group, Fotoform. A passionate educator, he taught graphic arts and photography at the School of Fine Arts, Berlin, his technical publications further strengthening his considerable influence. EL

André Kertész (b. 1894 Budapest, Hungary; d. 1985 New York City, New York, USA). Born Kertész Andor, Kertész purchased his first camera in 1912 while working as clerk at the Budapest stock exchange. Determined to establish a freelance career, he moved to Paris in 1925, where, under the name of André, he attained commercial success by publishing his photojournalistic work in European and English magazines and newspapers. Along with fellow Hungarians Brassaï and Robert Capa, Kertész immersed himself in the city's avant-garde artistic circles. While influenced by the theories of surrealism and dada, he maintained an observational approach to photography, which he used primarily as a medium for documenting everyday urban life. He produced several photographic books in the 1930s before immigrating to New York in 1936. zz

Rudolf Koppitz (b. 1884 Schreiberseifen, Duchy of Upper and Lower Silesia [now Czech Republic]; d. 1936 Perchtoldsdorf, Austria). Koppitz began his professional life in commercial studios before undertaking a photography course at Vienna's Institute for Applied Graphic Arts in 1912. He would later become director of the Institute's photographic department, and was an active member of the Vienna Photographic Society. In his personal practice, Koppitz concentrated on picturesque rural scenes and a series of nudes, shot in the Czech countryside. By the mid-1920s he was making nude studies using dancers from the Vienna State Opera; these languid forms, combined with dramatic composition and *fin de siècle* spirit, became his best-known works. In 1929 the landmark exhibition *Film and Photo* awakened Koppitz to the New Vision and although he returned to rural scenes, he relinquished his soft, pictorial style in favour of a crisper, modern aesthetic. EL

Dorothea Lange (b. 1895 Hoboken, New Jersey, USA; d. 1965 San Francisco, California, USA). Lange began her documentary work in the early 1930s, after the Wall Street crash of 1929 that precipitated America's Great Depression. Before then, she was working as a portrait photographer in San Francisco. Aware of the social and economic crisis, and its impact on all walks of life, Lange hit the streets with her 4 × 5 inch camera. In 1937 she was one of a number of photographers selected by the Farm Security Administration (FSA), part of President Roosevelt's New Deal, to express the crisis of rural areas. Genuinely concerned with their plight, it was through a mutual respect for her subjects that Lange was able to capture powerful images of the human condition with compassion and dignity. NH

Klara Langer (b. 1912; d. 1973 Budapest, Hungary). Upon gaining her degree in fine arts in Budapest, Langer pursued a career in advertising and graphic design before turning to photography. She worked as a studio assistant to the Hungarian illustrator and photographer Emery P. Révész-Bíró, whose modernist practice inspired her to experiment with photographic abstraction. In the 1930s she became involved with the Socialist Arts Group and turned her lens towards social documentation, concentrating on subjects such as displaced children and political refugees. She then joined the Budapest-based and Bauhaus-inspired photographic movement Szociofotó. Following a year in Paris in 1938, she returned to Budapest to take up a teaching position. Langer continued her photography and graphic design practice while working as a photojournalist for local newspapers and illustrating children's books. zz

Alma Lavenson (b. 1897 San Francisco, California, USA; d. 1989 Piedmont, California, USA). A self-taught photographer from San Francisco's Bay Area, Lavenson achieved success in the late 1920s with the regular publication of her work in the pictorialist magazine *Camera Craft*. Meeting Edward Weston and Imogen Cunningham, founders of the San Francisco-based Group f.64, in 1930, prompted a new, modernist direction and a focus on architectural and industrial forms. In 1933 Lavenson began photographing California's 'Gold Country' ruins, a subject she returned to often. Later, she travelled extensively and made black-and-white images of the cultures she encountered. Lavenson was

recognised throughout her career with solo exhibitions, including three at the San Francisco Museum of Modern Art (1942, 1948 and 1960). EL

Helen Levitt (b. 1913; d. 2009 New York City, New York, USA). In 1937, whilst teaching children photography as part of the Federal Art Project (a New Deal initiative), Levitt decided to photograph them at play. In doing so, she initiated what became her most enduring body of work within a career dedicated to documenting life on the streets of New York. Levitt had purchased her first Leica 35mm camera the previous year, following an inspirational meeting with Henri Cartier-Bresson. This allowed her to shoot spontaneously and unobtrusively in a much freer style. Her photographs of America during the Great Depression provided an intimate and revealing portrait of the country's social landscape. From the 1940s Levitt turned her attention to cinematography, through which she made a highly significant contribution to the documentary genre. EL

Herbert List (b. 1903 Hamburg, Germany; d. 1975 Munich, Germany). List's early photography, made during the 1930s, was informed by the literature and poetry of Paris surrealism. His taste for the unusual and subversive was apparent not only in his combinations of unexpected subjects in still-life compositions and his use of double exposure, but also in his depictions of otherwise benign subject matter, such as vernacular architecture. Throughout the decade he developed a distinctive, magical realist aesthetic, sympathetic to the contemporaneous Neue Sachlichkeit (New Objectivity) movement in Weimar Germany; it was also influenced by classicism, particularly Greek antiquity. The male nude featured as a subject throughout his photographic career. List was published in *Harper's Bazaar*, *Verve* and *Life* magazines and throughout the 1950s he worked almost exclusively in photojournalism, having become a member of Magnum Photos in 1951. EL

George Platt Lynes (b. 1907 East Orange, New Jersey, USA; d. 1955 New York City, New York, USA). Originally wanting to be a writer, Lynes discovered through the guidance of his Parisian friends of the 1920s, such as Man Ray and Gertrude Stein, that his true vocation lay in photography. Lynes was a self-taught studio photographer who focused on portraiture and nudes. His excellent technical abilities with a large format camera and lighting skills earned him a place amongst top studio photographers of the time. While he earned his living through portrait work for magazines and as chief photographer for the American Ballet Company, his nudes were a deeply private series, which he pursued throughout his life. Meticulously planned and sculpted, his compositions created an idealistic image of the human form, seen through a surrealist lens. NH

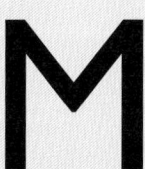

Dora Maar (b. 1907 Tours, France; d. 1997 Paris, France). French-Croatian Dora Maar, born Henriette Theodora Marković, spent her childhood in Buenos Aires, Argentina. Upon relocating to Paris at the age of nineteen, she enrolled in the Académie Julian where she studied painting and photography. By the 1930s, persuaded by figures such as André Breton and Man Ray, she became fully immersed in the city's surrealist activities. Her photographic work comprised dreamlike portraits, interiors and still lifes in which she practised experimental techniques such as double-exposure and collage. Maar became romantically involved with Pablo Picasso, and is acclaimed for her photographic documentation of the making of his 1936 painting *Guernica*. zz

Man Ray (b. 1890 Philadelphia, Pennsylvania, USA; d. 1976 Paris, France). Born Emmanuel Radnitzky, Man Ray was a leading figure in the dada and surrealist movements. Having met artist Marcel Duchamp in New York and collaborated with him on a proto-dada project in 1915, Man Ray soon relocated to Paris, where he would remain for much of his life. An introduction by Duchamp to André Breton and his surrealist circle positioned Man Ray in the centre of avant-garde activity, to which he contributed paintings, assemblages and photographs. In addition to his successful practice as a portrait and fashion photographer, he also pioneered innovative photographic techniques, such as his camera-less rayographs and solarisation. zz

Werner Mantz (b. 1901 Cologne, Germany; d. 1983 Eijsden, Germany) . Mantz first picked up a camera at the age of fourteen, and, following his service in the First World War, enrolled in photography courses in Munich. In 1921 he returned to his hometown of Cologne to establish a commercial portrait studio, which quickly rose to popularity among the city's elite. Due to an increasingly anti-Semitic climate in Germany, Mantz relocated to Maastricht, Netherlands, in 1932, where he completed a series of commission-based architectural photographs of modernist housing projects. While he maintained his portraiture practice throughout his career, Mantz later focused on architectural photography, inspired by the tenets of the Neue Sachlichkeit (New Objectivity) movement. zz

Adolph de Meyer (b. 1868 Paris, France; d. 1946 Los Angeles, California, USA). As a young man in Berlin, de Meyer encountered the twin influences of pictorialism and secessionism, and met the pioneer of modern photography, Alfred Stieglitz. On relocating to London in 1895, he ingratiated himself in the city's most fashionable and aristocratic circles; he also began to pursue photography seriously and was admitted to the Royal Photographic Society and two leading pictorialist groups: the Linked Ring (in Britain) and, later, Stieglitz's Photo-Secession (in America). In 1914 de Meyer immigrated to New York, becoming Condé Nast's first official fashion photographer for *Vogue* and *Vanity Fair* before moving to *Harper's Bazaar* in 1921. De Meyer was an early advocate of artificial lighting, with a distinctive style that was theatrical, exuberant and full of emotional intensity. His images revolutionised the aesthetic of early fashion and society magazines, establishing him as the preeminent commercial photographer of the period. EL

Tina Modotti (b. 1896 Friuli, Italy; d. 1942 Mexico City, Mexico). Born Assunta Mondini, Tina Modotti left her native Italy aged sixteen to join her father in San Francisco. After moving to Los Angeles in 1918, she met American photographer Edward Weston and soon became his model, lover and collaborator. The two relocated to Mexico City in 1923, where they joined the country's political and artistic avant-garde circles. In addition to formal experimentation, Modotti photographed architectural spaces, urban landscapes and portraits of fellow artists, workers and peasants. In 1929 the National Library of Mexico presented a selection of her work: *The First Revolutionary Photographic Exhibition in Mexico.* Modotti subsequently set aside her camera in favour of social activism, to which she remained committed until her untimely death. zz

László Moholy-Nagy (b. 1895 Bácsborsód, Austria-Hungary [now Romania]; d. 1946 Chicago, Illinois, USA). Moholy-Nagy was a seminal figure in the development of both European and American modern photographic practice. Following military service during the First World War, he abandoned his law studies and joined Budapest's avant-garde circles as a painter. In 1920 he relocated to Berlin, where he met members of dadaist and constructivist groups, as well as the architect and designer Walter Gropius. Gropius invited Moholy-Nagy to teach at the Bauhaus in Weimar until 1925, and Dessau until 1928, during which time he promoted visual experimentation through typography, photomontage, photocollage, photograms and photography. In 1937 he moved

to the United States as director of the New Bauhaus, Chicago, and later founded the Institute of Design. He worked as a freelance designer and artist until his death. zz

Marcello Nizzoli (b. 1887 Boretto, Italy; d. 1969 Camogli, Italy). A pioneering figure in Italian design, Nizzoli obtained his degree at the Fine Arts School in Parma, at which point he turned to painting and joined the Nuove Tendenze (New Tendencies), an artistic group influenced by the futurist movement. He began working as a graphic designer for the company Olivetti in the early 1930s, and soon moved from advertising to become head of product design. Nizzoli adopted the Bauhaus principle, unifying all the arts in pursuit of a re-imagined society. This led him to take up photography, which he promoted as a means of visually expressing the modern age. He continued to incorporate photographic practice into his design work throughout his career. zz

Dorothy Norman (b. 1905 Philadelphia, Pennsylvania, USA; d. 1997 East Hampton, New York, USA). Born Dorothy Stecker, to a wealthy family in Philadelphia, and married in 1925, Norman moved to New York City, where she became deeply engaged in socio-political issues, as expressed throughout her life in her photographs, her activism and her support for literary criticism and the visual arts. Norman began taking photographs seriously after meeting Alfred Stieglitz in 1927; they were later to become lovers and in 1931 he lent her a 4 × 5 inch Graflex camera. Whilst intensely intimate, her portraits also suggest a belief in the emancipatory possibilities of image-making. Throughout the interwar period Norman campaigned for American civil liberties and Indian independence. In 1973 she published *Alfred Stieglitz: An American Seer,* a biography of the photographer. SG

Paul Outerbridge (b. 1896 New York City, New York, USA; d. 1958 Laguna Beach, California, USA). After enrolling at the Clarence H. White School of Photography in New York City in 1921, Outerbridge established his commercial practice, specialising in advertising photography and graphic design. He published his work in fashion magazines such as *Vanity Fair* and *Vogue,* and in 1925 accepted a post with *Vogue* in Paris. There he met leading figures of the avant-garde, including Man Ray, Edward Steichen and Berenice Abbott. Outerbridge was also an early pioneer of colour photography, often with eroticised nudes as his subjects, and in 1940 released his influential book entitled *Photographing in Color.* zz

Norman Parkinson (b. 1913 London, UK; d. 1990 Singapore). One of the foremost fashion photographers of the twentieth century, Parkinson is revered for transforming editorial practice by removing his subjects from the context of the studio and placing them instead in unusual, and often outdoor, settings. Following an apprenticeship with English court photographers Speaight and Sons Ltd, Parkinson held positions at *Harper's Bazaar* and *Bystander* magazines before joining the Royal Air Force as an aerial photographer during the Second World War. His subsequent tenure at *Vogue* established him as a prominent portrait photographer, with subjects that included the British royal family, celebrities, artists and leading figures in film, theatre, politics and music. zz

Margaret De Patta (b. 1903 Washington DC, USA; d. 1963 San Francisco, California, USA). In tandem with her practice as a jewellery designer, De Patta began making photograms using the components of her 'wearable sculptures'. Already established as a leader in her field by 1935, the years 1939–41 marked a transformative period for her. She took a summer workshop led by Moholy-Nagy at Chicago's Institute of Design, then temporarily relocated from California to study at the Institute for one year. Her preoccupations with light, space, volume and motion intersected with the design principles of the Bauhaus, which she disseminated through her various teaching posts, published writings and inclusion in seminal exhibitions such as *An Exhibition for Modern Living* (Detroit Institute of Arts, Michigan, 1949). EL

Irving Penn (b. 1917 Plainfield, New Jersey, USA; d. 2009 New York City, New York, USA). With a degree from the Philadelphia Museum School of Industrial Art, Penn moved to New York City in 1939 to pursue a career as a commercial artist. His early engagement with the camera was inspired by the work of photographers Eugène Atget and Walker Evans, whose 1938 exhibition he had seen at the Museum of Modern Art, New York. Yet it was not until 1943 that Penn turned his full attention to photography, at the behest of his employer, the art director of *Vogue*. Penn's first *Vogue* cover, and the first still life in the magazine's history, was featured that year, after which he travelled frequently to Europe on assignment for the magazine. His corner portraits of the European and American modernists received great acclaim. ZZ

Arnošt Pikart (b. 1895 Mostar, Herzegovina [now Bosnia and Herzegovina]; d. 1932 Starý Smokovec, Czechoslovakia [now Czech Republic]). A classically trained musician and composer, Pikart's introduction to photography came in 1916 during service in the Austro-Hungarian army, when he and Czech photographer Josef Sudek met in military hospital. Throughout the 1920s he continued his photographic practice alongside his musical career and was an active member of the avant-garde Czech Photographic Society, founded by Sudek and Jaromír Funke. In his early work Pikart focused on rural genre scenes and landscapes, executed in the 'purist' pictorial style advocated by Drahomír Josef Růžička, the New York 'returnee' and founder member of Pictorial Photographers of America. Later, Pikart adopted a sharper, cleaner form of modernism, evinced in his precise still lifes and dynamic architectural shots captured from high vantage points. EL

Edward Quigley (b. 1898 Philadelphia, Pennsylvania, USA; d. 1977 Haddonfield, New Jersey, USA). Best known for his experiments with light abstractions, Quigley first began taking photographs at the age of eighteen. He joined the Photographic Society of Philadelphia in 1932, and thereafter his production was prolific with frequent submissions to salons and exhibitions. Although he never revealed his technical process, his formally driven practice sought to mirror the camera-less work of European figures such as Man Ray and László Moholy-Nagy. In addition to his engagement with modernism, Quigley also maintained a successful career as a commercial photographer, regularly publishing his work in local and national newspapers, magazines and journals. ZZ

Q

R

Albert Renger-Patzsch (b. 1896 Würzburg, Germany; d. 1966 Wamel bei Soest, Germany). Renger-Patzsch was a pioneering figure in the Neue Sachlichkeit (New Objectivity) movement, which emerged in German art, architecture and literature in the 1920s. Applying this philosophy to the field of photography, he embraced the camera's ability to produce a faithful recording of the world. Following a post as a staff photographer at the *Chicago Tribune*, Renger-Patzsch decided to pursue his photographic career full-time and established a freelance practice in 1925. His work, which included wildlife and botanical studies, formal arrangements of mechanical equipment, commercial still lifes, and landscape and architectural compositions, revealed the patterns, beauty and order in the natural and man-made worlds alike. ZZ

Aleksandr Rodchenko (b. 1891 St Petersburg, Russia; d. 1956 Moscow, Russia). One of Russia's most influential avant-garde artists, Rodchenko was instrumental in founding the socially driven constructivist movement in the 1910s and 1920s. After completing his artistic training at the Stroganov Institute in Moscow in 1914, his work was featured in the futurist exhibition *Magazin* (The Store), organised by influential architect and painter Vladimir Tatlin. Rodchenko engaged with a variety of media, including painting, sculpture, graphic design, photography and photomontage. His experimental photographic practice, which he felt most objectively conveyed modern times, sought to recast the notion of perception through the use of unusual camera angles, disorienting perspectives and abstracted compositions. ZZ

S

Toni Schneiders (b. 1920 Ubar, Germany; d. 2006 Lindau, Germany). After serving as a photographer for the Luftwaffe during the Second World War, Schneiders built a successful career as a commercial photographer. From 1957 he travelled extensively, photographing different cultures and landscapes for illustrated publications. His most important contribution to photography, however, was made through the Fotoform group that he founded with Otto Steinert and others in 1949, and the subjective photography it promoted throughout the 1950s. Unlike his Fotoform colleagues, however, Schneiders predominantly worked in-camera. The landscapes, people, flora and fauna found around Lake Constance, Germany, where he lived for over fifty years, were favoured subjects, and he was especially attentive to the qualities of light and water. Schneiders typically printed his works in high contrast to achieve clean, graphic forms and to emphasise pattern and texture. EL

Frederick Sommer (b. 1905 Angri, Italy; d. 1999 Prescott, Arizona, USA). Sommer was born in Italy to German-speaking parents, grew up in Brazil and moved to Arizona in 1931, eventually settling in Prescott in 1935. During the following decades, he experimented with a wide variety of media, producing drawings, collages and, above all, photographs, the most inventive part of his *oeuvre*. His photographic subject matter and technique were strikingly diverse, ranging from disorienting landscapes and macabre aspects of the natural world to surreal arrangements of found or hand-sculpted objects, and abstractions made in-camera. Yet all reflect his abiding belief that the medium was better suited to suggesting fantasy and imagination than it was to describing reality. EL

Emmanuel Sougez (b. 1889 Bordeaux, France; d. 1972 Paris, France). In 1911, having abandoned his studies in painting and art history in Bordeaux, Sougez moved to Paris where he pursued photography, opening his own studio in 1919. Best known for his still lifes and nude studies, he moved away from pictorialism in favour of 'pure' photography, the French equivalent of Neue Sachlichkeit (New Objectivity) in Germany. Sougez encouraged greater knowledge of the history of photography while continuing to experiment with the medium himself, significantly aiding the development of early colour photography. In the 1920s and 1930s he formed the group Le Rectangle (later Groupes des XV) and assisted young practitioners by publishing their work in the magazine *L'Illustration* (whose photographic department he established in 1926) and in *Arts et Métiers Graphique*, for which he worked from 1930 to 1939. SG

Elfriede Stegemeyer (b. 1908 Berlin, Germany; d. 1988 Innsbruck, Germany). After attending art school in Berlin, Stegemeyer relocated to Cologne in 1932. She enrolled in a photography course at the School of Applied Arts and became involved with the Kölner Progressive (Cologne Progressives), an artistic group allied to political activism that included photographer August Sander. Inspired by the creative climate of the Weimar Republic, she experimented by creating photograms, photomontages and multiple-exposure prints. Often these images featured still-life compositions of household objects. During her travels to Paris and Eastern Europe from 1935 to 1939, Stegemeyer also engaged in landscape and documentary photography as a means of capturing everyday life. Much of her work was destroyed during an air raid in 1943; from 1945 onwards, she concentrated on painting and drawing. zz

Edward Steichen (b. 1879 Bivange, Luxembourg; d. 1973 West Redding, Connecticut, USA). Born in Luxembourg but raised in Milwaukee, Wisconsin, Steichen purchased his first camera when aged sixteen. During an apprenticeship with a lithography firm, he discovered Alfred Stieglitz's publication on photography, and thereafter became Stieglitz's protégé. Steichen's work was regularly published in *Camera Work*, and he was praised for his technical virtuosity, experimentation and innovative printing methods. Alongside Stieglitz, he championed the work of European modernists, making frequent trips to Paris. A pioneer in American photography, Steichen worked in the realms of advertising, fashion and celebrity photography, becoming director of the department of photography at New York's Museum of Modern Art. In 1955 he curated the seminal exhibition *The Family of Man*, the most viewed photography exhibition to date. zz

Ralph Steiner (b. 1899 Cleveland, Ohio, USA; d. 1986 Hanover, New Hampshire, USA). Steiner gained recognition for his contribution not only to modernist photography but also to American avant-garde cinematography. After studying at the Clarence H. White School of Photography in New York City, he was employed at the Manhattan Photogravure Company before becoming a commercial photographer. In 1928 he met photographer Paul Strand, under whose influence he turned his lens towards formal relationships within the city's urban landscape. His interest in exposing the aesthetics of the everyday also translated to the moving picture; his 1930 film *Mechanical Principles* transformed industrial machinery into a study of geometric abstraction. Steiner continued to work in both film and photography until the mid-1970s. zz

Varvara Stepanova (b. 1894 Kaunas, Lithuania; d. 1958 Moscow, Russia). During the 1910s Stepanova received a formal art education and experimented with 'visual poetry' as well as the applied arts. Following the 1917 revolution, she and husband Aleksandr Rodchenko dedicated themselves to the Soviet cause; in 1921 they established the Working Group of Constructivists to promote graphic arts and design that would bolster the democratic goals of modern Russia. Stepanova translated the revolutionary zeal of the time into avant-garde designs for textiles, theatrical costumes and posters, her aesthetic heavily informed by cubism and futurism. Her photomontages, which combined photographs (often by Rodchenko) and graphic elements, a spare colour palette and dynamic composition, became exemplars of Soviet propaganda. EL

Alfred Stieglitz (b. 1864 Hoboken, New Jersey, USA; d. 1946 New York City, New York, USA). Having studied mechanical engineering in Berlin, Stieglitz returned to America in 1890 to pursue a career as a photographer in New York City. Influenced by European pictorialists, he explored the medium's expressive capacities, and devoted himself to promoting amateur photography. In 1902 he founded Photo-Secession, a group for which craftsmanship was paramount, and became editor of its authoritative journal, *Camera Work*. From 1905 he organised exhibitions at the Little Galleries of the Photo-Secession, known as '291', which included the work of not only American photographers but also leading figures in European modernism, such as Pablo Picasso, Constantin Brâncuși and Francis Picabia.

His lifelong support of the avant-garde informed his own practice, and his soft-edged pictorialist style gave way to formal geometric compositions that reflected modern urban life. zz

Paul Strand (b. 1890 New York City, New York, USA; d. 1976 Oregeval, France). As a teenager, Strand was introduced to the work of the Photo-Secessionists through his teacher, the sociologist and photographer Lewis Hine, with field trips to Alfred Stieglitz's famed 291 gallery. He determined to become a photographer and joined the Camera Club of New York, experimenting with different processes and perfecting his printing. Heeding Stieglitz's harsh critique of his early works, Strand started to create some of his most powerful images. He set out to capture the movement of the city and its people, and learned how to build an image skilfully with spaces and shapes. Known throughout his career as a master printer, his meticulous techniques for enriching tonality astonished his colleagues. Regardless of the subject matter, Strand's final interpretation of the print was both complex and modern. NH

Josef Sudek (b. 1896 Kolín, Bohemia [now Czech Republic]; d. 1976 Prague, Czechoslovakia [now Czech Republic]). When the loss of an arm during service with the Austro-Hungarian army ended his bookbinding career, Sudek turned to photography. He studied at the School for Graphic Arts in Prague and took advertising commissions throughout the 1930s, his sharply defined still lifes contrasting with the pictorial softness of his personal work. Focusing initially on the city, and later on studio compositions, he crafted a singularly atmospheric style distinguished by the play of light, and an absence of people or movement. Sudek's views of Prague were published to acclaim as *Praha panoramatická* (1959), and *The Window of My Studio*, a body of studio still lifes (early 1940s–1950s), is equally revered. In 1961 Sudek became the first photographer to receive the Artist of Merit Award from the Czech government. EL

Maurice Tabard (b. 1897 Lyon, France; d. 1984 Nice, France). Formerly a textile designer, Tabard left France aged seventeen to study at the New York Institute of Photography. On returning to Paris in 1928 as an aspiring commercial photographer, he met author Philippe Soupault, who introduced him to both the principles and key figures of the surrealist movement, including Man Ray. Tabard's photographs appeared in publications such as *Harper's Bazaar*, *Elle* and *Vogue*, but it was his experimentation with photomontage, double exposures, combination printing and, in particular, solarised photography that positioned him at the centre of avant-garde photographic practice. In 1929 his work was included in the pivotal photographic exhibition *Film and Photo* in Stuttgart, Germany. Tabard later returned to the fashion world, working as a freelance photographer until the 1960s. zz

Lloyd Ullberg (b. 1904 Minneapolis, Minnesota, USA; d. 1994 San Francisco, California, USA). Ullberg, a musician, took up photography during the Great Depression. He continued to photograph throughout his life, in a commercial and freelance capacity, mostly documenting the Philadelphia streets. During the 1930s his work was published in *Vogue* and *Fortune* magazines, and was included in the Second Philadelphia International Salon of Photography in 1932, overseen by Alexey Brodovitch. Ullberg was not associated with any of the self-defined photography groups or movements in the United States and although sophisticated, his style defied categorisation. Experimentations with solarised portraits, and worm's and bird's eye views, show the influence of the early European avant-garde; attention to texture, line and shadow echo the formal abstraction of the New Bauhaus; and the overarching sense of personal expression anticipated the subjective photography movement of the 1950s. EL

Umbo (b. 1902 Düsseldorf, Germany; d. 1980, Hanover, Germany). Born Otto Umbehr, Umbo began his career in photography as a student of the Bauhaus in Weimar in 1921, where he studied under László Moholy-Nagy. After establishing a portrait studio in Berlin in 1926, he joined the photojournalism cooperative Dephot (Deutscher Fotodienst) and subsequently published his photographs in myriad newspapers and magazines. Alongside his successful commercial practice, Umbo experimented with photomontage, collage, multiple exposures and camera-less photography, and in 1929 was included in the seminal avant-garde photography exhibition *Film and Photo* in Stuttgart, Germany. Few examples of Umbo's early work remain, as over fifty thousand negatives were destroyed in a bombing raid on Berlin during the Second World War. zz

James Van Der Zee (b. 1886 Lenox, Massachusetts, USA; d. 1983 Washington DC, USA). Primarily a portrait photographer, Van Der Zee is best known for chronicling the Harlem Renaissance, a period in which the New York City borough experienced the emergence of a middle class. He began taking photographs as a boy, and in 1916 opened a portrait studio on 135th Street. Its success spurred him on to found the Guarantee Photo Studio, where he produced theatrically composed portraits – replete with props, costumes and backdrops – of figures such as Bill Robinson, Florence Mills and Marcus Garvey. His photographs of Harlem's social transformation were featured in the historic 1967 exhibition *Harlem on my Mind* at the Metropolitan Museum of Art, New York. In 1978 his funeral portraits were published as *The Harlem Book of the Dead*. zz

Pim Van Os (b. 1919 Arnhem, Netherlands; d. 1954 The Hague, Netherlands). Van Os moved with his family from Arnhem to The Hague in 1914. He abandoned his schooling in 1925 in favour of working as an apprentice to local photographers, eventually becoming assistant to commercial photographer Willy Schurman. In 1931 he opened his own portrait studio, but with the advent of the Second World War he was forced into hiding in 1942. He later resumed his studio practice before travelling throughout Europe, camera in hand. During this period his photographic engagement with abstraction flourished, and in 1949 he joined the experimental Nederlandsche Fotografen Kunstkring (Dutch Art Photographers Circle). From the early 1950s until his untimely death, he returned to commercial photography and freelance journalism, contributing to publications such as the daily newspaper *The Fatherland*. zz

Carl Van Vechten (b. 1880 Cedar Rapids, Iowa, USA; d. 1964 New York City, New York, USA). Van Vechten was a prominent patron of the arts, literary critic and novelist before the gift of a 35mm Leica camera in 1932 prompted his decision to turn to photography. His close friendship with key protagonists of the Harlem Renaissance meant that he was well placed to make them his subjects, and over the next three decades he obsessively documented the period's leading artists, writers and musicians, his portraits forming an invaluable historical record. Less well known, and not revealed until after his death, was his private body of work featuring male nude studies and homoerotic interracial photographs. The critical dialogue they have sparked surrounding documentation of race and queer culture in relation to the Harlem Renaissance has cemented these images as an equally important part of his legacy. EL

Edward Weston (b. 1886 Highland Park, Illinois, USA; d. 1968 Carmel-by-the-Sea, California, USA). Brought up in the environs of Chicago, Weston received his first camera at the age of sixteen. By 1907 he had relocated to California to take up a career as a photographer. A key proponent of the 'straight' photography movement, Weston applied his unmanipulated, sharp-focused style to subjects that ranged from landscapes to portraits and still lifes. During the 1920s he travelled with Tina Modotti, his apprentice and lover, to Mexico, where he began to engage with social documentary photography. Alongside fellow photographers Ansel Adams and Imogen Cunningham, in 1932 Weston co-founded the influential San Francisco-based Group f.64, which promoted the monumentality of natural forms and everyday objects. zz

Minor White (b. 1908 Minneapolis, Minnesota, USA; d. 1976 Cambridge, Massachusetts, USA). It is hard to define White as solely a photographer. His multi-faceted practice spanned roles as a photography teacher, art critic and editor of *Aperture* magazine. Critically, though, it was the camera that provided him with a sense of self-discovery and spirituality (White first converted to Catholicism, later leaving the church for Eastern practices). Heavily influenced by Group f.64, White's approach to photography was formalistic and expressive. During this creative period of his life, he was extremely prolific and made one of his most important series, *The Temptation of St Anthony is Mirrors* (1948). Comprising some thirty-two images of his student, Tom Murphy, White used this series as a means of self-exploration, including his closeted homosexuality. NH

Iwao Yamawaki (b. 1898 Nagasaki, Japan; d. 1987, Tokyo, Japan). Born Iwao Fujita, Yamawaki studied architecture at the Tokyo School of Arts, after which he joined a construction company. At the same time he began experimenting with a 35mm camera. In 1930 he interrupted his architectural career and enrolled at the Bauhaus in Dessau, Germany, where he concentrated on photography, engaging in techniques and processes promoted by László Moholy-Nagy. Yamawaki explored the use of diverse camera angles and formal compositions, as well as combination printing and photomontage. In his travels throughout Europe, he documented details of modernist architecture and design. Although he returned to architecture once back in Tokyo, he continued to spread the Bauhaus philosophy as a teacher and through articles and exhibitions. zz

Willy Zielke (b. 1902 Lódz, Poland; d. 1989 Bad Pyrmont, Germany). Zielke studied railway engineering before moving with his family to Munich, Germany. From 1923 he attended the Bavarian State School of Photography, where he remained as a teacher until 1936. He primarily photographed nudes and still lifes, often exploring the optical effects of materials such as glass and water. In 1929 his work was included in the seminal exhibition *Film and Photo* in Stuttgart, Germany. He also cultivated an interest in the moving picture, and in 1932 produced his first film *Arbeitslos* (Unemployed), which documented social strife at the close of the Weimar Republic. Following the Second World War, he resumed his career as a filmmaker. zz

SELECTED BIBLIOGRAPHY

Mitra Abbaspour, Lee Ann Daffner and Maria Morris Hambourg (eds), *Object:Photo. Modern Photographs: The Thomas Walther Collection 1909–1949*, The Museum of Modern Art, New York 2014; www.moma.org/objectphoto

Dawn Ades, *Photomontage*, London 1976; 2nd edn 1986

Dawn Ades and Richard Francis, *Experimental Photography*, exh. cat., Arts Council of Great Britain touring exhibition 1979–80

Mary Street Alinder, *Group f.64: Edward Weston, Ansel Adams, Imogen Cunningham, and the Community of Artists Who Revolutionized American Photography*, New York 2014

Quentin Bajac and Clément Chéroux, *Voici Paris: Modernités Photographiques, 1920–1950: La Collection Christian Bouqueret*, Paris 2012

Péter Baki, Colin Ford and George Szirtes, *Eyewitness: Hungarian Photography in the Twentieth Century: Brassaï, Capa, Kertész, Moholy-Nagy, Munkácsi*, exh. cat., Royal Academy of Arts, London 2011

Geoffrey Batchen, *Emanations: The Art of the Cameraless Photograph*, exh. cat., Govett-Brewster Art Gallery, New Plymouth 2016

Walter Benjamin, *One-Way Street and Other Writings*, London 1979; first published in *Literarische Welt*, 1931

Walter Benjamin, *Illuminations: Essays and Reflections*, ed. Hannah Arendt, trans. Harry Zohn, London 1968

Walter Benjamin, *The Work of Art in the Age of its Technological Reproducibility, and Other Writings on Media*, ed. Michael W. Jennings, Brigid Doherty and Thomas Y. Levin, Cambridge MA 2008

Vladimír Birgus, *Czech Photographic Avant-Garde, 1918–1948*, Cambridge MA 2002

Richard Bolton, *The Contest of Meaning: Critical Histories of Photography*, Cambridge MA 1989

Christian Bouqueret and Andy Grundberg, *Paris, Capitale Photographique 1920–1940: Collection Christian Bouqueret*, exh. cat., Jeu de Paume, Hôtel de Sully, Paris 2009

Victor Burgin (ed.), *Thinking Photography*, London 1982

Stuart Cohen, *The Likes of Us: America in the Eyes of the Farm Security Administration*, Boston 2009

Emmanuelle de L'Ecotais and Alain Sayag (eds), *Man Ray: Photography and its Double*, London 1998

Leah Dickerman and Barry Bergdoll, *Bauhaus 1919–1933: Workshops for Modernity*, New York 2009

David Elliott, *Alexander Rodchenko*, exh. cat., Museum of Modern Art, Oxford 1979

Walker Evans, *American Photographs*, 1938; reprinted (75th anniversary edition) by The Museum of Modern Art, New York 2012

Horacio Fernández, *Fotografía Pública: Photography in Print 1919–1939*, exh. cat., Museo Nacional Centro de Arte Reina Sofía, Madrid 2000

Maria Morris Hambourg and Christopher Phillips, *The New Vision: Photography between the World Wars: Ford Motor Company Collection at the Metropolitan Museum of Art*, New York 1989

Robin Lenman, *The Oxford Companion to the Photograph*, Oxford and New York 2005

Anton Kaes, Martin Jay and Edward Dimendberg (eds), *The Weimar Republic Sourcebook*, Oakland CA 1994

Sarah Kennel, Diane Waggoner and Alice Carver-Kubik, *In the Darkroom: An Illustrated Guide to Photographic Processes Before the Digital Age*, Washington DC 2010

György Kepes, *Language of Vision*, Chicago 1944

Richard Kostelanetz (ed.), *Moholy-Nagy, Documentary Monographs in Modern Art*, Westport CT 1970

Rosalind Krauss, *The Optical Unconscious*, Cambridge MA 1993

Alexander Lavrentiev, Alexander Rodchenko and Varvara Stepanova, *Alexander Rodchenko. Possibilities of Photography*, exh. cat., Galerie Gmurzynska, Cologne 1982

Daniel H. Magilow, *The Photography of Crisis: The Photo Essays of Weimar Germany*, University Park PA 2012

Man Ray, *Writings on Art*, ed. Jennifer Mundy, London 2016

Lucia Moholy, *A Hundred Years of Photography 1839–1939*, London 1939

László Moholy-Nagy, *Painting Photography Film*, trans. Janet Seligman, London 1969; paperback edn, Cambridge MA 1973. Originally published as *Malerei Fotografie Film*, Bauhaus Books 8, Munich 1925

László Moholy-Nagy, *The New Vision: from Material to Architecture*, trans. Daphne Hoffmann, New York 1932

László Moholy-Nagy, *Telehor: The International Review New Vision*, nos.1–2, ed. Klemens Gruber and Oliver A.I. Botar, Zurich 2011

László Moholy-Nagy and Franz Roh, *László Moholy-Nagy: 60 Fotos*, Berlin 1930

Francis Naumann and Hector Obalk (eds), *Affectionately Marcel: The Selected Correspondence of Marcel Duchamp*, Ghent 2000

Beaumont Newhall, *Photography 1839–1937*, exh. cat., The Museum of Modern Art, New York 1937

Beaumont Newhall, *Photography: A Short Critical History*, New York 1938

Peter Nisbet et al., *El Lissitzky, 1890–1941*, exh. cat., Sprengel Museum, Hanover and Staatliche Galerie Moritzburg, Halle 1987

Elizabeth Partridge, *Dorothea Lange: Grab a Hunk of Lightning*, San Francisco 2013

Michael R. Peres, *The Focal Encyclopedia of Photography*, London 2007

Christopher Phillips, *Photography in the Modern Era: European Documents and Critical Writings 1913–1940*, New York 1989

Franz Roh, *Foto-auge: 76 Fotos der Zeit* (Photo-eye: 76 Photos of the Time), Stuttgart 1929

Aaron Scharf, *Art and Photography*, London 1974

Van Deren Coke, *Avant-Garde Photography in Germany, 1919–1939*, exh. cat., San Francisco Museum of Modern Art, 1980–1

Dziga Vertov, 'Kinoki. Perevorot' (Kinoki: A Revolution), *Lef*, no.3, 1923

Edward Weston, *The Daybooks of Edward Weston*, ed. Nancy Newhall, 2 vols, New York 1973

Matthew S. Witkovsky and Peter Demetz, *Foto: Modernity in Central Europe, 1918–1945*, exh. cat., National Gallery of Art, Washington DC 2007

ARTISTS' COPYRIGHT CREDITS

PHOTOGRAPHIC CREDITS

247

THE RADICAL EYE: MODERNIST
PHOTOGRAPHY FROM THE
SIR ELTON JOHN COLLECTION
EDITED BY SIMON BAKER
AND SHOAIR MAVLIAN
WITH NEWELL HARBIN

WITH CONTRIBUTIONS FROM
SIR ELTON JOHN, DAWN ADES,
SAMUEL GLANVILLE, JANE JACKSON,
EMMA LEWIS AND ZMIRA ZILKHA

TATE EDITION
EDITORS: SHOAIR MAVLIAN
AND SIMON BAKER
PROJECT MANAGER: KATE BELL
PRODUCTION MANAGER: BILL JONES
DESIGNER: MELANIE MUES,
MUES DESIGN
COPY EDITOR: DENNY HEMMING
PICTURE RESEARCHER: ROZ YOUNG

FIRST PUBLISHED 2016
BY ORDER OF THE TATE TRUSTEES
BY TATE PUBLISHING, A DIVISION
OF TATE ENTERPRISES LTD,
MILLBANK, LONDON SW1P 4RG
WWW.TATE.ORG.UK/PUBLISHING

ON THE OCCASION OF THE EXHIBITION
THE RADICAL EYE: MODERNIST PHOTOGRAPHY
FROM THE SIR ELTON JOHN COLLECTION
TATE MODERN, LONDON
10 NOVEMBER 2016 — 7 MAY 2017

THE QUOTATION ON P.20 FROM JULIAN BARNES,
KEEPING AN EYE OPEN: ESSAYS ON ART,
JONATHAN CAPE, LONDON 2015, IS REPRODUCED
BY PERMISSION OF THE PUBLISHER.

PAGES 10–11: IMOGEN CUNNINGHAM
OIL TANKS (DETAIL FROM PP.208–9)
PAGES 26–7: KLARA LANGER
RIBBON (DETAIL FROM P.222)
PAGES 46–7: ELFRIEDE STEGEMEYER
OTTO'S HANDS (DETAIL FROM P.153)
PAGES 224–5: TONI SCHNEIDERS
RAIL SPIDER, HAMBURG-ALTONA
(DETAIL FROM P.207)

MEASUREMENTS OF ARTWORKS ARE GIVEN
IN CENTIMETRES, HEIGHT BEFORE WIDTH.

KEY TO AUTHORS
SG SAMUEL GLANVILLE
NH NEWELL HARBIN
EL EMMA LEWIS
SM SHOAIR MAVLIAN
ZZ ZMIRA ZILKHA

APERTURE EDITION
MANAGING EDITOR: AMELIA LANG
PRODUCTION DIRECTOR:
NICOLE MOULAISON
ASSISTANT TO THE MANAGING
EDITOR: TAIA KWINTER
SENIOR TEXT EDITOR:
SUSAN CICCOTTI
PROOFREADER/COPY EDITOR:
SALLY KNAPP

ADDITIONAL STAFF OF THE APERTURE BOOK
PROGRAM INCLUDES:
CHRIS BOOT, EXECUTIVE DIRECTOR; SARAH
MCNEAR, DEPUTY DIRECTOR; LESLEY A. MARTIN,
CREATIVE DIRECTOR; KELLIE MCLAUGHLIN,
DIRECTOR OF SALES AND MARKETING; RICHARD
GREGG, SALES DIRECTOR, BOOKS

FIRST APERTURE EDITION, 2016
PRINTED BY DIE KEURE IN BELGIUM

LIBRARY OF CONGRESS CONTROL NUMBER:
2016949526

HARDCOVER EDITION
ISBN 978-1-59711-386-1
10 9 8 7 6 5 4 3 2 1

PAPERBACK EDITION
ISBN 978-1-59711-390-8
10 9 8 7 6 5 4 3 2 1

TO ORDER APERTURE BOOKS, CONTACT:
+1 212.946.7154
ORDERS@APERTURE.ORG

FOR INFORMATION ABOUT APERTURE TRADE
DISTRIBUTION WORLDWIDE, VISIT:
WWW.APERTURE.ORG/DISTRIBUTION

aperture

APERTURE FOUNDATION
547 WEST 27TH STREET, 4TH FLOOR
NEW YORK, N.Y. 10001
WWW.APERTURE.ORG

APERTURE, A NOT-FOR-PROFIT FOUNDATION,
CONNECTS THE PHOTO COMMUNITY AND ITS
AUDIENCES WITH THE MOST INSPIRING WORK,
THE SHARPEST IDEAS, AND WITH EACH OTHER
—IN PRINT, IN PERSON, AND ONLINE.

FSC
www.fsc.org
MIX
Paper from
responsible sources
FSC® C009115